THE FOLDING IMAGE

THE FOLDING IMAGE

SCREENS BY WESTERN ARTISTS OF THE NINETEENTH AND TWENTIETH CENTURIES

By Michael Komanecky and Virginia Fabbri Butera

with an introduction by Janet W. Adams

Yale University Art Gallery · National Gallery of Art

To Charles —
With deep gratitude
for your wise words
and interest —
Ginny
31 May 1984

The Folding Image: Screens by Western Artists of the Nineteenth and Twentieth Centuries

National Gallery of Art · Washington · 4 March through 3 September 1984

Yale University Art Gallery · New Haven · 11 October 1984 through 6 January 1985

*The publication of this catalogue was aided by a grant
from the National Endowment for the Arts, a federal agency.*

Published by Yale University Art Gallery
2006 Yale Station, New Haven, Connecticut 06520
March 1984

Design & Typography by Howard I. Gralla
Composed in Sabon types by Finn Typographic Service
Printed by Eastern Press and Bound by Mueller Trade Bindery
Production Supervision by Yale University Printing Service

CONTENTS

LENDERS TO THE EXHIBITION

Brooke Alexander, Inc., New York

Anonymous Collector

Kenneth Armitage, London

Art Gallery and Museums and The Royal Pavilion, Brighton

André Emmerich, New York

Mr. and Mrs. Roy Frangiamore, Atlanta

Hereditary Disease Foundation, Beverly Hills

Mrs. Patrick Higson, Glasgow

Castle Howard Collection, York

Dr. and Mrs. Ira J. Jackson, Houston

Jim Jacobs, New York

Felix Klee, Bern

Sydney and Frances Lewis Collection, Richmond

Sydney and Frances Lewis Foundation, Richmond

Giorgio Marconi, Milan

Městské Museum, Žamberk, Czechoslovakia

Metropolitan Museum of Art, New York

Philippe Morane, Paris

Dr. Seeley W. Mudd, II, Carmel

Musée National d'Art Moderne, Paris

Museum of Art, Carnegie Institute, Pittsburgh

Museum of Modern Art, New York

Lillian Nassau Ltd., New York

National Museum of American Art, Smithsonian Institution, Washington

Patsy Norvell, New York

Pace Gallery, New York

Mrs. Duncan Phillips, Washington

Private Collection, London

Private Collection, New York

Private Collection, Paris

Städtisches Museum, Mülheim an der Ruhr, West Germany

Städtisches Museum Abteiberg, Mönchen-Gladbach, West Germany

Stedelijk Museum, Amsterdam

Allan Stone, New York

Victoria and Albert Museum, London

Washburn Gallery, New York

Galerie Rudolf Zwirner, Cologne

PREFACE

This catalogue, like the exhibition it accompanies, is the first attempt to chronicle the role of the folding screen in European and American art from 1850 to the present. The screen is an artistic form usually associated with the Orient. As the exhibition makes clear, however, from the mid-nineteenth century onward, western artists also frequently designed or decorated screens. These works of art are as varied in design and spirit as are the artistic movements that gave birth to them. At first inspired by Japanese art, the functional screen gradually evolved into an independent form, dissociated from its traditional role as baffle or partition. Indeed, recent manifestations of the screen format have more nearly approximated independent sculpture. Taken together, the three essays and the forty-three catalogue entries in this book provide the first comprehensive survey of the history of folding screens in western art.

The idea for this exhibition was conceived by Michael Komanecky and Virginia Butera when they were both interns at the Philadelphia Museum of Art in 1978 under grants from the National Endowment for the Arts, a federal agency, which has also provided a generous grant to Yale University to help subsidize this project. We are grateful to Ms. Butera and Mr. Komanecky who not only wrote essays and entries for this catalogue, but also selected and organized the exhibition, and to Janet Adams, who graciously agreed to provide an introductory essay. The complex arrangements for the show were handled primarily by Michael Komanecky, assistant to the director of the Yale Univeristy Art Gallery. Linda Ayres coordinated the exhibition in Washington.

Most of the objects in the exhibition have never been exhibited before, and close to half of them come from private lenders in whose homes they are actually put to functional use. We are doubly grateful to those generous individuals who agreed to disrupt their private living spaces for the benefit of this exhibition.

J. Carter Brown, *Director*
National Gallery of Art

Alan Shestack, *Director*
Yale University Art Gallery

Catalogue entries 1-18, 20, and 24-27 were written by Michael Komanecky;
entries 19, 21-23, and 28-43 were written by Virginia Butera.
(fig.) refers to an illustration in the essay; these illustrations are numbered
consecutively throughout the three essays. (Cat.) refers to the catalogue entry
for an object in the exhibition. In both (fig.) and (Cat.) captions,
as well as the entry headings themselves, height precedes width,
with measurements given first in centimeters followed by inches (in parentheses);
these measurements include the frames. Medium, dimensions, and present location of the object
and/or the photograph source are given, when available.
Because there is virtually no bibliographical material on the history of
western folding screens, we have chosen to give relevant reference sources
in the footnotes to the essays and entries. All translations of
foreign language passages are by the authors, unless otherwise indicated.
The terms recto and verso are used to describe the two sides of a folding screen,
without any implication of priority.

FOREWORD

While in New York in early spring 1978 my colleague Virginia Butera and I made separate visits to the exhibition of works by American synchromist painters at the Whitney Museum of American Art. After our return to the Philadelphia Museum of Art, where we were then National Endowment for the Arts interns in the Print Department, we began discussing the many exciting objects we saw at the Synchromism show. One which to us stood out from all others was Thomas Hart Benton's *Screen with Abstract Sea Motif* (Cat. 22 and cover). Surprised that Benton ever did a folding screen, we realized that the Philadelphia Museum of Art also owned a lithographic screen by Pierre Bonnard, a painted screen by Donald Deskey, and had just exhibited a color serigraph screen by Jack Beal. At Ginny's suggestion, we began to consider whether there might be other western folding screens of significant quality and availability to warrant an exhibition. We soon learned that the centuries-old tradition of screenmaking in the West had never been studied in any meaningful way, and, to paraphrase William Morris, "with the conceited courage of young scholars, we set ourselves to reforming all that."

We then visited the Cooper-Hewitt Museum in hopes of finding screens in this national museum of design, and to discuss our ideas with their curator of decorative arts, David Revere McFadden. Although the Cooper-Hewitt did not possess any screens of interest for our exhibition, David encouraged us to continue working. Within weeks of our discussion, he informed us that Janet W. Adams had also come to speak with him about her work on western screens. Janet had just finished a book on the subject, and was eager to organize an exhibition. A few weeks later, we met with Janet in Philadelphia to talk about our mutual interests. We discovered we had much to offer and to learn from each other, and we decided to join forces.

In the six years that have passed since that series of fortuitous events in 1978, our research has taken us to private and public collections throughout the United States and Europe in search of folding screens by western artists of the nineteenth and twentieth centuries. The paucity of information on the existence and whereabouts of these screens was a formidable obstacle, and we were often called upon to be part scholar, part archaeologist, and part detective. The Franz Marc screen (Cat. 20), for example, had been broken up and its panels sold to three separate individuals in three different auctions in the late 1950s. The fact that screens were intended to be functional as well as decorative objects meant in addition that many had been damaged or even destroyed. Of the five folding screens known to have been done by Odilon Redon, only one survives. Of the three screens made by Edouard Vuillard, none remains entirely intact; one is mounted as a wall painting (Cat. 7), another has been cut down and lacks one of its panels, and all three are without their original frames. Our task was further complicated by the realization that dealers, in order to capitalize on the immense popularity of folding screens at and after the turn of the century, occasionally mounted painted wall panels in screen frames. Finally, the fragile condition and media of existing screens sometimes prevented their inclusion in the exhibition; such is the case for Redon's single extant screen, and for Whistler's only screen.

There were, of course, a number of discoveries which more than compensated for our frustration. The remarkable stained glass screen by Louis Comfort Tiffany (Cat. 11), long presumed to have been destroyed, miraculously reappeared just months before our catalogue went to press. The Franz Marc screen mentioned above has been reunited for this exhibition as well. Moreover, during the last fifteen years European and particularly American artists contributed toward a virtual renaissance of screenmaking in the West. We have discovered that more than 200 contemporary artists have done folding screens, only a very few of which could be included in this exhibition.

What success we have realized in our efforts must be shared with hundreds of scholars, dealers, collectors, and colleagues throughout the world. Our thanks goes first to all to the institutional and private lenders, whose cooperation and support have been extraordinary. In many instances they have been asked to lend objects which are rare, fragile, and difficult to handle and transport. Their positive responses to our pleas have been enormously gratifying. Private lenders have been especially generous, as they have agreed to part with screens that still perform their intended functional and decorative roles in private residences. We would also like to express our sincere thanks to Alan Shestack, Director of the Yale University Art Gallery, whose steadfast commitment to exhibitions of scholarly merit first encouraged us to approach him about *The Folding Image*. His willingness to accept this logistically, administratively, and financially demanding project has in many ways been courageous. Moreover, his keen sensitivity to issues of quality has been insightful if not inspirational. We are equally indebted to J. Carter Brown, Director of the National Gallery of Art, whose enthusiasm for this exhibition literally made it possible, and also enabled it to reach a national audience. In addition, through his personal involvement a number of loans vital to the success of the project were secured. In no small measure, it is due to their joint support that *The Folding Image* has come into being.

Many, many people have aided us in our research on western folding screens, not all of whom can be mentioned in this brief acknowledgement. A special note of appreciation must be proffered to Antoine Salomon, Felix Klee, Jiří Mucha, Dominique Maurice Denis, Claire Denis, Juliet Man Ray, Margaret Mansfield (Van Everen) Jaynes, and Luce and Elica Balla. They have each provided essential and often previously unpublished information on the screens made by their illustrious relatives. Jiří Mucha and Dominique Denis, in particular, deserve recognition for assembling invaluable primary research materials on their fathers' screenmaking activities, and for handling many administrative matters regarding the loan of the screens themselves. In addition, a large number of living artists who have done screens generously granted interviews to Virginia Butera, and their comments helped us formulate our understanding of the folding screen in the twentieth century.

We were aided in our research abroad by the following people: In Austria by Herbert Fux of the Museum für Angewandte Kunst, and Christian M. Nebehay, both in Vienna; in Czechoslovakia by Jiří Kotalík of the National Gallery of Prague, and Marie Bakešová of the Městské Museum, Žamberk; in England by L. R. H. Smith and Michael Collins of the British Museum, Anthony d'Offay of the Anthony d'Offay Gallery, Peter Cormack of the William Morris Gallery, Richard Ormond of the National Portrait Gallery, S. Martin Summers of Alex Reid & Lefevre, Phillipe Garner, Lucy Havelock-Allen and Nicola Redway of Sotheby Parke-Bernet & Co., Simon Jervis, Lionel Lambourne, Linda Parry, and Steven Astley of the Victoria and Albert Museum, and by Robert Key, M. A. Ford, J. S. Maas, Doris and Charles Saatchi, and Richard Shone, all in London; and elsewhere in England by Simon Howard and Judy Sladden at Castle Howard, John Morley and Jessica Rutherford at the Art Gallery and Museums and the Royal Pavilion in Brighton, and by Linda Hardiman at the Portsmouth Art Gallery; in France by Daniel Wildenstein of the Fondation Wildenstein, Jean Coural of the Mobilier National, Yvonne Brunhammer of the Musée des Arts Décoratifs, Jean Lacambre and Germain Viatte of the Musée National d'Art Moderne, Geneviève Lacambre of the Musée d'Orsay, Laurence Marceillac of the Musée Picasso, José Alvarez, Juliet Bareau, Huguette Berès, Klaus Berger, Florence Chauveau, Pierre Daix, Pauline Dejean, Jean Baptiste Denis, Charles Durand-Ruel, Michel Hoog, Marcel Jean, Giovanni Lista, Claude and Sydney Picasso, Daniel Templon, and Pierrette Vernon-Montredon, all in Paris, and Marie-Amélie Anquetil of the Musée du Prieuré, Saint Germain-en-Laye; in Germany by Rüdiger Joppien of the Kunstgewerbemuseum, Cologne, J. Gladders and Klaus Flemming of the Städtisches Museum Abteiberg, Mönchen-Gladbach, Karin Stempel of the Städtisches Museum, Mülheim an der Ruhr, and the late Veronika Schaeffer of the Stadtmuseum, Munich; in Holland by Joop Joosten of the Stedelijk Museum, Amsterdam, and S. Crommelin in Laren; in Italy by Carla Verri of Studio Marconi, Milan; in Portugal by Maria Helen Soares Costa of the Museum Department, Fundação Calouste Gulbenkian, Lisbon; in Spain by Juan Bassegoda Nonell, Barcelona; and in Switzerland by Sigrid Barten of the Museum Bellerive, and Thomas Ammann, both in Zürich.

Our American and Canadian colleagues have been equally generous with their time and expertise, among them: Pam Adler of Pam Adler Gallery, New York; Brooke and Carolyn Alexander of Brooke Alexander, Inc., New York; Kevin L. Stayton of the Brooklyn Museum; Kermit Champa, William Jordy, and George Landow of Brown University, Providence; Susan Caldwell of Susan Caldwell Gallery, New York; Jean Sutherland Boggs of the Canada Museums Construction Corporation, Ottawa; Henry Adams of the Museum of Art, Carnegie Institute, Pittsburgh; Alastair Duncan and Nancy White at Christie, Manson & Woods, New York; John Rewald, Annette Juliano, Mona Hadler, William B. Geerdts, and especially Linda Nochlin and Rose Carol Washton Long at the City University of New York; George Collins of Columbia University, New York; Sue Lawler of Condeso-Lawler, New York; Douglas Baxter of Paula Cooper Gallery, New York; David Revere McFadden, Elaine Evans Dee, and Christian Rohlfing of the Cooper-Hewitt Museum, New York; Roger Clisby of the Crocker Art Museum, Sacramento; Gary Reynolds of the Newark Museum; David Curry of the Denver Art Museum; Kathleen Pyne of the Detroit Institute of Arts; André Emmerich and Dorsey Waxter of the André Emmerich Gallery, Inc., New York; Ellen McGoldrick of the Equitable Life Assurance Co., New York; Barbara Fendrick of Fendrick Gallery, Washington; Wally Findlay and Helen T. Findlay of Wally Findlay Galleries International; Xavier Fourcade of Xavier Fourcade, Inc., New York; Yoshiaki Shimizu and Ann Yonemura of the Freer Gallery of Art, Washington; Randell L. Makinson of the David B. Gamble House, Pasadena; Barbara Gladstone of Barbara Gladstone Gallery, New York; Lucy Flint of the Solomon R. Guggenheim Museum, New York; Jaap van Liere of Haber-Theodore Gallery, New York; Bernard Lennon of the Harcus Gallery, Boston; Milton Wechsler of the Hereditary Disease Foundation, Beverly Hills; Donald C. Pierce of the High Museum of Art, Atlanta; Maury Leibovitz of M. Knoedler & Co., New York; Monique Knowlton and Linda Marchisotto of Monique Knowlton Gallery, New York; Antoinette Kraushaar of Kraushaar Galleries, New York; Robert Pincus-Witten and the late Richard Lerner of Lerner-Heller Gallery, New York; Frederick R. Brandt of the Sydney and Frances Lewis Collection, Richmond; Stella Paul and Stephanie Barron of the Los Angeles County Museum of Art; Pierre Matisse of the Pierre Matisse Gallery, New York; Mary Lorincz and Gary Tinterow at the Metropolitan Museum of Art, New York; Ruth Bohan at the University of Missouri, St. Louis; Hugh F. McKean and David Donaldson at the Morse Museum of Art, Winter Park, Florida; Clifford Ackley and Barbara

Schapiro at the Museum of Fine Arts, Boston; John Pultz, Riva Castleman, and J. Stewart Johnson at the Museum of Modern Art, New York; Gabriel P. Weisberg of the National Endowment for the Humanities, Washington; Carolyn Amiot, E. A. Carmean, Carroll Cavanagh, Dodge Thompson, Laurie Weitzenkorn, John Wilmerding, and Al Viebranz of the National Gallery of Art, Washington; Ralph T. Coe, Richard Gruber, Susan Hobbs, and Tom Bower at the National Museum of American Art, Washington; Anne Fabbri Butera of the Noyes Museum of Art, Oceanville, New Jersey; Harvey Jones at the Oakland Museum of Art; Arnold Glimscher and Jeffrey Hoffeld at the Pace Gallery, New York; Ellen Jacobowitz, Ann Percy, Anne d'Harnoncourt, Joseph Rishel, and Marge Kline at the Philadelphia Museum of Art; Sasha Newman at the Phillips Collection, Washington; Neil Prinz at the Rice University Art Museum, Houston; John Brancati at Rizzoli Gallery, New York; Paula Kirkeby of Smith-Anderson Gallery, Palo Alto; Marc Rosen, Ruth Ziegler, and Mary Bartow of Sotheby Parke Bernet, Inc., New York; Angela Westwater of Sperone Westwater, New York; Barbara Toll of Barbara Toll Fine Arts, New York; Edmund Gaultney of Tower Gallery, New York; Ken Tyler and Barbara Delano of Tyler Graphics, Bedford Village, New York; Joan Washburn of Washburn Gallery, New York; William G. Allman at the White House; Gail Levin of the Whitney Museum of American Art, New York; Harry A. Brooks, Jr. of Wildenstein and Co., Inc., New York; Merv Richard of the Winterthur Museum, Winterthur, Delaware; Theresa Fairbanks, Anne-Marie Logan, Duncan Robinson, and Anna van den Burg of the Yale Center for British Art, New Haven; Anne Coffin Hanson, Robert L. Herbert, George Hersey, and Kelly Simpson of Yale University, New Haven; David Barquist, Helen Cooper, Louisa Cunningham, Richard S. Field, Patricia Kane, Susan Matheson, and Mary Gardner Neill of the Yale University Art Gallery, New Haven; Phillip Dennis Cate and Jeffrey Wechsler at the Jane Voorhees Zimmerli Art Museum, Rutgers University, New Brunswick; and individually, Mary Alinder, Celia Betsky, Scott Braznell, Gary Carson, Michelle Cohen, Douglas Cooper, Karen Davies, Mr. and Mrs. Daniel B. Drachman, Lauren Zelinger Eisenberger, Barbara Gasper, Lloyd Goodrich, Andrea Gray, Charles Gregory, Carol Grissom, Melissa Harris, Joan Q. Hazlitt, Olive May Hibbert, Warren Howell, Robert Jameison, Richard Kirsch, Robert Koch, Les

Lang, Maud Lavin, Katherine Lynn, Mr. and Mrs. David McAlpin, Kneeland McNulty, Charles M. Mount, Marlene Park, Mrs. Duncan Phillips, Margaret Potter, Mrs. Charles Prendergast, John Pultz, Henry Reed, Zena Maria Ruddock, Bertha Saunders, Miriam Schapiro, Gertrude Stein, and Penelope Hunter Stiebel.

Research and the business of negotiating loans, of course, comprise only a small part of any exhibition. The decision to share the exhibition with the National Gallery of Art required that one person from that institution coordinate logistical and scholarly activities. Linda Ayres, assistant curator of American Art, was our liaison. Her efficiency, determination, and devotion to this project have been exemplary. Moreover, her gracious performance of countless tasks has earned our deep respect and heartfelt gratitude. We owe thanks as well to her capable assistant, Maria Mallus. From the beginning of this project, Gaillard Ravenel and Mark Leithauser of the design and installation department of the National Gallery responded eagerly to the formidable challenge of installing in one space forty-three folding screens of widely differing size, media, format, and style. The handsome result of their efforts can be seen in both Washington and New Haven. Frances P. Smyth and her staff edited the entire catalogue manuscript, skillfully and patiently synthesizing contributions from three different authors under a very demanding schedule. In addition, Ross Merrill, Victor C. B. Covey, and Ann Hoenigswald of the National Gallery conservation department offered their expertise on many occasions, and have supervised several restoration tasks.

We are fortunate to have been aided in similar tasks at the Yale University Art Gallery by an equally talented group of people. Foremost among them is Elise Kenney, who served as research assistant and editorial consultant. She was vigilant, encouraging, and admonishing, each in the proper measure to help us achieve the high end result for which all were striving. This colleague's deep personal commitment will long be remembered. Howard Gralla of New Haven designed this catalogue, and his pursuit of excellence under frequently changing parameters has been remarkable as it has been successful. Greer Allen and John Gambell of the Yale University Printing Service were responsible for supervising production of the catalogue, and their devotion and professional abilities are very much appreciated. Many of the photographs in the catalogue, including several special reconstructions of lost or damaged screens, were provided by Joseph Szaszfai and Geraldine T. Mancini, with the aid of William Cuffe; without their assistance, the value of this book would have been significantly lessened. The complex task of coordinating packing, transportation, and insurance for objects coming from eight countries and forty different lenders was superbly handled by Rosalie Reed, Sarah Cash, and Lisa Bornman-Davis of the Registrar's Office. They were aided by their counterpart at the National Gallery of Art, Kathleen Kelley. The demanding details of the installation were capably performed by Robert M. Soule, Robert C. Soule, Richard Moore, and Fred d'Amico. Special thanks go as well to Diane Hoose and Ethel Neumann, who selflessly took on many tasks during my long absences to write the catalogue and otherwise prepare the exhibition.

We would like to express as well our very sincere thanks and gratitude to Janet W. Adams, author of the introductory essay to this catalogue. From our first meeting with Janet, we found her to be a learned, dedicated, and generous colleague, whose enthusiasm for folding screens led her to write the first book devoted to this subject. Whatever contributions we have made with this exhibition and the accompanying catalogue could not have been possible without her groundbreaking research.

And finally, to Timothy Toy and Rosalie Reed, friends and partners who have tolerated incessant discussions about folding screens, who have shared our successes and failures over the past six years, and who have offered encouragement when it was most needed, go our deepest thanks.

THE FOLDING IMAGE

FIG. 1 and 2 Kano Naizen, Japanese, 1570-1616, *Pair of Six-Panel Screens*, early 17th century, watercolor on gold leaf on paper, 154.6 x 363.2 (60⅞ x 143), each screen. Kobe, Japan, City Museum of Namban Art.

Janet W. Adams

THE ORNAMENTAL BACKGROUND

It has been reported that the duke of Marlborough was so attached to a great Coromandel screen given to him by the Holy Roman Emperor that he carried it with him on his campaigns. There is no doubt that the duke lived in high style even in the shadows of the battlefield, for he enjoyed the services of his valet and carried with him great "pilgrim bottles of silver for wine and a vast wine cooler, all beautifully engraved with his coat of arms. This well-traveled Chinese screen, decorated with figures dressed in European clothes of the period, was given to him by the grateful emperor after the victory at Blenheim in 1704. It is still in his family's possession, and The Countess Spencer informs us that the screen was one of a pair commissioned by the Jesuits in China and given to Leopold I on the occasion of his election as emperor in 1658, and that he in turn gave it to the duke. This story of the attachment of an English general to his Chinese screen, carrying it into Dutch territory while engaging in combat with the French, is significant here because it involves several of the countries that played key roles in the history of the decorative folding screen.[1]

The tale begins with the opening of Japan to the West toward the end of the sixteenth century, although screens had existed in the East for many centuries prior to that time. A Chinese invention later adapted by the Japanese, the folding screen was so transformed during the centuries of its development that it became more closely associated with Japan than with its true place of origin. The earliest references to screens are in literary sources from the late Chou Dynasty (206 B.C.– 220 A.D.).[2] In the eighth century, the screen made its entry into Japan; rare examples from this period still remain in the imperial repository in Nara. Chinese dominance of Japanese art was most marked from the seventh to the tenth century, and early screens are consistent with this stylistic influence. Due to wars, fires, and natural deterioration, however, no screens made in Japan during these centuries have survived, and very few exist that predate 1450.[3]

Despite the closely interrelated development of Chinese and Japanese screens, they differed in their construction and uses. The architecture of the two cultures contributed to a large degree to the types of screens which evolved. In China houses normally had stationary walls upon which paintings or other decorations could be displayed; screens were therefore primarily functional, serving to provide privacy and to control the flow of air, space, and light within large rooms. Even in such a situation, though, screen painting in China was a fine art until the end of the Sung Dynasty (1279 A.D.). After that time, the Chinese tended to consider the screen almost exclusively a minor decorative object, to be done by skilled artisans rather than by serious scholar painters as had been the case in previous centuries.[4] The construction of early Chinese screens was poor: they were most often composed of separate panels hinged together clumsily by leather or cloth straps. Due to this hinging method, the design of each panel was physically self-contained, though usually related compositionally and thematically to the other panels. These screens were also heavy, and not meant to be moved easily or frequently.

In contrast, the traditional Japanese house lacked permanent walls, and was thus open to the elements. As a result, screens became an architectural necessity, and three distinct types evolved. The simplest and least important one esthetically was the single-panel stationary screen, called a *tsitsuae*, used at the entrance to a house. By its image such a screen announced to visitors something of the owner's wealth or status, or the nature of a particular ceremony or season which was being celebrated. The sliding panel screen, called a *fusuma*, was the most important functionally. Principally a Japanese invention, it was used as a movable wall which both controlled the amount of sunlight and cool air admitted to a room and afforded privacy. The folding screen, or *byobu*, was designed for flexibility and mobility; hence lightness, durability, and somewhat smaller scale were requirements. Part of the success of the Japanese folding screen lies in its construction. It was made of layers of very strong paper fibers stretched over a light frame, itself painstakingly crafted of carefully prepared wood. These layers were interlocked and overlapped from panel to panel, creating a flexible paper hinge. It was the ingenuity of this hinge which enabled the artist to conceive of the screen as a virtually continuous picture plane instead of a series of separate, vertical panels. Consequently, the Japanese came to consider the screen an eminently suitable platform for some of its most distinguished artistic accomplishments.

The form of a screen presents peculiar compositional problems of which the Japanese were keenly aware. Before all else an angular structure intended to stand by virtue of its angularity, the screen was not made to be mounted flat on a wall. Because it was meant to be moved, its form and the degree of the angles between its panels were always changing. Moreover, each panel was seen obliquely, usually by a viewer whose position was changing. Japanese screens always had an even number of panels, usually two to six, and when folded in a typically symmetric fashion, the center of the composition would necessarily be in an acute angle, the least visible position and the one of greatest visual distortion. Artists solved the challenge through masterful compositional arrangement, with extraordinary sensitivity to rhythm, balance, color, and movement. Until the latter part of the nineteenth century, these basic considerations of the unique problems of screen composition failed to concern western artists.

The art and customs of the Orient had fascinated the rare early traveler who penetrated that remote and isolated part of the world. It was not until 1543 that the first European ship arrived in Malacca, however, and not until thirty years later that trade between the East and West was established on a regular basis. Soon after the first ships arrived in Nagasaki from Lisbon, the Jesuits followed, intent upon spreading Christianity. The ensuing cultural intercourse between the Portuguese and the Japanese resulted in the development of a style of art called *namban*, literally meaning "southern barbarian." Neither oriental nor European, the style was the result of an intermingling of the two cultures. The screen was the principal but not the exclusive form of *namban* art. Always painted in pairs in the traditional manner, *namban* screens generally date from 1590 to 1630.[5]

A typical pair (fig. 1 and 2) shows the arrival of a Portuguese ship (*nao*) in the harbor, and the reception of the crew. In the background is a pavilion or chapel, set against a gold background which swirls around the blue water, whose abstractions make it difficult to define where land ends or sky commences. In the companion

FIG. 3 *World Map Screen* (one of pair with fig. 4), Japanese, ca. 1600-1650, watercolor on paper, 158.7 x 477.7 (62½ x 188). Kobe, Japan, City Museum of Namban Art. Presumably copied from Abraham Ortelius' *Theatrum Orbis Terrarum* (Antwerp, 1570).

screen, the procession of the arriving captain and his retinue is greeted by Jesuits in their long cassocks. In these screens, no attempt is made to achieve accurate perspective; the artist has relied for expression on minute representation of anecdotal details, carefully arranged across the surface. Painted in predominant shades of red, green, blue, black, and white on gold paper, these screens display "a completely convincing union of observant realistic detail within a large decorative framework, . . . and produce an inexhaustible combination of narration and decoration."[6]

The subjects of other *namban* screens reflect the efforts of the Jesuits to teach western geography and customs, as well as religious tenets, to the Japanese. A famous pair of screens was called *World Map* and *Four Major Cities of the World*. The *World Map* (fig. 3) was painted in a Jesuit art class in 1593 in a western style. It is profusely decorated with ships in the Atlantic, Pacific, and Indian oceans; with representations of the four hemispheres; and with images of the Ptolemaic universe at the corners.[7] The *Four Major Cities of the World* (fig. 4) depicts Lisbon, Seville, Rome, and Constantinople, each with recognizable topographical and architectural features. At the top of the panels are figures dressed in the fashion of their countries, as well as mounted knights, painted against a gold background. It is virtually certain that by

1590 the Jesuits had brought into Japan materials for western style painting and the tools necessary for working copper engraving plates. Both the printing of textbooks, and the production of works of art interpreting western themes were soon undertaken.[8] At the beginning, the Jesuits' Japanese students copied religious works, which were difficult to understand because of the enormous language handicaps. Later, secular themes such as landscapes were often preferred, as they were easier for the students to comprehend visually. The *European Genre Scene with Water Mill* screen (fig. 5) clearly shows its derivation from these circumstances. Such *namban* screens, generally done by modestly skilled artists working in the Kano school stylistic tradition during the Momoyama (1573-1615) and Edo (1615-1868) periods, do not deserve great distinction in the history of Japanese screen painting. Yet their role historically is extremely interesting both as a starting point in the East-West exchange, and for their marked similarity to some late nineteenth-century western screens.

During the early years of the seventeenth century, trade grew between the West and both Japan and China, with several European countries vying for the valuable cargo. The Dutch succeeded the Portuguese in obtaining the largest portion of the Japanese export trade, establishing the Dutch East India Company in 1602. England joined

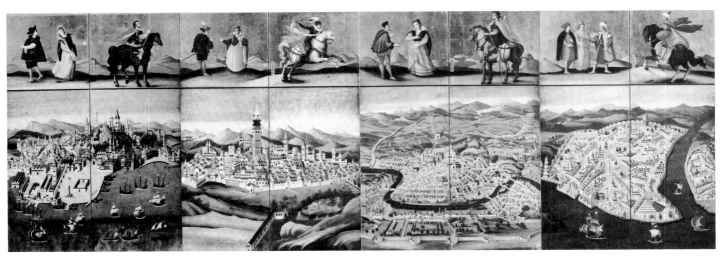

FIG. 4 *Four Major Cities of the World* (second of a pair with fig. 3), Japanese, ca. 1600-1650, watercolor on paper, 158.7 x 477.7 (62½ x 188). Kobe, Japan, City Museum of Namban Art. Presumably copied from Georg Braun and Franz Hogenberg's *Civitates Orbis Terrarum* (Cologne, 1572).

the competition, founding its own East India Company shortly thereafter, although English ships were forced by the powerful Dutch fleet to take a circuitous route, transferring goods at Coromandel, a section of the Madras coast. In 1614 the *Clove*, the first English ship to return from Japan, carried home a rich load including "Japanese wares, scritoires, Trunks, Beoubes (screens), Cupps, and dishes of all sorts and of a most excellent varnish."[9]

From that time forward, there are frequent references to oriental screens in numerous inventories. During Charles II's reign, huge twelve-panel lacquer screens were among the contents of Queen Mary's lodgings at Kensington Palace (1697), as were several "India" screens.[10] The records of the English East India Company reveal a letter written in 1697 to a Chinese factory requesting "20 sets of screens, 12 leaves to a set, 8, 9, & 10 feet high by 20-24 inches broad."[11] The frigate *Fleet* arrived in England with seventy packing cases of screens, indicating the great popularity of these objects. Instructions to the suppliers of the ship *Trumbull* being loaded at Amoy specified "What tonnage will yet remain to be completed, you may yet supply, with some more boards of sufficient thickness...lacquered on both sides, fit for screens, or panels to be done by the best artists, and of the finest Lacker & works procurable, or else none at all."[12] The diarist John Evelyn described a visit to a neighbor whose whole house was a cabinet of elegancies which included

"Japan" screens used as wainscot.[13] (During the seventeenth century, the terms India, Japan, and China were used indiscriminately and interchangeably, and it is impossible to know precisely the style or source of objects described as such.) By the end of the century, many of England's noble houses, such as Chatsworth and Hampton Court, had rooms paneled with wainscot of this desirable material.

The arrival of lacquer goods from the Orient during the seventeenth century did not mark the first appearance of lacquer in Europe. Venetian artisans had used the material since the preceding century, but it was of a different nature and lost favor soon after its introduction. The lacquer that arrived from China, however, enjoyed such immense popularity that supply rarely met prevailing demand. True lacquer is made of the resin that comes from the *Rhus vernicifera*, a tree that originated in China and was later transplanted to Japan. The crude lac is a grayish fluid that must be used quickly, as it dries and darkens upon exposure to air. For these reasons, raw lac could not be exported to Europe, but only the finished product. Preparation of a board to be lacquered was a lengthy process, surpassed only by the tediousness of the application of the lac itself. First the board was covered with a layer of linen, paper, or even clay, and grasses. Then the liquid lacquer was applied with a brush. To achieve the deep luster characteristic of fine lacquer, many coats of the liquid had to be applied, allowing

FIG. 5 *European Genre Scene with Water Mill*, Japanese, ca. 1600-1650, watercolor on paper, 101.7 x 262.2 (40 x 103¼). Osaka, Collection of Mr. Ichio Kuga.

FIG. 6 *Twelve-Panel Coromandel Screen,* Chinese, 17th century, black incised lacquer decorated with colors and gilt, 274.3 x 548.6 (108 x 216). New York, Collection of Dr. and Mrs. Sidney M. Cohen.

FIG. 7 *Six-Panel Coromandel Screen,* Chinese, 17th century, lacquered wood. Erddig Park, Clwyd, Wales. Photograph, National Trust.

several days between applications for each coat to dry thoroughly. The surface was then polished to a deep satin finish, a laborious process requiring skill and patience. Once prepared the board could be decorated in a number of ways.

The lacquer screen most desired by the Europeans was the Chinese Coromandel, so named due to its devious route via India to England. The distinguishing feature of this lacquer was its incised decoration. First a design was scratched onto the surface and then a cut was made into the lacquer with a very sharp knife. The exposed area was then filled with a water-soluble substance mixed with

color or gilt. The fresh colors used would likely appear garish to our taste, especially since we now know only their muted tones, mellowed by age and faded by exposure to light. Many colors were available for the gesso, just as various powders and dyes could be added to the liquid resin as it was applied. Black was the color most often preferred for lacquer goods, closely followed by vermilion, "tête de nègre," and aubergine.

This superb example of a Coromandel screen (fig. 6 recto and verso) is decorated on both sides, with totally unrelated designs as was the usual practice. On the recto is a scene of a birthday celebration, showing the pavilion where the fête occurred, the arrival of the guests by sea, and a mountainous landscape beyond. Typically, no attempt has been made to achieve linear perspective; decorative unity is attained through flowing line and glowing color. As in the case of Japanese prints from the late nineteenth century, such (to western eyes) compositional aberrations made these objects all the more intriguing and desirable. On the reverse is a landscape dominated by flowering shrubs, almond trees, and a variety of flowers including peonies and chrysanthemums. Coromandel screens of the seventeenth century, like this one, are usually enormous, from eight to nine feet tall, and extending to a width of as much as twenty feet. Their usefulness in the spacious mansions of the upper classes is evident. An interesting screen of a smaller scale was obtained by Elihu Yale while he was governor of Fort St. George in India (1687-1692) (fig. 7).[14] The central scene is again a mountainous landscape. The treatment of the borders is

FIG. 8 *Six-Panel Coromandel Screen* (one of a pair), Chinese, 17th century, lacquered wood with carved and gilded frame, 200.7 x 320.0 (79 x 126). Courtesy of The Countess Spencer.

especially pronounced. Wide borders almost always surround Coromandel screens, and here this space is decorated with vignettes containing vases of flowers, bowls, utensils, birds, animals, and calligraphy. This type of border image is referred to as "The Hundred Objects" and showed valued possessions believed to be needed by the screen's owner in the afterlife. It was not unusual either for a lacquer screen to be commissioned in China, as was the case for the great Coromandel screen mentioned at the beginning of this essay (fig. 8). The subject

matter of the panels is not of any particular significance, and the most distinctive feature of this screen is the wide, boldly carved gilt border which displays on each of its panels the double-headed Imperial Eagle of the Hapsburg family.[15]

While many lacquer screens were sent to Europe and cut up for reuse in other types of furniture, some were made specifically for export, such as the *View of Amsterdam* screen (fig. 9). Both the form and the number of panels indicate clearly that the screen was made for the

FIG. 9 *Nine-Panel Screen with a View of Amsterdam*, Chinese, 18th century, lacquered wood with carved and gilded frame, 210.8 x 297.1 (83 x 117). Montreal, Collection of Mr. Herbert Black.

European market; the Chinese would not have made for themselves a screen with an uneven number of panels, nor would they have made the panels slightly concave, or placed them within this elaborately carved gilt framework. In addition, the subject was almost certainly copied from a European engraving, although its rendition in the screen was undeniably orientalized.

Although the Coromandel screens were most in demand, there were many other means of decorating lacquer screens. Sometimes, materials such as mother-of-pearl or ivory were applied to the surface; ornamentation with inlay or appliqués of jade, coral, lapis lazuli, agate, or crystal was also desirable. Such Chinese lacquer screens continued to be imported into Europe in the last half of the nineteenth century, where they found great favor. The Coromandel technique was also known to the Japanese, but not often used. Instead, they chose to decorate on the surface of the lacquer, embellishing it with a kind of built-up gesso called *gofun*. This gesso was generally painted gold, and gold dust could also be sprinkled over the surface before the final application of lacquer. Other decorative materials might further adorn or substitute for the gesso.

As the seventeenth century progressed and trade between the Orient and the West prospered, the demand for lacquer screens increased dramatically; lacquer boards and other items of furniture, as well as screens, were arriving in record numbers. At the same time, some English joiners sent cabinets and tables to the East to be lacquered, or even incorporated lacquer panels in their cabinetry. By 1700, slightly more than a century after the first merchant vessel from Portugal (*nao*) arrived in Japan, the flood of eastern goods into England had actually caused a crisis. Their livelihood threatened by the presence of these goods in England, joiners petitioned Parliament for a halt on imports of this type. The same condition existed in France. Some of the finest rococo *menuisiers* and *ébénistes* frequently inserted black and gold lacquer cut from screen board onto the surface of cabinets and tables. A group of Parisian cabinetmakers were as alarmed as their English counterparts by the plentiful oriental lacquer wares, and they strove to develop a product which could compete with the popular Chinese screens.

The cabinetmakers who opposed the imports were faced with a basic problem—the fact that lac could neither travel to France, nor could its source, the *Rhus vernicifera*, be transplanted into another hemisphere. The only solution, it seemed, was to develop a native substitute for oriental lacquer. An Italian Jesuit, Filippo Bonanni, was the first to correctly analyze lacquer, while the Frenchman Antoni d'Emery developed one of the earliest recipes for a European substitute.[16] The different chemical composition of the native lacquer, however, did not require as long to dry or to polish. Although frequently it was not applied with the same care as oriental lacquer, this European imitation became quite popular. The most famous treatise on "japanning," as the new process was called, was written by John Stalker and George Parker and appeared in England in 1688. Theirs was primarily a pattern book, designed so that "the Nobility and Gentry might be compleatly furnish't with whole Setts of Japan Work, whereas otherwise they were forc't to content themselves with perhaps a Skreen . . . or some other odd thing."[17] In this example of an English "japanned" screen (fig. 10 recto and verso), it seems strange that the two outermost panels do not appear part of the otherwise continuous scene, and one is tempted to think they may be from another screen, or perhaps a later addition. The same treatment is found on the lower section of all six panels, however, and it is helpful to know that European cabinetmakers often deliberately did not match or use adjacent panels so as to lend to their works the same arbitrariness they perceived in oriental prototypes. Their use of noncontinuous panel compositions heightened the desired effect.[18]

In England another decorative screen type in the chinoiserie style soon found favor—the stamped, gilded, and painted leather screen. The art of decorating leather was known at least by the fourteenth century, and rare specimens date from the fifteenth century. These early examples are usually decorated hangings, mounted on frames and intended to be attached to walls. Stamping gave a relief effect to the leather, and the gilt served to reflect and augment the inadequate light of candles. The raised designs were often further articulated by paint and an oil glaze. Prior to 1800, most patterns were composed of scrollwork, flower, bird, or fruit designs. Early eighteenth-century trade cards indicate that many leathersmiths were working in London, including one William Barbaroux, "maker of all sorts of Gilt leather and screens in the newest and Genteelest taste."[19] This "newest taste" craved leather screens which imitated the Coromandel screens of the previous century. Exceedingly handsome,

FIG. 10 *Pair of Six-Panel Screens*, English, ca. 1680, Japanned wood. Photograph, Hamlyn Group.

FIG. 11 (?) Holford, English, active 18th century, *Six-Panel Screen*, ca. 1750, oil and gilt on leather. Photograph, Hamlyn Group.

leather screens embodied a number of special advantages. They were made by local craftsmen and therefore much more easily and cheaply obtained than imports. In addition, they could be ordered in any desired size, usually four to eight panels with a proportionally reduced height, as opposed to the huge, twelve-panel Chinese screens. Finally, design and color could be determined in advance by the patron. The styles could be as varied as the makers' skills allowed or the patrons' tastes dictated. Some designers of leather screens preferred vignettes with oriental motifs (fig. 11), while others copied on a smaller scale scenes of celebrations in architectural and landscape settings.

These leather screens also enjoyed popularity in the Netherlands, where a leather gilder's league had been active since the early seventeenth century. A six-panel screen from that period still has wide border designs in imitation of Coromandel screens (fig. 12). The main design contains exquisitely painted flowers and birds arranged in a flat, highly patterned design.

Italy, too, fell under the influence of the Orient, though with slightly different results as far as screens were concerned. The Italians generally preferred painted screens on either wood, silk, or leather. With a broad palette of vibrant colors, Italian artists and artisans captured the gaiety and exotic subject matter of Chinese pavilions, figures with parasols, and strange, imaginary birds and plants, as seen in an example painted on silk and mounted in an elaborately carved frame (fig. 13). Three other exceptional Italian screens deserve recognition, although they are not chinoiserie. Two of them, like the previous example at the Palazzina di Caccia at Stupinigi, were made by Giuseppe Maria Bonzanigo, one of Italy's greatest woodcarvers. These screens, with their elaborate gilded frames and silk panels decorated with garlands, ribbons, and flowers, rival any made in Europe. Bonzanigo received a number of royal commissions, including one for a screen for the marriage of Carlo Emanuele IV of Savoy in 1776. The fine carving of the bowed frame, the clearly articulated wreaths, and the acorn finials reveal why Bonzanigo was designated official woodcarver

to the crown.[20] The pattern of wreaths is repeated on the silk panels, which are further ornamented at the top with a drape of silk fringe and tassels (fig. 14). Similar wreaths, garlands, and ribbons appear in another screen by Bonzanigo, this time with panels containing a mythological subject (fig. 15).

The history of the screen in France is of special interest because it is so well documented. The French, under Colbert's direction, had established the Compagnie des Indes in 1660, and thereafter imported large quantities of goods from the Orient. In 1698 the *Amphritite* made its first voyage to China, returning with a cargo which included thirty-six screens, while a second voyage two years later yielded forty-five cases of *paravents*.[21] The *Journal du Garde-Meuble de la Couronne* shows that as early

FIG. 12 *Six-Panel Screen*, Dutch, 17th century, stamped, painted, and gilded leather, 199.4 x 327.7 (78½ x 129). London, Victoria and Albert Museum.

FIG. 13 *Four-Panel Screen*, Italian, ca. 1780, watercolor on silk with carved walnut frame. Stupinigi, Reale Palazzina di Caccia.

FIG. 14 Giuseppe Maria Bonzanigo, Italian, 1744-1820, *Five-Panel Screen*, ca. 1786, embroidered silk with silk fringes and tassels, and carved and gilded frame. Stupinigi, Reale Palazzina di Caccia.

FIG. 15 Giuseppe Maria Bonzanigo, Italian, 1744-1820, *Six-Panel Screen*, late 18th century, oil on panel with carved and gilded frame. Turin, Palazzo Reale. Photograph Francesco Aschieri.

as 1662, Anne of Austria had two large twelve-panel screens.[22] In the next few years, many entries appear listing screens of various materials, such as a six-panel *façon de la Chine* wallpaper example, and an eight-panel white satin embroidered screen with Chinese figures. Another listing describes a fabric screen with a painting of a Chinese fête set in a lacquer frame decorated with vases of flowers, wild animals, and assorted objects. An inventory of Versailles from 1708 lists twenty Chinese lacquer screens.[23] In the eighteenth century, Paris became a center for the creation of imitation lacquer as well. Its

most famous master was Robert Martin, who took out a patent for japanning "in relief in the style of Japan and of China," called "vernis martin." Martin's technique grew so famous under the patronage of Mme. de Pompadour that his name became synonymous with japanning. Voltaire even noted that "the cabinets of Martin have surpassed the art of China."[24]

Eighteenth-century French screens have a particular significance for this exhibition, as it is from this period that we first have records of distinguished artists—including Watteau, Boucher, Huet, and Lancret—painting folding screens. Some of these artists painted scenes in the Chinese style, following the fashion of the previous century, and some painted in more traditional European styles, while others worked in both modes. The French screens of the late eighteenth century also depict a curious development, the appearance of the *singerie,* a grotesque monkey often dressed in oriental robes and playing the role of a human. The popularity of these *singerie* figures signals yet another aspect of the oriental influence, yet in these pictures artists often were intent on mocking the Chinese source which engendered them. Christophe Huet in 1720 decorated two rooms in the Château de Chantilly, now the Musée Cluny, in this manner.[25] These superb

FIG. 16 Christophe Huet, French, died 1759, *La Toilette,* 1720, oil on panel, detail. Chantilly, Musée Condé. Photographie Giraudon.

examples of orientalist decorations are the "Grande Singerie," a salon, and the "Petite Singerie," a boudoir. In a panel from these decorations known as *La Toilette* (fig. 16), there is even a folding screen painted with vignettes of pagodas, landscapes, parasols, and dragons – in other words, all the paraphernalia usually associated with China and its screens. Seated in front of the screen is a monkey at a dressing table, assisted by two servants, in a paraody of virtually all aspects of the French fascination for things Chinese.

Singerie motifs also decorate a six-panel screen attributed to Alexis Peyrotte, formerly part of the Waddesdon Collection. Here, placed in a pastoral setting and dressed in European clothing, the monkeys frolic with other animals and marionettes and play musical instruments (fig. 17).[26] Screens which feature *singeries* were also made by the Savonnerie manufactory, after designs by Alexandre-François Desportes. In one of these screens (fig. 18), parrots, squirrels, birds, and monkeys are woven together against a gold background, painted in vivid shades of green, blue, cream, and red (fig. 18). The Savonnerie works were also responsible for a series of tapestries showing various animals and mounted on a screen as part of a suite of furniture for Louis XV in 1749 (fig. 19).[27]

Although most screens found in Europe prior to the late nineteenth century originated in the Orient or included decoration derived from eastern motifs, either honestly or in parody of them, some screens were also made in Europe. The earliest English examples were the more or less permanent architectural wall screens placed in the large halls of medieval buildings. Typically, at the end of a hall was a screen whose arched doorways led to a pantry, kitchen, buttery, or other work area. At a later date, wooden screens were even placed in front of such arches to conceal the activities in the kitchen; this traditional function of the screen is still with us today. Early furniture inventories from England, such as the one for Hardwicke Hall, list numerous screens, described only as "wicker skreynes." These objects could have been either firescreens or folding draft screens. There were other devices for combating the cold in English manor rooms; one was described as a "travice like a skreyne covered with violet Colored Cloth layde about with black lace." An inventory of 1603 lists "one great foulding skrene of seaven foulds," and in 1634 there is a similar mention of an "embroydered skreen gould lace."[28]

FIG. 17 Attributed to Alexis Peyrotte, French, 1699-1769, *Six-Panel Screen,* ca. 1760, oil on canvas, 152.4 x 342.9 (60 x 135). Collection of Baron Ferdinand de Rothschild, Waddesdon Manor. Photograph, National Trust.

FIG. 18 After Alexandre-François Desportes, French, 1661-1743, *Four-Panel Screen,* ca. 1720, wool and Savonnerie tapestry, 185.1 x 233.6 (72⅛ x 92). Malibu, J. Paul Getty Museum.

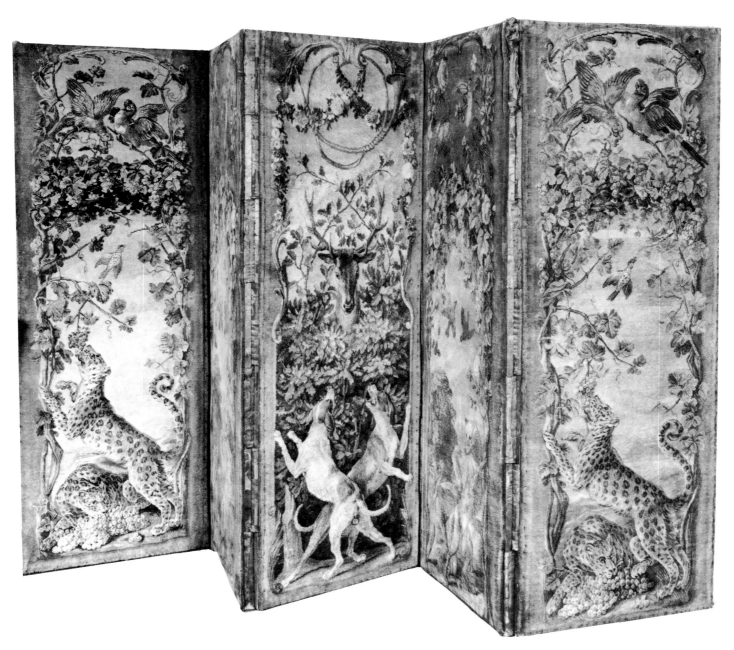

FIG. 19 *Five-Panel Screen,* ca. 1740, Savonnerie tapestry, 192.0 x 355.0 (74½ x 138½). Paris, Musées Nationaux: Musée du Louvre.

As the screens arriving from the Orient gained favor, Europeans began to look upon them as decorative as well as functional items. In England, early screens were often crudely constructed, sometimes including scenes depicting some phase of country life, such as a hunting vignette, or a simple landscape. These images tended to reflect the individualism of the upper-class Englishman, the informality of country life, and the naive style of the self-taught artist. As the eighteenth century progressed, English needlework screens gained in popularity. One such screen, worked by Julia, Lady Calverly in 1727, contained an image based on a passage in a 1693 edition of Vergil's *Georgics*. This six-panel screen was praised by Arthur Young in his *Northern Tour* (fig. 20).[29] Another English needlework screen is ornamented with realistically rendered floral bouquets, reflecting the traditional English love of flowers and gardens (fig. 21). In contrast, a French needlepoint screen from the same period with floral

FIG. 20 Julia, Lady Calverly, English, active 18th century, *Six-Panel Screen,* 1727, needlework on fabric. Photograph, National Trust.

motifs as its main design contains much more elaborate subsidiary decorations, including urns, cartouches, garlands, and ribbons (fig. 22).

Various aspects of eighteenth-century French life, especially "fêtes de campagne" and pastoral scenes, were favored subjects for screens from that country. Adaptations of Watteau's "Scènes Champêtres" appeared, in fact, in both English and French screens, probably because Watteau had gained fame in England before attaining it in France. Nicolas Lancret, a contemporary strongly influenced by Watteau, was a specialist in painting such fête scenes. When M. de Boullogne, commissioner of finances, bought a mansion in Paris located at the rue de la Paix and place Vendôme in 1728, Lancret was commissioned to decorate the salon. Here he created one of his most important decorative achievements.[30]

Some of the same elegant figures, delicate arabesques, and refined trellises from Lancret's ensemble were duplicated on a screen entitled *Les Quatres Heures du Jour* (fig. 23); a similar subject would be taken up, obviously in a much different style, some 170 years later by Alfons Mucha. François Boucher seems also to have done a folding screen: adorned with garlands, cartouches, and scenes of shepherdesses and milkmaids engaged in bucolic pursuits, it was presumably painted as a royal commission, as it bears the fleur-de-lis in its central panel (fig. 24). Screens and oriental bric-a-brac certainly appear in the backgrounds of paintings by Boucher, such as *La Toilette* (fig. 25). In this work a screen is prominently placed behind the young mistress who coyly adjusts her garter. The very same screen, framed in red lacquer and decorated with flowering fruit trees and birds in dull vermilion and green against a brown-gold background, also appears in a 1743 portrait by Boucher of his wife.[31] Jacques de Lajoue, another French artist from the circle of Lancret, is known to have done a seven-panel folding screen.[32] In it (fig. 26) shepherds and flute players are surrounded by curving consoles, canopies, and trellises; the panels are mounted in carved gilded frames. The fête scenes were evidently eminently suitable for these objects. Watteau, too, was a painter of folding screens, though the four examples in this genre listed in the catalogue raisonné of his paintings are lost.[33] Their subjects are unfortunately unknown. One source mentions that Watteau painted fans and screens which he gave to his friends, but again the nature of the decoration is a mystery.[34]

FIG. 21 Two panels from a *Four-Panel Screen,* English, ca. 1750, cross-stitch needlework. Photograph, Hamlyn Group.

FIG. 22 *Four-Panel Screen,* French, early 18th century, wool and needlepoint, 243.0 x 314.9 (96 x 124). New York, Metropolitan Museum of Art, Harris Brisbane Dick Fund, 1957.

FIG. 23 Nicolas Lancret, French, 1690-1745, *Les Quatres Heures du Jour,* ca. 1730, oil on canvas with gilded frame, 191.8 x 233.7 (75½ x 92).
London, Victoria and Albert Museum.

FIG. 24 François Boucher, French, 1703-1770, *Five-Panel Screen*, 1735-1760, oil on canvas, 180.3 x 241.3 (71 x 95). Photograph, London, P. & D. Colnaghi & Co. Ltd.

FIG. 25 François Boucher, French, 1703-1770, *La Toilette*, oil on canvas. Lugano, Thyssen-Bornemisza Collection.

FIG. 26 Attributed to Jacques de Lajoue, French, 1687-1761, *Seven-Panel Screen*, ca. 1730-1740, oil on canvas, 148.9 x 354.6 (58⅝ x 140). New York, Frick Collection.

"Conversation pieces" and paintings of interiors provide a rich source of material about different types of screens available in the eighteenth century, and of equal importance, about how they were used. Numerous watercolors and prints also show the ubiquitous presence of folding screens in domestic interiors. An engraving, *L'Assemblée au concert* by François Dequevauviller after a painting by Nicolas Lavreince, depicts a fashionable salon, with elegantly dressed and coiffed members of the court gathered for a musicale (fig. 27). In this interior is a low, eight-fold screen with panels of brocade or tapestry. Located at the right side of the scene, the screen partially shields the chair of a cellist as well as a table strewn with musical scores. This type of screen, usually about four feet high and extending to about eight to ten feet in width, was highly popular in eighteenth-century France. It was generally placed around a seated group to provide protection from drafts; Horace Walpole describes a dinner party in his *Paris Journal* of 1765 where such a screen was placed around the dining table to keep the cold from the guests' feet.[35] In any memoirs of court life in the eighteenth century, such as those of the Duc de Saint-Simon, one is constantly reminded of the essential role

of conversation and gossip as normal parts of palace intrigue. Such intimacies and exchanges no doubt flourished, and were even encouraged, in the privacy afforded by folding screens.

Possibly the most elaborate of all French screens was designed for the apartments of Louis XVI at Compiègne and further refined by recommendations made by the king himself. The design for this screen, requiring the skills of several master cabinetmakers, carvers, gilders, and upholsterers to execute, was delivered to Louis for his approval. After seeing it, he suggested to these craftsmen that it would be more elegant to have the frame cast in gilt bronze instead of the proposed wood. The result was a six-panel screen with silk-embroidered panels showing garlands of flowers and set into a gilded bronze frame (fig. 28). The following year some of the same master craftsmen made a similar screen for Marie Antoinette for her apartments at St. Cloud.[36]

The last highly formal folding screens made for a ruler of France were those woven at the Gobelins factory for the Grand Cabinet of Napoleon at the Tuileries. Gobelins delivered two complete suites of tapestries, each containing a folding screen and a single-panel firescreen. The earlier of the suites, dating from 1810, was rejected by Napoleon as being inadequate to express fully the richness of his reign. The second suite was designed with the collaboration of the famous neoclassical painter Jacques-Louis David; Pierre Fontaine, chief architect of the crown; and Vivant Denon, director of the French museums. In the latter suite was a screen consisting of richly embossed panels containing classical figures surrounded by laureled columns, imperial eagles, and crowns. After the Restoration of 1814, these last two royal symbols were replaced by helmets and fleur-de-lis, and the screen appears that way today (fig. 29).[37]

Folding screens seem to have lost their popularity as the century wore on. Cabinetmakers' design books of the early nineteenth century, such as Thomas Sheraton's *The Cabinet Dictionary* of 1803, in fact, do not contain designs for screens.[38] In drawings and watercolors of the same period, screens still appear in simple domestic scenes, but rarely in depictions of more formal interiors such as those by Percier and Fontaine in France, or Thomas Hope in England. In the eighteenth-century genre paintings, one frequently sees waist-high screens, usually portrayed without any attention to their decoration. Often the furniture in these works is painted with

FIG. 27 François Dequevauviller, French, 1745-1807, after Nicolas Lavreince, French, 1737-1807, *L'Assemblée au concert*, 1784, detail. New York, Metropolitan Museum of Art, Harris Brisbane Dick Fund, 1935.

FIG. 28 Hauré, Guérin, Forestier, Thomire, and Boulard, French, 18th century, *Six-Panel Screen,* 1786, embroidered silk with gilded bronze frame, 120.0 x 269.9 (47¼ x 106¼). Paris, Musées Nationaux: Musée du Louvre.

FIG. 29 *Six-Panel Screen,* Gobelins tapestry with gilded frame, designed by Pierre Fontaine, French, 1762-1853, and Jacques-Louis David, French, 1748-1825, 130.0 x 372.0 (51³/16 x 146½). Paris, Musée Mobilier.

such precision that existing pieces can be identified. The absence of detail in the screens depicted suggests that their importance was on the decline. After 1800, virtually no artist of importance attempted a folding screen anywhere in Europe. Whatever demand for these objects might have existed was probably met by examples that

survived from previous decades, if not generations. As this exhibition will demonstrate, however, the folding screen did not become extinct, even with greatly improved heating systems. It weathered at least a half-century period of disfavor to emerge during the second half of the nineteenth century in a new role.

NOTES

1. Janet W. Adams, *Decorative Folding Screens* (New York: Viking Press, 1982), 11.

2. Sherman E. Lee, *Japanese Screens from the Museum and Cleveland Collections* (Cleveland Museum of Art, 1977).

3. Elise Grilli, *The Art of the Japanese Screen* (New York and Tokyo: Weatherhill and Bijutsu Shuppan-sha, 1971), 151.

4. Grilli, *The Art of the Japanese Screen,* 151.

5. Shin'ichi Tani and Tadashi Sugase, *Namban Art* (exh. cat., International Exhibitions Foundation, 1973), 59.

6. Sherman E. Lee, *Japanese Decorative Style* (New York: Harper and Row, 1972), 95.

7. Yoshitomo Okamoto, *The Namban Art of Japan* (New York: Weatherhill, 1970), 139.

8. Okamoto, *The Namban Art of Japan,* 103.

9. Hugh Honour, *Chinoiserie* (London: John Murray, 1961), 43.

10. Percy Macquoid and Ralph Edwards, *Dictionary of English Furniture* (London: Country Life, Ltd., 1954), revised edition, vol. 3.

11. Margaret Jourdain and R. Soame Jenyns, *Chinese Export Art in the Eighteenth Century* (London: Country Life Ltd., 1950), Appendix D.

12. Jourdain and Jenyns, *Chinese Export Art,* Appendix D.

13. Honour, *Chinoiserie,* 71.

14. G. Jackson-Stops, "Erddig Park, Clwyd II," *Country Life* (13 April 1978): 972.

15. Note from The Countess Spencer, Althorp. See also Herbert Hall Mulliner, *The Decorative Arts in England* (London: B. T. Batsford, 1924), 35.

16. Hans Huth, *Lacquer of the West* (Chicago: University of Chicago Press, 1971), 23.

17. Herbert Cescinsky, *English Furniture of the Eighteenth Century* (London: George Routledge & Sons Ltd., 1911), 180.

18. Francis J. B. Watson, *The Wrightsman Collection* (New York: Metropolitan Museum of Art, 1966), 1: 174.

19. Victoria and Albert Museum, Department of Furniture and Textiles, Trade Card Collection.

20. Giuseppe Morazzoni, *Il Mobile neoclassico-italiano* (Milan: Editore Görlich, 1955), 19.

21. Jacques Romain Boulenger, *L'Ameublement français au grand siècle* (Paris: Les Arts Graphiques, 1913), 22.

22. H. Belevitch-Stankevitch, *Le Gout chinois en France* (Paris: Jean Schemit, 1910), 87.

23. Belevitch-Stankevitch, *Le Gout chinois en France,* 137.

24. Adolf Reichwein, *China and Europe* (London: Routledge and Kegan Paul Ltd., 1968), 35.

25. Gustave Macon, *Château de Chantilly* (Parc-St.-Maur: A. Garcet, 1925), plates 40 and 41.

26. Geoffrey DeBellaigue, *Furniture, Clocks, Gilt and Bronzes, The James A. de Rothschild Collection at Waddesdon Manor* (London: National Trust for Places of Historic Interest or Natural Beauty, 1967), 2: no. 135.

27. For these Savonnerie screens, see Gillian Wilson, *Decorative Arts in the J. Paul Getty Museum* (Malibu: J. Paul Getty Museum, 1977), 35; and Carle Dreyfus, *Catalogue sommaire, mobilier et objets d'art au XVIIe et du XVIIIe siècle,* 2d ed. (Paris: Musées Nationaux, Palais du Louvre, 1922), plate 53.

28. Macquoid and Edwards, *Dictionary,* 56.

29. John Cornforth, "Wallington, Northumberland II," *Country Life* (23 April 1970): 922-926.

30. *George Petit,* sale catalogue, 27 May 1896.

31. *Frick Collection, An Illustrated Catalogue, The Paintings* (New York: Frick Collection), 2: 3.

32. *Frick Collection,* 2: 141-146.

33. Jean Ferré, *Watteau. Catalogue raisonné* (Madrid: Editions Artisiques Athena, 1972), 4: 1210.

34. Adolf Rosenberg, *Antoine Watteau* (Bielefeld and Leipzig: Velhagen and Klasing, 1896), 17.

35. Paget Toynbee, ed., *The Letters of Horace Walpole* (Oxford: Clarendon Press, 1903-1905), 2: 133.

36. Pierre Verlet, *Le Mobilier royal français* (Paris: Les Editions d'Art et d'Histoire, 1945), 105.

37. M. Fernand Calmettes, *La Manufacture des Gobelins* (Paris: Imprimerie Nationale, 1912), 434.

38. Thomas Sheraton, *The Cabinet Dictionary* (London: W. Smith, 1803).

Michael Komanecky
'A PERFECT GEM OF ART'

INTRODUCTION

Our ancestors made great use of folding screens, and it is truly sad that this type of furniture is falling little by little into disuse, no doubt because of the small size of our apartments, which would soon be encumbered by them.

So wrote the French critic, historian, and publisher Charles Blanc in 1881.[1] The ancestors he refers to are most likely those of the previous century, when folding screens were commonplace fixtures in the spacious and drafty residences of the upper classes. Indeed, due partially to the decreasing size of domestic interiors, and perhaps as well to the inclinations of artists themselves, there were very few folding screens of any esthetic or historical significance done in France in the first half of the nineteenth century. Yet Blanc's assessment was not entirely accurate: in the 1850s both the established dean of landscape painting, Jean Baptiste Camille Corot, and the fledgling painter Paul Cézanne made folding screens. In Blanc's defense, it must be said that he would have had little opportunity to have seen either of these screens, since they were both kept in the artists' families and were almost certainly never exhibited publicly. The fact remains, however, that they were done, and that for the first time in nearly a century, reputable French artists were experimenting with the screen format.

In retrospect, Corot's and Cézanne's screens signal a revived interest in this genre which has continued virtually unabated to the present day. Blanc would not have suspected that in the two decades following his lament, the Nabi painters Pierre Bonnard, Edouard Vuillard, Maurice Denis, and their self-appointed esthetic leader Odilon Redon would make Paris the center of screenmaking activity in the West. Nor could Blanc have suspected that the Nabis would be joined in their efforts by architects, furniture designers, and painters throughout Europe and even in America. William Morris, Edward Burne-Jones, and Laurens Alma-Tadema in England; Charles Rennie Mackintosh in Scotland; Paul Klee in Switzerland; Josef Hoffmann in Austria; Carlo Bugatti in Italy; Antonio Gaudí in Spain; and Thomas Wilmer Dewing in America, as well as the American expatriate James McNeill Whistler would each do one or more folding screens in the years between 1870 and 1910.

What was responsible for this interest in the folding screen, an interest which transcended national boundaries as well as those sometimes artificial boundaries placed between the so-called fine and decorative arts? To be sure, these artists were motivated by different reasons in their decisions to make screens. Some were commissioned, some were made by the artists for use in their own studios, while still others were made for the commercial market, often as parts of larger decorative environments. In England, William Morris' desire to restore the quality of household goods by emphasizing the artists' and artisans' roles in both design and production was a significant factor. Morris' ideas found acceptance in one fashion or another throughout Europe, and had a powerful effect on American craftsmen such as Gustave Stickley. In France, as we have seen, there was already a strong tradition of screenmaking in the eighteenth century. By the latter part of the nineteenth century, in fact, there was a renewed interest in the rococo, much heralded and encouraged by the critics Edmond and Jules de Goncourt. At least one important late nineteenth-century screen was heavily influenced by the interest in eighteenth-century French decorative arts. The Nabis were also in sympathy with an often-quoted dictum proclaimed by one of Paul Gauguin's followers, Jan Verkade: "The war cry went up from studio to studio: 'No more easel pictures! Away with useless bits of furniture! Painting must not usurp a freedom which cuts it off from the other arts! The painter's work begins where the architect decides that his work is finished. . . . There are no such things as pictures, there is only decoration!'" As we shall see, not only did the Nabis find walls to paint; they also produced some of the most arresting and important folding screens of their era.

And by the turn of the century, one hardly needs to look for explanations of the screenmaking phenomena. The desire, even demand, for folding screens had spread from its centers in London and Paris throughout western and eastern Europe, and as far as Australia. There was hardly a single middle- or upper-class home that did not have at least one of these versatile pieces of furniture.

If there was any overriding reason for the ubiquitous interest in folding screens in the second half of the nineteenth century, however, it is to be found in the art of the Orient. As in so many other aspects of European and to a lesser degree American art, Japan exerted a strong influence on the western folding screen. The extent of this influence certainly varied from artist to artist and from one time to another, but it is notable that a large number

of western artists who made folding screens also owned Japanese screens. It was not so much that western artists were attracted to the compositional or design elements of Japanese screens; for the most part the oriental screens that they saw were far inferior in quality to the much better-known Japanese woodblock prints. On the contrary, western screenmakers were interested in a specific object type which, as they learned, had been the special province of Japanese artists for a millennium: the multipaneled folding screen. What attracted many of them was the very notion of a functional object whose surface could be decorated according to the artist's predilections, on one side or two. More importantly, a screen had to fold in order to function. The compositional ramifications implied by this idea of a folding image were consid-

FIG. 30 Jean Baptiste Camille Corot, French, 1796-1875; Charles Daubigny, French, 1740-1830; and Armand Hubert Simon Leleux, French, 1818/1820-1885, *Souvenir de Roquemaure (Gard)*, 1853; originally oil on canvas, 180.0 x 324.0 (70¼ x 126⅜). In Alfred Robaut, "Corot: Peintures décoratives," *L'Art* 31 (15 October 1882).

erable. Some artists chose to make their compositions continuous over several panels of a screen, almost always taking into account what effect folding would have. Others chose to relegate the image to a relatively small portion of the screen's surface, emphasizing instead ornamental patterns or motifs, often executed in luxurious materials. Still others ignored the role of image altogether, preferring to subordinate the screen within the design constraints of a larger decorative interior scheme. Regardless of the particular solutions, however, it was the formal challenge inherent in this simultaneously decorative and functional object which would command the attention of some of the West's foremost painters, architects, and designers between 1870 and 1910. What resulted from their efforts was a virtual golden age of screenmaking, which at times rivaled even the greatest achievements of their oriental predecessors.

THE WESTERN TRADITION: BEGINNINGS

The centuries-old tradition of screenmaking in the West was frequently nourished by a long-standing familiarity with oriental folding screens of both Chinese and Japanese origin. Even in the second half of the nineteenth century, though, when so much attention was focused on collecting and understanding the art of Japan, the eastern and western traditions existed side by side. Two important examples of the latter tradition must be mentioned if we are to properly assess the impact of Japanese folding screens during this period.

Two major French artists, Jean Baptiste Camille Corot and Charles Daubigny, both accomplished landscape painters of the Barbizon school, were responsible for one of the most important folding screens done after the mid-nineteenth century. Together with their lesser-known countryman Armand Leleux,[2] they painted in 1853 a six-panel screen entitled *Souvenir de Roquemaure (Gard)* (fig. 30).[3] It was done as a gift for Leleux's father-in-law, a man named Girard, who lived in the Swiss town of Dardagny in the canton of Geneva. Corot painted the four central landscape panels; Daubigny painted the left portion of the foliated trellis; and Leleux did the remaining upper and right portion of the trellis. The screen was later dismantled and only Corot's central landscape panels have survived, making it difficult to assess the

original impact of the whole. From a late nineteenth-century wood engraving reproduction of the screen, however, one can see that Corot's composition of gently rolling, wooded hills flows smoothly across the four central panels. In style, this landscape is largely typical of most Barbizon school works of the late 1840s or early 1850s. Daubigny and Leleux's foliated trellis, on the other hand, is somewhat unusual in its subject. Not only does the trellis function as an internal decorative frame for Corot's landscape, but it also evokes the effect that the viewer is looking through a window into this landscape.[4]

In the composition as a whole, there is very little concern for the special folding structure of a screen. The design extends across the surface as it would in an easel painting. The frame created by the trellis in the first and last panels might be enhanced by the screen's folding, whereas Corot's landscape undoubtedly would be fragmented. Of course, there is little in the Barbizon esthetic that would have led Corot to such concerns. The screen's most important aspect is that an artist of Corot's stature consented to decorate it, for nearly a century had elapsed since any of his countrymen had made a similar attempt.[5]

The issues raised by the second example are far more revealing terms of the past history of the western folding screen. In 1859, the young Paul Cézanne painted a number of works for his father's newly purchased seventeenth-century house, Jas de Bouffan, located near Aix-en-Provence. These included decorative panels, *The Four Seasons;* a wall decoration copied from a painting by Lancret; and a six-panel, double-sided folding screen called *Les Environs d'Aix-en-Provence* (fig. 31 and 32).[6] The recto of the screen shows two figure groups in eighteenth-century dress, one drinking and the other simply conversing. They are situated in a densely wooded Aix landscape; at the left the façade of Jas de Bouffan is visible in the background. This naive fête is framed first by dark and light bands and then by a wide floral border; it was probably painted to look like a tapestry mounted across the panels of a folding screen. The idea for the screen itself may have been suggested by an eighteenth-century prototype which was exhibited at the Musée Granet in Aix while the artist was a child. Cézanne borrowed the figure motifs for his screen from a painting by Lancret.[7]

The verso is even more dependent on eighteenth-century sources for its subject, a fanciful compendium of floral and architectural elements and portrait medallions.

FIG. 31 Paul Cézanne, French, 1839-1906, *Les Environs d'Aix-en-Provence* (recto), 1858-1860, formerly a six-panel screen but now mounted as a wall painting, oil on canvas, 249.9 x 403.9 (98⅜ x 159). Collection Wally Findlay, Palm Springs.

FIG. 32 Paul Cézanne, French, 1839-1906, *Les Environs d'Aix-en-Provence* (verso), 1858-1860. In Lionello Venturi, *Cézanne* (1936), 2: Fig. 1 and 2.

The subject recalls, in fact, an eighteenth-century needle-point screen mentioned in the previous essay (fig. 22). The vertical compositional orientation in each panel and the repetition of design motifs across the verso of the screen evidence the strong hold which the prevailing rococo revival had on Cézanne.[8] In any case, neither side indicates that he was at all concerned with how the folding structure would affect his compositions. In fact, the composition seems to have been chosen for its ability to present self-sufficient fragments in each panel whose pictorial integrity does not depend on their relationship to the other panels in the screen.

The evolution of Cézanne's screen was partially influenced by his friendship with Emile Zola, a childhood schoolmate. The two had exchanged letters, Cézanne writing from the Jas de Bouffan to his friend in Paris. In these letters Cézanne composed somewhat awkward

poems in which he frequently described his dreams of romantic love, and the pleasures of bathing, fishing, and drinking – all of which reappear as themes on the screen's recto.[9]

Zola at the time was just beginning his own career; his first book appeared in 1864. By 1866 he had decided finally to become a writer, and in the same year he published the first of several articles praising the work of a young painter in Paris, Edouard Manet. In gratitude for these reviews, and as an expression of the friendship that developed between the two men, Manet painted Zola's portrait in 1868 (fig. 33). Zola is shown seated, nearly in profile, reading a book at his desk. He is surrounded by several items which signal important aspects of Manet's art: a photograph of Manet's then-scandalous painting *Olympia*, an etching after a Velázquez painting, a Japanese print, and at the left edge one panel of an oriental folding screen. Despite a lengthy debate, it remains uncertain whether the painting shows Zola in his own apartment or in Manet's studio.[10] The answer is not that important to our discussion, for by 1868, when Manet finished the portrait, either he or Zola presumably owned this gold-ground, silk bordered Japanese screen. When or from whom the screen was purchased is unknown, as is its present location.

THE EASTERN INFLUENCE

Over the next two decades, oriental screens entered European markets and collections at an ever-increasing rate. Considerable scholarly effort has been devoted to discerning the various ways in which Japanese prints influenced European and American art in the second half of the nineteenth century.[11] Yet remarkably little attention has been paid to the fact that Japanese screens were also quite popular from at least 1860 on in Europe, and slightly later in America. It is certain that many western screenmakers, such as Whistler and the Nabis, were heavily dependent for their images on the design and compositional elements in Japanese prints. It is equally certain that their decisions to do screens were initially prompted by the increased presence of oriental examples in both public and private collections prior to the turn of the century.

The word oriental has been chosen deliberately here, for as we shall see, there was considerable confusion even

FIG. 33 Edouard Manet, French, 1832-1883, *Portrait de Zola*, 1868, Paris, Musée d'Orsay, Galerie du Jeu de Paume.

among critics and connoisseurs as to what was Japanese and what was Chinese. The distinctions between objects produced by these two great eastern cultures became clearer as the century came to a close, but for many the distinctions even when recognized were not that important, at least in the case of folding screens. Blanc himself wrote that:

Folding screens are never better decorated than by Chinese or Japanese subjects which are colored with opulent costumes, exotic flowers, highly colored coats of arms; fantastic birds with glistening plumage; [and] improbable quadrupeds with remarkable coats. . . . A glance at this type of folding screen transports you to imaginary countries at the other end of the world.[12]

Chinese and Japanese screens alike, to the late nineteenth-century viewer, had certain qualities in common. They showed exotic subjects, portrayed with unusual compositional asymmetry, and were frequently made of sumptuous materials. Each of these characteristics made such screens eminently desirable objects to own. Even in the context of screens, however, Japan's influence seems to have been dominant, supplanting the long-established European familiarity with Chinese screens discussed earlier.

As a result of Commodore Matthew Perry's official visit to Japan in 1853, for the first time in more than two centuries that country permitted commercial contacts with the West.[13] In addition to reestablishing trade, Japanese rulers also decided to send official entries to the various international industry and art exhibitions so popular in the second half of the nineteenth century.[14] Beginning with the famed 1850 International Exhibition at the Crystal Palace in London, and continuing for the next half-century, manufacturers, craftsmen, and artists alike had the opportunity to show their products to millions of visitors. The first systematic display of Japanese art took place at the London International Exhibition in 1862 when Britain's minister to Japan, Sir Rutherford Alcock, showed his personal collection of lacquer, bronze, and porcelain.[15] Although no screens seem to have been shown in this exhibition, the objects which were included excited one visitor who would later become an important commercial retailer of Japanese screens: Arthur Lasenby Liberty. Liberty was working at that time for Farmer & Rogers' Great Shawl and Cloak Emporium in London. He was so struck by the Japanese objects at the exhibition that he managed to purchase some of them for Farmer & Rogers' oriental warehouse.[16] When Liberty opened his still extant shop in London in 1875, he continued to sell Japanese goods of all kinds.[17] The quality and selection of Japanese objects at Liberty's were soon noticed by the influential architect and designer Edward W. Godwin: "If it [Liberty's] only had a little decent furniture, an artist might almost decorate and furnish his rooms from this one shop. There are matting and mats, carpets and rugs for the floor; Japanese papers for the walls; curtain stuffs for windows and doors; folding screens, chairs, stools, and so forth."[18] At least in London, then, the International Exhibition served to make the public aware of the curious goods arriving from Japan, including screens, and stimulated their wide availability through entrepreneurs like Liberty.

The next major display of Japanese products took place at the 1867 Exposition Universelle in Paris. The Japanese government-sponsored entry consisted of 1,308 objects, a small portion of which were devoted to the pictorial and decorative arts. Several folding screens were

FIG. 34 Japanese section, Exposition Universelle, Paris, 1867. In Fr. Ducuing, *Exposition Universelle,* 1867.

included in this entry.[19] Many of the objects were sold after the exhibition closed so that the Japanese government could recoup some of the expense of sending its entries. The sale catalogue from the Japanese section mentions, in fact, a six-panel screen consisting of "a curious series of Japanese scenes forming pendants. The personages are dressed in colored and embroidered silk."[20] A wood engraving by Dieudonné Lancelot published in one of the many illustrated guides to the exhibition may show this very screen (fig. 34).[21] In addition, at least eight other folding screens were mentioned in the sale catalogue.[22] These screens attracted the attention of Philippe Burty, a well-known critic and himself a collector of Japanese objects.[23] In a review of the exhibition, he wrote, "There was in the Japanese house of which we speak a magnificent lacquered folding screen made of two panels skillfully hewn from the trunk of an ancient tree, and decorated with an aquatic plant in which warblers make the stems bend." Burty also mentioned "folding screens of gilded paper with paintings of formidable roosters, and of landscapes where the crater of Mt. Fuji smokes."[24] Unfortunately, none of the screens listed in the sale catalogue has been linked with existing objects. Regardless, the listings indicate the variety of screen types

publicly available: there were lacquered wood screens and silk embroidered screens, as well as the more traditional gilded paper screens, all with various kinds of framing elements. Almost incredibly, not a single artist is mentioned in this list, and even to a relatively experienced connoisseur such as Burty the paucity of information about the screens' authorship seems not to have been the slightest bit disturbing. The fact that these exotic, intriguing examples of Japanese culture were on view was sufficient in itself.

China also sent an entry to the 1867 Exposition Universelle, including at least one folding screen. Purchased in 1869 by the South Kensington Museum (today the Victoria and Albert) in London, which only seven years before had been the site of the first large-scale public display of Japanese objects, this double-sided five-panel embroidered silk screen with lacquered wood frames (fig. 35) shows seated, standing, and riding figures in a landscape on the recto. The verso is decorated with trees, birds, and butterflies in blue featherwork upon a gold ground. The exotic imagery and rich materials of this mid-nineteenth-century Chinese screen seem to modern eyes not appreciably different from the characteristics of those screens described by Burty. One should remember

FIG. 35 *Five-Panel Screen* (recto and verso), Chinese, 19th century, embroidered silk with lacquered frame, 168.9 x 266.7 (66½ x 105). London, Victoria and Albert Museum.

that the critical and public reaction to oriental screens in this period, though enthusiastic, did not reflect a sophisticated understanding of their venerable pictorial heritage.

Strangely, no screens were included at the 1869 Paris exhibition, the so-called Musée Oriental, devoted solely to Japanese art.[25] But at the 1878 Exposition Universelle, the Japanese government again sent an official artistic contribution.[26] The selection of objects was augmented, however, by loans from some of France's most avid Japanophiles, including Burty, Jules Jacquemart, Samuel Bing, and Emile Guimet. These objects were apparently shown in spaces adjacent to the official Japanese entries. From the various catalogues and commentaries on the exhibition, it is possible to reconstruct the variety of the screens shown. The critic Ernest Chesneau was struck by one screen in particular:

There is not a visitor who has not admired in the first floor showcase the grand salon furnishing in the form of a four-panel folding screen where four compositions in a marvelous style showing bushes of flowers, long branches, and curved reeds are isolated by a black lacquer base. These incomparable images are executed by means of juxtapositions and encrustations of mother-of-pearl and of precious metals: bronze, silver, and gold patinated in different ways. The absolute perfection of the handwork, which leaves nothing to chance and which suffers no negligence in the application of sumptuous materials, from which unforeseen and magnificent effects of coloration proceed, constitute here the fundamental elements of a masterpiece.[27]

This remarkable passage does reveal to us one important aspect of the growing popularity of Japanese screens—namely that they were appreciated as much for their superb craftsmanship as for their compositional or design principles. And perhaps for the first time, a screen's maker is known: Minoda Chojiro. The absence of biographical information on Minoda implies that he was an artisan whose work has merited little attention.

Among the Japanese objects in western collections shown at the 1878 Exposition Universelle were a number of screens which attracted the attention of Edmond Duranty.[28] In his brief review, he mentioned only in passing

FIG. 36 *Six-Panel Screen*, Japanese, Kano school, 18th century, watercolor and gold leaf on paper. Paris, Musées Nationaux: Musée Guimet.

"the curious folding screens owned by Messieurs Davis and de la Narde," but he discussed at length a screen owned by Emile Guimet: "M. Guimet has brought back a very precious screen which allows us to establish the time periods in the making of Japanese art. *The artist* [Duranty's emphasis] has represented a debarkation of the Portuguese, received by the Jesuits, then established in the country. The Shōgun Yeyas,[29] persecutor of the Christians, some time later had the figures of the Jesuits scratched out. This screen is incontestably from the end of the sixteenth century, and it clarifies for us certain points of design such as it was then understood, and such as it had been practiced previously in Japan."[30] Within a year after this screen was shown, the industrialist and collector Emile Guimet had founded his own museum of Far Eastern art in Lyon. In 1884 he gave the museum and its collection to the state. It was transferred in 1887 to Paris, where the screen described by Duranty, which Guimet probably purchased during his 1876-1877 trip to Japan, still resides (fig. 36). Now recognized as an eighteenth-century Kano school product, the screen is an example of so-called *namban* art. In this instance, the subject is the arrival of Portuguese traders while Japan still allowed these contacts and while Jesuit missionaries were still permitted.[32]

It is important to distinguish between the vastly different situations posed by Minoda's and by this *namban* screen. Minoda's screen was a government-sponsored entry to an international exhibition, done by an artist who attained no particular reputation for the quality of his work. And, according to the description provided by Chesneau, one may presume the screen was notable more for its precious materials than for its subject matter or style. Considering how many oriental objects were made specifically for export to the West, it is likely the screen's appearance was even determined by the audience for which it was intended. The latter screen, however, drawing as it does from Kano school stylistic and compositional sources, is far closer to the justifiably famed tradition of Japanese screens established by Ogata Korin, Nonomura Sotatsu, and members of the Kano family.[33] The linear rhythms, the bold light and dark patterns, the continuous composition, the generous use of gold, and the relatively simple border and frame are all typical of traditional Japanese screens. Yet this type was not the one most often seen or collected by western Japanophiles. The most important and esthetically distinguished

Japanese screens were considered family heirlooms, and they remained in families' hands for generations.

Chesneau also commented further on the distinction between different oriental cultures: "The long-standing confusion which exists between Chinese decor and Japanese decor [is a] confusion which still persists in the souls of inattentive fools."[34] His anger is better understood in view of the considerable number of Chinese screens that were being imported into Europe. Some of these screens were shown at the same 1878 Exposition Universelle: there were screens made of embroidered silk, black carved lacquer, embroidered satin, and even stone.[35] Duranty, too, differentiated between the products of the two Asian cultures, but with some advice for the uninitiated: "I know we have too often depreciated Chinese art in order to exalt the Japanese . . . the remarkable folding screens from Canton, partly ancient types, catch one's attention and equal at certain points the good Japanese paintings. . . . The beauty, the variety of vegetation, of trees, of landscape, of terrain, of fabrication; the groups and incidents so diverse from public or private life that take place and unfold there. All this makes these screens very interesting."[36] As we have seen such Chinese screens were in great favor in eighteenth-century France and England. Perhaps due to the new-found interest in Japanese screens, they too maintained their popularity.

Japanese screens were also imported into other European countries. The official catalogue to the 1873 Weltausstellung in Vienna lists "folding screens with paintings" and "folding screens with paintings on paper and silk" among the objects shown in the Japanese section.[37] The following year the Orientalisches Museum was founded in Vienna, no doubt responding in part to the surge of interest in Far Eastern cultures generated by the Japanese entries at the Weltausstellung. Sometime between 1874 and 1907, when its collections became incorporated into what is today the Österreichisches Museum für Angewandte Kunst, the Orientalisches Museum acquired seven Japanese screens dating from as early as the seventeenth century to perhaps as late as 1874.[38] The lack of precise acquisition information permits only broad generalization about their potential impact. Initially, one is again struck by the general low quality of the screens. Two six-panel Kano school screens (fig. 37 and 38) are actually pastiches made up of narrative battle scenes[39] whose panels do not even present the battles in sequence. This totally unorthodox grouping[40] leads one to believe

FIG. 37 and 38 *Pair of Six-Panel Screens,* Japanese, Kano school, 18th century, ink and color on silvered paper, 166.0 x 353.5 (64¾ x 137⅞), each screen. Vienna, Österreichisches Museum für Angewandte Kunst.

that the panels were rearranged, perhaps with some missing, and that the screens may even have been put together by a dealer for undiscerning customers. Another screen dating from the eighteenth or nineteenth century (fig. 39) depicts on its two panels a dynamic arrangement of Japanese fans against a gold background. It is not difficult to imagine how the floral, wave, and abstract design motifs shown in these fans, as well as the lively surface pattern across the screen, would have interested artists and collectors alike.[41] A third screen from this group (fig. 40) surely dating from the nineteenth century, portrays two armed warriors in pursuit of a man whose only protection is a long staff. Such a subject was undoubtedly more familiar to an audience whose knowledge of Japan and its art was introduced primarily by seventeenth- and eighteenth-century *ukioye* prints. In addition, the richly patterned costumes, asymmetrical compositional arrangement, and slightly overhead viewpoint are characteristics which were also found in these readily available woodblock prints. The familiarity of these motifs may have made the screen desirable for its western purchaser. Clearly, few if any truly high quality Japanese screens were available at the time.

FIG. 39 *Two-Panel Screen*, Japanese, 18th-19th century, twenty colored fans mounted on gold leaf on paper, 180.0 x 180.0 (70¼ x 70¼). Vienna, Österreichisches Museum für Angewandte Kunst.

FIG. 40 *Six-Panel Screen*, Japanese, 19th century, ink and color on gold-sprinkled paper, 154.0 x 839.0 (60⅛ x 327¼). Vienna, Österreichisches Museum für Angewandte Kunst.

A similar situation prevailed in England, at least as far as existing documentation indicates. In 1886, the British Museum received a number of oriental screens from the physician William Anderson (1842-1900). He probably acquired them when he served as a professor of anatomy and surgery at the newly founded Imperial Naval Medical College at Tokyo between 1873 and 1879.[42] One of the screens (fig. 41) is a six-panel ink painting of high quality which Anderson described as follows: "The picture is a good example of the Usa-Zaishiki, or thinly-coloured painting, a style which the early artists of the Sesshiū, Chinese, and Kano schools had adopted from the masters of the Sung and Yüen dynasties. Painted by Ka-no Yasunobu. Two seals. Seventeenth century."[43] Anderson seems to have been a discerning collector who recognized that even the Kano school artists of Japan, like many of their countrymen before them, had imitated Chinese painting styles in their screens.[44] In its imitation of such a style, Anderson's screen offers evidence that traditional types of Japanese screens became more available in the marketplace and in public collections as the century drew to a close.

Two other screens acquired by Anderson indicate further the level of knowledge about Japanese screens in the late nineteenth century (fig. 42 and 43). In a lengthy descriptive passage, Anderson states that the two screens show a river festival at Nagoya, Owari Province: "These pictures, which belong to the end of the seventeenth century, are valuable as records of dress and customs, and, despite the conventionality of drawing, possess considerable artistic beauty."[45] In these two screens, we see the same subject type, generically speaking, found in the *namban* screen purchased by Emile Guimet in Japan at very nearly the same time. A dense pattern of gold-leaf-covered clouds reveals glimpses of a busy port, bustling with daily activity. One can only presume that the combination of bold overall compositional pattern with minute anecdotal detail was highly valued. More important, however, is the fact that Anderson managed to purchase a *pair* of screens. Almost all traditional Japanese screens were executed in pairs, in which subjects and composition were closely related if not totally continuous across the panels of both screens. This fact was either unknown or largely ignored by western collectors of Japanese

FIG. 41 Kano Yasunobu, Japanese, active 18th century, *Six-Panel Screen*, 180.3 x 373.4 (70⅜ x 145½). London, British Museum.

FIG. 42 and 43 *Pair of Eight-Panel Screens,* Japanese, 17th century, watercolor on paper, 151.1 x 468.6 (59½ x 184½), each screen. London, British Museum.

screens, however, and only the American Thomas Wilmer Dewing was to follow the traditional Japanese method, executing at least three pairs of painted screens around 1900 (see Cat. 10).

America, too, shared Europe's fascination for oriental art. The International Exhibition of 1876 in Philadelphia served to increase this country's awareness of both Chinese and Japanese cultures. Even before then, some American collectors had already begun to acquire oriental screens. In Philadelphia itself, the merchant Nathan Dunn amassed a substantial collection of Chinese objects, and in 1839 he published a catalogue to document it.[46] Among the many objects exhibited in a large building at Ninth and George (now Sansom) Streets were several Chinese screens.[47] One in particular deserved special mention:

In the vestibule which separates the vestibule from the grand [salon], we have an admirable specimen of Chinese screen work. It is richly and tastefully gilded; the portion of the wood-work not covered with gold is painted of delicate green; and the silk inserted in the panels is as gay as can be rendered by a profusion of the most delicate and magnificent of eastern flowers. The whole view is redolent of the spirit and beauty of spring. The drawings and colourings of the flowers are admirable, and show the perfection which has been attained in these branches of their art by Chinese painters. Besides the floral delineation, there is also a row of silk panels, if we may be allowed the expression, exhibiting the views of naval architecture, both curious and instructive.[48]

It would seem obvious from this description that collectors in Philadelphia, like those in many other eastern cities, were familiar with oriental screens from the vast Chinese export trade that flourished in America at the end of the eighteenth and the beginning of the nineteenth century. Dunn's collection, in fact, was of such interest that he exhibited it in London in 1842; at least one hundred thousand copies of the catalogue were sold in the two cities.[49]

To the International Exhibition of 1876, both China and Japan sent numerous official entries, including several screens. From the scanty information provided in the catalogue it would seem that the Chinese screens were made by Canton furniture firms rather than by established artists.[50] Japan's screen entries fall into the same category.[51] The few available illustrations of these screens and the brief descriptions of them in the catalogue make it clear that contemporary rather than ancient or traditional oriental screens were the rule.[52] The taste for such contemporary Japanese and Chinese products spread throughout America with the help of the many guides to home decorating which were published shortly after the Centennial Exhibition. In Clarence Cook's 1878 *The House Beautiful*, for example, is a six-panel oriental screen showing figures in a landscape (fig. 44). From the subject of the screen it is difficult to tell whether it is Chinese, or a Japanese interpretation of a Chinese scene. Cook was apparently even more confused, for the caption beneath the illustration describes it as "a charming Indian screen."[53]

To Cook and others the usefulness of such screens was obvious:

If any one shall be led by it to think it a good notion to divide a large room up by screens and curtains instead of always by formal and permanent partitions, the little picture will be doing a part of its duty. To many people a large room is a great pleasure. Indeed, I think, most people like to have plenty of space in which to move about, but as we all like privacy sometimes, and seclusion from the doings of others, if for no other end than to have the temptation to talk and look about us removed, it is good to have easy ways of attaining our object. The long, narrow parlors that are such an affliction to New-York housekeepers are much more elegantly divided by screens, which may be made as rich or as plain as we choose.[54]

FIG. 45 Dining Room, Mr. and Mrs. James Lancaster Morgan, Jr., House, Brooklyn, New York, as seen in 1888. Museum of the City of New York.

Late nineteenth-century photographs of upper middle-class and upper-class homes throughout America attest to the popularity and availability of oriental screens. Whether in Brooklyn, St. Paul, or Chicago (fig. 45, 46, 47), such screens became standard fixtures in domestic interiors. They were found in the White House (fig. 48)[55] and continued to be seen at exhibitions such as the 1884-1885 World's Industrial and Cotton Centennial in New Orleans (fig. 49). Japanese screens, it seems, had reached virtually every major urban center in America by the late 1880s.

This excursion through the great international exhibitions makes it clear that Japanese and Chinese screens were increasingly abundant in both Europe and America toward the end of the nineteenth century. Western artists, some of whom themselves made folding screens, were interested in them as well. Manet's *Portrait of Zola* (fig. 33) is only one of many paintings from the period which include oriental screens as part of their subject. We know

FIG. 46 Dining Room, George Finch House, St. Paul, Minnesota, as seen in 1884. Minnesota Historical Society.

FIG. 47 Apartment of Arthur Dana Wheeler, Mentone Apartment House, Chicago, Illinois, as seen in April 1891. Chicago Historical Society.

FIG. 48 Red Room, the White House, Washington, as seen in 1889. Photograph, the White House.

FIG. 49 Japanese section, World's Industrial and Cotton Centennial, New Orleans, 1884. New Orleans, Louisiana State Museum.

from the inventory of Manet's belongings taken after his death that he owned "one small Chinese folding screen, valued 40 fr."[56] Manet's more overtly Japanophile contemporary James Jacques Joseph Tissot also included Japanese screens in his paintings of the 1860s, most notably in *Young Women Looking at Japanese Objects,* from 1869 (fig. 50). The painting is one of several in which Tissot displayed his essentially archaeological approach toward both Japanese and Chinese objects.[57] The only object here clearly identifiable as Japanese is the gold-ground folding screen at the left. Even though very little of the screen is visible, the bold design fragments as well as the traditional hinging method employed in the screen indicate a relatively high quality example, probably of eighteenth-century Japanese origin. Where these screens were obtained is not known, but Parisian shops like La Porte Chinoise in the rue Vivienne and M. and Mme. Desoye's curiosity boutique in the rue de Rivoli are likely sources.[58] Many other European and American artists who owned oriental screens can be cited as well: Alfred Stevens,[59] Jean-Léon Gérôme,[60] Paul Serusier,[61] Edouard Vuillard,[62] Alfons Mucha,[63] in France; J. F. Weir[64] and William Merritt Chase[65] in America owned them. Sir Laurens Alma-Tadema in England had at least ten

FIG. 50 James Jacques Joseph Tissot, French, 1836-1902, *Young Women Looking at Japanese Objects,* 1869. London, Private Collection.

Japanese screens.[66] In London such screens likely could have been purchased from the Oxford Street firm of Bontor and Collins, which opened in 1872, or from the store which Arthur Lasenby Liberty opened in 1875.[67]

Perhaps the best-known examples of these documentary pictures are those of James McNeill Whistler. This expatriate American artist shuttled back and forth between Paris and London in the late 1850s and early 1860s, and thus had ample opportunity to see and collect oriental objects then being imported in great numbers to the two art centers. Whistler did purchase some oriental objects from the Desoye shop in Paris, which opened in 1860 and which Manet, Tissot, and the critics Jules and Edmond de Goncourt and Théodore Duret were also known to have frequented. In 1864 Whistler painted two pictures which reflect his great interest in oriental objects, especially Japanese folding screens.[68] The first, entitled *Rose and Silver: The Princess from the Land of Porcelain* (fig. 51)[69] shows a woman dressed in a kimono standing on an oriental rug, and in front of a five-panel oriental screen. Whistler owned this screen until 1880, when bankruptcy forced him to sell his recently completed White House in Tite Street along with many of its furnishings.[70] Described in the sale catalogue as "Handsome Japanese Screen of 5 folds, with panels of silk, painted with flowers, glazed, and gilt wood frame," the screen is surely the same one shown in a photograph of Whistler's first studio at Cheyne Walk in London (fig. 52) where the artist lived from 1867 until June 1878 when the Tite Street house was completed. The second painting by Whistler is

FIG. 52 Room in Whistler's House, Cheyne Walk, London. *American Magazine of Art* 12 (September 1921).

FIG. 51 James Abbott McNeill Whistler, American, 1834-1903, *Rose and Silver: The Princess from the Land of Porcelain*, 1864. Washington, Freer Gallery of Art.

appropriately titled *Caprice in Purple and Gold, No. 2: The Golden Screen* (fig. 53).[71] Again a female figure in Japanese attire is shown, this time in front of what is probably a Tosa school screen whose literary subject is borrowed from such works as the *Tales of Genji*.[72] Both paintings document Whistler's understanding of the design heritage of Japan as conveyed by Japanese prints and costume, as well as by the screens themselves. There can be little doubt that in the second half of the nineteenth century many curious and exotic oriental screens attracted the serious attention of critics, collectors, and artists alike. For this last group, these screens were seen not only as versatile utilitarian objects, but also as tremendously challenging exercises in design. It was through exposure to oriental screens that western artists were inspired to revitalize a tradition of screenmaking that had nearly died out in the West. Corot's and Cézanne's efforts might very well have remained anomalies had it not been for the arrival of oriental screens in Europe during this period.

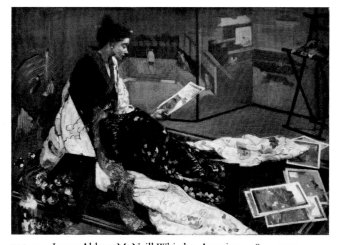

FIG. 53 James Abbott McNeill Whistler, American, 1834-1903, *Caprice in Purple and Gold, No. 2: The Golden Screen*, 1864. Washington, Freer Gallery of Art.

THE WESTERN TRADITION: MATURITY AND FRUITION

How the oriental tradition was initially translated to the West is indicated by two screens made in London, the first by William Eden Nesfield in 1867, and the second by James McNeill Whistler just five years later. Nesfield was known primarily as an architect whose early work was closely tied to the medievalism of Pugin then prevailing in London.[73] He made several trips to the continent in the 1850s with his friend and fellow architect Richard Norman Shaw to study firsthand the great Gothic churches. Beginning in 1863 Nesfield and Shaw shared an office, and from 1866 to 1869 they were partners.[74] On the occasion of Shaw's marriage on 16 July 1867, Nesfield designed a six-panel double-sided folding screen (see Cat. 1) which was executed by James Forsyth, a sculptor and carver on good terms with both architects.[75] The screen is a rich blend of authentic Japanese design motifs, including twelve unattributed and probably contemporary Japanese goldground paintings of buds and flowers mounted on the recto and verso. Above and below the paintings are gilded, carved, and painted decorations, subdivided by and mounted in an ebonized wood frame. The wealth and variety of these decorations tend to minimize the effect of the paintings, despite the prominence accorded them by their very size. It is notable that the paintings do not contain continuous scenes; they consist instead of individual panels joined only for the purposes of this screen. Such panels were by all means as available as oriental screens. If the Orient was the ultimate inspiration for this screen, Nesfield adapted the ideas considerably, compartmentalizing the whole into a series of equally weighted individual panels whose continuity derives from repetition of similar patterns and from the structure provided by consistent handling of the framing elements. Japan may be recalled in individual motifs, but the overall result is a tightly organized exercise more typical of English interpretations of the Orient than of the Orient itself.[76]

The joining of noncontinuous Japanese paintings served as at least a partial basis for another even more important screen done in 1872 by James McNeill Whistler. This two-panel, double-sided folding screen (fig. 54 and 55) may have been commissioned in 1871 by Frederick F. Leyland, a Liverpool shipping merchant who was Whistler's most important patron in the 1870s.[77] For

FIG. 54 James Abbott McNeill Whistler, American, 1834-1903, *Blue and Silver: Screen with Old Battersea Bridge* (recto), 1872, tempera on brown paper on canvas, 195.0 x 182.0 (76¾ x 71¾). Hunterian Art Gallery, University of Glasgow, Birnie Philip Bequest.

FIG. 55 Verso of fig. 54. Nampo Osawa, Japanese, born 1845, *Two Flower and Bird Paintings*, 1867, watercolor on silk, 195.0 x 182.0 (76¾ x 71¾). Hunterian Art Gallery, University of Glasgow, Birnie Philip Bequest.

Whistler's screen shows a nocturnal view of Old Battersea Bridge with a golden moon rising from behind. The bridge is seen from the south bank of the Thames, almost directly across the river from Whistler's house at 2 Lindsey Row (96 Cheyne Walk). The lighted clock-tower of Old Chelsea Church is visible at the left, and the partially constructed Albert Bridge is in the distance at the right. Painted in tempera on paper laid on canvas, the bridge image is surmounted by a narrow gilded wooden frame decorated by Whistler with a four- and five-petal flower pattern painted in two shades of green. The two panels are joined by three pairs of leather hinges and supported by four squat rectangular legs, simple continuations of the vertical framing elements. At the bottom, the screen originally had a series of two, then three, horizontal slats connecting the legs in each panel (fig. 57). These slats surely would have added a horizontal emphasis to the screen, corresponding to an extent to the horizontal orientation of Whistler's image. They also would have provided a gentler transition between the floor and the screen itself. In this sense, then, Whistler shared Nesfield's concern for the integration of the image within the overall screen structure.

reasons unknown the screen remained in Whistler's hands at his various London and Paris homes until his death in 1903 (fig. 56). One side shows birds and flowers against a gold ground dominated by a blossoming orange tree. Both panels, done in a vaguely Chinese style, are signed by the woman artist Nampo and dated 1867.[78] Once again it was contemporary rather than ancient Japanese art which provided the stimulus. Moreover, the two panels, though certainly related in subject as were those in the Nesfield screen, do not depict a continuous scene. They may be fragments of a larger composition cut down to fit into Whistler's screen format, but it is equally likely that the panels were obtained by Whistler just as they are.[79] Whatever the exact circumstances, by including them in the screen, Whistler was not only stating his appreciation for the perceived abstractions in these Japanese landscape paintings; as an owner of oriental screens, he was also paying homage to the tradition that inspired the creation of his own screen.

FIG. 56 Whistler in his Paris studio, ca. 1892. Washington, Freer Gallery of Art.

Whistler's treatment of Old Battersea Bridge was a radical compositional departure from his earlier conceptions.[80] It may very well have been derived from Japanese prints such as Hiroshige's *Kyo Bridge* (fig. 58), from which Whistler borrowed the gently arching bridge motif, with emphasis on the vertical pilings, and even the prominent, rising moon. He also greatly simplified and abstracted his subject, however. In a preliminary drawing for the screen (fig. 59) dating from ca. 1872, Whistler rendered the scene relatively accurately, including such details as the railing on the bridge and a spectator peering down to the river below, and sketching in the Albert Bridge and various structures on the opposite shore. He also paid close attention to the actual construction of the bridge supports. Uncertainty about the final composition led him to outline the shore twice at the left, and more conspicuously to include not one but two moons at the level of the bridge railing. A later pastel (fig. 60) shows Whistler moving closer to establishing the composition.

FIG. 58 Andō Hiroshige, Japanese, 1797-1858, *Kyo Bridge*, ca. 1857, woodblock print, 35.3 x 24.0 (13⅞ x 9⁷/₁₆). Cologne, Museum für Östasiatische Kunst.

FIG. 57 Detail of screen hinge. Whistler, *Blue and Silver: Screen with Old Battersea Bridge*, 1872. Photograph, Hunterian Art Gallery, University of Glasgow.

The bridge support is depicted more abstractly, its vertical and near horizontal elements even recalling Japanese calligraphy. The shoreline and moon appear almost exactly as they do in the screen. Only the railing and figures on the bridge would be removed in the final version, and all that remained for Whistler to do was to elongate the composition slightly at the bottom. Painted in broad, subtle washes of verdigris blue and deep greens, with the golden moon at the upper right offset by the lighted clock tower at the lower left, the screen shows the result of Whistler's own inventiveness as much as it does his reliance on any specific Japanese source.

There are several reasons why Whistler's screen assumes such significance. The inclusion of Japanese paintings on one side allowed the artist to acknowledge the oriental source of his inspiration. But for the other side, Whistler deliberately chose a recognizable, even mundane subject – a much-used bridge lying at the edge of a bustling city. Then for the sake of purely formal and compositional concerns, he stripped it of all but the most basic identifying features. In doing so he was proclaiming that a western folding screen could succeed on its own terms, with its own subjects and its own stylistic features.

Whistler was, moreover, highly cognizant of the special structure of a folding screen. His first study for this work (fig. 59) consists of two nearly identically sized sheets joined at the middle along an even vertical seam. Why did he use two sheets when he just as easily could have cut down a larger sheet to any size he needed? A logical and compelling explanation is that Whistler sketched the composition on the two separate sheets before they were

FIG. 59 James Abbott McNeill Whistler, American, 1834-1903, *Old Battersea Bridge*, ca. 1872, charcoal with touches of white chalk and gray wash on paper, 26.7 x 35.5 (10⅝ x 14). Buffalo, Albright-Knox Art Gallery, Gift of George F. Goodyear.

FIG. 60 James Abbott McNeill Whistler, American, 1834-1903, *Old Battersea Bridge*, ca. 1872, pastel on paper, 18.5 x 28.1 (7¼ x 11¹/₁₆). Washington, Freer Gallery of Art.

permanently joined so that he had the opportunity to discover how folding would affect the final visual result. A screen, after all, must fold to stand upright. Whistler must have known that when folded, each half of the composition would be thrust out of plane. The panels would then relate to one another on a different basis, each possible folded position having its own set of dynamic sensibilities. These concerns almost certainly contributed to Whistler's decision to simplify his composition, so that the abstract qualities of the T-shaped bridge would dominate without being dramatically altered by folding. Whistler was therefore among the first western artists to experiment with the screen as a unique type of folding image.

London was again the site for the creation of yet another early folding screen, one which posed a much different alternative for the screen's development in the West. In late 1869 Sir Laurens Alma-Tadema, whose first wife had died, met the young and pretty Laura Epps. The daughter of a wealthy physician, she soon became the focus of the artist's attention. Alma-Tadema, then thirty-three, had already established a considerable reputation as a skilled painter of scenes from ancient Egyptian and classical times, rendered with astounding archaeological accuracy. When Laura Epps expressed to Alma-Tadema her desire to learn more about the craft of painting, he was probably only too happy to oblige.[81] The painting lessons eventually resulted in a six-panel folding screen done largely by Alma-Tadema (see Cat. 2).

The screen is a group portrait of the Epps family, with Laura's father Dr. George Napoleon Epps seated at the left; her mother, three brothers, four sisters, and their families are included as well. Laura is seen in profile in the sixth panel with the bearded Alma-Tadema just to her right, gazing from behind at the woman whom he would marry in July 1871. There is no known precedent in the nineteenth century for such a portrait screen, and the formal problems presented by this undertaking may account at least partially for the screen's unfinished appearance.[82] Even so, ample evidence exists to show that these problems were largely resolved by Alma-Tadema's formidable compositional abilities.

Alma-Tadema united the panels by a broad, red, L-shaped border, whose horizontality is echoed above by the long, white tablecloth. This border acts as a common denominator, so to speak, across the screen, mitigating the potentially disquieting effects of different sized portrait groups above. Moreover, the vertical portion of the L in the first panel brilliantly counteracts the procession-like entrance of figures from the right side of the screen. The artist's audacity and confidence are nowhere more evident than in the very first panel, where he confronts the viewer with a nearly purely abstract arrangement of red, white, and brown rectangles. There was no precedent in either eastern or western art for such a solution. The screen is enframed by this red border below and by the gold ground inscription at the top.[83] The vaguely gothic script in this inscription is matched in the border below by trompe l'oeil nameplates, not all of which were completed. The character of the inscription and nameplates, along with the compositional effect of the red border, tends to lessen the imposing scale of the screen, making it appear more like an enlarged (and modern) manuscript illumination.

But to what extent did Alma-Tadema consider how the folding structure would alter the decidedly horizontal nature of his composition? When the screen is arranged in a symmetrically folded position (Cat. 2), the verticality of the individual panels certainly counter-balances the lateral flow of the work as a whole. But the parenthetical opposition of the first and second panels with the last panel suddenly loses much of its purposeful force. Relationships between figure groups, such as those in the fourth and fifth panels, seem diminished rather than enhanced by the folding, despite Alma-Tadema's obvious intent to join the two panels by the careful placement and pose of Emily Epps. The breaks between panels are not extremely disconcerting, but it cannot be said that the artist consciously made the composition more dynamic by folding. The screen probably read better when groups of panels were folded at right angles. It would be fair to conclude, then, that while Alma-Tadema minimally considered the effects of folding on his composition, the final outcome is nevertheless somewhat arbitrary. The complexities for Alma-Tadema in a six-panel folding screen were of course far more demanding than those for Whistler in his two-panel screen. A six-panel screen has many more compositional variations – it need not be folded symmetrically, and groups of panels could even be shown flat depending on what purpose the screen was intended to serve at any given time. To a certain extent, then, it should not be presumed that the screen or its composition had any optimal folded position. Perhaps the most innovative aspect of Alma-Tadema's screen is that the artist chose a group portrait as its subject, and

that oriental traditions uncharacteristically seem to have played no part in its development.

The domination of figures in Alma-Tadema's composition and the emphasis on decorative designs in Nesfield's screen provided two coexistent possibilities for the development of the screen in England for the remainder of the century. Both possibilities were explored in time by one of the West's greatest design geniuses, William Morris. He fervently desired to revitalize nearly all aspects of decorative art in England, and even attempted furniture making in the 1850s. Morris himself did not do his first screen until 1887, and then under rather unusual

FIG. 61 Royal School of Art Needlework, *Three-Panel Screen*, ca. 1876. In Walter Smith, *Masterpieces of the Centennial International Exhibition* [1876-1877], vol. 2.

FIG. 62 Royal School of Art Needlework, *Four-Panel Screen*, ca. 1876. In Walter Smith, *Masterpieces of the Centennial International Exhibition* [1876-1877], vol. 2.

circumstances. In that year Morris reconstituted individual embroidered hangings made originally around 1860 for his Red House in London as a three-panel folding screen for Lady Carlisle. It is not known whether Morris or Lady Carlisle, wife of George Howard, ninth earl of Carlisle and one of Morris' most devoted clients, initiated the project. The resulting screen (Cat. 3) shows female heroines borrowed apparently from classical legends. Figural aspects dominate here in a composition where considerations for folding were largely unnecessary. Morris' early fascination with decorative pattern and detail is evident in the exquisitely rendered costumes and repetitive floral backgrounds. His use of figure types common among the Pre-Raphaelites precludes the possibility of any oriental influence. Much like Cézanne, Morris seems to have come to the screen form with a historical perspective, here adapting a type of wall hanging to a new use rather than responding to any eastern inspiration.

Morris' well-known goal of improving the quality of hand-crafted goods, especially fabrics, resulted at least indirectly in several other folding screens done in the 1870s. His interest in embroidery led to the foundation of several societies dedicated to the renewal of this "lost" art. In 1872 the Royal School of Art Needlework was started in London with the "aim of restoring ornamental needlework for secular purposes, to the high place it once held among decorative arts, and to supply suitable employment for poor gentlewomen."[84] Morris, Burne-Jones, Walter Crane, and Selwyn Image were among the many well-known artists who were commissioned to supply designs for the Royal School. Other similarly motivated societies were formed shortly thereafter, notably the Ladies Work Society founded around 1875, and the Leek Embroidery Society founded in 1879.

Each of these groups produced folding screens, admittedly of varying quality. In 1876 the Royal School sent at least three folding screens as part of their entry to the Centennial Exhibition in Philadelphia.[85] Two of them show a clear dependence on oriental (and possibly Japanese) design motifs, albeit reinterpreted in English fashion (fig. 61 and 62). The four-panel screen[86] with a blossoming orange tree and peacocks next to a fish-filled stream is particularly fascinating. It is possible that oriental screens made for export, either Japanese or Chinese and obviously readily available in London by the 1870s, could have provided the source for the subject. In 1875,

of course, Whistler did his celebrated Peacock Room in Frederick Leyland's London home, and he was merely one of several artists in the 1870s who popularized this Japanese-inspired motif.[87] But like William Nesfield, the unknown designer of the Royal School screen reinterpreted and reorganized decorative motifs of the East, especially in the borders and framing elements. Nurtured by a healthy dose of Morris' enthusiasm for embroidery, Anglo-Japanese screens continued to thrive through the 1880s.[88]

Morris' influence affected virtually all the "minor arts." The simultaneous revival of English craftsmanship and the interest in oriental design led to two very closely related screens done probably in the mid-1880s. The first is a stained glass screen representing the *Four Elements* and attributed to Edward Burne-Jones (fig. 63).[89] The stylistic features of the figures and the handling of the background elements, however, are too dry and uninspired to have been designed by him. Enough affinities between these aspects of the screen and windows from the circle of Burne-Jones do exist, though, to confirm its

FIG. 63 Attributed to Sir Edward Coley Burne-Jones, English, 1833-1898, *Four Elements*, ca. 1885, stained glass with oil on panel in ebonized wood frame, 180.0 x 206.0 (64 x 70⅜). Cologne, Kunstgewerbemuseum.

origin in this milieu. The screen shows in each panel a female personification of one of the elements with her attributes: Earth with a bowl of fruit; Air with the winged staff or caduceus of Hermes; Fire with a burning cauldron and down-turned torch; and Water carrying a pail in one hand and jug atop her head. Each figure is shown against a floral background of fruit-bearing orange trees, and each window is bordered by a mixture of various classically-inspired architectural elements. Framed in ebonized wood, the screen also contains painted panels below the stained glass windows. On the recto these panels show precisely described flowers;[90] on the verso are similarly accurate depictions of fish swimming through aquatic plants and reeds, in combination with a band of stylized chrysanthemum roundels, all done in bronze-colored paint (fig. 64 and 65).[91] These latter designs are unquestionably borrowed from Japanese

sources, perhaps transmitted indirectly through such books as Christopher Dresser's 1886 *Modern Ornamentation* (Cat. 4.4).

The designer of the screen was not thinking in terms of a folding image. Its allegorical subject is presented serially, with each panel treated as a separate field, and joined by numerous compositional devices. The figures themselves turn in pairs toward each other: Earth and Air are facing; Fire leans her head and bends toward Water, who approaches nearly in profile. This figure of Fire also focuses her glance down and in the opposite direction. These nuances of pose and gesture diminish the vertical emphasis in the composition, uniting the figures across the panels. The screen's designer has combined an allegorical theme deriving from classical antiquity, executed in stained glass as part of a medieval craft revival, with Japanese-inspired decorative motifs. This unusual

FIG. 64 Attributed to Sir Edward Coley Burne-Jones, English, 1833-1898, *Four Elements*, ca. 1885, detail (recto).

FIG. 65 Attributed to Sir Edward Coley Burne-Jones, English, 1833-1898, *Four Elements*, ca. 1885, detail (verso).

mixture could only have arisen in the forgiving climate of the esthetic movement in England.

Surprisingly, there is a nearly identical variant of the screen executed in oil on pine panel (Cat. 4). The figures of the four elements, though not in the same order here (earth, water, fire, and air), are exact copies, line for line, of those in the stained glass screen, and were done at the same size. The creator of this screen, possibly American, certainly knew the version from the circle of Burne-Jones, and freely adapted some of its design elements, most notably in the background for the figures, in the stylized fish and plant motifs on the recto and verso (Cat. 4). The verso of the painted screen shows a more deliberate debt to Japan in the inclusion of a fruit-bearing orange tree which reads from right to left in oriental fashion.[92] Regardless of the differences between the two screens, their designers shared a similar approach: their subject is a classically-inspired allegory depicted in serial fashion, and naturalistic and geometric elements, including those borrowed from Japan, serve to elaborate this central theme.[93]

This survey of English folding screens would be incomplete if it failed to mention one of Morris' contemporaries who shared his goal to improve the quality of English design and craftsmanship. In 1882 Arthur Mackmurdo founded the Century Guild in order "to render all branches of art the sphere no longer of the tradesman, but of the artists . . . [and to] restore building, decoration, glass painting, pottery, wood carving and metal to their rightful place beside painting and sculpture."[94] One of Mackmurdo's early accomplishments from the Century Guild was a diminutive two-panel screen (fig. 66) done around 1884, designed by Mackmurdo himself and executed by Wilkinson and Sons.[95] The repetitive pattern of curving papyrus fronds is done in golden yellow silk and gold thread on a blue silk ground, now somewhat faded and worn. A satinwood frame surrounds the embroidered panels. The architectural quality of the framing elements—flat pilasters within and simply fluted columns at the edges of each panel, surmounted by capitals with leaf designs—and their careful proportions impart a surprising monumentality to the screen. The scale of Mackmurdo's repetitive fabric design is quite different from that of Morris, far less sedate but also less innovative.

The importance of this screen lies instead in its size and use. It is similar to so-called dwarf screens used by the

FIG. 66 Arthur Heygate Mackmurdo, Scottish, 1851-1942, *Two-Panel Screen*, 1884, silk and gold thread on silk in satinwood frame, 125.0 x 109.0 (49³/16 x 42¹⁵/16). London, William Morris Gallery, Walthamstow.

Japanese, such as those owned by Whistler and Manet. The function of these dwarf screens is far more understandable in Japan where occupants of a house were accustomed to sitting on the floor. No such custom could have been conceivable in an English Victorian home. How, then, could it have been used? An advertising photograph of the Century Guild's products which appeared in the Guild's own publication, *Hobby Horse*, in 1887 suggests a few possibilities (fig. 67). The small-scale screen, placed next to the elaborately carved couch, could have offered a modicum of privacy to its reclining occupant. It may also have functioned as a firescreen, shielding sitters from the heat of a fireplace and deflecting the heat to either side. By the mid-1880s, though, it is just as likely that the screen was simply a familiar accoutrement of the middle- and upper-class household, its use left to the imagination of the owner. In this context, the screen

FIG. 67 Arthur Heygate Mackmurdo, Scottish, 1851-1942, Music Room in Century Guild Inventions Exhibition, 1887. In *Hobby Horse* 2 (April 1887).

Morris and Mackmurdo, insofar as their screens are concerned, seem to have been unaffected by the tremendous interest in Japan. But Morris' interest in embroidery still resulted in a number of English folding screens whose subjects were chosen from Japanese sources.

What is "western" about these various screens, then, if we are to speak of the origin of a new tradition or at least the revitalization of a dormant one? Above all else, the artists who did them felt no compulsion to imitate in any way the subject matter or style of either Japanese or Chinese screens. Even Nesfield, whose screen relies more completely than the others on oriental design motifs, combined them in an undeniably English manner. And it is certain that where he was using oriental motifs, they were not present in any eastern screens known to have been available at the time. Moreover the subjects for these western screens made in England were as varied as the personalities of the artists who created them: a modern city bridge, a group portrait, allegorical figures from classical antiquity, and purely decorative designs abstracted via Japan from the world of nature. There were obviously not any preconceived notions as to what was considered suitable subject matter for screens. It was

was intended to be part of the overall interior decoration, compatible in scale, design, and materials with the room or house as a whole. This latter notion is reinforced in another period photograph, this one showing the drawing room at Stanmore Hall, renovated by Morris and Co., 1888-1896 (fig. 68).[96] Although largely decorated and designed by John Henry Dearle rather than Morris himself, the room still shows a more or less typical approach used by the firm. The folding screen at the left, covered with a Morris fabric, is designed to harmonize with the various design motifs used throughout the interior. Even in its large size, it almost disappears into the flurry of decorative patterns used in the wallpapers and carpets.

The early development of the western folding screen took place in England between 1870 and 1890, and followed no consistent course. The Orient, and Japan in particular, played a significant design role in Nesfield's and Whistler's screens; Japan also played a lesser role in the development of the two *Four Elements* screens. And even in the most western of these screens, Alma-Tadema's *Portrait of the Epps Family,* it is known that the artist who painted it was an avid collector of Japanese screens. Only

FIG. 68 Drawing Room, 1888-1896, Stanmore Hall, Middlesex, England. Photograph, London, National Monuments Record.

more important that these folding screens could serve a multitude of uses in English Victorian homes. The two enduring concepts about folding screens that originated in England came from Whistler and Morris. Whistler was the first western screenmaker to experiment with the concept of a folding image, while Morris (along with Mackmurdo) saw the screen as an object which, given its multiple uses, would be integrated within a larger decorative interior scheme.

In the 1890s, a new generation of artists exploited both ideas to their fullest, not in England, but in France. More than thirty years had passed since Corot and Cézanne made their screens; not a single French artist of stature followed their examples. The hiatus can be explained here only in the broadest of contexts. Neither of these screens could have been known by the artists' contemporaries; consequently they could not have had much influence. Cézanne's work was not well known except perhaps among the narrow circle of impressionist painters. Moreover his screen was a private object, made for himself. It served a specific pictorial as well as functional purpose, reappearing in the background of several of his paintings even as late as the 1890s.[97] Corot's screen was a gift to the family of one of the three artists who worked on it, Armand Leleux. By 1885 it had already been broken up by the owners, no longer existing as a screen but as an easel painting. And as far as is known, neither Cézanne's nor Corot's screens were ever exhibited in the nineteenth century.

The larger issue is that in the two decades in between 1860 and 1880 in France, those artists whom we now recognize as leaders of the modern movement—Manet, Degas, Monet, Pissarro, Renoir, and even Cézanne—were almost entirely occupied with traditional easel painting. These impressionist artists and their lesser-known associates were forging new responses to the long established (and sometimes academic) traditions of portraiture, landscape, and still life. The idea of having such talented painters design and decorate functional household objects, so strongly advocated by Morris in England, caught on much later in France. Accomplished artists such as Delacroix and Puvis de Chavannes, even if interested in decoration, limited their activities to making large-scale murals for public and religious buildings. Yet it was precisely during this period from around 1860 to 1880 that the art of Japan gained enormous popularity in

FIG. 69 Camille Pissarro, French, 1830-1903, *Vue de Rouen*, 1885, watercolor and gouache over traces of pencil on silk, mounted on board, 20.0 x 67.3 (7⅞ x 26½). Yale University Art Gallery, Stephen Carlton Clark, B.A. 1903, Fund.

FIG. 70 Claude Monet, French, 1840-1926, *La Japonaise*, 1876. Boston, Museum of Fine Arts.

France. Manet and Tissot, as we have seen, and likely many others, owned Japanese screens. The impact of Japanese prints and albums was even greater.

The Impressionists were certainly interested in Japanese objects other than paintings, but were apparently reluctant to make or decorate such items themselves. Their few experiments in object-making, however, were restricted to a genre where Japan's influence was pivotal: fans. Degas, Monet, Whistler, Pissarro, and later Seguin, Gauguin, Bonnard, Denis, Toulouse-Lautrec, and many others did designs for several hundred fans.[98] These impressionist and post-impressionist painters were motivated partially by a desire to create what were thought to be salable objects, whose popularity as accoutrements of fashion was measurably increased by the recent importation of Japanese fans. It should be realized, however, that very few fan designs (fig. 69) were actually mounted as fans. One need only look at Monet's *La Japonaise* of 1876 (fig. 70) to see what an impact these oriental objects had on French painters' imaginations. The creators of fan designs may very well have been interested as much in the formal possibilities of the unusual arched fan shape on a rectangular sheet as in the completed object itself.

The Impressionists' and Post-Impressionists' interest in these small-scale objects is but one indication of the gradually changing attitudes of the avant-garde toward decoration in France in the 1880s. Although their dedication to the traditions and pictorial issues in easel painting probably prevented the Impressionists from doing folding screens, they nevertheless attempted a small number of larger decorative projects. In 1882 Claude Monet began work on a series of decorative panels commissioned by the picture dealer Paul Durand-Ruel for his rue de Rome apartment in Paris.[99] The taste for such panels was apparently on the rise; Renoir had already received a similar commission in 1876 from a Dr. Blanche for his residence in Dieppe.[100] The special character of Monet's project demonstrates more clearly than these others the formal relationship between decorative panels and folding screens.

The artist was asked in May 1882 to provide painted panels to be set into each of the two-part doors in Durand-Ruel's dining room. The project occupied Monet until 1885, when the thirty-six paintings were handed over to Durand-Ruel. The panels were eventually installed in doors in the grand salon. Each half of the

FIG. 71 Claude Monet, French, 1840-1926, Six decorative panels for door A, Durand-Ruel Apartment, Paris, 1883-1885, oil on canvas. Photograph Durand-Ruel & Cie.

two-section doors contained a tall vertical panel at the top; a narrow horizontal panel in the middle, just below the door latch; and a medium-height vertical panel at the bottom (fig. 71). The panels were linked visually throughout the room by their regular placement within the doors, and by their similar flower and fruit subjects. The overall effect is shown clearly in a period photograph of the apartment (fig. 72). No longer simply necessary architectural constructs, the decorated doors enlivened the appearance of an already luxurious interior. Every aspect of the apartment – the furniture, carpets, paintings, and painted decorations – seems to have been joined in a carefully considered ensemble. In contrast to the homogeneous stylistic products offered by firms like Morris and Co. in England, the "look" of Durand-Ruel's apartment was the result of collecting habits and obviously wide-ranging tastes. This more individualistic approach to interior decoration was to prevail throughout most of the 1880s and early 1890s in France, at least as far as contributions by its avant-garde painters were concerned. The only large-scale decorative projects undertaken by Monet prior to the 1890s, these panels for Durand-Ruel were among the very few projects of this nature done by the impressionist group.

The conceptual step from vertical decorative wall panels to the mutiple, connected, and freestanding panels of a folding screen was a significant one. Although one cannot deny that wall panels by their imagery change the visual quality of an interior space, they remain an essentially two-dimensional form of decoration with no other purpose than decoration itself. The functional purposes of a folding screen, on the other hand – to partition larger spaces into more intimate ones, to offer relief from drafts, and to provide privacy – might be served at any one time. From a decorative standpoint, there are always two surfaces which might be adorned. Moreover, because a fold-

ing screen by definition must fold in order to stand, it presents at the outset formal compositional problems which never confront the painter of decorative panels. If the composition is to be continuous, how should one cope with the breaks caused by the folds? Because the screen can be put to any number of generally predictable uses, its manner of folding in any particular situation is not foreseeable. In addition, once a screen divides an interior space, it becomes not a two-dimensional but a three-dimensional object.

All these issues were taken up to varying degrees by the next generation of artists in Paris known as the Nabis.[101] Among the group, Pierre Bonnard, Edouard Vuillard, Maurice Denis, Paul Ranson, Armand Seguin, and Ker-Xavier Roussel either designed or actually produced one or more folding screens in the years between 1890 and 1910. All of them except Seguin studied together in 1888 in the relatively liberal atmosphere of the Académie Julian in Faubourg St. Denis in Paris.[102] Enormously interested in literature, music, and theater as well as the visual arts, they formed relationships which grew more intimate in the next few years both professionally and personally. In 1890, Bonnard, Vuillard, and Denis began sharing a studio at 28, rue Pigalle with the dramatist Lugné-Poë, for whom the artists would later design set decorations. Denis became the chronicler of the group's activities through his letters and frequent publications. Roussel and Vuillard, who had been childhood schoolmates, continued their friendship as fellow artists. In 1893 Roussel married Vuillard's sister Marie, forging another link in the chain of relationships among various members of the Nabi group.

The stylistic searches undertaken by this group have attracted considerable scholarly attention, although their role as the most productive western screenmakers of their time has not. As a group they were evidently attracted to theoretical ideas and practical examples of decoration evolving from Gauguin and his circle.[103] The Nabis themselves were book and magazine illustrators, set designers, printmakers, and decorators of domestic interiors. Unfortunately, they wrote and spoke little of their screenmaking activities. Only Bonnard seems to have commented on this aspect of their art, recalling much later in his life that "our generation sought to link art with life. At that time [the 1890s] I personally envisaged a popular art that was of everyday application: fans, furniture, screens. . . ."[104] This simple declaration tells us nothing of

FIG. 72 Claude Monet, French, 1840-1926, Small Salon, Durand-Ruel Apartment, Paris, Photograph, Durand-Ruel & Cie.

FIG. 73 Pierre Bonnard, French, 1867-1946, *Femmes au jardin,* four panels for a screen, 1891, oil on paper mounted on canvas, 160.0 x 48.0 (63 x 18⅞), each panel. Cannes, Collection of Mrs. Frank Jay Gould.

their attitudes toward screens, leaving the works themselves as the only remaining evidence. Regrettably, not all their screens have survived, and of those which have, many no longer appear in their original state.

Bonnard was the first of the group to attempt a folding screen. Perhaps as early as 1890 and no later than 1891 he began work on a four-panel folding screen entitled *Femmes au jardin* (fig. 73),[105] which he showed at the

1891 Salon des Indépendants in Paris. It consists of four separate compositions depicting modishly attired young women in a garden setting, either strolling or reading in the company of friends and their pets. As André Fermigier has accurately noted, "Here there is neither depth nor receding planes, neither shadow nor modeling. The forms are delineated by clearly drawn outline, space is entirely arbitrary.... The stylization of fabric patterns is carried to an extreme, the composition and color elements distributed in a purely decorative manner."[106] It is likely that Bonnard borrowed some of these decorative patterns, such as the wave motifs in the background of the second panel, from Japanese sources.[107] Bonnard was, after all, known as the "Nabi très japonard," because of his deep interest in Japanese prints.[108] What unifies the panels, aside from the similarity in subject matter, is the rich patterning of both costume[109] and landscape. Rather uneven connections between the panels persist, however, and the patterning does not overcome them. Bonnard himself may have been somewhat dissatisfied with the result, for he never joined the panels together and chose to show them at the Indépendants exhibition as four decorative panels.[110]

This screen type, consisting of equal-sized, tall rectangular panels decorated with related though not continuous subjects, was used by Bonnard in two later works neither of which has survived in its original state. Around 1894 Bonnard painted the so-called *Ensemble Cham-*

FIG. 74 Pierre Bonnard, French, 1867-1946, *Ensemble Champêtre,* three panels of a four-panel screen, 1894-1896, oil on brown twill lined with canvas, 167.0 x 50.8 (65¾ x 20), each panel. New York, Museum of Modern Art, Gift of Mr. and Mrs. Allan D. Emil.

pêtre (fig. 74),[111] intended as a four-panel landscape screen with blooming trees and flowers, and humorously populated with chickens and rabbits. A similar compositional treatment and light-hearted attitude is seen in another four-panel screen dating from about 1899. It shows Parisian street scenes with mothers and children bustling along the sidewalk, carriages riding by with their passengers, and dogs playing in the street.[112] In each of these three screens, Bonnard has shown no compulsion to join the panels in a continuous compositional space but seems rather to have been content to allow each panel to exist within its own pictorial domain.

In 1892/1893 Armand Seguin, sometime follower of Gauguin and companion of the Nabis, painted his only folding screen, *The Delights of Life* (Cat. 5). Very possibly he followed the example of Bonnard's first screen in deciding to do one of his own. He set out to depict a lively café scene, borrowing stylistic features from the works of both Bonnard and Denis. The important difference between Bonnard's screen and Seguin's, however, is that Seguin chose to show two continuous scenes in the café, one in the first two panels and another in the last two panels. He also repeated the gaslights in the first and third panels, thereby forging subject and spatial links. Moreover, Seguin's extension of the composition onto the intrados of the frame indicates at least an awareness of the formal compositional problems in a screen's dynamic, planar surfaces. By painting the frame in this fashion, he was clearly attempting to lessen the potentially disruptive effects brought on by folding. In doing so, Seguin, though not considered a stylistic innovator among his Nabi peers, nevertheless made an important contribution to the development of the western folding screen.[113]

Seguin's consideration of the folding nature of a screen composition may have influenced Bonnard, who in 1894 painted his four-panel *Promenade des nourrices, Frise des fiacres* screen (fig. 75). It shows in the foreground a nanny accompanying her three charges along a Parisian street; the Eiffel Tower is faintly visible in the upper corner of the first panel. The two eldest children at her far left and right busily roll hoops across the pavement, while the youngest walks closely by her side, stopping to look at the playful dog in front of them. The composition, continuous across all four panels, is decidedly asymmetric and reflects Bonnard's assimilation of organizational principles of Japanese prints.[114]

FIG. 75 Pierre Bonnard, French, 1867-1947, *Promenade des nourrices,*
Frise des fiacres, 1894, distemper on canvas with carved wood frame,
147.0 x 180.0 (57⅜ x 70), New York, Private Collection.

which all other elements of the scene appear. This technique, though ultimately derived from Japanese prints, can be seen in some of Bonnard's earlier lithographs such as *Quadrille* (fig. 76), done in 1893 as part of the series *Petites Scènes familières.* In this lithograph, one sees the artist's interest in energetically outlined figures shown in horizontally disposed street scenes. The concept and subject for the *Promenade* screen probably evolved at least partially from this series of lithographs.[115] Finally, at the very left and right edges of the screen, fragments of branches and leaves subtly protrude into the picture field, partially cut off by the frame. Bonnard repeated this leaf motif in the decoration of the carved wood frame, creating a certain level of ambiguity between the painted and the carved images (fig. 77).[116]

The figures enter boldly from the right, their movement offsetting the tranquil group of standing female figures at the upper left next to a balustrade. This group establishes a second layer of space in the nonperspectival composition. At the very top of the screen is a long line of horse-drawn carriages which determines the most distant spatial area. Like all other objects in the screen, they are painted in a thickly-applied distemper; the flat handling reemphasizes the plane of the picture itself. What is perhaps the most unusual aspect of the screen is that the image consists largely of unpainted canvas, which is used to represent the pavement and pictorial ground against

FIG. 77 Pierre Bonnard, French, 1867-1947, *Promenade des nourrices,*
Frise des fiacres, 1894, detail, left panel, New York, Private Collection.

FIG. 76 Pierre Bonnard, French, 1867-1947, *Quadrille,* one of two illustrations for Claude Terrasse, *Petites Scènes familières,* ca. 1893, lithograph, 35.3 x 27.0 (13⅞ x 10⅝). New York, Museum of Modern Art, Purchase.

The composition as a whole consists of a series of counterbalancing groups placed on the surface as well as in space. Depending on how the screen is folded, the movement of the woman-child group in the third panel is either halted, corresponding to the intent of the nanny to control her young companions (fig. 78); or conversely, this movement is exaggerated as the group is thrust forward toward the picture plane, corresponding to the desire of the children to follow the rolling hoops (fig. 79). In either case, a new set of asymmetrical balances is established between the single figure in the first panel and the group in the third panel, and between the group in the second panel and the single figure in the fourth. In general, how a screen may be folded depends on its only vaguely foreseeable functions. Due to the even number of panels in a four-leaved screen, however, the few possible positions are symmetric. Bonnard was apparently so satisfied with his effort that he undertook to have the screen reproduced in a color lithograph version, thereby assuring an even wider audience for it.[117] The evidence is strong, indeed, that Bonnard considered the various compositional relationships in creating this remarkable folding image.

FIG. 79 Pierre Bonnard, French, 1867-1947, *Promenade des nourrices, Frise des fiacres*, 1894. New York, Private Collection.

FIG. 78 Pierre Bonnard, French, 1867-1947, *Promenade des nourrices, Frises des fiacres*, 1894. New York, Private Collection.

In 1902 Bonnard painted his last screen, actually a pair of three-panel screens (fig. 80) in which he offered yet another solution to the formal and compositional problems posed by this object type. The screens show a cluster of rabbits hopping playfully across the lower two-thirds of the surface against a grayish-silver ground, recalling the subjects of Bonnard's slightly earlier *Ensemble Champêtre*. The upper third is a dark, amorphous cloud layer through which one sees glimpses into a (connected?) cityscape, while in the clouds themselves nymphs and satyr couples romp lasciviously, their fecundity blatantly implied as well by their proximity to the rabbits below. What is unusual about the screens is that Bonnard did a pair of them, thereby becoming one of the very few western artists and the only member of the Nabis to do so. This decision suggests strongly that Japanese screens served as a model for the artist's conception; we know that Vuillard owned at least one Japanese screen, and by 1902 there would have been ample opportunity for a Parisian artist to see numerous Japanese screens in public collections, in exhibitions, and on the market. Bonnard's Japonisms are visible not only in this imitation of the western screenmaking tradition, but also in his use of a continuous composition across both three-panel halves. Moreover, the inclusion of a cloud-filled sky through which one sees vignettes of a distant cityscape is also a conscious borrowing of Japanese pictorial motifs found in screens known to have been in Europe as early as the 1870s (fig. 42 and 43). In fact, the screen which Emile Guimet brought back from his trip to Japan in 1876/1877 and which eventually entered the Musée Guimet in Paris (fig. 36) contains just this type of cloud-filled composition. Even the grayish-silver ground in Bonnard's screens recalls silver-leaf Japanese screens available at the turn of the century. This rare instance in which a western screenmaker so directly relied on several aspects of the Japanese screenmaking tradition justifies more than ever Bonnard's reputation as the "Nabi très japonard."

Similar compositional concerns obviously occupied Maurice Denis when sometime around 1902 he painted his only screen, the four-panel *Screen with Doves* (Cat. 8). Denis, a devout Catholic, depicted a subject with religious significance and included several Christian symbols relating to the rewards of Christ's love.[118] An enclosed garden is created by a wood fence running diagonally from left to right and from back to front. The fence shifts direction several times in the screen, first sideways then forward. Each time except the first, these changes occur precisely at the breaks between the panels. In designing his screen, Denis intentionally conceived his composition to use the folding surface structure to the best advantage.

Vuillard, too, tried his hand at screenmaking and was

FIG. 80 Pierre Bonnard, French, 1867-1947, *Pair of Three-Panel Screens,* 1902, oil on paper on canvas, 161.0 x 405.0 (63⅜ x 159⁷/₁₆). Saint Germain-en-Laye, Musée du Prieuré.

responsible for three and perhaps even four screens between 1892/1893 and 1918. Though compositionally and stylistically related to other Nabi screens, Vuillard's were set apart from those of his colleagues in one significant respect. Bonnard's screens, as far as we know, were not created for any specific purpose, at least no more than any of his other easel paintings. His first screen was exhibited at the Salon des Indépendants in 1891, and another was shown at Durand-Ruel's Paris gallery in 1896.[119] One presumes that screens were generally in demand, and that Bonnard was hoping to sell them as he might any other work. Denis' screen, if not done in hopes of sale, may have been done for himself; it was in his rue de Mareil studio in Saint Germain in 1904 and has remained in his family's collection.[120] Certainly, the Nabis as a group

were committed to doing all types of decorative projects for commercial consumption. Denis explained their hopes in 1892: "One of the exhibitors [at the gallery owned by the dealer Le Barc de Bouteville, where the Nabis began showing in 1891] might do fanciful and attractive posters. Another could make wallpapers of imaginative design, very modern tapestries and furniture of unusual style. A third might produce somber mosaics or dazzling stained glass windows. Where is the industrialist who might willingly avail himself of the valuable collaboration of these decorators, so as to consume a little of the time they devote to the execution of far too many paintings?"[121]

Although Denis' plea for a French counterpart to William Morris was not met, Vuillard found a personal

FIG. 81 Edouard Vuillard, French, 1868-1940, *Five-Panel Screen,* 1892-1893, Photograph, Antoine Salomon.

means to pursue his interests in painted decoration. Along with most of the other Nabis, he became good friends with the Natanson brothers and their families. Alexandre was the founder of the influential literary and art journal *La Revue blanche,* to which Bonnard and others contributed illustrations. Alexandre and his brothers Thadée and Alfred, through their commissions and contacts, were the strongest early supporters of Vuillard's work. When Stéphane Natanson, a cousin of these brothers, designed a home for his brother-in-law Paul Desmarais in Paris, Vuillard was commissioned to provide decorations for it.[122] In late 1892 or early 1893 he painted six large horizontal panels and a five-panel folding screen for the dressing room. The Desmarais panels consist of three pairs of related subjects: two park scenes, two outdoor terrace scenes, and two densely populated, richly patterned dressmaker shop scenes.[123] The screen, seen here in a contemporary photograph showing the original frame (fig. 81),[124] also focuses on the atelier of a dressmaker, and thus was directly related by subject to one pair of the decorative wall panels. These subjects seem particularly appropriate for a dressing room. Using the sharply receding perspective of the tiled floor, Vuillard related the screen compositionally to the pair of terrace scene panels also containing this spatial device. As for the screen image itself, one cannot claim that it was designed to be a folding image in the same sense as Bonnard's 1894 *Promenade* screen. Even though the scene is continuous across the screen surface, folding would only interfere with the perspective emphasis created by the tiled floor. Vuillard surely recognized this fact, and he therefore let each panel exist as an independent composition depicting a single figure. Unlike other Nabi screens, however, Vuillard's screen for the Desmarais was completely integrated by subject and composition into a larger, planned decorative environment. And also unlike his contemporaries, he broke from the tradition of equally-sized panels. Alternating the heights of the screen's panels could have served two distinct purposes. Even from a short distance within the dressing room the screen's uneven panel heights would have permitted a far more energetic view of the decorative panels in the room. Vuillard probably wanted to avoid the potential monotony created by the long horizontal decorative panels which one presumes were all hung at the same level. In addition, a screen having uneven panel heights would have afforded either partial or total privacy while dressing or undressing according to

the user's height or preference. Vuillard's innovations in screen format and function within a larger environment would become the hallmark of nearly all art nouveau screens.

Vuillard received another commission for a screen from Stéphane Natanson around 1895.[125] The four-panel work, illustrated in a contemporary photograph with its original frame (see Cat. 7), shows Stéphane and Misia Natanson seated in an interior. The space is viewed from above, and again Vuillard has made use of a sharply receding tiled floor plane, this time at the rear rather than the foreground of the composition. Here again, the screen's panels are not all the same height, though the images within them are. The screen is not known to be related to any larger decorative scheme, which perhaps accounts initially for its slightly less arresting appearance. It is apparent, however, that Vuillard was more conscious in this case of the notion of the screen as a folding image. The figures of Stéphane and Misia are relegated largely to the second and fourth panels, Stéphane at the back and Misia in the front. The first and third panels, composed of strongly asymmetric views of furniture in the interior, act as buffers between the figures. The sense of separation of the figures is reduced by the folding, while at the same time their spiritual togetherness is increased by it and by the glance exchanged between them. Just as in Bonnard's 1894 *Promenade* screen, which Vuillard certainly knew, the symmetrical arrangements possible in such a four-panel configuration seem to connect the composition dynamically and three-dimensionally.

Vuillard's last screen was done for a Mlle. Chapin in 1911, and a series of letters written by the artist between 30 April and 12 June record his progress.[126] The references in these letters to the screen indicate his concern for the surface qualities of the paint, for its backing materials, and for its ultimate installation in Mlle. Chapin's Paris apartment. The five-panel *Place Vintimille* screen (fig. 82) shows a section of the oval-shaped park (now Place Adolphe-Max), seen from above and populated with adults, children, vendors, and horse-drawn carts. A bright sun shines on resplendent foliage. The sight was extremely familiar to Vuillard; he moved in 1907 to 26, rue de Calais, where his fourth floor apartment looked down on the Place Vintimille.[127] The park was also the subject of several earlier paintings, most notably a series of eight decorative panels that Vuillard did for the playwright Henry Bernstein (fig. 83).[128] These vertical panels

FIG. 82 Edouard Vuillard, French, 1868-1940, *La Place Vintimille*, 1911, distemper on canvas, 230.0 x 302.0 (90¾ x 118¾). Private Collection.

were surely a precedent for the screen, the only difference being that the rich verdure obscured the tall, narrow buildings beyond the park. The basic proportions of the compositions are otherwise identical.

The greater number of permutations in how a five-panel screen may be folded – as compared to one with four panels – with no one position more sensible than another, leads one to believe that Vuillard was probably not thinking in terms of a folding image in quite the same terms as in the Natanson screen. Yet it is certain that the composition was chosen carefully with a folding struc-

ture in mind. The sweeping curve of the street at the bottom of the picture cuts through the foreground and leads the viewer first in, then across, and then out of the picture space. Depending on how the screen is positioned, the angles of the panels shift either to counteract the spatial and surface movement, or to accentuate it. While it is true that these effects were necessarily arbitrary, Vuillard's comprehension of the spectrum of possible effects caused by folding is nonetheless undeniably brilliant. A master of composition and format, Vuillard was able to visualize the screen as part of a larger environ-

ment. He was without question the most innovative screenmaker at the turn of the century.

Odilon Redon was not a member of the Nabi group in the strictest sense. Instead, nearly thirty years older than the Nabis, he was an artist whose work they gradually came to know and eventually revere in the 1890s.[129] Beginning about 1900, Redon embarked on a series of decorative projects including wall panels as well as screens.[130] Unfortunately, not all of the folding screens have survived: two panels from the three-panel *Pegasus* done in 1902 for the Princess Cystria disappeared in Paris during World War II;[131] another screen for Olivier Sainsère done probably in 1902-1903 has not been seen since 1926; one for an unknown Englishwoman in Paris has also been lost;[132] and one which Count Kessler commissioned from Redon sometime after 1910 was apparently never finished.[133] Only one remains intact: the famous three-panel *Red Screen* done between 1905 and 1908 for Redon's most enthusiastic patron, André Bonger (fig. 84). Extensive correspondence between Bonger and Redon from December 1905 to July 1908 reveals the fascinating process by which this screen developed.[134]

A letter of 23 October 1906 is the first indication that Bonger wanted Redon to make a screen: "Of course I will make you a folding screen, with great pleasure. You only have to tell me, at your fancy, what seems best to you for the dimension of the panels, [and] their number. . . . The important thing is that it should be mounted very simply with a quality fabric, [either] matching or prominent; create something with Mme. Bonger's agreement and tell me about it. We will succeed." On 18 December Redon discussed his concern about the size of screen. If he followed Bonger's suggested width (190 cm) for the three-panel screen, Redon understood it must not be too tall or it would tip over. He even included a small sketch in the letter (fig. 85) showing how it would look folded, suggesting to Bonger that he make the panels a little wider and stating: "I think that with the dimensions you gave me, the screen would only be stable with a quite heavy frame . . . in the next instance, I am indecisive as to the height. Must it conceal a view? Be taller than the height of a man? Or shorter?" Redon prevailed in the matter of its width (234 cm in its finished state).

FIG. 83 Edouard Vuillard, French, 1868-1940, *La Place Vintimille*, 1908-1910, distemper on cardboard mounted on canvas, 200.0 x 69.5 (78¾ x 27⅜). New York, Solomon R. Guggenheim Museum, Justin K. Thannhauser Collection.

FIG. 84 Odilon Redon, French, 1840-1916, *Red Screen,* 1905-1908, distemper on canvas, 173.0 x 234.0 (68 x 92). Otterlo, The Netherlands, Rijksmuseum Kröller-Müller.

The screen's subject is ostensibly Pegasus, the legendary winged horse who appears in the upper portion of the third panel. Redon treated this same subject many times in drawings, pastels, lithographs, and paintings, as well as in the earlier screen for Princess Cystria, each time emphasizing one aspect of the mythological story or another.[135] Here Redon seems to have chosen to show Pegasus victorious over his captor Bellerophon and rewarded with a place in the heavens. As many critics have pointed out,[136] Redon chose his religious and mythological subjects mostly to provide his fantastic compositions with some connection to reality. As the artist himself said: "My originality consists in bringing to life, in a human way, improbable beings and making them live according to the laws of probability, by putting—as far as possible—the logic of the visible at the service of the invisible."[137] His letters to Bonger, in fact, clarify the development of the screen's true subject. In the same 18 December 1906 letter mentioned earlier Redon concluded by saying, "Otherwise bravo for the choice of red as the dominant color"—as if the color were more important than the theme itself. Writing on 3 March 1908, when the screen was largely completed, Redon amplified his feelings: "I think that it carries the time of my impressions of the summer in the mountains. It is a sort of chaos in the peaks, perceived through the amorphous rays of the sun. There are several cold grays and tinges of blues which I never had [before] and which I undoubtedly brought back from my travels in Switzerland and stored in my subconscious."[138] For Redon, then, the subject was merely a vehicle for expression—expression derived from the experience of nature.

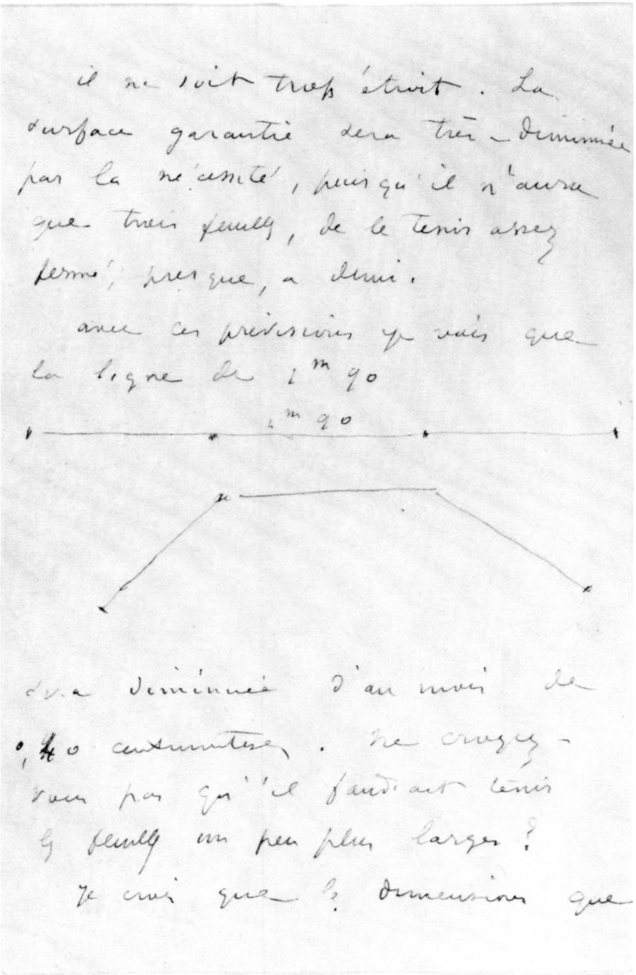
il ne soit trop étroit. La surface garantie sera très diminuée par la nécessité, puisqu'il n'aura que trois feuilles, de le tenir assez fermé; presque, à demi.

avec ces prévisions je vois que la ligne de 1m90

1m90

sera diminuée d'au moins de 0,40 centimètres. Ne croyez-vous pas qu'il faudrait tenir les feuilles un peu plus larges?

Je crois que les dimensions que

FIG. 85 Letter from Odilon Redon to André Bonger, 18 December 1906. Amsterdam, Rijksprentenkabinet.

As the screen progressed, the artist communicated to Bonger his concern for all its details. Like at least two of Redon's other screens,[139] Bonger's was painted in distemper on a fine linen canvas. Distemper consists of pigment mixed with water and size. Redon expressed his liking for the medium in his correspondence with Bonger, the first time in a letter of 28 December 1905: "[distemper] requires, in my opinion, all the freshness of improvisation and of the first thought.... I have just seen my screen again at the Princess Cystria's and found it softened and perhaps more harmonious; time leaves something which completes these simple substances, better than in oil, assuredly with none of the surprises which chemical reactions sometimes disagreeably give." And, in a letter dated 4 July 1908, "it will improve with age the same as all works in distemper."[140] Finally, in an undated letter from Madame Redon to Madame Bonger, "Redon asked me to tell you ... that he is very happy that the screen is in good harmony with the room it occupies, that the red does not cry out too much, moreover that in a painting on gesso *(colle)* the red will improve after several months." The still brilliant, almost phosphorescent coloring of the *Red Screen* is a testament to Redon's technical skills.

In a 3 March 1908 letter the artist consulted Bonger about another matter: "What kind of fabric will you put on the verso? The choice of shade will be important to obtain the right effect. But for the rest, the simplest frame [would do]; even hinges of fabric would be good. You will see; Madame Bonger, here, will also be obliged to help us and to collaborate." Their joint decision was to use a subtle, beige fabric with a slightly raised pattern to "frame" the painted panels, to back them, and to cover the hinges (fig. 86). The fabric was purchased by Redon from a merchant named Vasseur.[141]

Redon's attentiveness to all these details resulted in a superbly crafted folding screen. The fabric harmonizes with the vibrant hues of the painted panels, making the transitions between panels as unobtrusive as possible. The quietly patterned verso offers as well a dramatic contrast in mood and temperament to the Pegasus image; approaching the screen from behind, one no doubt would have been all the more amazed by Redon's painted creation. Of course, it is the incredible color fantasy of the

FIG. 86 Odilon Redon, French, 1840-1916, *Red Screen*, 1905-1908, detail of hinge. Otterlo, The Netherlands, Rijksmuseum Kröller-Müller.

Pegasus side which is the very heart of the screen. The artist seems not to have been very concerned with how folding would affect his expansive image. Certainly, there was no need to consider the various architectural, perspectival, or figural elements inherent to Bonnard's and Vuillard's screen compositions. The landscape is a continuous one, and by placing the relatively diminutive Pegasus figure near the edge of the third panel, the composition builds dramatically from left to right. The intended impact of the screen may be best understood, however, if one can imagine how it would feel to be seated in a chair in front of it. One would be secluded from the larger spaces beyond it, enveloped in Redon's mystery-filled vision of "chaos in the peaks, perceived through the amorphous rays of the sun." "Enclose yourself with nature," the artist is purported to have said.[142] No other object could have achieved this goal so effectively, so dramatically, or so completely as the *Red Screen*. It totally transforms its immediate environment, drawing the viewer into the world it creates.

The picturesque Swiss landscape which so inspired Redon's *Red Screen* was also the prime inspiration during this period for another painted folding screen, but one done by an artist physically and psychologically quite removed from the esthetic inventions of the Paris art world. In late spring 1900, the twenty-one-year-old Paul Klee returned to Bern from Munich, where he had just learned that his diligent studies in art had gained him a place for the fall in Franz Stuck's painting class at the Munich Academy. Shortly after his arrival in Bern, Klee was commissioned by a friend of his mother to make a painted folding screen (Cat. 9).[143] The young artist responded with a five-panel work whose subjects are scenes of the Aare River winding its way through the rising hills near Bern. The most evident visual effect of the screen is that the landscape is not continuous, showing instead five separate though related views. The second and fourth panels' compositions, in fact, are mirror images of each other. What might have prompted Klee to opt for such an unorthodox approach to the angled surfaces of a folding screen?

The answer lies in two distinct areas – his visual sources for the screen and his expressive intentions. By 1900 folding screens were common household objects, fulfilling as we have seen both decorative and functional ends. During his stay in Munich, Klee would have had ample opportunity to see screens designed by participants of the recently born *Jugendstil* movement. His own screen, however, bears no resemblance to the linear or sculptural stylizations usually associated with that group. Instead, Klee borrowed the salient compositional features of his panels from vertical format landscapes then popular with both older artists like Carl Spitzweg and younger contemporaries like Joseph Damberger. Klee seems to have joined five such separate vertical landscape panels which function together as a decorative ensemble only by the relative similarity of subject, composition, and coloration.

But there was surely another reason for Klee's unusual landscape depiction. Devoid of any anecdotal or human elements, the screen's silent landscape may have been designed to elicit a sympathetic emotive response from the viewer. Indeed, the expressively contoured shapes within the panels seem to emphasize the loneliness and isolation so evident in the landscapes. An entry in Klee's diary from 1900, when the screen was just or nearly completed, gives us an insight into the artist's creative process: "The comparison of my soul with the various moods of the countryside frequently returns as a motif. My poetic-personal idea of the landscape lies at the root of this."[144] Each of the screen's depictions, then, can be understood as a symbolic expression of the artist's emotional states as conveyed by different aspects of the familiar Aare River Valley landscape. The individuality of these expressions, implied on one level by the discontinuous nature of the compositions, is emphasized also by the very fact that folding separates them further. Placed before this screen, the viewer is forced to reevaluate his or her relationship with each landscape scene. Even in the case of the mirror image second and fourth panels, where the artist has made an obvious attempt to impart a compositional unity to the screen as a whole, the two panels were nevertheless painted in different hues so as to indicate different landscape moods. His screen was as a result almost surely conceived with its folding nature in mind. Klee's already well-developed sense of his artistic goals, however, led him to treat the screen differently than his Nabi contemporaries. It does not purport to relate to a comprehensive interior decoration. Instead, Klee used the screen more or less as a vehicle for his personal and poetic ideas about landscape. The screen's folding structure allowed him to seek an unusually innovative means of expression, means which were not to find a parallel until Jim Dine's *Landscape Screen* nearly seventy years later.

The generally widespread demand for folding screens in the last quarter of the nineteenth century was paralleled by a dramatic shift in attitude by a group of painters centered primarily in Paris. The screen, like many other household objects, was deemed increasingly worthy of the painter's attention. Spurred on by fortuitous commissions, Whistler, the Nabis, Redon, and Klee in a mere three decades raised the artistic value of the folding screen to a level approximating that of its oriental predecessors – and far above that of the oriental screens then known in Europe. As the nineteenth century came to a close, a talented group of architects, designers, and craftsmen also responded to the increasing demand for folding screens. Far more than their Nabi contemporaries, however, they viewed the folding screen as an object whose framing elements and very form were considered as important as the choice of image. Under the general stylistic rubric of art nouveau,[145] artists in France, Belgium, Holland, Germany, Austria, Italy, Spain, and Great Britain reexamined the nature of the folding screen and its role in the surrounding environment.

One screen in particular, designed by Czechoslovakian-born Alfons Mucha, demonstrates vividly the alternate esthetic responses toward the screen between 1895 and 1905. Mucha, whose training and earliest commissions were for large-scale decorative projects, achieved his reputation in France as a color lithographer.[146] His prints and posters, perhaps more than those of any other artist, have become synonymous with the stylistic characteristics of art nouveau. As early as 1897, Mucha began to mount and frame some of his vertical format color lithographs as folding screens, showing the *Four Seasons* series as a screen in the 1897 Salon des Cent in Paris.[147] Having already had several lengthy stays in Paris, Mucha may have been aware of Bonnard's 1896 lithographic version of the painted *Promenade des nourrices* screen of a few years earlier. In any case, he understood the commercial prospects for producing such screens and contracted with a furniture firm in Prague to mount his lithographs into their frames, thereby making his folding screens available to a wider audience.

The success of Mucha's venture is also revealed by this unique four-panel screen (Cat. 12) done around 1900 for Jarka Charfreitag, a beerhall owner who lived in the

Bohemian town of Žamberk. Charfreitag asked his friend Josef Rous, a sculptor with a considerable local reputation, to make a screen frame for Mucha's lithographic series, the *Four Times of Day*. Rous responded with a frame whose floral and geometric motifs derive from the patterned borders of the lithographs. The curvilinearly symmetric shape of the frame, and its brightly painted and gilded decorations very nearly overpower the relatively static images within, and the result appears to the modern viewer to be a blend of "Bohemian baroque" and French art nouveau styles. What is important, however, is that this screen signals a departure from the traditional rectangular format. In the ensuing decade, relationships between a screen's image, its frame, and its surrounding environment would evolve dramatically throughout Europe.

"The display of 'Art Nouveau Bing' [is] one of the most perfect pieces of combined decorative art-work in the whole Exhibition. It does the highest honour alike to the creative artists and to him who inspired them."[148] The critic who wrote these praises was referring to a small pavilion among the many displays of contemporary French decorative arts at the 1900 Exposition Universelle in Paris.[149] The display had been organized principally by Samuel Bing, a Hamburg-born entrepreneur who settled in Paris as a dealer in oriental objects, later including the works of some of France's most talented designers in his shop. The critic who made these remarks was attracted in particular to the *Boudoir de l'Art Nouveau Bing* (fig. 87), and his comments convey the sense of excitement inspired by this new art:

All the woodwork in the furniture of this room is gilded, and everything has its distinct individuality. The chairs are covered with silk embroidery; the walls are hung with brocade; while the fireplace of white marble is designed in the form of stalks, which support the mantlepiece. Around the hearth is a strip of opaline, framed in repoussé brass. In a large bay, and ornamented with a bordering of pale coloured glass, is a little divan covered with a brocade similar to that on the walls. On the floor are silken carpets here and there, and in one corner stands a screen, a perfect gem of art.[150]

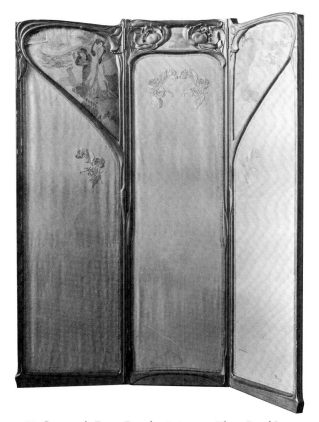

FIG. 88 Georges de Feure, French, 1868-1943, *Three-Panel Screen*, 1900, with brocades by Anaïs Faure, embroidered silk with gilded wood and gesso frame, 120.0 x 103.0 (46⅞ x 40¼). Paris, Musée des Arts Décoratifs.

FIG. 87 *Boudoir de l'Art Nouveau Bing*, 1900, with decorations by Georges de Feure, French, 1868-1943. In *Studio* 20 (1900).

That "perfect gem of art," along with all the other furniture in the boudoir, was designed by Georges de Feure. His screen (fig. 88), with brocades by Anäis Faure, consists of three panels covered with silk and bordered with an exquisitely carved gilded frame. The panels are unusually subdivided by the frame, creating a sort of drop-shaped section at the top of the left and right panels, and a small horizontal, rectangular section at the top of the central panel. Aside from the embroidered silk roses in the main portions of the screen panels, it is to these sections that the screen's images have been confined. In the first panel, two elegantly dressed ladies take a stroll in a park, and each of them is about to toss a ball for her dog to fetch. The third panel, where two similarly attired women watch three dogs at play, appears to be a continuation of that scene.[151] In the background of each scene is a pond or fountain, and in the central panel de Feure has cleverly implied the continuity between the images to either side by inserting a meandering stream between the stylized carved roses of the frame.

De Feure's design for the screen is ingenious in several respects. It was conceived as part of and in relation to a planned decorative environment where furniture, walls, and carpets all have strong decorative patterns of their own. By relegating the figures to a relatively minor portion of the screen, de Feure provided an unobtrusive backdrop against which they could stand out. Positioned at the topmost portion of the screen, these images also stand above the level of the decorated chair and love seat backs. That de Feure meant to isolate the screen and its images to their best advantage is also suggested by his placement of it in front of an undecorated fabric curtain.[152] Thus, even where the screen is linked so closely to an active decorative ensemble, de Feure still stressed its individual design qualities, thereby assuring the viability of its images wherever it might be placed. It is a unique solution to the idea of a folding image within a larger decorative ensemble.

De Feure's fellow designers Louis Majorelle[153] and Charles Plumet[154] also made folding screens, as did the poster artist and painter Jules Cheret.[155] One of the more interesting examples of French art nouveau screens was done in Nancy by Jacques Gruber. Born in 1870, Gruber studied in Paris in the 1890s; there he first became exposed to the art nouveau style as practiced by de Feure, Majorelle, Guimard, and others. In 1899 he did a three-panel screen (fig. 89) which, like most other designers'

FIG. 89 Jacques Gruber, French, 1870-?, *Three-Panel Screen*, ca. 1899, carved and inlaid wood with etched glass panels, 170.0 x 183.0 (66⅜ x 71⅜). Munich, Stadtmuseum.

screens of the period, was part of an ensemble of salon furniture.[156] It is notable for the richness of its decorative detail and the quality of its craftsmanship. The stylized ornamental plant motifs incorporated into the screen's image, so to speak, are done in several media. Vines "grow" up the legs of the carved wood frame, culminating in blossoms which stand out in superbly carved relief against a background of lighter colored clematis and Alpen violets inlaid into strongly grained wood panels (fig. 90). The gently curved arched top of the screen contains further elaboration of the basic floral motif, where blossoming clematis vines are etched into pinkish-hued stained glass.[157] Clearly, little attention is paid to the effect of folding on the screen's image. If anything, the latter was designed precisely to avoid such considerations. The wealth of decorative detail and the general similarity of motifs in each panel more than compensate for any disruption caused by folding. Far and away, the screen's dominant visual feature is its unusual curved tripartite shape.

Some art nouveau designers carried these ideas to the extreme, subjugating even further the decorative role of a folding screen to the larger demands of a decorative environment, and showing remarkable inventiveness for materials as well as design. One such artist was the Italian Carlo Bugatti.[158] Born in Milan, he worked as a furniture designer and cabinetmaker. Between 1888 and 1904, when he moved to Paris, Bugatti made at least five folding screens and a design for a sixth. His first folding screen, done in 1888, was shown at the Italian Exhibition in

FIG. 91 Carlo Bugatti, Italian, 1856-1940, *Two-Panel Screen*, 1888, painted leather. In *Journal of Decorative Art* 7 (1888).

FIG. 90 Jacques Gruber, French, 1870-?, *Three-Panel Screen*, ca. 1899, detail. Munich, Stadtmuseum.

London that same year (fig. 91). It seems conventional enough in its adaptation of an asymmetrical design of painted Japanese-inspired plant and bird images. The two-panel screen is broken, however, by a curious, framed mirror set into its left half. Even more peculiar are the four metal and ebony disks at bottom, below which are five pairs of short, stout columns which raise the screen slightly off the floor. One can explain the presence of the mirror as a practical concession—albeit wittily conceived—for an object which was often used to offer privacy while dressing or undressing. Having said this, however, one is at a loss to describe the particular qualities in the screen that together make up Bugatti's style. "Japanese" one critic called it, while others searched the Near East for cultural descriptions such as Turkish, Eastern, Arabian, and Algerian.[159]

A second Japanese-inspired screen, shown in the 1902 Turin Esposizione Internationale, is even more unusual in its form (fig. 92). It too contains painted floral and bird motifs across its two panels, though arranged symmetrically. Recollections of Japan are almost immediately nullified by the immense flowerlike copper repoussé disk at the top, intersected by a metal-encrusted wooden stem, complete with its own floral pattern. Disk motifs are used in the base as well, elaborated by a low-relief, step design inlaid with pseudo-Arabic inscriptions. Unfortunately the screen seems not to have survived. Because it is known only from this period photograph, one cannot say how the massive disk at the top moved when the screen folded. It does not appear to have been divided down the middle, so perhaps it stayed in place with one or the other screen panel. Regardless of the particular solution, Bugatti was responsible for several truly original screens, not just in terms of their materials or execution, but especially for their overall format.

In 1900 Bugatti designed a bedroom for Lord Battersea's London home (fig. 93). The opulent interior car-

FIG. 93   Bedroom of Lord Battersea, London, 1900. Designed by Carlo Bugatti, Italian, 1856-1940. Photograph, Editions du Regard, Paris.

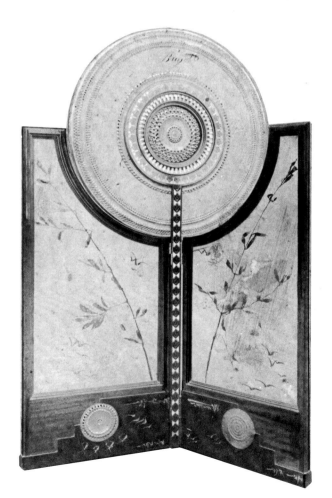

FIG. 92   Carlo Bugatti, Italian, 1856-1940, *Two-Panel Screen*, 1902. Photograph, Editions du Regard, Paris.

ries all the hallmarks of Bugatti's style: large medallions and disks, often decorated with inlay or repoussé and placed in a piece of furniture or on the ceiling; pairs of columns supporting broad arches in decidedly unusual places; and tassels and spires as final, witty touches to the ensemble. Almost unnoticed in this explosion of decorative detail is a small, two-panel folding screen, no longer extant, positioned at the right just beyond the bed. Judging from Bugatti's other furniture of the period, it was probably made of parchment, with elaborate inlays and repoussé work. Isolating the screens as we have done is helpful in understanding their visual components, but Bugatti, like de Feure, Gruber, and William Morris, almost always conceived his screens as mere parts within an integrated whole. In fact, images gradually disappeared entirely from Bugatti's screens, reinforcing their interdependent decorative role.

Like Bugatti, the Spanish architect Antonio Gaudí was an astonishingly innovative and idiosyncratic designer. Gaudí only occasionally designed furniture for the interiors of his buildings, and his only known screen, actually a pair of screens, (Cat. 16) was done around 1905 for the Milà family apartment in the Casa Milà in Barcelona. This is a rare instance when a western artist did a pair of screens; the close formal and structural relationship between each half implies that Gaudí intended them to work together as a unit. The screens might well have been used as a sort of a flexible partition across a doorway or between two rooms. They could be opened or closed as much as one chose, with the rippled, rose-colored (originally green) glass windows allowing light to pass through but still providing a modicum of privacy. The decorative role of the screen is clearly subordinated to its primary functional role, and to the larger interior scheme envisioned for the Casa Milà. The screens consist of a series of irregular, biomorphically shaped panels. No two of the ten panels duplicate one another in either overall shape,

the form or placement of their windows, or their carved oak decorations. The panels swell in height and breadth outward from their meeting points, growing organically as if of their own volition. Gaudí's screens, more than any others done at the turn of the century, are linked by decoration and function to the interior space they inhabit. On a separate level, they also anticipate the current trend to treat the folding screen as a potentially functional type of floor sculpture.

Folding screens were such popular and useful items of interior decoration that architects, designers, and furni-

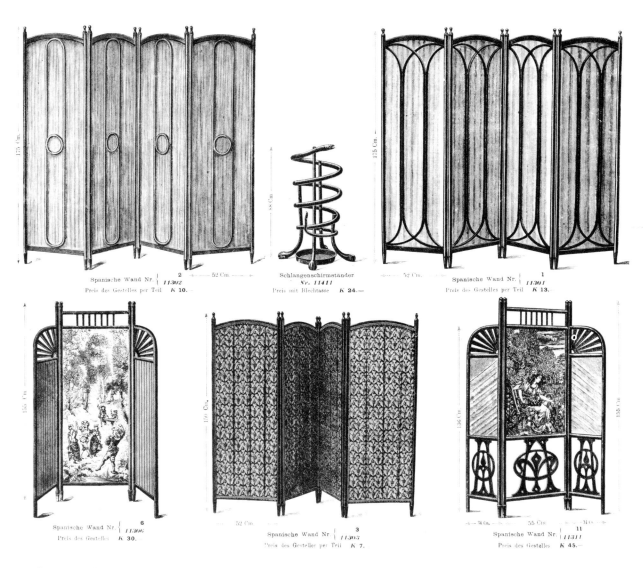

FIG. 94 Illustrations from Gebrüder Thonet, *Thonet Bentwood & Other Furniture: The 1904 Illustrated Catalogue*, introduction by Christopher Wilk.

ture manufacturers all over Europe experimented with the format. The renowned makers of bentwood furniture, Gebrüder Thonet in Vienna, included several different types of folding screens in their catalogues from the turn of the century.[160] Some, such as numbers 11302 and 11301 (fig. 94) consisted of simple bentwood frames with fabric panels. Others, such as numbers 23 and 24, used similar bentwood frames (fig. 94), only with cut-out designs in the wooden panels at the bottom. The slotted wooden panels at the top allowed one to insert prints or photographs in a slightly more elegant variety of the traditional scrap screen. The most elaborate and therefore most expensive versions are numbers 33 and 34 (fig.

95). These elegantly curved three-panel screens contained applied or inlaid decoration, even including a continuous seascape scene. Such objects were readily available to what must have been an eager middle-class clientele.[161]

In Vienna, the most innovative screens of the period came from a group of avant-garde architects and designers who formed the Vereinigung bildender Künstlers Österreich, commonly known as the Vienna Secession. One of its founders, Josef Maria Olbrich, is known to have done three designs for foldings screens between 1899 and 1903. The earliest was done for Dr. Friedrich Spitzer, whose Vienna apartment the architect remodeled in 1899.[162] The huge, eight-panel screen (fig. 96) presum-

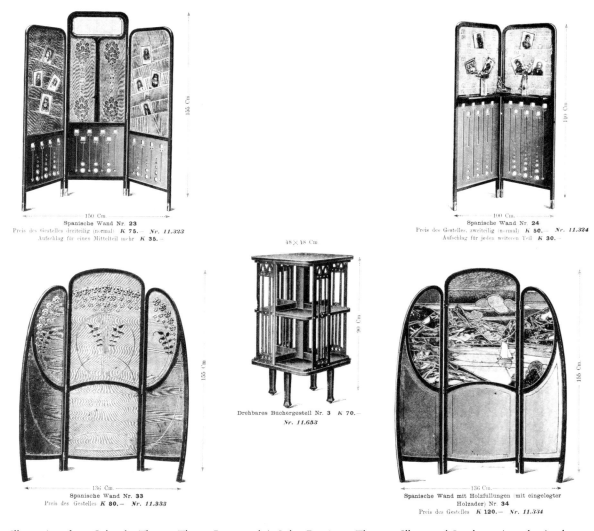

FIG. 95 Illustrations from Gebrüder Thonet, *Thonet Bentwood & Other Furniture: The 1904 Illustrated Catalogue*, introduction by Christopher Wilk.

FIG. 96 Josef Maria Olbrich, Austrian, 1867-1908, *Study for Decoration of Dining and Music Rooms, Dr. Friedrich Spitzer Apartment, Vienna*, 1899, crayon, ink, and watercolor on paper. Berlin, Kunstbibliothek.

classical Greece. The panels contain gilded, incised leather inserts with repeating decorative motifs which almost certainly were not from Hoffmann's hand; as with most of the screens made by these furniture companies, the purchaser probably had a choice of decorative inserts, and in the central panel, there was even a large rectangle into which one could place another image. Whatever may have been included, Hoffmann's screen bears little if any relation to the concept of the folding image as espoused by his contemporaries in France. To him, the screen was largely a design exercise which made use of architectural elements such as the square-topped columnar "strings" of the cithara at the top, and the glyphlike protrusions at the bottom. Although Hoffmann's screen was not actually done as part of a larger decorative ensemble, as were Gaudí's and Bugatti's, his inclusion of these motifs established another kind of formal architectural relationship.

In Germany the demand for folding screens at the turn of the century led to the availability of both native and foreign products. The German government sent numerous contributions to the 1900 Exposition Universelle,

ably of wood and glass, fulfilled primarily an architectural role in the apartment, separating the music room from the dining room in the same spot where there once had been a wall. Its arched field for decoration relates it to the arched door beyond which it rests. Once again, the screen was subordinated in decoration and function within a fully integrated domestic interior scheme. Olbrich was probably also the designer of a small three-panel glass firescreen made around 1899,[163] and in 1903 he designed a three-panel screen to be manufactured by the Viennese furniture firm of Ludwig Alter, though no example is known to have survived (fig. 97).[164]

Olbrich's colleague and friend from the Secession, Josef Hoffmann, also did at least two folding screens. Both were based on a single design of 1898/1899 and were probably produced by the Viennese furniture manufacturer A. Förster. The ebonized wood frame of this three-panel screen (Cat. 13) recalls at the top the shape of a cithara, a stringed instrument resembling a lyre from

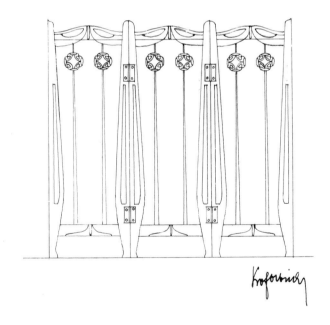

FIG. 97 Josef Maria Olbrich, Austrian, 1867-1908, *Study for a Screen*, 1903, ink on transparent paper. Berlin, Kunstbibliothek.

FIG. 98 Richard Riemerschmid, German, 1868-1957, *Three-Panel Screen,* 1900, embroidery by Hanna and Otto Ubbelohde, active ca. 1900. In *Deutsche Kunst und Dekoration* 7 (October 1900-March 1901).

FIG. 99 Richard Riemerschmid, German, 1868-1957, *Sketch for a Screen,* ink and pencil on transparent paper. Munich, Architektur-sammlung der Technischen Universität.

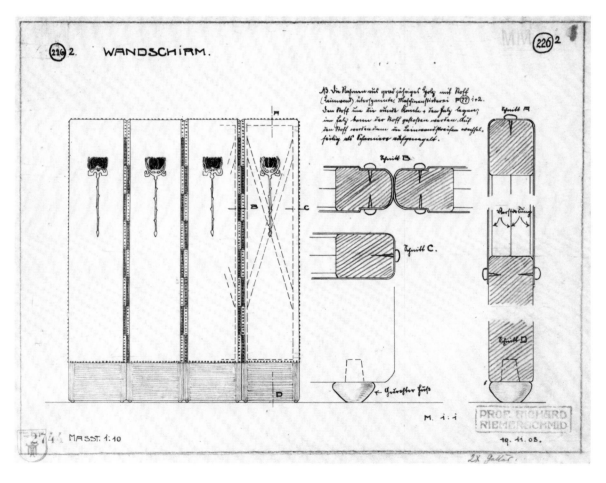

including the so-called *Room for an Art-Lover,* conceived by the furniture designer Richard Riemerschmid (fig. 98). The curving lines of the room were enhanced by a three-panel screen with embroideries by Anna and Otto Ubbelohde. Riemerschmid designed the curved, bracketlike frames for the embroideries as well as the elaborate hinges connecting the panels.[165] Riemerschmid himself also designed a very simple folding screen whose decoration consisted of understated, stylized linear floral motifs near the top of each fabric-covered panel (fig. 99). A variation of this screen was produced in 1910 by the Munich- and Dresden-based Deutsche Werkstätten, although the original design probably dates from a few years earlier.[166] Riemerschmid's contemporary Bruno Paul is also known to have done at least one folding screen, though of no particular distinction.[167]

The international nature of art nouveau revealed itself not only in stylistic but also in commercial terms. A number of ambitious artists responded to the great demand for folding screens by selling their wares in foreign markets. Henri Van de Velde was a Belgian architect and designer who in the 1890s pioneered the emerging stylistic principles of art nouveau in Brussels. His work became further known from exhibitions and from reproductions of it in the many new periodicals devoted to contemporary art. In 1899 Van de Velde showed a three-panel wood and glass screen at the Munich Secession (fig. 100), in one of several rooms he designed for that exhibition. There are no images on this screen, and decorative details are kept to a minimum, reflecting the artist's position that "only utility can regenerate beauty."[168] How the screen would meet the demands of utility is unclear, however. The large angular glass panels at the top of the screen could not have offered much privacy, but one must concede they would have allowed light to enter the intimate seating space created by the screen in the arrangement illustrated. A second screen associated with Van de Velde and dating from ca. 1899 (fig. 101) is visible in an advertisement for the Berlin showroom of Keller and Reiner, dealers in contemporary painting and especially decora-

FIG. 100 Henri Van de Velde, Belgian, 1863-1957, Folding screen in study, 1899. In *Deutsche Kunst und Dekoration* 5 (October 1899-March 1900).

FIG. 101 Henri Van de Velde, Belgian, 1863-1957, Decorative Arts Display Room, Keller & Reiner, Berlin, ca. 1899. In *Pan* 12 (1899).

tive arts. The screen at the right can be attributed securely to the artist on the basis of the caption accompanying the advertisement, describing Keller and Reiner's "Hall for decorative arts, designed and furnished by H. van de Velde, Brussels." [169] The decorative details of the screen recall the one done by Anna and Otto Ubbelohde for Richard Riemerschmid very nearly at the same time. The rather uninspiring stylistic character of this second Van de Velde screen aside, it is noteworthy that the demand for folding screens was sufficient to warrant a Berlin dealer to show the products of a Brussels designer. Van de Velde's reputation in Berlin soon flourished, and in 1900 he was commissioned by Count Kessler to design a folding screen. The four-panel white lacquered wood screen which resulted, decorated with colored tin appliqués, is known only from an illustration in *Studio* (fig. 102). [170] The abstract, curvilinear designs within the panels recall Van de Velde's early work in Brussels rather than the styles of his two other screens. Even though Van de Velde allowed decoration to appear on the surface of this screen, he accorded it a lesser role: the symmetry of the screen structure is far more striking than the decoration within.

The development of the folding screen followed a similar path in Holland as the century drew to a close.

FIG. 103 Gerrit Willem Dijsselhof, Dutch, 1866-1924, *Three-Panel Screen*, 1894, batik on silk with oak frame, 200.0 x 246.0 (78¾ x 96⅞). Amsterdam, Stedelijk Museum.

Though substantially influenced by stylistic and material principles of the English Arts and Crafts Movement, Dutch art nouveau (or Nieuwe Kunst) artists maintained a sense of independence from their European contemporaries. [171] The Dutch painter and designer Gerrit Willem Dijsselhof did a folding screen in 1894 (fig. 103). Its frame is constructed of oak, decorated at the top with curvilinear vegetal motifs and at the bottom with very simple carved rectangular panels. Within the frame is a stylized design with peacocks, a symbol of esthetic refinement since the 1860s. The image flows continuously across the three panels in an asymmetric pattern of strongly contrasting, tightly controlled linear gestures. The ornamental quality of the image is further enhanced by the stylized plant motifs that inhabit the spaces between the main body of the peacock scenes and the frame itself. While there seems to be little consideration for how the image might be affected by folding – the basic similarity between each panel being so strong – there can be no doubt whatsoever that Dijsselhof was far more concerned with the role of the image in his screens than any of his architect and designer contemporaries on the continent.

What is most remarkable about Dijsselhof's screen is that the image was executed in batik, a stencil-printing process which the Dutch learned from their Indonesian colonies. [172] Dijsselhof was among the first to experiment

FIG. 102 Henri Van de Velde, Belgian, 1863-1957, *Four-Panel Screen*, 1900, white lacquered wood with tin appliqués. In *Studio* 18 (1900).

with the technique, along with Thorn Pryker. Their contemporary Chris Lebeau was even more accomplished in his use of batik. This Amsterdam-born artist may have done as many as eleven folding screens, all of them in batik, and sometimes with the collaboration of the Dutch framemaker Jacob van den Bosch.[173] Two of these screens demonstrate the level of Lebeau's technical skill as well as his concept of the screen as a type of folding image. The first is a three-panel, double-sided example done in collaboration with van den Bosch around 1903/1904 (fig. 104). The mahogany and ebony inlaid frame, slightly curved at the top of each panel, encloses on the recto a rigidly symmetric maroon, black, and white design of standing storks. The central images of the storks are further surrounded in each panel by a dense, repetitive-pattern border. On the verso is a purely geometric and also symmetric design in brown, white, and green of heavily stylized roundels. The large rectangles at the center of each panel are almost completely unadorned, while the top portions are the most elaborately decorated of the verso. The two sides of this imposing screen (more than two meters tall) offer two distinct image types: the nature-inspired stork figures on the front and the purely decorative, rectangle-dominated fields on the verso. Amazingly, both these images have been printed in batik on parchment in what must be considered a technical tour-de-force.

Lebeau's interest in batik led to a second three-panel screen done around 1904, this time on silk and on a much-reduced scale. Just over a meter high, the screen again includes on its recto storks playing against an even more highly stylized decorative background (Cat. 17) of blue, white, and gold. Upon closer examination, however, one can read this decorative background as a series of smaller or larger "trees" with geometric roundel patterns as their foliage. Below, the storks stand on a marshlike "ground" consisting of layers of bluish-tinged arches. Lebeau's technical skill is equally visible in the decorative details throughout these images. Like his earlier screen, this one also has an image on the verso, though radically different in conception. The screen folds so that it may be stored with only one panel showing, and that panel contains a boldly rendered image of the winged Icarus approaching the sun, just before his fatal plunge. The drama of the scene, contrasting stylistically and emotionally with the sedate storks on the recto, was enhanced all the more by the clever way in which the

FIG. 104 Chris Lebeau, Dutch, 1878-1944, *Three-Panel Screen* (recto and verso), ca. 1903, batik on parchment with mahogany, satinwood and ebony frame, 203.0 x 201.0 (79¹⁵/₁₆ x 79⅛). Frame by Jacob van den Bosch. Amsterdam, Stedelijk Museum.

image on one side folded or unfolded to reveal the image on the other. In choosing this arrangement, Lebeau posited yet another alternative for the screen as a type of folding image.

In Great Britain, Morris and Burne-Jones continued to make folding screens, one of which was shown in 1899 at Hirschwald's Gallery in Berlin (fig. 105). Lesser-known artists, craftsmen, and craftswomen such as Frank Brangwyn, Kate Eadie, and Amy Sawyer also did screens there in the 1890s and early 1900s.[174] And at Liberty's, where oriental screens had been sold in the 1860s, screens by contemporary art nouveau designers were also available.[175] By the turn of the century, however, the center of screenmaking activity had passed from London to Glasgow, where Charles Rennie Mackintosh was responsible for many of the stylistic innovations in architecture and decoration associated with the Glasgow

FIG. 105 William Morris, English, 1834-1896, and Sir Edward Coley Burne-Jones, English, 1833-1898, Arts and Crafts Exhibition, Hirschwald's Gallery, Berlin, ca. 1899. In *Studio* 16 (1899).

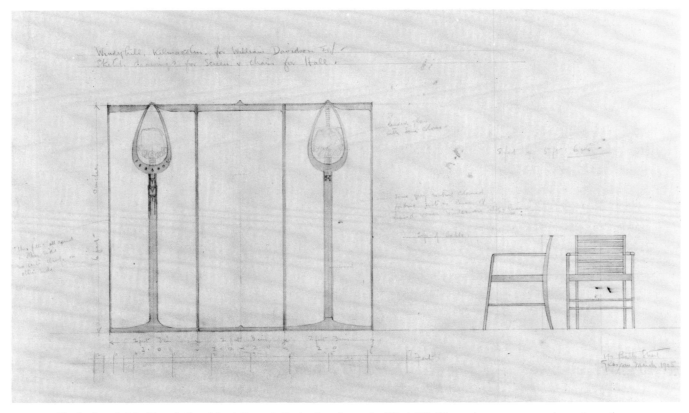

FIG. 106 Charles Rennie Mackintosh, Scottish, 1868-1928, *Design for a Screen for Windyhill, Kilmacolm*, 1905, watercolor and pencil on paper, 31.7 x 49.8 (12⅜ x 19). Hunterian Art Gallery, University of Glasgow, Mackintosh Collection.

style. In 1916 Mackintosh did his only folding screen; a 1905 design for another screen was never realized (fig. 106).[176] Most of Mackintosh's screens were fixed wall partitions. Whether straight or curved, they permanently divided an interior space and sometimes even allowed access through openings in them.[177] It would seem that his interiors were conceived with spatial and visual flow determined by the architectural elements themselves, with no need for the flexibility of function offered by folding screens.

By contrast, Mackintosh's contemporaries were eager and enthusiastic designers of folding screens. J. Herbert McNair's three-panel screen from 1897 (fig. 107) and E. A. Taylor's three-panel screen (fig. 108) shown in the 1902 Turin Esposizione Internationale, share some stylistic features with Mackintosh's design of 1905. The main portion of the panels is basically unadorned except for simple vertical framing or design elements, with the upper third reserved for decoration. McNair's screen contains squarish lead panels, each with an owl design worked in repoussé and restricted to an elongated oval. Just below,

FIG. 108 E. A. Taylor, Scottish, ca. 1870-1951, *Three-Panel Screen*, 1902, stained glass and wood. In *Studio* 26 (1902).

FIG. 107 J. Herbert McNair, Scottish, 1869-1955, *Three-Panel Screen*, 1897, wood, glass and metal repoussé. In *Studio* 11 (1897).

carved into each panel are two-part horizontal ovals which mimic the shape of the owl's eyes above. Both the owl's eyes and the "eyes" in these wood panels are made of green glass.[178] Taylor's screen, though its central panel is taller than those to either side, is quite similar. At the top of each panel is a stylized tulip shape containing stained glass designs. The vertical wood strip running up the center of each panel becomes the stem for the flower above. The similarity between Taylor's screen and Mackintosh's 1905 drawing is striking: Mackintosh also planned to use stained glass, and he allowed the flower tip to protrude above the otherwise horizontal upper edge of the frame.

By far the most elaborate and original of the Glasgow style screens was made by George Logan, like Taylor's, for the 1902 Turin exhibition (Cat. 14). This three-panel screen follows the same basic design principle as the others, a vertical stem rising up a relatively unadorned lower portion of each panel and culminating in a more highly decorated upper portion whose frame is broken by a slightly pointed protrusion. The stems in this case are relief moldings applied to the screen's matched walnut veneer, and they surround the top portion in a square. The moldings are decorated further with silver roses at the top. Where they "drop" back down the screen, they are tipped with silver hearts. The screen's upper portion is an inventive combination of solid and void, flat image and three-dimensional relief decoration. The center panel contains a watercolor by Jesse King entitled *Princesses of the Red Rose*. Although the issue of folding does not arise here, the watercolor was obviously included to serve as a stylistic and thematic adjunct to the screen as a whole. In the left and right panels an oval is actually cut out from the solid wood panels. This treatment marks the first time an artist has literally pierced the screen's surface, thereby suggesting that decorative concerns might outweigh functional ones. The cutouts themselves are bordered with silver, covered partially with three vertical silver bars at their centers, and topped with turquoise-studded silver chains that hang down from the top. The delicacy of ornament, the sumptuousness of materials, and the cohesion of the overall design make Logan's screen one of the masterpieces in what was probably the most fertile period in the history of the western folding screen.

This group of Scottish artists around and including Mackintosh also sought to improve the quality of all types of household goods. As in Morris' England, embroidery received special attention from the reformers. As early as 1894 embroidery classes taught by Jessie Newberry were held at the Glasgow School of Art,[179] for which Mackintosh would design a new building three years later. Among those who studied there, Muriel Boyd,[180] Anna Macbeth and B. F. Maitland,[181] and Eliza Kerr are all known to have done folding screens incorporating embroidered panels. Kerr's screen of about 1910 is the most interesting (fig. 109). The embroideries are set into arch-topped cutouts within rectangular shaped panels. The solidity of each panel is broken at the top left and right by small rectangular perforations, recalling similar decorative motifs in many pieces of Mackintosh's furniture. Perched atop a fence railing in the left and right panels, the symmetrical embroidered peacocks face each other. Their resplendent plumage cascades down, draping the fence in an abstract feather design. In the center panel, a highly stylized, oval-shaped design containing papyrus plants breaks the potential continuity of the composition. Remarkable for the quality of its embroidery, the screen is unusual in that it is virtually the only Scottish example to place such emphasis on the image, and a near-continuous one at that.

What can one conclude about the development of the folding screen in Europe between 1895 and 1905, insofar as these art nouveau designers are concerned? First of all, the variety of esthetic and material approaches in this decade is no less than astonishing. Further, the role of the image in these screens fluctuated considerably: in screens by Gaudí and Van de Velde, for example, the image was excluded altogether. In others, like Hoffmann's, the image could be chosen by the purchaser of the screen,

FIG. 109 Eliza Kerr, Scottish, active ca. 1906-1912, *Three-Panel Screen*, ca. 1910, embroidered panels with wood frame. Glasgow Museums and Art Galleries.

even from the manufacturer. Often limited in size, an image might be related directly to the overall decorative scheme, as in Logan's screen; or it might be full-sized and on both sides of the screen, part of a carefully conceived ensemble, as in Lebeau's work. In general, there was a far greater emphasis on the esthetic and structural interplay between the screen and its surrounding environment, as evidenced, for example, by de Feure's screen. As much as these European architects and designers adapted the screen to their own individual styles, they also brought to it an unparalleled inventiveness of form. Bugatti's, Logan's, and Gaudí's screens all stand out in this regard. In addition, there was a penchant for luxurious if not exotic materials: stained glass, silver, mother-of-pearl, copper repoussé, parchment, and batik. Whatever the specific form or materials, the vitality of approaches and execution in these screens, including those by Bonnard, Vuillard, Redon, and Klee, resulted in what was by far the most creative era of European screenmaking that had yet taken place.

THE AMERICAN RESPONSE

The development of the folding screen in America was governed by a different set of conditions from those in Europe. The new nation obviously could not draw on a native tradition of screenmaking, at least not until the very end of the nineteenth century and even then this tradition was strongly influenced by European examples. The country's taste for such objects was informed almost entirely by its familiarity with oriental screens. An unknown author writing in 1859 was able to report that

Folding screens, to keep off draughts of cold air, seem to be of Chinese or Japanese origin, if we may judge from the paintings with which they used to be decorated. They are now little used, since the finishing of our houses has been so much improved. Still, there are cases where they are found to add much to comfort.... [182]

The usefulness and popularity of folding screens in America at mid-century reported here recalls the situation in France described by Blanc in 1881. As we have seen, the first screens to come into this country were Chinese export products, ususally Coromandel lacquer screens. At the 1876 Centennial Exhibition in Philadel-

phia, visitors saw not only contemporary Chinese screens, but also those from the newly opened ports of Japan. Throughout the 1880s and even into the 1890s, America's demand for folding screens was met largely by these oriental examples.

At the 1876 Centennial Exhibition, however, Americans also saw for what was probably the first time some of the most recent products of the English Arts and Crafts movement. London's Royal School of Art Needlework, a group of amateur and semiprofessional craftswomen formed under the inspiration of William Morris, sent several folding screens as part of their exhibit. One screen (fig. 62) whose design was obviously derived from oriental sources made a noticeable impact. This peacock subject screen was reproduced in a full-page wood engraving as the frontispiece in Harriet Prescott Spofford's *Art Decoration Applied to Furniture*. Her influential book was one of several written after the Centennial Exhibition

FIG. 110 Ella Rodman Church, *How to Furnish a Home*, 1881, Fig. 18.

FIG. 111 Dining room from Grant-Kohrs Ranch, Deer Lodge, Montana, ca. 1916. Photograph, Montana Historical Society Collection.

intended to instruct primarily upper middle-class American women about the proper and tasteful way to decorate a home. Judging by Spofford's remarks, by 1876 the situation regarding the usefulness and desirability of folding screens had changed significantly: "The customary folding screen is valuable for its effect both through its beauty and its use in breaking space, and it affords opportunity for the exercise in fancy, with gilded glass, with peacock plumes and velvet, with frames of finely woven brass wire, or with panels of embroidery."[183] Ella Rodman Church, author of a similar volume on home furnishing, was even more specific in her recommendations: "A screen is always a graceful and agreeable object in a room. 'They quiet the glare of blazing lights,' says a writer, 'subdue harsh angles, shut out unsightly views, and placed here and there about a room, serve to give charming variety,' etc. A screen also affords good opportunity for the display of home skill in embroidery." Accompanying Church's remarks was "an example of screen, with embroidery or satin . . . from the Society of

Decorative Art" (fig. 110).[184] Homemade screens apparently found favor even in the far west; a period photograph from the turn of the century shows a peacock subject screen, probably made in Chicago, similar to the Royal School of Art Needlework example exhibited in Philadelphia (fig. 111).[185] As Church indicates, many different types of screens were possible, and, in her estimation, tasteful.

Various are the materials used in screenmaking, some very rich ones having the panels entirely filled in with coarse but effective canvaswork. This, however, requires a large outlay of time and money. Others are done in Cretonne work, and are also very handsome, but open to the same objection in a lesser degree. A beautiful one may be made, with less worth and less expense, by using the Japanese or Chinese crape pictures recommended for brackets, and finishing with a border of black velvet or velveteen put on with gilt-headed nails. Scrap-pictures of all sorts, colored or otherwise, are used; and these are sometimes arranged to present the seasons, and sometimes in a state of purposed confusion. . . . A screen of plain crimson felt, finished with brass headed nails, is quite as satisfactory as many more elaborate ones, and gives a rich, bright glow to a quietly furnished room. Peacock feathers are much used, both for screens and small hangings, curtains for cabinets, etc., and they have a look of elegance in almost any combination.[186]

Church's revelations are fascinating, for they indicate that the presence of actual oriental screens was supplemented by amateur versions decorated with individual panels, paralleling the more adventurous examples made in London by Nesfield and Whistler around 1870. Scrap screens, too, are mentioned in a description which calls to mind the verso of Alma-Tadema's *Epps Family* screen.[187] The taste for homemade screens evidently continued toward the end of the century; the American painter Frederic Church is known to have purchased in 1889 a four-panel screen containing four early nineteenth-century Spanish or Portuguese paintings on canvas mounted in an oak frame (fig. 112).[188]

The relatively limited but growing demand for folding screens in America in the 1880s may have been met partially by furniture manufacturers as well, though evidence is scarce. A small three-panel stained glass screen (fig. 113) is one of the few known examples of this genre

FIG. 112 *Four-Panel Screen*, 19th century, oil on canvas with oak frame, 169.6 x 240.7 (66⅝ x 94). Photograph, New York State Office of Parks, Recreation and Historic Preservation Bureau of Historic Sites, Olana State Historic Site, Taconic State Park Region.

from the period, and its design is clearly influenced by oriental and perhaps Anglo-Japanese precedents.[189] The carved, fretted ornament at the bottom of the frame and the incised molding with roundels in the frame itself both recall the Japanese-inspired decorative motifs of Nesfield's 1867 screen. The two different overlapping arch motifs in the stained glass panels are simplified versions, in fact, of painted and carved decorations in his screen, suggesting that a design pattern book like Owen Jones' *Grammar of Ornament* may have been their mutual, though perhaps distant, source.

The late 1870s were a watershed for the development of the folding screen in America. Chinese, Japanese, and Anglo-Japanese screens had all been shown at the Centennial Exhibition, and a number of other screens were produced by both amateur and commercial makers. It was also during this period that Albert Pinkham Ryder became the first American artist of any stature to experiment with the screen format. Ryder is known to have done three folding screens,[190] only one of which survives intact (fig. 114), although no longer in its original frame.[191] Due to the artist's unorthodox working methods—the screen is painted leather—there are now numerous cracks in the surface which blur the image. The three-panel screen was made around 1876/1878, either as a commission or as a wedding gift for Mrs. William C.

Banning, an acquaintance of Ryder who owned one other painting by the artist.[192]

In the left and right panels against a steeply sloped, continuous landscape background, two pairs of unclad children play with rabbits. In the central panel, perched on a small plateau in the rocks, a nude woman with her long hair tied on top of her head holds a young deer in her lap. The idyllic, Eden-like subject matter, though consistent with the artist's decidedly romantic pictures, may have had a specific purpose here, for the innocence and fecundity implied in this paradisaical setting would have been perfectly appropriate for either a bride or bride-to-be. Indirect references to Japanese prototypes are made through the inclusion of flowering and fruit-filled orange trees in the left and right panels. Similar motifs are visible in Royal School of Art Needlework screens, and in the example reproduced in Ella Rodman Church's home decorating book. In addition, the foliage is painted in a broad manner reminiscent of plant motifs in other oriental screens known to have been in America a few years later. Whatever the screen's near or distant antecedents may have been, however, Ryder adapted them to his own subject and style, with some concessions to the particular

FIG. 113 *Three-Panel Screen*, American, ca. 1880-1885, stained glass with cherry frame, 96.0 x 114.6 (38 x 45⅛). New York, Metropolitan Museum of Art, Edgar J. Kaufman Charitable Foundation Fund, 1969.

nature of a folding structure. The continuous landscape is organized so that emphasis falls on the female figure in the central panel. The breaks between panels occur in relatively unimportant areas, where the steep hills rise to the top of the canvas edge. One cannot speak of a true folding image, though, in that the same compositional qualities might have been found in a triptych. The small size of this screen suggests as well that it may have been intended to function as a firescreen rather than a room divider. The end result is a somewhat tentative but nevertheless auspicious beginning of what has become a century-old tradition of American folding screens, into which oriental precedents and influences have been absorbed both stylistically and iconographically.

Remarkably few American artists seem to have followed Ryder's example,[193] and it was not until the turn of the century that an important artist attempted a folding screen. Beginning in the late 1890s, Thomas Wilmer

Dewing produced at least three two-panel and four three-panel screens.[194] All but one were done on commission either for the Detroit industrialist and collector Charles Freer, or for Freer's business partner and friend Colonel Frank Hecker. Between 1890 and 1893, Freer and Hecker had new homes built for themselves on adjacent lots on Ferry Avenue in Detroit, and Dewing's screens were intended for these residences. The story of how these screens came about is fascinating not only for what it reveals about the various sources Dewing drew upon for his imagery and his concept of the screen in a domestic interior but also for the light it sheds on the recurring role of Japanese art in the development of western folding screens.

Freer became acquainted with Dewing's art sometime in the late 1880s, when he was responsible for organizing exhibitions of contemporary American painting for the Detroit Club. After having met Dewing in 1891, Freer

FIG. 114 Albert Pinkham Ryder, American, 1847-1917, *Three-Panel Screen*, 1876-1878, oil on leather, 97.8 x 154.3 (38½ x 60¾). Washington, National Museum of American Art, Smithsonian Institution, Gift of John Gellatly.

102 / *The Folding Image*

invited him and his fellow painter Dwight Tryon to participate in planning the interior decoration for his new home.[195] Tryon did a number of wall paintings for the entrance hall, while Dewing was responsible for the parlor, where a portrait of his own daughter was to be hung.[196] Dewing also made suggestions on plantings for the garden.[197] The house was finished by mid-1893, as were most of the decorative schemes, but Freer continued to ask both artists to provide needed "finishing touches."

Sometime in spring or early summer 1896, Freer commissioned Dewing to make a folding screen for him; the result was the pair of two-panel screens entitled *Four Sylvan Sounds* (fig. 115). The screens were begun in the summer when Dewing was living in the artists' colony of Cornish, New Hampshire.[198] While working in that forested retreat the artist was inspired to do a number of paintings in which figures are placed against densely foliated or flowering backgrounds, as in the screen. In August Dewing wrote to Freer, expressing his satisfaction with his environment: "I am having the great pleasure of painting something that I enjoy more than anything for a long time. The four forest notes – the Hermit Thrush, the sound of running water, the woodpecker, and the wind through the pine trees."[199] Dewing admired the poetry and philosophy of Ralph Waldo Emerson, and it is possible that Emerson's verse entitled *Woodnotes* inspired the screen's allegorical subject matter.[200] The classically dressed figures may each represent a different "sylvan" sound. In each of the four panels, a female figure holds a musical instrument: a lyre, signifying the wind rustling through the pines; a drum, recalling the woodpecker's tapping; a xylophone, symbolizing the "sound of running water"; and a flute, to mimic the hermit thrush's call. The transcendental subject matter of the screens is elegantly portrayed here with a lyrical handling of paint. The restrained character of the images is further enhanced by the simple, unadorned gilded frame which surrounds them.

It is interesting to speculate on what precedents, if any, Dewing may have relied for the idea and appearance of his early screens. On his first trip to Europe in 1894-1895, Dewing visited Whistler's London studio and may very well have seen *Blue and Silver: Screen with Old Battersea Bridge* (fig. 54).[201] Indeed, the correspondences between their screens are striking. Each consists of two panels in a relatively square overall configuration. Dewing's simple gilded strip frame recalls at least the form of Whistler's. It

is likely Dewing understood the compositional complexities in Whistler's screen caused by folding, although his own solution is somewhat less adventurous. The scenes in *Four Sylvan Sounds* are unified by a continuous foliated background, but in accordance with the symbolic theme, the figures are placed individually within each panel. Dewing therefore did not have to confront the problem of having his image altered by folding. He did turn the figures toward each other, though, so that when the screen is folded, they face each other even more completely. And, as in all of Dewing's screens, there are no framing elements between the hinged panels which might have interrupted the continuity of his composition.

Although the style of the *Four Sylvan Sounds* has little to do with the Japonisms of Whistler's screen, Japan did play an important role in Dewing's art in general and in his subsequent screens. The artist became familiar with the eastern tradition through Freer, who was an avid and knowledgeable collector of oriental art. Dewing actually became Freer's agent in New York, helping to find oriental objects for the industrialist's collection.[202] Between 1896 and 1900 Freer purchased twenty-seven Japanese folding screens, including six pairs of screens. No doubt responding to this eastern influence, Dewing almost always chose to paint pairs of screens, in true Japanese fashion, rather than single screens, as did virtually every ther western screenmaker in the nineteenth and early twentieth centuries. Freer was also beginning to collect Whistler's art in earnest by this time and some of the decorative, semiabstract qualities of Dewing's paintings and screens could have been gleaned from Whistler's liberal interpretations of Japanese art in paintings that Freer owned.[203] The economy of figural and landscape elements and the corresponding emphasis on these elements' roles in Dewing's screen design are indebted partially to Whistler and partially to Japanese painting.

Dewing's next screens were done for Freer's friend and business partner Colonel Frank Hecker, who commissioned two pairs of three-panel screens for his French Renaissance-style Detroit mansion, almost certainly after seeing the *Four Sylvan Sounds* in Freer's nearby home.[204] Unfortunately, only one half of each pair has survived, making it difficult to reach any substantial conclusions about how each pair functioned as a compositional unit. The remaining three-panel screen from the first pair, known as *Classical Figures* (fig. 116), was done between 1897 and 1898 for the drawing room of Hecker's home.

Reminiscent of *Four Sylvan Sounds*, classically inspired female figures are seen against a foliated background, though in this case the women are standing and the background is far more sketchily rendered. The source for Dewing's languidly posed females were fourth- and third-century B.C. Greek Tanagra figures that Hecker began collecting in the 1890s.[205] The classicisims of Dewing's screen were emphasized further by the architect Stanford White's magnificent gilded frame. After Hecker received *Classical Figures* in August 1898, however, he began to share Dewing's concern that the screen's tonality was too dark for its intended setting. So in 1899 he asked Dewing to do a second pair of screens for the same drawing room. The following year Dewing finished the pair entitled *Morning Glories* and *Cherry Blossoms,* of which only the former survives (Cat. 10). The palette is much brighter than that of *Classical Figures,* and Hecker

was apparently pleased with the result, for he installed the screens in the drawing room and had the first pair moved to a nearby room and mounted on the wall.[206] In *Morning Glories* the artist again relied on the Tanagra statues for his figures, although they convey less emotional intensity than do the previous ones. Possibly Dewing wished to soften the mood as well as the tonality of this second pair of screens. To that end he placed the figures against a background of blossoming morning glories (and presumably cherry blossoms in the lost pendant). A flowering branch drifts into the lower half of the composition, proclaiming its Japanese forebears not only by its very inclusion but also by its right to left orientation.[207] Dewing could very well have borrowed this motif from Whistler, who used it with great effectiveness in *Variations in Flesh Colour and Green: The Balcony* (fig. 117), a painting Freer purchased in 1892.

FIG. 115 Thomas Wilmer Dewing, American, 1851-1938, *Four Sylvan Sounds,* 1896, oil on panel, 175.7 x 153.0 (69¼ x 60¼) each two-panel pair. Washington, Freer Gallery of Art.

FIG. 116 Thomas Wilmer Dewing, American, 1851-1938, *Classical Figures*, 1897-1898, oil on panel with gilded carved frame, 165.1 x 180.3 (65 x 71). Detroit Institute of Arts, Gift of Mr. and Mrs. James O. Keene in memory of their daughter, Sandra Mae Long.

FIG. 117 James Abbott McNeill Whistler, American, 1834-1903, *Variations in Flesh Colour and Green: The Balcony*, 1864. Washington, Freer Gallery of Art.

Once again Dewing employed Stanford White to make the frames for this pair of screens. The frame for *Morning Glories* consists of two fluted columns with pseudo-Corinthian capitals supporting an incised entablature with medallions. The base is raised off the floor by four ball feet. White's vocabulary, certainly in keeping with the classical sources for Dewing's figures, was equally well suited to the restrained elegance of the screen's overall design. But it is clear there was an additional purpose in choosing the architectural motifs used in the frames. Hecker's mansion was designed in a French Renaissance style by the German-born architect Louis Kamper, whose embellishments in the drawing room included a pair of fluted columns with Corinthian capitals and a significant number of other classically inspired ornaments. That White's frame and Kamper's architectural elements are so familiar is not surprising; Kamper studied with White before forming his own firm in Detroit. An even more likely explanation for their similarity, however, is that

Dewing wanted White's frame to harmonize with the screens' intended environment. Decorated in white and gold, the drawing room was filled with gilded Louis XVI furniture purchased from Duveen.[208] The rigid architectural nature of White's frame, together with the simple symmetry of the *Morning Glories* composition, obviously blended well with the formal elegance of Kamper's drawing room.[209] Although there is nothing in Dewing's screens to remind us overtly of simultaneous developments in Europe, the artist did share with art nouveau designers their concept of the screen as part of a larger decorated environment, even if only subconsciously. Dewing's eclectic fusion of classical sources, allegorical subject matter, and certain Japanese design principles makes his screens unique among American examples. Unquestionably America's foremost screenmaker, Dewing in this genre rivaled his European contemporaries.

At the same time Dewing was providing screens for Freer and Hecker, a group of artists and craftsmen working as far apart as California and New York began to show a growing interest in folding screens. A number of American furniture designers such as Gustave Stickley traveled to Europe to discover for themselves the continuing impact of the revolution brought on by William Morris' fervent desire to produce quality objects for household use. Stickley, in fact, visited the English designer Charles F. A. Voysey in 1898 and saw others in England and on the continent before returning to his own furniture company in Eastwood, New York.[210] He is known to have made several screens, including one example from 1906 (fig. 118).[211] At least two others were produced by his fellow furniture maker Charles Rohlfs (fig. 119), whose small shop was located in Buffalo.[212] Stickley's simple three-panel screen was one of two versions announced in the February 1905 issue of *The Craftsman:*

The soft olive green of the panel color suggests the deep tones of the hazel wood of which the frame is made, and in contrast we have introduced, as the appliqué of the rose form, a bloom linen of richest gold – this again finding a place in the little space enclosed at the base of the stem lines. The tapering leaves of the rose, singularly decorative in line, are carried out in an appliqué of this clear green and outlined in a golden brown which also is again repeated in the stem lines, and the markings of the petal forms of the flower.

FIG. 118 Gustav Stickley, American, 1858-1942, *Three-Panel Screen*, 1905, linen panels in oak frame, 147.3 x 137.1 (58 x 54). Collection of James and Janeen Marrin.

The rather plain long-stemmed flower motif is common to a number of contemporary European screens, notably those designed by Mackintosh and his circle in Scotland and Riemerschmid in Germany. A slightly earlier screen by Rohlfs, one of two he designed for his own home in 1900, places a similar emphasis on simplicity of design and quality of craftsmanship.

Even more austere in its decoration is the three-panel screen made in 1906 for the California home of William T. Bolton by the architect and designer Charles Sumner Greene (fig. 120).[213] In 1901 Greene visited England, where he became interested in the English country home. Whether he saw any European screens on that trip is not known, but he did keep up with developments in European architecture and decorative arts through a subscription to *Studio*, where many folding screens were illustrated.[214] Like Rohlfs and Stickley, the latter of whose work he probably knew from *The Craftsman*, Greene scrupulously avoided the use of excessive decorative detail in his screen. A symmetrical arrangement of tiny, stained glass squares bordered in ebony provides the only breaks in the otherwise smooth mahogany panels.

FIG. 119 Charles Rohlfs, American, 1853-1936, *Four-Panel Screen*, 1900, oak, 182.9 x 223.5 (72 x 88). Atlanta, High Museum of Art, Gift from Virginia Carroll Crawford.

FIG. 120 Charles Sumner Greene, 1868-1957, *Three-Panel Screen*, 1906, mahogany, ebony, and stained glass, 161.3 x 167.6 (63½ x 66). Pasadena, Randell L. Makinson.

What these American arts and crafts movement screens have in common is an almost puritanical avoidance of ornamental detail. This predilection for unadorned articles of household furniture was based on both philosophical and economic considerations. Like Morris in England, these American craftsmen sought what they termed an honesty in furniture-making materials – primarily native hardwoods – whose attractiveness lay in their natural qualities. The silver appliqués and mother-of-pearl inlays in George Logan's screen, and even more the exotic combinations of copper, parchment, and other materials of Bugatti's screens, would have been anathema to American screen designers. This esthetic bent may account as well for the total absence not only of folding images, but almost any images at all on their screens. In addition, furniture makers like Stickley, Rohlfs, and Roycroft wanted to make their products accessible to a middle-class audience. The application of costly materials such as silver would have defeated this purpose.

Another name which must be added to the list of American screenmakers is that of Louis Comfort Tiffany. Although one would presume that this masterful designer and craftsman of lamps, vases, and stained glass windows surely did folding screens in substantial numbers, examples by him are in fact quite rare. Tiffany did send an impressive three-panel folding screen with stained glass panels to the 1900 Exposition Universelle in Paris (Cat.

11). Probably made as a showpiece, it has survived only in this single example. The screen is particularly remarkable for the richly decorated, fruit-bearing foliage in the windows, hallmarks of Tiffany's style. The design of the screen itself is rather awkward and seems simply an attempt to use the colored glass windows in a screen format. Tiffany's studios did produce another type of folding screen of which several examples are extant (fig. 121). This so-called tea screen is less than a foot high and as its name implies was apparently intended to shield a steeping teapot from drafts. Of course these table-top screens must have been desirable from a purely decorative standpoint as well, imitating in miniature their larger, more common ancestors. Tiffany made this particular screen himself for his niece, using a relatively plain type of glass similar to that used in the lower portions of the larger 1900 screen. There must have been a fancy for these diminutive screens; the Gorham Manufacturing Company produced an example in silver around 1900 (fig. 122).

The first half-century of American screenmaking came to a close with the work of two artists whose common ground was the now legendary Armory Show of 1913. In that exhibition several one-panel and multi-panel folding screens by Robert Winthrop Chanler were shown. While Chanler is now nearly forgotten, his screens were received with great praise by reviewers of the Armory Show.[215] The artist trained first in Rome and then in Paris in 1900 with Jean-Léon Gérôme at the Académie Julien – coincidentally where Bonnard, Vuillard, and their Nabi colleagues had studied just a few years earlier.[216] Chanler returned to the United States in 1902, but

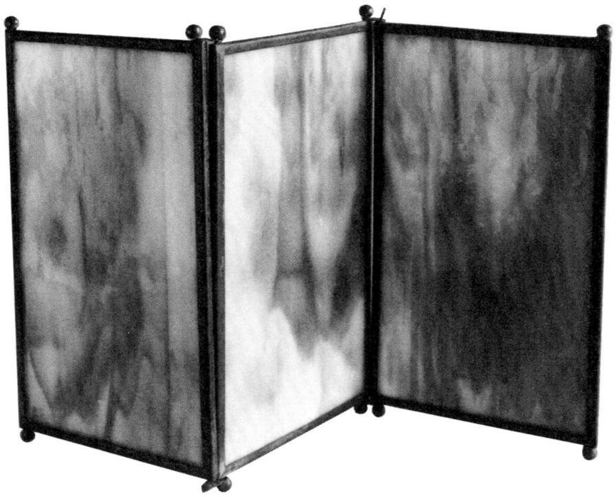

FIG. 121 Louis Comfort Tiffany, American, 1848-1933, *Three-Panel Tea Screen*, ca. 1900, green and white glass with copper plated brass frame, 10.2 x 17.8 (4 x 7). Winter Park, Florida, Morse Gallery of Art.

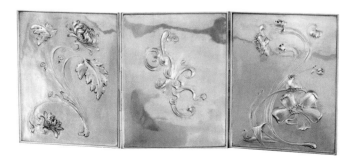

FIG. 122 *Three-Panel Tea Screen*, 1900, Gorham Manufacturing Company, Providence, Rhode Island, sterling silver, 19.5 x 43.3 (7½ x 17 1/16). Yale University Art Gallery, Gift of Dr. L. J. Camuti.

three years later he went back to Paris, where he showed one of his painted panels at the Salon d'Automne. His first known exposure to folding screens occurred during this visit when he chanced upon a Chinese lacquer screen in a shop in the Place St.-Georges[217] and was so captivated that he bought it.[218] Once again, we encountered the familiar influence of oriental screens; it is interesting to note that another Parisian shop handling Chinese lacquer screens would later spark the young Eileen Gray's interest (Cat. 24).

Between 1910 and 1925 Chanler did several folding screens, exhibiting them with great success at the Albright (now the Albright-Knox) Art Gallery in Buffalo,[219] and in the Belmaison Gallery at Wannamaker's in New York in the 1920s (fig. 123).[220] The exotic subject matter of Chanler's designs made his screens and decorative panels highly sought after by New York patrons such as Mrs. Gertrude Payne Whitney and the Colony Club. Chanler did not, however, influence the development of the folding screen in America; as we shall see, his achievements were far surpassed by American art déco designers such as Donald Deskey.

Chanler's screens at the Armory Show may have provided a stimulus to at least one other American artist.

FIG. 123 Installation photograph of the Chanler Exhibition, Paris. In *The Mentor* (June 1927).

Charles Prendergast, younger brother of Maurice, the more well-known painter and printmaker, began his career as a framemaker.[221] In 1912 at the age of fifty he decided to become an artist, but his previously-learned skills were called for in 1913 when he was asked to provide frames for objects in the Armory Show. A few years later, probably between 1916 and 1920, Prendergast did the first and what must be considered the best of his three folding screens (Cat. 18). In this three-panel, double-sided, painted and gilded work he drew upon Persian miniatures and native American folk art for the curious unidentifiable subjects on the recto. The viewer yearns to make sense of the seated, riding, haloed, and winged creatures inhabiting the Eden-like setting. Yet despite Prendergast's known use of Biblical subject matter, and despite the unmistakable depiction of full-sized standing angels on the verso, it seems that the artist chose his subjects simply to evoke a sense of charm and mystery. As is true in Chanler's screens, the artist has constructed his design with little concern for how folding might affect the composition. Instead, the density of the decorative patterns across the recto and the rigid, iconlike restriction of each figure to a panel on the verso were expected to impart cohesiveness to each side of the screen.

America's involvement with folding screens was on the whole far less consuming than Europe's. On the one hand, the country was without any existing tradition of screenmaking, except for the influential oriental tradition: when Americans wanted such objects, they frequently turned to the Orient to meet their demand. Nor did America possess any guiding figure in the mold of Morris who could stimulate an entire generation of artists, craftsmen, and consumers to consider the merit of well-made, even artistic, household goods. By the time American artisans such as Stickley finally mounted their assault against shoddy, machine-made products, their esthetic biases forced them to view the screen more as furniture than as art. And with the exception of Dewing, rarely did America's craftsmen or painters consider the screen part of a consciously designed domestic environment. Consequently, the early history of American folding screens is marked by occasional but generally isolated forays by artists of vastly differing stylistic and decorative approaches. Not until the middle of the twentieth century did any genuinely American tradition of folding screens evolve.

The circumstances in Europe were of course much different. There the folding screen was considered from a number of interrelated viewpoints. Artists like Morris, de Feure, Gaudí, or Bugatti saw their screens principally as accountrements – albeit useful ones – in planned decorative environments. The visual impact of their screens was achieved usually through varied emphases on exotic forms, or costly and unusual combinations of materials, not to mention their relationships to the three-dimensional spaces which they would occupy. The fantasies of shape and wealth of materials that characterize so many European art nouveau screens were simply not to be found in American examples.

In addition, Europe was blessed with a number of extremely talented artists for whom the folding screen was a formidable and intriguing challenge. Beginning with Whistler, and continuing on to the Nabis, the screen was considered a unique type of painted furniture: a folding image. Whatever relationship the screen may have enjoyed with the surrounding environment, it still had to be confronted first on formal terms. To what extent would folding alter the appearance of a screen composition? Could a compositon be chosen that would work equally well in all the various positions in which a folding screen could be erected? Whistler, Bonnard, Vuillard, and Denis in particular not only confronted these issues but resolved them with astounding originality and success. Never before had artists of their caliber experimented so freely with the screen format. The conspicuous lack of commentary on folding screens by the artists who made them suggests they considered it perfectly natural to embark on this type of decorative project. Certainly, screens were by no means as common in domestic interiors as paintings and prints, nor for that matter as common as chairs. It is evident, though, that such artist- and architect-designed screens were highly desirable objects which only a privileged few could hope to own. Whatever the motivation of these artists and designers, their contributions forever altered the development of the western folding screen, renewing a tradition which continued to find new means of expression throughout the twentieth century.

NOTES

1. Charles Blanc, *Grammaire des arts décoratifs: Décoration intérieure de la maison* (Paris: Librairie Renouard, 1882), 233. Similar sentiments were voiced even earlier in Pierre Larousse, *Grand Dictionnaire universel du XIXe siècle*, vol. 2 (Paris: Administration du Grand Dictionnaire Universel, 1874), s.v. *paravent* (screen). "Today screens have almost passed from usage; they are no longer used, except as a backdrop in elegant theaters to present a proverb or a small comedy that requires very little mise en scène. . . ." Larousse also relates a colloquialism then common in France, *Chinois de paravent* (a Chinaman in a screen), that is, "a figure ridiculed in a tableau, by comparison to the Chinese often represented on screens." Blanc also comments on this phenomenon, "If called upon, our school of painting will make available delightful motifs found in the faunesque comedies of Gillot, the *fêtes galantes* of Watteau and his pupils – motifs seemingly conceived for the express purpose of decorating panels, screens and fans." Blanc, *Grammaire*, 234.

2. Armand Leleux (1818-1885) was born in Paris and became a student of Ingres. He was active as a genre and portrait painter, etcher, and author.

3. See Alfred Robaut, "Corot: Peintures décoratives," *L'Art* 31, no. 4 (15 October 1882): 49-52, in particular, and Alfred Robaut, *L'Oeuvre de Corot*, 4 vols. (Paris: Léonce Laget, 1965), 2: no. 1073. According to Robaut, the screen belonged to the Leleux family, who "had the unfortunate idea to have the work mounted on a canvas in order to make it into an [easel] painting and, at the same time, to eliminate the surrounding areas attributable to the collaboration of Corot's two friends. Daubigny's signature still remains, but that of Leleux has disappeared; the work of both of these artists no longer exists. The painting in its actual state measures approximately 1.3 x 2.1 m. After this transformation of around 1885, the painting passed into the hands of MM. Goupil and Sedelmeyer. It surfaced in 1891 in London in an exhibition organized by MM. Hollender and Cremetti." See also *National Gallery of Ireland: Illustrated Summary Catalogue of the Paintings* (Dublin: Gill and Macmillan, Ltd., 1981), 28, no. 950.

4. A similar trompe l'oeil trellis motif can be seen in Edouard Muller's block printed wallpaper, *The Garden of Armida*, 1854, reproduced as no. II-16 in *The Second Empire: Art in France under Napoleon III* (exh. cat., Philadelphia Museum of Art, 1978). In this context, the screen is as much a Second Empire as a Barbizon object.

5. Corot, in fact, did a number of vertically oriented decorative panels as well. See Robaut, "Corot," 45-53.

6. See Lionello Venturi, *Peintures: Période académique et romantique, 1858-1871*, vol. 1 of *Cézanne: Son art – son oeuvre* (Paris: Paul Rosenberg, 1936), 69, nos. 1-7. These illustrations show both sides of the screen as it originally existed. The verso panels have disappeared, according to Wally Findlay, the screen's present owner. The screen has

since been broken up and mounted as an easel painting. See also Edgar Munhall, *Paul Cézanne, "Les Environs d'Aix-en-Provence"* (New York: Wally Findlay Galleries, 1974), unpaginated.

7. Munhall, *Cézanne,* second page. The woman under a parasol with an admirer in the screen's fifth panel is taken from Lancret's *Près de vous, belle Iris,* which Cézanne may have known from Hortemel's engraving. Theodore Reff has claimed that the groups in the second and third panels derive from the same Lancret source; see Theodore Reff, "Pictures within Cézanne's Pictures," *Arts Magazine* 53 (June 1979): 97 and note 35.

8. Reff suggests that Cézanne may have done other screens with designs based on eighteenth-century French wallpapers and that there may have been additional screens at Jas de Bouffan owned by the artist's father. See Reff, "Pictures," 96-97.

9. Munhall, *Cézanne,* first and second pages and accompanying notes.

10. S. Lane Faison, Jr., has claimed the portrait was done in Manet's studio, based on knowledge that Zola's precarious financial situation would not have allowed him such sumptuous surroundings. In a February 1868 letter to Duret, Zola stated that he sat for the portrait in Manet's studio; see Faison, "Manet's Portrait of Zola," *Magazine of Art* 42 (May 1949): 163-166. Jean Adhémar concluded the portrait showed Zola in his own apartment because some of Zola's personal possessions are shown; see "Le Cabinet de travail de Zola," *Gazette des Beaux-Arts* 56 (November 1960): 285-298. Theodore Reff convincingly concluded that "the setting in the portrait of Zola is not only 'un décor suggérant l'idée du travail intellectual' in realistic detail. It is also a symbolic statement, contrived of objects in Manet's possession and executed in his studio where Zola himself said he posed in February 1868." See Theodore Reff, "Manet's Portrait of Zola," *Burlington Magazine* 117 (January 1975): 35-44. More recently, Anne Hanson has accepted Faison's and Reff's arguments that Zola is shown in Manet's studio; see *Manet and the Modern Tradition* (New Haven and London: Yale University Press, 1977), 74-75. This view is again contradicted by Geneviève Lacambre's entry on the portrait of Philadelphia, *Second Empire,* 331, no. VI-83. Citing only Adhémar's article, Lacambre reiterates her claim that objects such as the inkstand owned by Zola indicate the portrait was done in Zola's rue Moncey apartment. The most recent publication on this painting accepts Reff's contention that the scene contained mostly objects from Manet's studio, including the screen. See *Manet: 1832-1883* (exh. cat., Paris, Grand Palais, 1983), 282.

11. The most useful of these efforts are *Japonisme in Art:* (Committee for the Year 2001, 1980), a series of essays by several authors, edited by Yamada Chisaburō for the Society for the Study of Japonisme; *Japonisme: Japanese Influence on French Art* (exh. cat., Cleveland Museum of Art, 1975), with contributions by Gabriel P. Weisberg, Philip Dennis Cate, Gerald Needham, Martin Eidelberg, and William R. Johnston; *Japanese Influences in American Art, 1853-1900* (exh. cat., Williamstown, Mass: Sterling and Francine Clark Art Institute, 1981), by Sally Mills; Benjamin Rowland, Jr., "The Interplay between American and Japanese Art," in *The Shaping of Art and Architecture in Nineteenth-Century America* (New York: Metropolitan Museum of Art, 1972); Colta Feller Ives, *The Great Wave: The Influence of Japanese Woodcuts on French Prints* (New York: Metropolitan Museum of Art, 1974); and C. V. Yamada, ed., *Dialogue in Art: Japan and the West* (Tokyo, New York, and San Francisco: Kodansha International, 1976).

12. Blanc, *Grammaire,* 233-234. Siegfried Wichmann's recent book, *Japonismus: Ostasien-Europa, Begegnungen in der Kunst des 19. und 20. Jahrhunderts* (Herrsching: Schuler Verlag, 1980), although a valuable source of Japanese images, is not entirely accurate in the implica-

tions suggested by the comparisons. For a review of Wichmann's book, see Gabriel Weisberg in *Antiques* (August 1982): 254-256.

13. Dutch traders were allowed to remain in Japan even after the trade ban went into effect in 1640 under the Shōgun Ieyasu Tokugawa. Some Japanese goods did find their way to Europe, as Deborah Johnson has convincingly shown in her article, "Japanese Prints in Europe before 1840," *Burlington Magazine* 124 (June 1982): 343-347; clearly, so much emphasis should not be placed on the period directly after 1854, for Japanese prints, at least, were far more prevalent and accessible than previously recognized.

14. For a general overview of these exhibitions, see John Allwood, *The Great Exhibitions* (London: Studio Vista, 1977), and for more specific information, Elizabeth Gilmore Holt, "The Documentation for the Contribution of Three Mid-Nineteenth Century Exhibitions to the Popularization of Japanese Art," in *Art, the Ape of Nature: Studies in Honor of H. W. Janson* (New York: Harry N. Abrams, Inc., 1981), 639-650.

15. Even prior to this exhibition, Japanese goods made their way into London. According to Elizabeth Aslin, when the Department of Practical Art, a forerunner of the present Victoria and Albert Museum, was established in 1852, some Japanese and Chinese objects were already in its collection. In 1854, there was also a fairly large exhibition of Japanese applied art held in the gallery of the Old Water Colour Society in Pall Mall East; the display, however, seems not to have had a noticeable impact on the London art world. See Elizabeth Aslin, *The Aesthetic Movement: Prelude to Art Nouveau* (1969; reprint, New York: Excalibur Books, 1981), 80.

16. Alison Adburgham, *Liberty's: A Biography of a Shop* (London: George Allen & Unwin, Ltd., 1975), 13.

17. Oriental departments could be found at a number of other large retail establishments, including William Whiteley's Debenham & Freebody, and Swan and Edgar. The architect and designer Christopher Dresser opened his own Japanese warehouse in London in 1879. See Adburgham, *Liberty's,* 23-24.

18. Adburgham, *Liberty's,* 22.

19. See *Exposition Universelle de 1867 à Paris: Catalogue général publié par la commission impériale* (Paris: E. Dentu and London: J. M. Johnson and Sons, n.d.), under "Groupe III. Meubles et autres objets destinés à l'habitation," 438-439. Among the entries listed, "Fsy Sodjero in Yeddo—decorated folding screens, . . . Haségawa Kihée, in Yeddo—folding screens painted and highlighted with gold and silver. (Shown by MM. Roczaémom and Ousabouro, in Yedda [sic]); . . . S. A. Le Taishiou of Satsouma—folding screens with artistic paintings."

20. *Catalogue de produits et objets d'art japonais composant la collection envoyée du Japon pour l'Exposition Universelle* (Paris: Renou et Maulde, 1868), no. 4. This catalogue lists the items designated for sale by the Japanese government. See also Geneviève Lacambre, "Les Milieux Japonisants à Paris, 1800-1880," in Chisaburō, ed., *Japonisme,* 44-45.

21. Illustration from Fr. Ducuing, *L'Exposition Universelle de 1867 illustrée: Publication internationale autorisée par la commission impériale* (Paris: Administration, 1867), 1: 333. Lancelot (1822-1894) was active in Paris as an illustrator.

22. *Catalogue de produits et objets d'art,* 1868, "No. 45 (just as 43 and 44)—Black lacquered wood screen, landscape subject, six panels; . . . No. 119 (just as 120)—Paper screen, six panels, black lacquer wood, metal ornamentation representing various Japanese screens; . . . No. 130—Two panel wood screen, frame lacquered, with applications of metal and incised, gilded escutcheons; the base represents gilded bamboo in relief with a great effect; . . . No. 173—Six panel screen, black lacquered wood, representing a Japanese farm; . . . No.

175 – Six panel screen, 2m 65 in height, of very great richness, black lacquered wood with ornamentation, gilded incised metal. The middle of each panel is decorated with a daylight shade of bamboo; . . . No. 181 – Six panel screen with paintings representing a view of Japan."

23. See Gabriel P. Weisberg. "Philippe Burty and a Critical Assessment of Early Japonisme," in Chisaburō, ed., *Japonisme*, 109-123; *Collection Ph. Burty: Catalogue de peintures et d'estampes japonaises, de kakemonos, de miniatures indopersiens et de livres rélatifs à l'Orient et au Japon*, preface by Ernest L. Leroux (Paris, 1891); and *Collection Ph. Burty: Catalogue objets d'art japonais et chinois*, introduction by Samuel Bing (Paris: Durand-Ruel, 1891). As with most collections dispersed at the end of the nineteenth century, including those of the Goncourts and Bing, it is almost impossible to know when specific objects were first acquired.

24. Philippe Burty, "Le Mobilier moderne," *Gazette des Beaux-Arts* 24 (1868):28. My thanks to Geneviève Lacambre, conservator at the Musée d'Orsay, whose 1964 thesis, "Le Role du Japon dans l'évolution de l'habitation et de son décor en France de la 2e moitié du XIXe et au début du XXe siècle," first declared the connection betwen Burty's comments and the screens in the 1867 Exposition Universelle.

25. For a brief summary of this exhibition, see Weisberg, "Burty," 112-116.

26. See *Catalogue de la section japonaise à l'Exposition Universelle de Paris 1878*, under "Groupe III. Mobilier et Accessoires," 6-20. Among the items listed: "A. Matsouda, Tokyo. Plain folding screens; . . . Z. Acano, *département* of Hichi, province of Owari. Folding screen with panels in *nourishippo* (lacquered porcelain with designs); . . . R. Tanaka, Tokyo. Folding screens with *noumé-shu-sou* (a kind of satin); . . . Simple folding screens in *kin-dei-sou-kashi* (wood gilded, then lacquered in such a way that the coat of lacquer allows the gold to show through), made by S. Sougiryama."

27. Ernest Chesneau, "Le Japon à Paris," in *Exposition Universelle de 1878: Les Beaux-Arts et les arts décoratifs, I. L'Art moderne* (Paris: Gazette des Beaux-Arts, 1879), 476-477.

28. Edmond Duranty, "L'Extrême Orient: Revue d'ensemble des arts asiatiques à l'Exposition Universelle," in *Exposition Universelle de 1878 . . . II. L'Art ancien*, 507-544.

29. Presumably Ieyasu Tokugawa, the shōgun who, in 1640, banned foreign trade and travel.

30. Duranty, "Revue," 509-510.

31. See Yoshitomo Okamoto, *The Namban Art of Japan* (New York: Weatherhill, 1970).

32. Duranty was accurate in assuming that at least the subject of the screen was early; the Portuguese came to Japan in 1542 and continued to trade with Japan until ca. 1640.

33. For the most recent general studies on Japanese screens, see Sherman E. Lee, *Japanese Screens from the Museum and Cleveland Collections* (Cleveland Museum of Art, 1977); Julia Meech-Pekarik, "Twelve Japanese Screens," *Metropolitan Museum of Art Bulletin* (Fall 1979); Elise Grilli, *The Art of the Japanese Screen* (New York and Tokyo: Weatherhill and Bijutsu Shuppan-sha, 1971); and Miyeko Murase, *Byōbu: Japanese Screens from New York Collections* (New York: Asia House Gallery, 1971).

34. Chesneau, "Le Japon," 470.

35. See *Catalogue of the Collection Exhibited in the Palais du Champ de Mars, Universal Exhibition, Paris 1878, Published by Order of the Inspector General of Customs*, Imperial Maritime Customs. III – Miscellaneous Series: No. 5 (Shanghai: Statistical Department of the Inspectorate General, 1878), 6-9. The introduction to the section entitled "Troisième Groupe. Mobilier et Accessoires. Classe A" states "Shanghai exhibits here very beautiful folding screens, of which the panels painted on silk have been executed in Shanghai."

36. Duranty, "Revue," 538-539.

37. *Welt-Ausstellung 1873 in Wien. Officieler Kunst-Katalog. Zweite vermehrte und verbesserte Auflage* (Vienna: Verlag der General-Direction, Druckerei des Journals "Die Presse," 1873), 188 and a previous unnumbered page with headings, "Timbuctu," "Persien," and "Japan."

38. Inv. Nr. 20232, Or. 3422 by Yoskikai (Kimei) Komitsu, dated either 1814 or 1879; Inv. Nr. 20692, Or. 3882, late eighteenth century; Inv. Nr. 20693, Or. 3883, early eighteenth century; Inv. Nr. 20694, Or. 3884, eighteenth-nineteenth century; Inv. Nr. 20697, Or. 3887, late eighteenth century; and Inv. Nr. 20698, Or. 3888, seventeenth century. My thanks to Dr. Herbert Fux, Director, Österreichisches Museum für Angewandte Kunst, for supplying this information.

39. According to Dr. Yoshiaki Shimizu of the Freer Gallery of Art, the screens in fig. 8 and 9 show scenes from the famous 1180 battle at Yashima leading to the fall of the Taira clan. They depict one of several versions of this historic battle and could date as early as the seventeenth century.

40. See for example, the Tosa school screen depicting the famous seventeenth-century *Battles of Hogen and Heiji*, in Meech-Pekarik, "Twelve Screens," 14-21.

41. This type of screen was known from the late fifteenth century, and unlike this example, usually consisted of fans made by the same studio. Here the fans seem to date from the early seventeenth to late eighteenth century. The fan shape itself was exploited by many impressionist and post-impressionist artists in numerous fan designs done between 1875 and 1910. Interest in this object type has been thoroughly documented and analyzed by Marc Gerstein in "Impressionist and Post-Impressionist Fans" (Ph.D. diss., Harvard University, 1978). Some correlation does exist between the western artists' fascination for fans and folding screens. Interest in these objects stems at least partially from an eighteenth-century French tradition which found revitalized currency in France after mid-century. Quite obviously, both objects also demonstrate the undeniable rage for things Japanese at the same time. Unlike screens, however, fans were almost never actually made from the many designs which were done, perhaps suggesting it was more the novelty of the semicircular fan form that interested their designers than their actual function. Moreover, designers of fans, unlike designers of folding screens, never had to consider how the folding structure would affect the reading of the composition. Even when the fans were mounted, their numerous folds could achieve the overall effect of a rippling image, whereas with screens, the impact of recognizable focal points in the composition was altered – presumably consciously – by the predictable breaks between panels.

42. William Anderson, *Descriptive and Historical Catalogue of a Collection of Japanese and Chinese Paintings in the British Museum* (London: Longman Co., B. Quaritch, Trübner & Co., 1886). nos. 442-447, 1573, 1717-1718. For a general overview of the collectors and critics of Japanese art in this period, see Elisa Evett, "The Critical Reception of Japanese Art in Europe in the Late Nineteenth Century" (Ph.D. diss., Cornell University, 1980).

43. Anderson, *British Museum*, 327, no. 1573.

44. Lee, *Japanese Screens*, especially 4-5.

45. Anderson, *British Museum*, 374-375, nos. 1717-1718. Dr. Yoshiaki Shimizu of the Freer Gallery of Art believes the screen may actually depict the Hi'e Festival on Lake Biwa, east of Kyoto. The presence of the Tori gate at the right fig. 43 indicates a large city rather than a small town such as Nogoya.

46. Nathan Dunn, *"Ten Thousand Chinese Things": A Descriptive Catalogue of the Chinese Collection in Philadelphia* (Philadelphia: Printed for the Proprietor, 1839).

47. Dunn, *"Ten Thousand Chinese Things,"* 83-89, nos. 906, 938, 962, 1024, 1040, and 1057.

48. Dunn, *"Ten Thousand Chinese Things,"* 3-4.

49. Between 1839 and 1847, at least ten editions of the catalogue were published. For further information on Dunn's collection, see J. Thomas Scharf and Thompson Westcott, *History of Philadelphia 1609-1884*, 3 vols. (Philadelphia: L. H. Everts & Co., 1884), 2: 948-949. According to William B. Langdon, curator of the collection, who authored an 1844 edition of the catalogue, Nathan Dunn was "an extensive and successful merchant... [who] resided in China for a period of twelve years.... He was assisted moreover, in his commendable labors, by Houqua, Ting-qua, and other Hong merchants of considerable note." See William B. Langdon, *"Ten Thousand Chinese Things"* (London, 1844), 13.

50. *United States Centennial Commission: International Exhibition 1876 Official Catalogue, Revised Edition* (Philadelphia: Published for the Centennial Catalogue Company by John R. Nayle and Company, 1876), 241-242, nos. 21, 24, and 66. Screens by Fow Loong, Canton (listed as blackwood screens); Lien Shing, Canton (also blackwood screens); and watercolor paintings on silk by Wang Kien-ting (listed as "for screens") are mentioned.

51. *United States Centennial Commission,* 245, no. 66c: "Blinds and screens by the Kirin-Kosho-Kuwaisha, First Japanese Manufacturing & Trading Co., Tokio."

52. See Frank Henry Norton, ed., *A Facsimile of Frank Leslie's Illustrated Historical Register of the Centennial Exhibition, 1876,* introduction by Richard Kenin (London: Paddington Press Ltd., 1974), 161, 270, and 309.

53. Clarence Cook, *The House Beautiful: Essays on Beds and Tables, Stools and Candlesticks* (New York: Scribner, Armstrong and Company, 1878), 181.

54. Cook, *The House Beautiful,* 181-182.

55. Four inventories taken from 1865 to 1876 indicate that at least ten sceens, some of which were oriental, were in the White House collections. An inventory of 1 January 1849 lists "Door-screens" in six rooms, which almost certainly meant folding screens since three of the rooms did not have exterior doors. Whether they were eastern or western screens, however, is not known. My thanks to William B. Allman at the White House for providing this documentation.

56. Paul Jamot and Georges Wildenstein, *Manet,* 2 vols. (Paris: Les Beaux Arts Editions d'Etudes et de Document, 1932), 1: 106. By its size alone, the screen would not seem to fit the description in the inventory.

57. See Michael Justin Wentworth's fascinating study, "Tissot and Japonisme," in Chisaburō, ed., *Japonisme,* 127-146, especially 127-133 and accompanying notes.

58. See Lacambre, "Milieux," in Chisaburō, ed., *Japonisme,* 45-46, where the two shops are conclusively shown to be separate enterprises, a source of much confusion in previous studies of Japonisme.

59. See Stevens' paintings, *The Blue Dress* and *The Visit,* both in the Sterling and Francine Clark Art Institute, Williamstown, Mass.

60. Ronnie L. Zukon, *The Artist and the Studio in the Eighteenth and Nineteenth Centuries* (exh. cat., Cleveland Museum of Art, 1978), Fig. 6. This photograph is in the Slide and Photography Collection, Art and Architecture Library, Yale University.

61. Charles Chassé, *The Nabis and Their Period* (London: Lund Humphries, 1969), Fig. 4.

62. Thadée Natanson, *Le Bonnard que je propose* (Geneva: Pierre Cailler, 1951), Fig. 1.

63. *La Plume: Littéraire, Artistique et Sociale. Numéro Consacré à Alphonse Mucha,* no. 197 (1 July 1897): no. 92, includes two photographs of the artist in his studio. In the background of each of these photographs, an oriental screen is visible.

64. A portion of a painted oriental screen, probably Japanese, is visible at the top of Weir's painting, *His Favorite Model,* 188?, in Theodore E. Stebbins, Jr. and Galina Gorokhoff, *A Checklist of American Paintings at Yale University* (Yale University Art Gallery, 1982), no. 1703, illus.

65. *The Open Air Breakfast,* ca. 1888, in *The Toledo Museum of Art: American Paintings* (Toledo Museum of Art, 1979), plate IV (color) and plate 92.

66. See *Catalogue of the Well-Known and Interesting Collection of Antique Furniture and Objets d'Art* (London: Hampton & Sons, 1913) from Alma-Tadema's collection, nos. 1440-1448. One six-panel Kano school screen, claimed to be from Lord Leighton's collection, is illustrated. Although Alma-Tadema's interest in Japanese art may have been significant as early as the 1870s, neither the date nor source of purchase of these screens is known. My thanks to Vern G. Swanson for references and a copy of the 1913 sale catalogue.

67. Robin Spencer, *The Aesthetic Movement: Theory and Practice* (London: Studio Vista/Dutton Picture book, 1972), 76.

68. See especially Robin Spencer's article, "Whistler and Japan: Work in Progress," in Chisaburō, ed., *Japonisme,* 57-82.

69. Andrew McLaren Young, Margaret MacDonald, and Robin Spencer, *The Paintings of James NcNeill Whistler* (New Haven and London: Yale University Press, 1980), 26-27, no. 50.

70. Sotheby, Wilkinson, and Hodge, *Catalogue of the Decorative Porcelain, Cabinets, Paintings, and Other Works of Art of J. A. McN. Whistler* (London, 12 February 1880), no. 66. An annotated copy of this catalogue in the Glasgow University Library indicates the screen was sold to Charles Augustus Howell, a friend of Whistler. My gratitude to David Curry, who provided me with a copy of this rare catalogue and called my attention to the screen references.

In addition, no. 67 from this sale catalogue mentions a "Pair of dwarf screens, painted with landscape and figures, on gold grounds"; according to a handwritten annotation it was sold to Jarvis.

71. Young, et al., *Whistler,* 34, no. 60.

72. Young, el al., *Whistler,* 34, no. 60, and Spencer, "Whistler," in Chisaburō, ed., *Japonisme,* 61 and note 34. The *Tales of Genji* was the subject of many important traditional Japanese screens. The screen is certainly not either of the dwarf screens listed in the 1880 sale catalogue, and its ultimate disposition is unknown.

73. Nesfield's life and career still have not attracted the attention of any biographers. The best source for information is Andrew Saint, *Richard Norman Shaw* (New Haven and London: Yale University Press, 1976).

74. Saint, *Shaw,* 44.

75. Saint, *Shaw,* 21. For a more detailed analysis of questions of attribution and of sources for various design motifs, see Cat. 1.

76. E. W. Godwin also designed a folding screen in the Anglo-Japanese style around 1877, although its decoration is much less ornate than Nesfield's. For an illustration, see Edward W. Godwin, *Art Furniture and Artistic Conservatories* (1877; reprint, New York: Garland Publishing, Inc., 1978), plate 2.

77. E. R. and Joseph Pennell, *The Whistler Journal* (Philadelphia: J. B. Lippincott Company, 1921), 121 and 302. In 1875, Leyland commissioned the artist to do decorations for the famed Peacock Room. See also Young, et al., *Whistler,* no. 139 and accompanying bibliography. Condition problems with the surface painted by Whistler (tempera on brown paper laid on canvas) prevented its inclusion in this exhibition.

78. See Isao Nakayama's article on the artist who painted these panels, identified tentatively as Nampo Osawa, in *Tokai Joshi Daigaku Kiyo,* 2 (1983). Nakayama suggests that the two paintings formed part of a larger screen, or parts of two screens, and were done in the *Nanga*

style. My thanks to Martin Hopkinson, Hunterian Art Gallery, University of Glasgow, for this reference.

79. Several individual panels are listed as being in Whistler's possession in the 1880 sale; see Sotheby, et al., *Whistler,* nos. 68, 71, and 72.

80. Sotheby, et al., *Whistler,* nos. 33, 139, and especially 140 for other bridge subjects. A telling comparison showing Whistler's stylistic and compositional liberties is offered by two additional images: a photograph, ca. 1877, of Old Battersea Bridge reproduced in Spencer, *Aesthetic,* 86, and an 1874 painting by Whistler's companion and student of sorts, Walter Greaves, entitled *Old Battersea Bridge,* now in the Tate Gallery, London (no. 3598).

81. Laura Epps had already studied with Cave Thomas and William Bell Scott. See Ellen C. Clayton, *English Female Artists* (London: Tinsley Brothers, 1876), 2:6. My thanks to Vern G. Swanson, author of a forthcoming catalogue raisonné of Alma-Tadema's paintings, for providing the factual information concerning this screen.

82. Obviously, the third panel lacks what was possibly a group of children standing in front of the table. Such a group would have been a compositional counterbalance to the figure of Emily Epps standing in front of the table in the fourth panel. In addition, the screen is sketchily painted in some areas, like the portrait of Dr. Epps in the second panel. For a more detailed analysis of the screen, see Cat. 2.

83. The inscription is a plea for familial cohesion, made all the more appropriate by the fact that Rowland Hill and his wife, Louisa Epps Hill, were forced to flee England to Argentina in 1871 because of a stock market scandal. The standing figure of Rowland was apparently painted out of the fifth panel and instead, inserted peering from behind a door in the same panel; the pentimento is now clearly visible.

84. Barbara Morris, *Victorian Embroidery* (London: Barrie & Jenkins, 1970), 113; see especially 113-207.

85. Professor Walter Smith, *The Masterpieces of the Centennial International Exhibition – Illustrated* (Philadelphia: Gebbie & Barrie [1876-1877]), 2: 143, 249, 372, illus.

86. The illustration shows a third panel perpendicular to the picture plane and is therefore somewhat confusing, but the orientation of the panel at the far right makes it clear that the screen must consist of four panels.

87. Aslin, *Aesthetic Movement,* 83, 93, 98, 176. E. W. Godwin, in particular, utilized the motif, borrowing it from a Japanese crest. Whistler's friend and fellow artist, Dante Gabriel Rossetti, even kept peacocks in his garden. See Susan Hobbs, *The Whistler Peacock Room* (Washington: Freer Gallery of Art, 1980), 18.

88. The Ladies Work Society, an offshoot of the Royal School of Art Needlework, is known to have done several screens, including one "with a Japanese type of design of sprays and bunches of blossom" done in two versions around 1887. Selwyn Image also designed a Four Seasons screen for the Royal School in 1887-1888. See Morris, *Victorian Embroidery,* 117-118, 136, and Fig. 17, 54, 55, and 56.

89. See Rüdiger Joppien, "Paravent und Armsessel," *Museen in Köln Bulletin* 12 (December 1977): 1579-1583. In this article, the screen design is ascribed to Burne-Jones, with Henry Holliday suggested as its maker. Burne-Jones is known to have treated similar allegorical themes in both stained glass and oil, including a window with a personification of Earth. See A. Charles Sewter, *The Stained Glass of William Morris and His Circle* (New Haven and London: Yale University Press, 1974), 291. A comparison of Burne-Jones' *Four Seasons* windows in nos. 271-274, however, clearly shows marked stylistic differences from the screen windows.

90. From left to right, the flowers in the lower register are: *Cattleya* or "corsage orchid," a cultivated genus which does not grow wild in North America or Europe; either the *Campanula* (blue bellflower) or a type of lily; *Clematis* or "virgin's bower"; and the *Cypripedium* orchid known as lady's slipper. On the verso, the plants are somewhat more stylized but still recognizable: buttercups; an aquatic plant, rushes or papyrus; unidentifiable palmlike plant; and cattails. My thanks to James E. Rodman, associate professor of biology, Yale University, for his help in identifying the flowers. Although the plants on the recto are accurately depicted, there does not seem to be any iconographic significance in their inclusion: there is no tradition which would link floral symbolism with the theme of the four elements.

91. At the left side of the Fire window is a three-legged stand from whose bowl-like top a fire smolders. A similar type of stand was actually made for Morris and Co. and can be seen at the left center of fig. 105.

92. A similar fish motif can been seen in fig. 62 at the bottom of the embroidered panels; the blossoming orange tree background for the stained glass figures is also present in the earlier embroidered screen.

93. For a more thorough comparison of the two screens, including a discussion of their mutual attribution problems, see Cat. 4.

94. Quoted from Gillian Naylor, *The Arts and Crafts Movement: A Study of Its Sources, Ideals, and Influence on Design Theory* (London: Studio Vista, 1980), 117. See pages 115-120 for an insightful analysis of the theoretical and practical differences between Morris' and Mackmurdo's positions.

95. The catalogue of the Arts and Crafts Society's first exhibition in 1888 lists the screen (no. 128) as made by Wilkinson & Sons.

96. Linda Parry, *William Morris Textiles* (London: Weidenfeld and Nicolson, 1983), 143-144.

97. See note 7 regarding Reff, "Pictures."

98. See Gerstein, "Impressionist Fans," cited in note 41.

99. Daniel Wildenstein, *Claude Monet: Biographie et catalogue raisonné,* 3 vols. (Lausanne-Paris: La Bibliothèque des Arts, 1974-1979), 2: 138-149, nos. 919-954. Durand-Ruel apparently acquired four other panels from Monet intended for, but not used, in decorating two additional doors; see Wildenstein, *Monet,* 2: 150, nos. 955-958.

100. See Elda Fezzi, *L'Opera completa di Renoir nel periodo impressionista, 1869-1883* (Milan: Rizzoli Editore, 1972), nos. 258-259 and nos. 349-353.

101. The self-chosen name *Nabi* derived from a Hebrew word meaning "prophet," signaling the young artists' confidence that their art offered something new and important to the constellation of styles, theories, and movements already marking the 1880s. Also in the group were Paul Sérusier, who preached the expressive aims of Gauguin's art to the extent that he understood them; a painter, Henri Ibels; a sculptor, Georges Lacombe; and Jan Verkade, who later gave up his painting career and joined a monastery.

102. For a brief discussion of the training they received there, see John Rewald, *Post-Impressionism* (New York: Museum of Modern Art, 1978), 272-275.

103. Gauguin and his group at Le Pouldu in Brittany had by 1889 already done easel paintings and murals to decorate Marie Henry's inn where they were staying. Rewald, *Post-Impressionism,* 294-300, believes these early attempts at decoration may have led Gauguin to try his hand at sculpture, bas-reliefs, ceramics, and designs for plates and fans. Emile Bernard, one of Gauguin's followers, designed tapestries, and the Dane, Willumsen, was taught by Gauguin to make polychrome wooden reliefs. It is known that Gauguin visited Bonnard's studio in Paris in 1890, and Gauguin may have inspired, or at least encouraged, the decorative impulses of the Nabis. It is interesting to note that Gauguin himself seems never to have done a folding screen. Christopher Gray, in his book, *Sculpture and Ceramics of Paul Gauguin* (Baltimore: Johns Hopkins Press, 1963), illustrates a three-panel folding screen whose attribution to Gauguin he rightfully doubts. Gray never saw the screen,

and therefore did not know that it is, in fact, double-sided. After examining the screen in July 1982 at the shop of a Paris dealer, the author noted that the central panel of the screen had been reversed; stylistically and compositionally, the panel actually belongs to the two verso panels. Although the screen has appeared several times in exhibition literature as an authentic work by Gauguin, neither Richard S. Field (in conversation), Merete Bodelsen (by letter), nor John Rewald (also in conversation) accepts this attribution. The screen is said to have been done for Olivier Sainsère, who did collect several paintings by Gauguin, and who commissioned a screen from Redon in 1902/1903. Repeated attempts to verify the provenance through the present owner have been unsuccessful.

104. Quoted in Francis Bouvet, *Bonnard: The Complete Graphic Work* (New York: Rizzoli International Publications, Inc., 1981), 5-6.

105. Jean and Henry Dauberville, *Bonnard: Catalogue raisonné de l'oeuvre peint*, 4 vols. (Paris: Editions Bernheim-Jeune, 1966), 4: no. 01716. Bonnard also prepared near full-scale studies for the screen which are listed as no. 01715 in Dauberville. Although planned as a screen, the panels were never joined as such and were shown at the Salon des Indépendants as four decorative panels. See André Fermigier, *Pierre Bonnard* (New York: Harry N. Abrams, Inc., 1969), 22 and 68; Denys Sutton, *Pierre Bonnard* (London: Royal Academy of the Arts, 1966), 12-13, no. 7; and Mary Anne Stevens in *Post-Impressionism: Cross-Currents in European Painting* (exh. cat., London, Royal Academy of Arts, 1979), nos. 30, 31. The studies for the screen were on view most recently in the exhibition *Pierre Bonnard* (Hamburg: Kunstverein, 1970), nos. 1 and 2. Ursula Perruchi-Petri, in *Die Nabis und Japan: Das Frühwerk von Bonnard, Vuillard und Denis* (Munich: Prestel Verlag, 1976), 45-46, argues that the *Femmes au jardin* screen is also a representation of the four seasons. She cites a lengthy nineteenth-century pictorial tradition for the theme, including works by Böcklin, Marées, Puvis de Chavannes, Burne-Jones, and Hodler; of course, Mucha even did a screen with this subject (Cat. 12). She states: "In the woman with a dog—probably personifying Spring—[he expresses] the dynamic and expansive side of Nature awakened to a new life, while in the woman with a cat—apparently a symbol of Winter—[he expresses] the withdrawn and passively waiting side [of the season]. It is somewhat similar for both other seasons, although it is not expressed so clearly." Besides being unable to clarify the symbolism of the last two panels, Perucchi-Petri also fails to explain the unorthodox Spring-Winter (Summer-Fall?) order of the seasons. Her arguments are consequently unconvincing.

106. Fermigier, *Bonnard*, 68.

107. See Sherman E. Lee, *The Genius of Japanese Design* (Tokyo and New York: Kodansha International, 1981).

108. See also Perucchi-Petri, *Die Nabis*, 37-38 in particular.

109. Such costumes were clearly in vogue among the lady friends of the Nabis. A photograph of 1894 taken at Eragny by Edouard Vuillard shows two women in similarly patterned dresses. See Annette Vaillant, *Bonnard* (Greenwich: New York Graphic Society, 1965), 25. Of course, Vuillard's mother was a dressmaker, and, given the close relationship among the Nabis, Bonnard had ample opportunities to keep up with current fashions.

110. John Rewald, *Pierre Bonnard* (exh. cat., New York, Museum of Modern Art, 1948), 14, cites a letter by Bonnard: "I am working on an important picture which is progressing well and which will be exhibited, I hope, at the Indépendants. In addition, I am planning to do a screen which will also be shown at the exhibition."

111. Dauberville, *Bonnard*, 1: no. 128.

112. The screen is listed in Dauberville, *Bonnard*, 1: no. 205, as dating from ca. 1899. It is also illustrated in Rewald, *Bonnard*, 64, but dated

there as 1891/1892, which seems far too early, given the emphasis on strong, flat color patterns in Bonnard's work of the early 1890s. Unfortunately the screen was broken up sometime after 1948 when it was still intact in the collection of Louis Carré. The screen's second panel is now in the hands of Galerie Beyeler, Basel.

113. Margaret Potter, in her forthcoming catalogue to the David Rockefeller Collection, repeats a dealer's claim that Seguin may have painted the screen as part of the decoration at the Pension Gloanec, Pont-Aven. He was there in 1892, and probably returned to Paris in late 1892 or early 1893. Evidence about Seguin's activities is so scanty that one cannot be certain exactly when or where the screen was done, and whether he had it in Paris. Stylistically, the screen has more affinities with Nabi works than with those of Gauguin and his followers at Pont-Aven. See especially Richard S. Field, *The Prints of Armand Seguin, 1869-1903* (exh. cat., Middletown, Conn., Davison Art Center, Wesleyan University, 1980).

114. Perucchi-Petri, *Die Nabis*, 71 and notes 237-238, suggests Hiroshige, *Shono, Rainshower* from *Fifty-Three Stations of the Tokaido*, and Kuniyoshi, *The Poet Yasuhide*, as possible sources for the composition. Ives, *Japanese Woodcuts*, 64-66, suggests a Kiyonaga woodcut which served as the cover illustration for *Le Japon Artistique* (February 1899), as the source for the group of children and an adult. Although one cannot deny that the right to left orientation of the scene, the active silhouetting of dark figures against a light ground, and the vertically disposed spatial recessions are ultimately derived from Japanese sources, it would seem more instructive to consider how the screen is integrated into the rest of Bonnard's oeuvre, where these various compositional devices had already become relatively commonplace.

115. See Bouvet, *Bonnard*, nos. 5-24. The series was published by Claude Terrasse in 1893.

116. This integration of frame and image indicates clearly that Bonnard was the maker; he even signed and dated the screen in the frame at the upper portion of the fourth panel. Decorative borders and frames appear frequently in his work, most notably in the 1890 *Portrait of Andrée Bonnard* (Dauberville, *Bonnard*, 1: no. 12); the ca. 1891 *Young Woman with a Cat* (Dauberville, *Bonnard*, 1: no. 21); the 1892 *Portrait of a Young Woman (Berthe Schaedlin)* (Dauberville, *Bonnard*, 4: no. 01730); and in the ca. 1892 *Woman Hanging Out the Linen* (Dauberville, *Bonnard*, 1: no. 35). The screen frame was probably executed by means of pyrogravure, a technique in which designs were literally burned into a surface. For information on this technique, see Blanche Everard, *Traité de pyrogravure sur bois, cuir, ivoire, velours, toile, carton, etc., ses aplications diverses à la décoration* (Paris: S. Bornemann, n.d.); and Jean Closset, *La Pyrogravure et ses applications* (Paris: H. Laurens, n.d.). My thanks to Margaret Potter for indicating the use of this method in the frame decorations.

117. The lithographic version was announced and illustrated in *Studio* 9 (October 1896): 67-68. The following advertisement appeared in the first issue of *L'Estampe et l'affiche* (15 March 1897): "Bonnard—paravent: Edit chez Molines, 20, rue Lafitte. P. Bonnard. Paravent sur 4 feuilles lithographiques en cinque coleurs ... en feuilles 40 fr. monté 60 fr." According to Claude Roger-Marx, *Bonnard: Lithographe* (Monte Carlo: Editions du Livre, 1952), no. 47, the screen was printed in an edition of 110, of which 40 were mounted as screens. My thanks to Barbara Schapiro of the Museum of Fine Arts, Boston, for information on this screen.

118. See Cat. 8 for a more complete discussion of the dating and an intrepretation of the screen's iconography.

119. Paris, Durand-Ruel, *Pierre Bonnard*, January 1896, listed in no. 52 as "Paravent." My thanks to Margaret Potter for this reference.

120. Letter from Dominique Maurice Denis, 18 March 1983.

121. Maurice Denis, under the pseudonym Pierre Louis, "Pour les jeunes peintres," *Art et Critique* (20 February 1892). Since Denis attempted works in nearly all these media, the statement may reflect his own sentiments, rather than those of his fellow artists. Paul Ranson, who did at least one screen (now in the Sydney and Frances Lewis Collection, Richmond), also did several tapestry designs. Both Bonnard and Vuillard made stained glass window designs for Louis Tiffany around 1897.

122. An excellent overview of this and the following commissions can be found in Roseline Bacou, "Décors d'appartements au temps des Nabis," *Art de France*, no. 4 (1964): 190-205, and in Claire Frèches-Thory, "Jardins publics de Vuillard," *La Revue du Louvre et des Musées de France*, no. 4 (1979): 305-312.

123. The six oil on canvas panels, all in a French private collection, are: *Nannies and Children in a Park, Gardening, Petting the Dog, A Dressmaker's Shop* (two different scenes), and *A Badminton Game*. All measure 48.5 x 114.3 cm. They are illustrated in *Edouard Vuillard – Xavier Roussel* (exh. cat., Munich, Haus der Kunst, 1968), nos. 66-71.

124. My sincere thanks to M. Antoine Salomon for providing this rare photograph. The screen has since been broken up, losing its original frame and the upper and lower painted panels. The first four panels appeared in a Sotheby's New York sale catalogue (5 November 1981, no. 4742M), no. 210; the fifth panel was sold at Sotheby's, London (15 April 1970), no. 20.

125. According to M. Salomon, the screen was *not* done for Mme. Desmarais in 1898 as recorded by Achille Ségard, *Peintres d'aujourd'hui: Les Decorateurs,* 2d ed. (Paris: Société d'Editions Littéraires et Artistiques, 1914), 321.

126. These letters are kept in Vuillard's "journal" at the Bibliothèque de l'Institut in Paris. Mlle. Chapin published a literary review called *Commerce,* and it seems that the screen was made on the occasion of her marriage. The screen is dated 1911 by Segard, *Peintres,* p. 321, and certainly was done no later than April 1912, when it was exhibited at Bernheim-Jeune's Paris gallery as no. 29 in their show *Edouard Vuillard.* The dense foliage implies that it was at least conceived in late spring or early summer of 1911. Segard claims incorrectly that the screen was "for Mme. La Princesse Bassiano"; Vuillard did write to the Princess about the screen on 31 March 1912. My thanks to M. Antoine Salomon for providing these references.

127. This apartment was only a few blocks west of the rue Pigalle studio which Bonnard, Vuillard, and Denis shared beginning in 1890.

128. For a thorough review of these panels, see Vivian Barnett, *The Guggenheim Museum: Justin K. Thannhauser Collection* (New York: Solomon R. Guggenheim Museum, 1978), 200-205, including references for additional illustrations.

129. See John Rewald in *Odilon Redon, Gustave Moreau, Rodolphe Bresdin* (exh. cat., New York, Museum of Modern Art, 1962), 35. More thorough studies are Rosaline Bacou, *Odilon Redon: La Vie et l'oeuvre. Point de vue de la critique au sujet de l'oeuvre,* 2 vols. (Geneva: Pierre Cailler, 1956); Klaus Berger, *Odilon Redon: Fantasy and Colour* (New York: McGraw-Hill, 1965); and Richard Hobbs, *Odilon Redon* (Boston: New York Graphic Society, 1977). However, Rewald's essay is still the most succinct and insightful analysis of Redon's art.

130. Bacou, *Redon,* 1: 165. Berger, *Redon,* 204-205, lists sixteen screens by Redon, many of which were of the single panel variety.

131. The sole surviving panel is now in the *Reader's Digest* Collection in Pleasantville, New York. See also Bacou, *Redon,* 1: 166: "For the Princess Cystria, a lady of refined culture who has gathered around her musicians and writers, Redon executed a folding screen: 'You did not

wish to see either figures or flowers represented there. What was left for me to do? You can easily guess. The whole chimeric world!'"

132. Bacou, *Redon,* 1: 167.

133. In a letter to David Rust of the National Gallery of Art, 19 January 1965, Roseline Bacou reported: "Redon, who had executed a certain number of screens – among others, screens for Olivier Sainsère, André Bonger, and the Princess Cystria...."

134. My sincere gratitude to S. Crommelin and the Rijksprentenkabinet, Amsterdam, for granting permission to reproduce these letters.

135. The story of Pegasus comes from Ovid's *Metamorphoses,* 4.605 and 5.1. The winged horse was born to Medusa and Poseidon. When Perseus beheaded Medusa, a task ordered by King Polydectes so that Perseus could marry Danaë, Pegasus sprang from Medusa's body and flew up to the heavens, where he became the steed of Zeus. Another section of the story relates that when Pegasus struck his hoof on the ground, he caused the spring Hippocrene to gush forth on Helikon, the wooded mountain in Boetia, sacred to the Muses, those daughters of Zeus who were goddesses of song, music, poetry, art, and the sciences. Later on, when Pegasus was quenching his thirst at the spring Pirene on the Acropolis of Corinth, he was captured by Bellerophon, who needed him to slay the monster Chimera. Athena sent Pegasus to Bellerophon for this task, to help him in his battle against the Amazons. Made presumptuous by his victories, Bellerophon tried to climb Mt. Olympus but was repulsed by the shafts of Zeus. Pegasus then threw Bellerophon and continued his ascent up Olympus, where he was accorded a place in the stars.

136. See, for example, Hobbs, *Redon,* 106-110, and Rewald, *Redon,* 39.

137. *Odilon Redon, A soi-même, journal (1867-1915), notes sur la vie, l'art et les artistes,* 1922 (Paris, 1961), especially 11-30.

138. The letter continues with a self-warning of sorts: "Nevertheless it would be dangerous for a painter to nourish himself often with the grandiose spectacle of mountains. At least that is my opinion. Its effects on a simple decor are not to be feared, but it should not be misused to produce something mediocre and limited." One may therefore infer that the "grandiose spectacle of the mountains" was more appropriate to the large-scale requirements of decoration.

139. The screen of Princess Cystria and the one for an unknown Englishwoman.

140. Redon may have been correct in his observations about the effects time would have on the quality of colors in distemper. His contemporaries were very much taken by distemper and similar non-oil media. Bonnard's 1894 *Promenade* screen is also done in distemper on canvas; many of Vuillard's decorative panels and screens were distemper on size (Frèches-Thory, "Vuillard," 305 and note 16). Denis, too, often worked in the similar medium of tempera, as did Whistler on his screen. The great problem with all of these water-based media is that the finished objects painted with them are extremely sensitive to changes in humidity. Although current technology allows us to protect these works in most museums and even some properly equipped domestic environments, the surfaces of such works are fragile under the best conditions. Consequently, neither Whistler's *Old Battersea Bridge* screen nor Redon's *Red Screen* could be included in this exhibition.

141. Undated letter from Madame Redon to Madame Bonger: "M. Vasseur still has not sent us the bill for the framing and for the cloth, but the price agreed upon was 135 F. for the frame and 15 F. for the cloth. This upholsterer does very good work."

142. Reported by André Gide in 1904 and quoted in Hobbs, *Redon,* 125.

143. For greater detail about the commission, as well as about Klee's sources for the screen, see Cat. 9.

144. Cat. 9.

145. The genesis of art nouveau is thoroughly documented in Stephen Tschudi Madsen, *Sources of Art Nouveau* (New York: G. Wittenborn, 1956), and in Peter Selz, *Art Nouveau: Art and Design at the Turn of the Century* (New York: Museum of Modern Art, 1975).

146. See Cat. 12 for a description of Mucha's decorative commissions and his early attempts at the folding screen format.

147. See *La Plume*, no. 197 (1 July 1897): no. 92.

148. Gabriel Mourey, "Round the Exhibition.— I. The House of the 'Art Nouveau Bing,'" *Studio* 20 (1900): 164-180.

149. For an overview of the exhibition, see Philippe Julian, *The Triumph of Art Nouveau: Paris Exhibition 1900* (New York: Larousse & Co., Inc., 1974).

150. Mourey, "Art Nouveau Bing," 180.

151. There is at least a generic stylistic similarity between de Feure's figures and those of Bonnard and Vuillard. In addition, both of the latter by 1900 had done either painted or lithograph scenes of elegantly dressed ladies in parks; these scenes may very well have been known to de Feure.

152. It must be pointed out that the photograph shows the idealized arrangement of an exhibition display. Of course, if one purchased such an ensemble, the actual everyday placement of the screen could not be so inviolable, as it were, since the screen's popularity and usefulness derive from its ability to function in a variety of situations. As an exercise in pure exhibition design, however, it would be difficult to argue with this interpretation of de Feure's intent.

153. See Laurence Buffet-Challé. *The Art Nouveau Style* (New York: Rizzoli International Publications, Inc., 1982), 25, no. 37, illus.

154. See *Studio* 10 (1897): 119; and 11 (1897): 41.

155. See the sale catalogues *Ecole des Beaux-Arts: Exposition des acquisitions et des commandes de l'état entrées en 1911* (Paris, December 1911), no. 550, and Palais Galliera (Paris, 20 March 1971), no. 45.

156. For an illustration of the Salon, see *La Lorraine Artiste* 18 (1900): 76. See also J. A. Schmoll, *Nancy 1900: Emile Gallé und der lothringische Jugendstil zwischen Historismus und Art-Déco* (exh. cat., Munich, Stadtmuseum, 1980), 329, no. 356.

157. The central stained glass panel has been lost and is now replaced with mirrored glass.

158. The most important sources for information about this artist are l'Ebé Bugatti, *The Bugatti Story* (London: Souvenir Press, 1967); Simon Jervis, "Carlo Bugatti," *Arte Illustrata* 10 (December 1970): 80-87 and 114-115; Philippe Garner, "Carlo Bugatti 1856-1940," in *The Amazing Bugattis* (exh. cat., London, Design Council, 1979); and Philippe Dejean, *Carlo-Rembrandt-Ettore-Jean Bugatti* (Paris: Editions du Regard, 1982). Carlo was the father of the sculptor Rembrandt Bugatti and the car designer Ettore Bugatti.

159. Jervis, "Bugatti," 114.

160. Christopher Wilk, *Thonet Bentwood and Other Furniture: The 1904 Illustrated Catalogue* (New York: Dover Publications, 1980) is a useful reproduction of this catalogue.

161. The Viennese firm Jakob and Josef Kohn also sold similar mass-produced screens. See *Erste Österreichische Aktiengesellschaft für Erzeugung von Möbeln ausgebogenem Holze: Der Katalog von 1916* (Munich: Dr. Graham Dry, 1980). Listed as "Bettschirme" or bed-screens, 110-114, nos. 1045-1047, 1053, 1055, 1057-1059. As with Thonet's screens, Kohn's could be purchased with more luxurious fabrics, provided by the manufacturers at an increased price of course.

162. See Karl Heinz Schreyl, *Josef Maria Olbrich: Die Zeichnungen in der Kunstbibliothek Berlin, kritischer Katalog* (Berlin: Gebrüder Maria Verlag, 1972), 54-55, no. 10717. My thanks to Professor Robert Judson Clark of Princeton University, who provided references to Olbrich's screens from his doctoral dissertation on the artist.

163. Illustrated in the exhibition catalogue, *Möbel von Josef Maria Olbrich un Josef Niedermoser: Architekt und Tischler. Beispiel einer Symbiose* (Vienna: Galerie am Graben, 1982).

164. Schreyl, *Olbrich*, 275, no. 11711.

165. See Sonja Günther, *Interieurs um 1900* (Munich: Wilhelm Fink Verlag, 1971, 49, no. 1h.

166. Reproduced in *Deutsche Werkstätten G.M.B.H. II. Auflage 1910 Handgearbeitete Möbel*, 124, no. 152. For other screens by the artist, see Winfried Nerdinger, ed., *Richard Riemerschmid: Vom Jugendstil zum Werkbund, Werke und Dokumenta* (Munich: Prestel Verlag, 1983), nos. 81 and 270.

167. Bruno Paul's folding screen with decorated fabric panels was part of a dining room set. It is illustrated in Roberta Waddell, ed., *The Art Nouveau Style* (New York: Dover Publications, Inc., 1977), 157, no. 379.

168. "G.F.," who reviewed the 1899 Secession exhibition of decorative art in which Van de Velde's wood and glass screen appeared, praised this esthetic viewpoint highly: "One must find new art forms [based] purely on constructive line, without the help of ornamental images. The beauty of constructive form, which Van de Velde cultivates, appeals to the same esthetic perception that is expressed when we find an elegantly built English lorry, a sailing yacht, or a bicycle 'beautiful.'" See G.F., "Angewandte Kunst in der Münchener Sezession," *Deutsche Kunst und Dekoration* 5 (October 1899-March 1900): 14.

169. The title of the advertisement reads: "Keller and Reiner: Art merchant and permanent art exhibition. Berlin W. 122, Pottsdamerstrasse. Constantly changing exhibition in enclosed spaces. Modern painting and sculpture. Furniture, fabric, tapestries, carpets, decorative metalwork, glass painting, etc. Native and foreign ceramics." The page was an inset bound into a copy of the periodical *Pan* 2 (1899). The periodical with the advertisement can be seen at the Arts of the Book Collection, Sterling Memorial Library, Yale University. Neither of the Van de Velde screens is known to have survived.

170. *Studio* 18 (1899): 207.

171. Madsen, *Sources*, 57-58.

172. See Cat. 17 and its note 4 for a more thorough explanation of this technique.

173. Van den Bosch was born in Amsterdam in 1868; his death date is unknown.

174. A three-panel wood marquetry screen attributed to Brangwyn and showing a stork and peacock in a landscape setting is in the museum at Brighton. Another "screen" by Brangwyn is illustrated in *Studio* 18 (1899): 110, although it does not fold and appears more like a triptych. Kate Eddie's ca. 1902 incised, stained, and gilded wood screen of three-panels showing the *Three Fates* is in the Victoria and Albert Museum (70/2197). Amy Sawyer's four-panel painted screen showing several female figures in pseudoclassical dress is also illustrated in *Studio* 2 (1893): 25.

175. See plate 11 in Victor Arwas, *The Liberty Style* (New York: Rizzoli International Publications, Inc., 1979).

176. For a discussion of these screens, see Roger Billcliffe, *Charles Rennie Mackintosh: The Complete Furniture, Furniture Drawings, and Interior Designs* (New York: Taplinger Publishing Company, 1979), 177, 214, and 224, nos. 1905.2, 1905.3, and 1916.12. See also Cat. 14 in this exhibition.

177. Billcliffe, *Mackintosh*, nos. 1900.G, 1900.H, 1903.D, 1904.49, 1906.16, 1916.4, and 1916.6.

178. See Gleeson White, "Some Glasgow Designers and Their Work: Part II," *Studio* 11 (1897): 225-229.

179. See Fiona C. MacFarlane and Elizabeth F. Arthur, *Glasgow School of Art Embroidery 1894-1920* (Glasgow Museums and Art Galleries, 1980).

180. MacFarlane and Arthur, *Glasgow School*, no. 12.

181. MacFarlane and Arthur, *Glasgow School*, no. 45.

182. *The American Family Encyclopedia* (New York: Parkes, Webster, 1859), 282.

183. Harriet Prescott Spofford, *Art Decoration Applied to Furniture* (New York: Harper & Brothers Publishers, 1878), in the section entitled "The Drawing Room," 221.

184. Ella Rodman Church, *How to Furnish a Home* (New York: D. Appleton and Company, 1881), 60-61. The book was part of a series entitled Appleton's Home Books. Church was certainly familiar with Spofford's book; she quotes the passage cited in note 183 on page 109, without citing her source. For a similar screen, see also Rhoda and Agnes Garrett, *Suggestions for House Decoration in Painting, Woodwork, and Furniture* (Philadelphia: Porter & Coates, n.d. [1877?]), 63, illus. only.

185. The screen is still in the Grant-Kohrs Ranch in Deer Lodge, Montana. According to Rodd L. Wheaton (Chief, Branch of Historic Preservation, Rocky Mountain Regional Office, National Park Service), the screen was a housewarming gift to Conrad and Augusta Kohrs in 1890 from Joseph Rosenbaum, a Chicago friend and business partner. The screen was installed in the dining room of the ranch in 1889/1890. The recto contains three oil on canvas bird subject paintings, and the verso consists of much smaller-scale vignettes of Japanese figure groups, silkscreened on a heavily textured silk fabric. The panels are all set in an oak frame. One of the painted panels carries the monogram "E TH(?) R," perhaps the mark of the still-unidentified maker. My thanks to Rodd Wheaton for providing this information.

186. Church, *Home*, 108-109.

187. See Cat. 2.

188. Church purchased the screen to decorate his home on 4 May 1889 from the New York dealer, L. A. Lanthier, for $200. The undated, unsigned paintings are attributed to an unknown Spanish or Portuguese painter of the early nineteenth century. The screen frame is of quartersawn oak, topped with a spindled frieze and a carved floral and foliated crest. According to James Ryan, curator of Olana, the screen was most likely made in America around the time Church purchased it. My thanks to James Ryan for providing this information.

189. See *19th Century America: Furniture and Other Decorative Arts* (exh. cat., New York, Metropolitan Museum of Art, 1970), no. 208. The screen is unattributed, but a furniture firm "like that of Christian Herter" is suggested as the maker.

190. *A Stag Drinking* and *A Stag and Two Does,* with a central panel by Homer D. Martin entitled *Beech Trees near a Pond,* are reproduced by Lloyd Goodrich in *Albert P. Ryder* (New York: George Braziller, Inc., 1959), nos. 51 and 52. According to Goodrich, "Ryder painted a number of such decorated screens, probably for Cottier & Co." The stained glass designer and furniture maker Daniel Cottier had worked in London and Glasgow before Ryder met him sometime between 1877 and 1882. The Ryder and Martin screen is undated and has been broken up. Martin's central panel has been missing since at least 1947 when the two Ryder panels were shown in *Albert P. Ryder: Centenary Exhibition* (exh. cat., New York, Whitney Museum of American Art, 1947), nos. 41 and 42. The two panels by Ryder are now in a private collection in Denver. Another screen, listed as "Idylles – 2 (set into a screen)" is mentioned in Frederic Newlin Price, *A Study of Appreciation* (New York: William Edwin Rudge, 1932), no. 67, as the property of Mr. John F. Braun, Philadelphia. The screen remains unlocated.

191. This sole surviving screen was eventually purchased by the famed collector John Gellatly in 1923 from the estate of the original owner. At that time, the panels were framed together as a screen. According to Ralph Seymour, Gellatly's curator, in 1928 the panels were removed from the original frame and reframed separately in gilded and carved wood frames made by E. A. Milch.

192. Mrs. Banning (née Helen Josephine Mellen) obtained the screen and one other small landscape from Ryder, according to a letter from her son Kendall Banning in the files at the National Museum of American Art, Washington.

193. There is a small, five-panel painted screen of flower subjects, dated 1882 and attributed to Elizabeth Bigelow Greene in the Robert Schoelkopf Gallery in New York. It is signed with a monogram which may or may not be that of Greene. Only thirty-six inches tall, the screen's five panels each contain precise renderings of various flowers.

194. An excellent analysis of Dewing's activities as a screenmaker is provided by Kathleen Pyne in "*Classical Figures,* A Folding Screen by Thomas Dewing," *Bulletin of the Detroit Institute of Arts* 59 (Spring 1981): 4-15.

195. For information on Freer's mansion and the artist's involvement in the interior decoration, see Thomas W. Brunk, "The House That Freer Built," *Dichotomy* 3, no. 4 (1981): 10-25 and 37-38.

196. Brunk, "The House That Freer Built," 10-17.

197. Brunk, "The House That Freer Built," 37-38.

198. My thanks to Susan Hobbs, whose research on these screens for the Freer Gallery of Art provided much of the factual information for this section.

199. Letter from Dewing to Freer, 12 August 1896, letter 74, Freer Gallery of Art, Washington.

200. See Susan Hobbs, page 1 of her unpublished, three page paper on the screens at the Freer Gallery of Art.

201. Pyne, "Dewing," 9 and note 27.

202. Mary Ellen Hayward, "The Influence of the Classical Oriental Tradition on American Painting." *Winterthur Portfolio* 14, no. 2 (1979): 126.

203. Hayward's astute analysis of Orientalisms in Dewing's art recognizes the emphasis on the abstract nature of the artist's figural compositions, where in outdoor settings these figures function as part of the overall pattern and design. All of the artists whom Freer patronized – Whistler, Tryon, Dewing, and Abbot Thayer – were chosen precisely because their works displayed compositional and temperamental affinities to oriental art. See especially Hayward, "Influence," 126-132.

204. Pyne, "Dewing," 6-7.

205. Pyne, "Dewing," 10-12.

206. Pyne, "Dewing," 8.

207. As we have seen, Japanese-inspired floral designs such as this were considered ideal subject matter for screen panels. See fig. 110 and the related text in this essay.

208. Pyne, "Dewing," 9.

209. Although it is not know whether Dewing's *Four Sylvan Sounds* screen for Freer was intended for any specific location, it is nevertheless evident that the screen's plain gilded strip frame was also in keeping with the simpler architectural features of Wilson Eyre's design for the mansion. See Brunk, "The House That Freer Built," 6-10, for illustrations of the interior of Freer's residence. Some classical elements were used by Eyre, but the overall effect recalls the work of architects such as C. F. A. Voysey and Charles Rennie Mackintosh.

210. See Robert Judson Clark, *The Arts and Crafts Movement in America* (Princeton: University Art Museum, 1972), 37.

211. They were originally shown in Stickley's 1910 *Catalogue of Craftsman Furniture,* nos. 83 and 91, and are reproduced in a reprint of this catalogue entitled, *Stickley Craftsman Furniture Catalogues* (New

York: Dover Publications, Inc., 1979); see also David M. Cathers, *Furniture of the American Arts and Crafts Movement* (New York: New American Library, 1981), 242, for a 1913 all oak screen with vertical boards joined by butterfly joints in each panel.

212. For information on Rohlfs, see Clark, *Arts and Crafts,* 28-31. The Roycroft firm was also known to have produced folding screens; see Nancy Hubbard Brady's facsimile of the 1912 catalogue, *Roycroft Hand Made Furniture* (East Aurora, New York: House of Hubbard, 1973), 32.

213. General references for the work of both Greene brothers are Randell L. Makinson, *Greene and Greene: Furniture and Related Designs* (Santa Barbara and Salt Lake City: Peregrine Smith, 1979), and Randell L. Makinson, *Greene and Greene* (Los Angeles: Municipal Art Gallery, 1977).

214. Greene kept bound copies of the *Studio* up to the 1902 issue in his library (Makinson, *Greene,* 1977, 10).

215. A backhanded compliment by today's standards, to be sure. See Milton W. Brown, *The Story of the Armory Show* (Greenwich: New York Graphic Society, 1963), 104, 108-109, 166, 171, 182, and nos. 1023-1031 in the accompanying reproduction of the exhibition catalogue.

216. Ivan Narodny, *The Art of Robert Winthrop Chanler* (New York: William Helbrun, Inc., 1922). Narodny's book is the only biography of the artist, though the repetitive and inflated rhetoric the author uses in analyzing Chanler's work makes it of minimal value.

217. Narodny, *Chanler,* 11.

218. Narodny, *Chanler,* 12.

219. "Exhibition of the Art of Robert Winthrop Chanler at the Albright Art Gallery," *Academy Notes* 16 (January-June 1921): 3-11.

220. See a review of the Wannamaker show by Henry McBride, *New York Herald,* 18 November 1923.

221. See Ruth Kedzie Wood, "He Mixes His Colors with Magic," *Mentor* (June 1927): 24-25. The most useful study on Charles Prendergast's life and work is Richard J. Wattenmaker, *The Art of Charles Prendergast* (New Brunswick: Rutgers University Art Gallery, 1968).

Catalogue I : 1867-1916

1.1

I

Design attributed to

WILLIAM NESFIELD

English, 1835-1888

made by

JAMES FORSYTH

Scottish, 1826-1910

SIX-PANEL SCREEN, 1867
*Watercolor on paper paintings in an ebonized
wood frame with gilded, carved, and painted decorations. 207.0 x 233.0 (81 1/2 x 91 1/4)
Victoria and Albert Museum, London*

INSCRIPTIONS:
(Panel One, Recto) All are Architects / of Fate Working on these / walls of time / Some with massive deeds & / great Some with / ornaments of Rhyme
(Panel Three, Recto) Richard & Agnes Shaw AD 1867 / From James Forsyth
(Panel Six, Recto) Nothing Useless is / or low Each thing / in its place is best / And what seems / but idle Show & / Strengthens and supports the rest
(Panel One, Verso) Favour is deceitful and / beautie is vaine but A / Woman that feareth / the Lord she shall be praised / Give her of the fruit of her / hands & let her own work / praise her in the Gates
(Panel Four, Verso) Richard & Agnes Shaw AD 1867 / From James Forsyth
(Panel Six, Verso) Many waters cannot quench / Love neither can the / Floods drown it if A / Man would give all ye / Substance of his House / For love it would / Utterlie be contemmed

This six-panel, double-sided screen (1.1 and 1.2) was made by James Forsyth, cabinetmaker and sculptor, who was on close terms with many of the most important English Aesthetic Movement architects and designers.[1] A wedding present for one of the most successful architects in this group, Richard Norman Shaw, the screen displays a wealth of Japanese painted and carved motifs which

indicate that its designer was indeed familiar with oriental ornament. There is no precedent in Forsyth's work for these motifs, and it is presumed that Shaw's partner William Nesfield was responsible for the screen's design. Nesfield had already produced several pieces of furniture, and was the greatest enthusiast of the three for oriental art, even decorating his office with "a very jolly collection of Persian, Indian, Greek, and Japanese things."[2] The relationship between Nesfield and Forsyth was also a close one: Forsyth named his son James Nesfield Forsyth.[3]

The screen documents clearly the multiple oriental influences upon which western screen artists first drew for their inspiration. Its "image" consists of twelve vertical Japanese paintings mounted on both recto and verso. These unsigned and unattributed paintings date from the late eighteenth or early nineteenth century.[4] They depict various birds perched upon blossoming branches of small trees and shrubs. Chrysanthemums, lilies, pinks, peonies, and perhaps magnolias can be seen. The consistency of handling and format in the paintings points to the work of a single artist, probably following Chinese prototypes for the decorative arrangement of these flower and bird subjects. It is also likely that these twelve paintings make up a thematically related group, although the subjects are not so easily identifiable as, for example, the twelve months. What is significant is that in choosing to use

Japanese paintings as the major visual components of the design, Nesfield was obviously responding to oriental precedents for the very idea of his screen.

His innovation lay in how he incorporated these colorful painted compositions into the screen's structural framework. The paintings are surrounded by an incised ebonized wood frame with a small horizontal strip of open fretwork at the top; there is a larger area of diagonal and perpendicular frets at the bottom. Between the black fretwork at the top and the paintings themselves is a band of gilded, carved motifs of Japanese origin. Accompanying the verses in the first panel (1.2) is the very common key-fret motif known as *sayagata,* with highly stylized flower or circle patterns at the center of each of the three Buddhist swastikas. In the second panel, against a background of *uzumaki* or spirals, are three different chrysanthemum medallions, one of which is painted black. Next to the black medallion is a type of family crest,[5] and to its right is a small concentric circle roundel. The third panel is dominated by a free combination of both the *sayagata* and *uzumaki* motifs, with a single large chrysanthemum at the lower left. There are in addition various stylized geometric and floral medallions. Even the

plaques bearing the Shaws' and Forsyth's names are "held" in place by an abstract vine design known as *karakusa.* A woven lattice work with hourglass-shaped openings forms the ground in the next panel, against which are two chrysanthemum medallions and a single stylized daisy roundel at the top center. In the lower left corner is another variation on the *sayagata.* Two other medallions carry Shaw's initials, and his wife's first name. The background of the fifth panel shows overlapping concentric circles with two different chrysanthemum designs. A delicate combination of bamboo leaves with a single plum blossom at its center can also be seen. Finally, in the sixth panel, there is a rare display of symmetry: the *sayagata* motif from the first panel is repeated.[6]

The splendid asymmetric rhythm of these carved patterns is matched in the painted sections beneath the Japanese paintings. There are two areas of painted decoration here, a narrow horizontal band above a larger horizontal rectangle in each screen panel.[7] In the first (1.3), there is a stylized wave motif in the upper band. Below, against another variation of the *sayagata,* are two more permutations on the ever-present chrysanthemum. The petals of the one at the left are made up of overlap-

1.3 Detail, lower register, first verso panel.

1.4 Detail, lower register, second verso panel.

1.2 Verso.

1.5 Detail, lower register, third verso panel.

1.6 Detail, lower register, fourth verso panel.

1.7 Detail, lower register, fifth verso panel.

1.8 Detail, lower register, sixth verso panel.

ping concentric circles, and its center actually contains a single bellflower known as *kikyō*. The second panel (1.4) has an upper band of overlapping circles or "pies" containing highly stylized alternating floral patterns (perhaps sunflowers). Below is yet another *sayagata* ground, this time with seven *genji* derived from the *I Ching*. Within a vertical rectangle is a relatively naturalistic rendering of daisies in the grass along a stream, virtually the only portion of the screen which does not seem directly dependent on a Japanese model. In the adjacent circle is an unidentified design showing a group of utensils bound together; this group of objects may be a symbol of Shaw's architectural profession.

Panel three (1.5) contains some of the richest combinations of ornamental patterns. In the upper band, there is a background of two different arrow designs known as *yagasuri*, with a pattern of rippled waves in the center. Medallions of highly stylized, six-petaled blossoms (apricot plum?) are laid over this background at the left and right, while in the center there is a medallion consisting of a chrysanthemum over a bellflower. The panel below has for its ground an abstract design of hexagons formed by three-legged arrows that resemble the starlike hemp pattern known as the *asa-no-ha*. Seven oranges are still attached to their short branches and surround another chrysanthemum medallion. The remaining two six-petaled flowers cannot be identified with any certainty. The next panel (1.6) repeats the wave pattern from the same position in the first panel, and the larger rectangle below has a *sayagata* ground. Six bellflowers, each subtly different in their details, are placed in squares around still another variation of the chrysanthemum, whose center consists of a lattice inscribed in a circle. A medallion with bamboo leaves and plum blossoms is located to the left, outlined with a variation of the *karakusa* or vine motif. At the top of the next panel (1.7) is a diaper pattern of alternating black and gold triangles overlaid with three stylized plant medallions, of which only the bellflower at the center is recognizable. The larger rectangle below contains an abstract ground made up of a repetitive diamond pattern. The eight medallions made up of three rotating commas are actually family crests known as the *tomoe*. The large roundel at the left center contains a bound sheaf of autumn grasses, while the rectangle to the right shows a sunflower in a *t'ing* type three-legged pot of Chinese origin; this particularly rigid rectangular format may be more English than oriental.

Finally, in the sixth panel (1.8), there is in the upper band another variation on the *sayagata*, this time with an overlay of three sunflower medallions. In the bottom section is a ground of a slightly different *karakusa* design, with two identical roundels that probably show a scraggly leafed species of chrysanthemum. Between them is what may be a highly abstract chrysanthemum design. At the bottom center is a small, newly opened blossom which again may be a version of this flower.

The obvious question is where could Nesfield, or Forsyth for that matter, have borrowed this wealth of authentic Japanese design motifs? Certainly, some of the patterns such as the *sayagata* were indigenous to several ancient eastern cultures, including Japan, China, and Greece. Many variations on this key-fret motif can be found, for example, in Owen Jones' *The Grammar of Ornament*.[8] First published in 1856, Jones' book was probably the best known of all such studies on ornament available to English designers of the 1860s and 1870s. Some of the more unusual motifs may have been borrowed from Japanese ceramics, which Nesfield easily could have seen, or even owned. A small lacquer box owned by Sir Rutherford Alcock and exhibited in the 1862 London International Exhibition contains a utensil design relatively close in flavor to that in the screen's second panel.[9]

The intricacy of the several painted and carved panels, however, suggests strongly that they came from a single

1.9 Detail, hinge.

source. On the whole, the asymmetric arrangement of stylized circular and rectangular patterns against contrasting types of background motifs is far too accomplished to have been achieved by an English artist in the 1860s, particularly if one assumes that these motifs were drawn from even a small group of different sources and then assembled on the screen. The complex layering of motifs creates a spatial definition that cannot be found on any other Anglo-Japanese objects from the period. Since many of the decorative patterns from the screen also appear frequently on Japanese textiles, it may very well be that Nesfield had access to either a pattern book or even stencils used for making such textiles.[10] The repetition of painted patterns on both the recto and verso of the screen also indicates the possibility of Nesfield's reliance on some sort of stencil.

Insofar as the overall design is concerned, Nesfield conceived of the screen not as a field for a continuous composition, but rather as a series of fields which were linked visually by the location of similar ornamental motif combinations. The precise execution of these designs also reveals Forsyth's considerable technical expertise, even in the metal hinges (1.9), where incised and punched decorative details enhance these purely functional pieces of hardware. The artist's debt to Japan is unabashedly acknowledged in the screen, yet the compartmentalization of painted and carved ornaments reveals an essentially western sensibility.

1. A short obituary on Forsyth appeared in *Building News* (11 February 1910). He is also discussed briefly in Andrew Saint's authoritative biography, *Richard Norman Shaw* (New Haven and London: Yale University Press, 1976), 21.

2. Letter from Simeon Solomon to the poet Swinburne, probably late September 1869, in *The Swinburne Letters*, ed. Cecil Y. Lang (New Haven: Yale University Press, 1959), 2:33, no. 310A.

3. Saint accepts the attribution of the design to Forsyth, albeit reluctantly: "His was the undisputed place of sculptor and carver to the friends in the years of their early successes, though he was more intimate with Nesfield. He could design, it seems, if he was really both author and craftsman of the Japanese screen he gave Shaw as a wedding present in 1867" (Saint, *Shaw,* 21). The screen is also published as the work of Nesfield, without elaboration, in Charles Spencer's *The Aesthetic Movement* (London: Academy Editions, 1973), 36, cat. no. 19.

4. My sincere thanks to Dr. Yoshiaki Shimizu of the Freer Gallery of Art and to Louisa Cunningham of the Yale University Art Gallery for their observations on these paintings, and for their help in identifying the various decorative motifs discussed in the following section of this entry.

5. See Sherman E. Lee, *The Genius of Japanese Design* (Tokyo and New York: Kodansha International, 1981) for an overview of Japanese crests and other design motifs found in the screen.

6. The motifs are virtually identical on both sides of the screen, since they were carved completely through the wood panels. Some minor details, such as those in the medallions, are painted black on one side and left gilded on the other.

7. As in the carved panels at the top of the screen, these painted decorations are repeated on both sides of the screen. In the narrow horizontal bands, the design in panel one recto (1R) is identical to that in panel four recto (4R); 2R is the same as 6V; 3R the same as 2V; 4R the same as 1R; 5R the same as 4V; 6R the same as 3V; and the design on 1V is the same as in 5V. As for the designs in the larger horizontal rectangles below these bands, 1R is identical with 1V; 2R is unique; 3R is the same as 3V; 4R the same as both 4V and 2V; 5R the same as 5V; and 6R the same as 6V.

8. Owen Jones, *The Grammar of Ornament* (London: Day and Son, 1856), plates 15 and 59.

9. See J. B. Waring, *Masterpieces of Industrial Art and Sculpture at the International Exhibition, 1862* (London: Day and Son, 1863), 3: plate 282. Some of the other ceramics illustrated in this plate also contain the key-fret motif and stylizations of the chrysanthemum that appear in the screen. These and other motifs are abundant in the many pieces illustrated by George A. Audsley and James L. Bowes' *Keramic Art of Japan,* 2 vols. (London: Henry Sotheran & Co., 1875), even on the stands which held the ostensibly more important ceramics.

10. See Frances Blakemore, *Japanese Designs through Textile Patterns* (New York and Tokyo: Weatherhill, 1978).

2

SIR LAURENS ALMA-TADEMA

Dutch, 1836-1912

and

LADY LAURA EPPS ALMA-TADEMA

English, 1852-1909

PORTRAIT OF THE EPPS FAMILY, *1870-1871*
*Oil on canvas (recto) with block-printed
wallpaper and découpage (verso). 182.9 x 472.2 (72 x 186)
Victoria and Albert Museum, London*

INSCRIPTION:

It was the hap of a very honest man to be the father of a brood of children. He call'd for a bundle of arrows and bad 'em take it and try one after another with all their force, if they could break it. They try'd and could not. Well says he, unbind it now, and take every arrow of it apart, and see what you can do that way. They did so, and with great ease, by one and one, they snap'd it all to pieces. This says he is the true emblem of your condition. Keep together and y'are safe.

In December 1869 the recently widowed Laurens Alma-Tadema met seventeen-year-old Laura Theresa Epps. Alma-Tadema's dealer, Ernest Gambart, wrote in a letter to the painter Holman Hunt: "Tadema went last Boxing Day [26 December 1869] to a dance at Madox Browns, fell in love at first sight with Miss Epps, the surgeon's daughter, and is going to marry her as soon as she names the day – it plays havoc with his painting; he cannot turn to work since."[1] Laura Epps, like her sister Emily, was interested in becoming an artist and had already received drawing lessons from Thomas Cave, William Bell Scott, and Ford Madox Brown.[2] Alma-Tadema agreed to teach her how to paint, and the result of their lessons was this six-panel screen portrait of the Epps family (2.1). It was probably painted in 1870 and certainly no later than July 1871, when Laura and Laurens were married.[3]

The family is shown just about to be seated for a midday meal. At the head of the table is Dr. George Napoleon Epps, with his wife Anne Charlotte Bacon. Mary Ann Camille Epps, her husband Dr. Hahnemann Epps, and their two seated children are seen next. Then come Ellen Epps (who later married Edmund Gosse, one of Alma-Tadema's biographers); Charles Pratt and his wife Amy Epps; and Rowland Hill, standing behind his wife Louisa Epps, who holds their daughter Charlotte. Because of a stockmarket scandal, Rowland and Louisa were obliged to flee to Argentina in 1871, and because of the disgrace, Sir Laurens or Laura painted his figure out and depicted him peering from around the door. The inscription at the top, a plea for familial unity, unexpectedly took on even greater meaning. Over time, the upper paint layers have become transparent, leaving the obvious pentimenti. Next is Frances Epps, her husband Dr. Washington Epps, and his sister Laura Theresa. Through the door there is a self-portrait of the adoring Alma-Tadema, followed by Franklin Epps and his wife.

Some areas were left unfinished, most notably the large whitish section in the third panel. The name inscriptions across the lower register were also left incomplete, suggesting that Sir Laurens became occupied with another project. The participants in the portrait obviously knew each other, indicating that these "nameplates" were included for future generations of the Epps family, who were likely to inherit the screen as a family heirloom.

The finished portions of the screen reveal the carefully planned composition and occasionally brilliant execution that the Victorian public came to expect of Laurens

Alma-Tadema. The bold L-shaped border unites the panels horizontally and provides a ground for the names of the figures who appear above. This large border also emphasizes the horizontal nature of the composition, as does the long white dining table. Parallels for this orientation may be found in the artist's more familiar Greco-Roman pictures such as *The Education of the Children of Clovis* (1869), *The Vintage Festival* (1870), or even *The Roman Art Lover* (1870).[4] As in these works, the screen figures here are carefully interspersed in related groups, forming a procession across the picture plane and receding only slightly into space. The figure of Emily Epps in the fourth panel, for example, is brought close to the picture plane and is the only figure on the viewer's side of the table. Posed slightly diagonally, with her back to us and highlighted by the warm, cream color of her dress, Emily functions as a *repoussé* figure. A drawing for this figure, virtually identical to that in the finished painting, indicates its importance to Alma-Tadema.[5] The composition as a whole is parenthetically conceived: the near-abstract rectangle of the first panel and the seated, pro-filed figure of Dr. Epps in the second are counterbalanced by the standing group at the far right, where Laura is shown in profile facing in the opposite direction.

Some areas are painted in a sketchy, impressionistic style,[6] while others such as the almost inconspicuous still life at the far right of the sixth panel are richly detailed and brilliantly executed. There is as a result a compo-sitional and painterly rhythm across the width of the screen. The apparent somberness of this Victorian domestic scene is not without comic relief, however: in the third panel, just above Anne Epps' head, and un-known to her, a spider dangles from its web.

The verso of the screen (2.2) is equally fascinating. A rich collage of printed cutouts from various sources were pasted against a gold paper ground, probably over a period of many decades, by the screen's different owners. This collage represents an older folk tradition of scrap screens, which has been wedded to the modern innova-tions of Alma-Tadema's painted group portrait on the recto. Recent restoration efforts have also revealed that William Morris' *Pomegranate* wallpaper was adhered to the screen's presumably original plain fabric backing (2.3). This paper, most visible in the first verso panel on the recto (i.e., the sixth recto panel), was one of Morris' earliest papers.[7] Dating from 1864, it may very well have been installed on the verso of the screen by the Epps family.

2.2 Verso.

2.1

1. Much of the factual information concerning the screen comes from the files in the Department of Furniture and Woodwork, Victoria and Albert Museum, provided by Vern G. Swanson.

2. Ellen C. Clayton, *English Female Artists* (London: Tinsley Brothers, 1876), 2:6. Laura Epps had an artistic career of her own that began in 1872 when she showed a painting at the Paris Salon. From 1873 on she was a regular exhibitor at the Royal Academy as well. See also *Art Journal* (1883): 345-347.

3. Unlike nearly all of Alma-Tadema's pictures, the screen does not bear an Opus number, the means by which the artist consecutively numbered his painted works. Because the screen was done in collaboration with Laura Epps, he no doubt excluded it from those works that he considered entirely his own.

4. See Vern G. Swanson, *Alma-Tadema: The Painter of the Victorian Vision and of the Ancient World* (New York: Charles Scribner's Sons, 1977), 17, plates 4 and 5. Swanson's monograph is the most accurate; he is presently preparing a catalogue raisonné of the paintings, in which the screen will be included.

5. Although it is certain both Laura and Laurens worked on the screen, compositional and stylistic factors suggest strongly that the elder professional artist played the dominant role in its creation. The existence of the study led Vern Swanson to state that Laurens drew it as a guide for Laura. The quality of paint handling in the finished portrait, however, seems far too accomplished to have come from Laura's hand.

6. There are several factors which would explain this deviation from Alma-Tadema's usually precise painting style. The obvious one is that the screen is far larger than any of his other pictures, perhaps necessitating a freer handling throughout. A second is that the artist could have been aware of both Manet's and Monet's works by this time; Alma-Tadema visited Paris late in 1864, and in 1869 he planned to have a house built for himself there. The death of his first wife, followed by the outbreak of the Franco-Prussian war, led him to London instead in 1870. Monet, Sisley, and several other French artists also moved to London in that year to flee the hostilities in Paris, and it is possible Alma-Tadema could have become familiar with their freer styles at that time.

7. See Peter Flood, "Dating Morris Wallpapers" in *Architectural Review* (July 1959): 14-20.

3

WILLIAM MORRIS

English, 1834-1896

THREE-PANEL SCREEN, *ca. 1860-1887*
Wool, silk, and gold thread on serge with oak frame. 170.2 x 213.4 (67 x 84)
From the Castle Howard Collection, Yorkshire

While a student in theology at Exeter College, Oxford, William Morris became fascinated with medieval tapestries he had seen on journeys to France and the Low Countries in 1854 and 1855. Both he and his fellow student Edward Burne-Jones, who accompanied him on one of these trips, chose to abandon their plans to enter the church and instead to "begin a life of art." Morris entered the office of gothic revival architect George Edmund Street, whose embroidered altar frontals certainly influenced the young artist.

By 1856, however, Morris was discouraged with his architectural career, and he left Street's firm to try his hand at painting. Early in 1857 Morris and Burne-Jones moved into rooms in Red Lion Square, and shortly after his marriage in 1859, Morris moved again, this time into the so-called Red House (Bexley Heath), designed by Philip Webb, whom Morris met while in Street's office. Reflecting in 1883 upon those early years, Morris explained, "I got a friend to build me a house very medieval in spirit in which I lived for five years, and set myself to decorating it; we found ... that all the minor arts were in a state of complete degradation especially in England, and accordingly in 1861 with the conceited courage of a young man I set myself to reforming all that."[1]

His efforts at reform began a few years earlier when he and Burne-Jones made their own furniture for their rooms in Red Lion Square. Among the furnishings for this house was a set of embroidered panels intended to form a narrative border around the outer walls of the drawing room. The panels were no doubt executed after Morris' designs by his wife Jane Burden or her sister Elizabeth (Bessie) Burden. The series as originally planned may have consisted of as many as twelve panels whose subjects were derived, albeit loosely, from Geof-frey Chaucer's *Legend of Good Women*.[2] The eight existing panels from the set and the four known designs for them all depict historical female figures: St. Catherine, Isoude, Penelope, Eve,[3] Venus, Ariadne, Hippolyte, and Helen of Troy. The last two appear in the second and third panels of the screen. The forlorn figure holding a sword in the first panel may be Lucretia, whose story is related in Chaucer's poem. The embroideries were to be done on plain linen, then cut out and applied to a heavy silk velvet background, reminiscent of late medieval and early Tudor tapestries with which Morris was familiar.[4]

The screen (3.1) was not assembled as such until 1887, however, in a rather unusual set of circumstances. George Howard, the ninth earl of Carlisle, had previously engaged Morris and Co. from 1872 to 1882 to provide decorations for his London home at 1 Palace Green,[5] and was one of Morris' most enthusiastic clients. On 30 August 1887 Howard sent Bessie Burden a check for £80 in payment for the "three needlework figures which you have sent to Messrs Morris to be framed."[6] Unfortunately, nothing more is known about the commission, but it is clear that Morris was not at all reluctant to reconstitute the panels from the Red House as a screen. By 1887 Morris' firm had produced several folding and single-panel firescreens, for the most part using floral patterned fabrics mounted onto wooden frames (3.2).[7] Such fabric screens were common enough in England, having been made in the late 1870s and the early 1880s not only by Morris but also by the Royal School of Art Needlework and the Leek Embroidery Society.[8] In 1884 Arthur Mackmurdo, founder of the Century Guild, also made his own small-scale, three-panel fabric screen (fig. 66).

In making this screen for George Howard, Morris had to contend with the obvious problem of joining together

3.2 William Morris, *Four-Panel Screen*, ca. 1890, colored silk on canvas in stem and darning stitch, 163.0 x 155.0 (64⅛ x 61). Photograph, Cecil Higgins Museum, Bedford, England.

three separate embroidered panels intended as wall hangings.[9] The panels, of course, were designed to relate to one another on the walls of the Red House, and have certain features in common. Each of the long-haired women is shown full-length against identical floral background designs. They stand on flower-filled plots of grass bordered in front by a four-rowed brick wall, slightly above a row of flowers. Each figure is attired in medieval garb, wearing a richly brocaded gown and a crown of either gold or laurel leaves. In addition, each figure holds a sword, lance, or torch which acts as a vertical accent. The similarity of these details provides compositional continuity across the panels, and the simple oak frame provides structural uniformity.

More important, however, is how the figures relate to one another. Lucretia in the first panel faces slightly toward Hippolyte in the center, while Helen leans her head toward the center of the screen. Hippolyte, posed frontally with her feet extending over the brick wall in front of her in an obvious reference to medieval repre-

sentational devices, anchors the screen both compositionally and physically: the richness and variety of materials in her costume naturally draw the viewer's attention. She is shown in chain mail and armor, wearing an ornate gown with a pattern of encircled flowers and eagles, and a full-length cape. Details such as the unbuttoned collar, the red and gold patterned belt hanging loosely from her waist, and the gold-threaded scabbard demonstrate fully how Morris and his co-workers earned their reputations as superb craftsmen and craftswomen. Like Nesfield and Whistler before him, Morris was able to bring together disparate elements into a cohesive finished product.

1. Linda Parry, *William Morris Textiles* (London: Weidenfeld and Nicolson, 1983), 7. I am deeply indebted to Mrs. Parry for answering my many questions about Morris' activities as a screenmaker.

2. Of the identifiable figures in the various panels and preliminary drawings, only Ariadne and Lucretia appear in Chaucer's poem; Cleopatra, Thisbe, Dido, Hypsipyle, Medea, Philomela, Phyllis, and Hypermnestra are the other characters in the *Legend*. Morris' scheme as a result does not recall the Ovidian or Vergilian prototypes revived by Chaucer, but instead freely mixes classical, Christian, and medieval personages. The relationship between all these panels and a series of designs for embroidery by Burne-Jones for John Ruskin, also based on Chaucer's *Legend*, will be the subject of a forthcoming article by Linda Parry.

3. For an illustration of the Eve figure, see Barbara Morris, *Victorian Embroidery* (London: Barrie & Jenkins, 1970), 153, plate 43. Morris also mentions a design for an embroidered panel showing Guinevere, now in the Victoria and Albert Museum.

4. Parry, *Textiles*, 13-14. The screen panels were not executed in this fashion, however.

5. Parry, *Textiles*, 66-67, 89-90, and especially 137; and Morris, *Victorian Embroidery*, 110.

6. This letter is in the Sandy and Helen Berger Collection, Carmel, California.

7. Linda Parry also lists two embroidered screens at the Museum Bellerive, Zürich (see Parry, *Textiles*, 34 and 178-179). Another three-panel floral pattern screen, dating from the 1890s, is in the Victoria and Albert Museum (Circ. 848-1956). A photograph of the drawing room at Stanmore Hall (fig. 68) shows one more folding screen designed by Morris and Co., with an ebonized wood frame; and there is a single screen panel illustrated in the Century Guild's publication, *Hobby Horse* 3 (1888).

8. Morris, *Victorian Embroidery*, 116-118, 120, and 135-136. A crewel work screen on silk from ca. 1879, after designs by Walter Crane, is illustrated on page 179, plate 54, and is now in the London School of Economics.

9. Morris and Burne-Jones did another group of tapestry panels with figure subjects joined together as a three-panel folding screen (fig. 105), showing Saints Agnes and Cecilia. The panels were originally woven in 1887 for Thomas Wardle; the location of this screen, considered unique by Linda Parry, is unknown.

3.1

4.1 Recto.

4
ARTIST UNKNOWN

Probably American, active ca. 1875-1900

FOUR ELEMENTS, *ca. 1885*
Oil on pine with ebonized wood frame. 180.3 x 166.3 (71 x 66¹/4)
Collection of Mr. and Mrs. Roy Frangiamore, Atlanta

The designer of this four-panel screen (4.1 and 4.2) certainly knew the *Four Elements* stained glass and painted screen done by an artist in the circle of Burne-Jones (fig. 63-65 and 4.3). The individual figures of the elements in the two screens are virtually identical, line for line, and are nearly the same size. In addition, many of the design features, such as the stylized plant and fish motifs in the lower registers of the painted screen, derive from those in the stained glass version. Because the wood in the painted screen is American pine, it has been presumed that the maker was American.[1] While it was probably designed by an American artist, this screen's nearly total dependence on its English predecessor makes it difficult to be certain about such an attribution.

There are significant differences between the two *Four Elements* screens, the most obvious being that the order of the figures is not the same. The more orthodox Earth-Air-Fire-Water arrangement in the stained glass version has been altered to Earth-Water-Fire-Air. In addition, in the painted screen each figure is also identified by an inscription, suggesting perhaps the copyist anticipated that his audience might not be entirely familiar with the allegorical theme. The transposition of the Air and Water figures does not detract greatly from the unity of the composition, since both face toward the center of the screen, thereby uniting the group parenthetically across the surface as in the stained glass composition. The personification of Air, though, with her caduceus held high to the right, does not close the composition as effectively as does the leftward-striding personification of Water. As a result, the subtle gestural and formal cohesiveness that characterizes the arrangement of figures in the glass screen has been lessened.

The painted screen is also embellished with more elaborate decorative motifs. Behind each figure, for example, are bamboo leaves against a blue ground, replacing the highly patterned orange tree background in the glass panels. And above each figure, there is a semicircular arch draped with a garland of fruit and a stylized leaf motif, again differing from the symmetrical floral

4.3 Circle of Sir Edward Coley Burne-Jones, English, 1833-1898, *Four Elements*, ca. 1885, stained glass with oil on panel, 180.0 x 206.0 (64 x 70³/8). Cologne, Kunstgewerbemuseum.

designs above the figures in the glass prototype. Below the figures, the Renaissance-style plant ornaments of the prototype have been replaced with an additional band of flowers lying beneath a semicircular arch; this arch is framed and decorated in nearly the same way as are the arches at the top. The painted example also contains a combination of cherry blossoms, bamboo, and a highly stylized geometric pattern of triangles, circles, and circles within circles at the very bottom portion of the screen, again in contrast to the treatment accorded this section of the glass screen. Yet even these details derive ultimately from the English example, whose verso also contains similar motifs painted in a golden bronze against a black ground. The common source for these Japanese-inspired motifs may very well have been a plate in Christopher Dresser's *Modern Ornamentation* of 1886 (4.4). Of course, William Nesfield's 1867 screen (Cat. 1) also included such Japanese design features, and by the 1880s when the two *Four Elements* screens were made, these features were abundantly available from Japanese objects themselves as well as from English interpretations of them.[2]

Finally, the designer of the painted screen also appropriated to the lower register the fish and plant motifs which appear in the same location on the stained glass example. Once again, there is a minor deviation from the source: the fish are brightly painted in realistic colors, and the reeds are rendered in naturalistic greens, both in

contrast to the bronze-on-black handling of these motifs in the glass screen. While there can be no doubt the designer of the painted screen worked closely from the English model, he chose to elaborate considerably upon the subsidiary decorative details.

The painted *Four Elements* screen differs significantly from its predecessor in that it is double-sided, with a separate set of images on the verso. Across the central section of the panels is a fruit-laden orange tree branch, depicted from right to left in oriental fashion; whether the source was Japanese, Chinese, or even an American or English interpretation is impossible to say. Above and below the branch are bands of stylized leaf and roundel decorations surmounted by rather generalized, non-specific representations of birds. Each of these birds is perched on a branch within a circle set into a diamond. The symmetric arrangement of the horizontal bands frames the orange branch segment of the composition and further emphasizes the flow across the screen's surface. Both the recto and verso have their own character, the iconic and serially-ordered *Four Elements* side contrasting with the continuous but equally densely patterned composition on the verso.

On the whole, the painted *Four Elements* screen is an eclectic, if not somewhat less elegant, rendition of its stained glass predecessor. The latter has by virtue of its medium a sparkling, jewel-like quality which of course could not be achieved in oils on a wood support. By decorating both sides and by including more elaborate decorative details, however, the designer of the painted version attempted to compensate for the character of his chosen medium. In any event, the close formal and thematic relationship between the two screens demonstrates one aspect of America's interest in the English arts and crafts movement.

4.4 Christopher Dresser, *Modern Ornamentation*, 1886.

1. *A Thing of Beauty: Art Nouveau, Art Deco, Arts & Crafts Movement and Aesthetic Movement Objects in Atlanta Collections* (exh. cat., Atlanta, High Museum of Art, 1980), 52, 64, and cat. no. F.1.

2. Another rich source for Japanese design motifs was George A. Audsley and James L. Bowes' *Keramic Art of Japan*, 2 vols. (London: Henry Sotheran & Co., 1875); and G. A. Audsley, *The Ornamental Arts of Japan*, 2 vols., (New York: Charles Scribner's Sons, 1885). Both of these books reproduce dozens of Japanese objects which contain design elements one sees in the two screens. At the very least, they indicate the frequency with which certain types of motifs appeared and therefore would have been known in England and America.

4.2 Verso.

5.1

5

ARMAND SEGUIN

French, 1869-1903

THE DELIGHTS OF LIFE, *1892-1893*
Oil on canvas with painted and gilded frame. 159.1 x 256.5 (62 5/8 x 101)
Private Collection, New York

The Delights of Life (5.1) is Seguin's only attempt in the screen format. He chose as his subject the physical and sensual pleasures of human existence, portrayed in the gaslighted environs of a Paris café. At the very left of the first panel, a woman in a green dress, lighted cigarette in one hand, pours wine for an unseen customer whose playing cards lie face up on the table. Behind her a billiards player attempts a massé shot, with a gaslight above illuminating the scene. To the right in panel two, a black-gowned pianist plays for the dancing couples beyond, whose haunting, flat shapes make them seem more like apparitions than flesh and blood figures. In the third panel, a waitress serves a meal to her customer, while a light-bearded man watches from behind, calmly smoking his pipe. Again, a gas lamp at the upper left casts its glow over the scene. This bearded figure spreads across to the fourth panel, as does the patterned tabletop below. To those "delights" of life already shown – drinking, smoking, card playing, billiard playing, music making, dancing, and eating – Seguin adds sexual pleasure: a scantily clad waitress engagingly stares out at us as she carries a tray onto which her near-naked breasts appear to fall.

Seguin spent most of his creative life reacting to the strong influence of Gauguin and his circle at Pont-Aven, and to the chic Parisian world of the Nabis. In this work, Seguin's borrowings from the latter group are abundantly clear. It is likely that the idea for making the screen came from Bonnard whose first attempt, *Femmes au jardin* of 1891, (fig. 73), was exhibited late that year at the Salon des Indépendants in Paris,[1] where Seguin probably saw it. Moreover, the energetically outlined "Valse" music sheet in the second panel is a motif Seguin may very well have taken from Bonnard's painting *Suite pour piano* of 1891.[2] Finally, although Denis' *Danse Breton*

has been suggested as a possible source for the repetitive dancing figure shapes in this panel,[3] this motif too could have been borrowed from Bonnard, who used it in his *La Partie de croquet* painting of 1892.[4] This evidence, coupled with Seguin's demonstrated interest in Parisian café scenes, strongly suggests a date of 1892-1893 for the screen.[5]

Whatever his borrowings from Bonnard and Denis may have been, Seguin still managed to bring several important nuances to the screen format. Unlike Bonnard in his first screen, in which each panel is occupied by a single full-length female figure, Seguin attempted to unite the four panels by both compositional and narrative means (5.2). The bodies of the pianist and the pipe-smoker both extend across the panels, gaining a certain

5.2 *The Delights of Life*, folded position.

compositional prominence by virtue of their active shapes and contours. The narrative, of course, is not continuous across all the panels, and it is broken by the relatively wide painted and gilded frame. Even within the framing elements, however, Seguin still worked to join the panels. The painted intrados of the frame emulate to a certain degree the pattern and coloration of the various picture fields. In the first and again in the second panel, compositional elements run over onto the painted frame: first the pianist's gown, and then the curvilinear contours of the music sheets. And in the third panel, where the wine bottle on the table is divided by the frame, Seguin surprises us by making no effort to join the two halves, instead remaining content to allow the continuity to be implied.

In stylistic terms, Seguin carefully balanced those elements which largely define his entire artistic output: the heavily outlined, internally modulated shapes of cloi-sonism,[6] and the richly patterned, actively contoured interior scenes favored by the Nabis. The resulting screen is justifiably considered the best painting from the artist's tragically short career, and it may well have influenced Bonnard to attempt a continuous composition in his second folding screen (fig. 75).

1. See "A Perfect Gem of Art," 72-73.

2. Ursula Perruchi-Petri, *Die Nabis und Japan: Das Frühwerk von Bonnard, Vuillard und Denis* (Munich: Prestel Verlag, 1976), 66, ills. 22 and 23.

3. See *The Prints of Armand Seguin, 1869-1903* by Richard S. Field (exh. cat., Middletown, Conn. Davison Art Center, Wesleyan University, 1980), 12. Although this catalogue is devoted to Seguin's activities as a printmaker, Field's insightful essay on the life and work of the artist is the best to date.

4. Jean and Henry Dauberville, *Bonnard. Catalogue raisonné de l'oeuvre peint*, 4 vols. (Paris: Editions Bernheim-Jeune, 1966), 1: no. 38.

5. Field, *Seguin*, 12.

6. See Field, *Seguin*, 5-6, for Maurice Denis' still accurate evaluation of Seguin's stylistic development as demonstrated in the latter's 1895 exhibition.

6

PIERRE BONNARD

French, 1867-1947

PROMENADE DES NOURRICES, FRISE DES FIACRES, *1896*
Color lithographs in modern frame
150.0 x 200.0 (59 x 78 3/4)
Collection of Dr. and Mrs. Ira J. Jackson, Houston (Washington)
Museum of Modern Art, New York, Abby Aldrich Rockefeller Fund (New Haven)

In 1894 Bonnard painted his second folding screen, a Parisian street scene with a nanny and her charges in the foreground and a line of horse carriages in the background (fig. 75). In proceeding from the static, single figure per panel configuration in his first screen (fig. 73) to the continuous and dynamic folding image in the *Promenade* screen, the artist had taken a vast conceptual stride. Like Whistler two decades before, Bonnard grasped the special nature of a folding screen and arranged his composition to take full advantage of it.[1]

Just two years after the painted *Promenade* screen was completed, Bonnard undertook to do a color lithographic version of it which has survived in numerous examples (6.1). No doubt sensing the commercial possibilities of producing the screen in this relatively inexpensive and thus far more accessible medium, he had 110 examples published by Molines in Paris.[2] Advertisements for this lithographic version appeared in an 1896 issue of *Studio*,[3] and in the very first issue of *L'Estampe et l'affiche* in 1897.[4] In this latter periodical the screen was offered as follows:

Bonnard—folding screen: Published at Molines, 20, rue Lafitte. P. Bonnard. Folding screen in four panels lithographed in five colors... in sheets 40 francs, mounted 60 francs.

According to Roger-Marx, only forty examples from the entire edition were actually mounted as screens.[5] Presumably, those who bought the lithographs unmounted planned to have it framed elsewhere or to mount it themselves. Similar practices were followed by Alfons Mucha, whose color lithograph series such as the *Four Seasons* and *Four Times of Day* could be purchased framed as screens from the Prague furniture seller F. Topič.[6] Josef Hoffmann's screens were also commercially available, through A. Förster's luxury store in Vienna,[7] indicating just how popular folding screens were throughout Europe at the turn of the century.

For Bonnard, however, the decision to do this lithographic screen was not based solely on economic grounds, at least not in the usual sense. All of the Nabis—including Vuillard, Denis and Roussel as well as Bonnard—consciously strove to apply their talents to the creation of household objects. As Bonnard later stated, "Our generation sought to link art with life. At that time [the 1890s] I personally envisaged a popular art that was of everyday application: fans, furniture, screens...."[8] This position is strikingly similar to that taken by William Morris in England thirty years earlier, and probably derives at least in part from his influence. In contrast to Morris, however, Bonnard and the other Nabis never attempted to become decorators on the same scale or with the same fervor; this distinction may very well correspond to the different world views of the painter and the designer. Moreover, the Nabis' decorative projects were almost always the result of commissions from friends and supporters such as the Natanson brothers, and all centered around the Parisian art world.

All differences aside, Bonnard's lithographic screen is still best understood in this populist context. This approach remains with us today: Jim Dine, Marc Chagall, Jack Beal, and David Hockney have each done printed screens in limited editions.[9]

1. See "A Perfect Gem of Art," 72-76. We are indebted to the Museum of Modern Art, New York, for lending their version of the lithographic screen to the New Haven showing of the exhibition.

2. Claude Roger-Marx, *Bonnard: Lithographe* (Monte Carlo: Editions du Livre, 1952), no. 47.

3. *Studio* 9 (October 1896): 67-68.

4. *L'Estampe et l'affiche* (15 March 1897).

5. Roger-Marx, *Bonnard*, no. 47.

6. See Cat. 12.

7. See Cat. 13.

8. Quoted from John Rewald, *Pierre Bonnard* (exh. cat., New York, Museum of Modern Art, 1948), 14.

9. See Cat. 37, 39, and 40. The Marc Chagall screen has not been included in this exhibition.

6.1

7.1

7

EDOUARD VUILLARD

French, 1868-1940

FOUR-PANEL SCREEN, *ca. 1895*
Distemper on canvas (remounted as a wall painting). 120.0 x 170.0 (47^1/$_4$ x 66^{15}/$_{16}$)
Private Collection, London

Although Bonnard was a more prolific screenmaker than was Vuillard, it can be said that Vuillard enjoyed a far greater familiarity with this object type than any of his contemporaries. Vuillard lived amidst the trappings of his mother's dressmaking shop, where simply decorated folding screens were often used to provide privacy for those changing into and out of costumes in need of alteration. Many of the artist's early paintings focus on this environment and show such screens, as in the 1891 *L'Essayage*,[1] the 1897 *La Dame en bleu à l'enfant*[2] and *Le Déjeuner à Villeneuve sur Yonne*,[3] and the 1898 *Les Deux Fauteuils*.[4] Vuillard's first screen, in fact, shows a group of women at work in his mother's atelier (fig. 81). In addition, Vuillard owned at least one Japanese screen,[5] offering yet another source of inspiration.

In his second screen (7.1), Vuillard continued to concentrate on the domestic interior, but shifted from a genre subject to portraiture. Done around 1895, this four-panel screen was done for Stéphane Natanson and shows him and Misia (née Godebski) Natanson seated in a room with a dark and light tiled floor.[6] Seen from above with quickly receding perspective, the floor serves the same compositional purpose as in Vuillard's first screen: to establish the physical confines of the three-dimensional space. The composition overall is much more open, however, so much so in fact that Stéphane, shown in the left background in the second panel, and Misia, shown in the right foreground at the right edge of the fourth panel, appear isolated from each other even in their tranquil surroundings. In the slightly earlier painting *La Vie conjugale* of 1894, Vuillard depicted a couple in a domestic setting with a similar emphasis on the physical, and apparently psychological distance that separates the figures.

The important distinction between this wall painting and the screen, of course, is that the latter is a folding structure whose composition as a result becomes three-dimensionally dynamic. Four-panel screens such as this normally can be folded in one of two symmetrical positions, with the V-shape formed by the two central panels either protruding forward or receding back into space. The effect on the composition (7.2) is iconographically important here. Regardless of the position of screen, Stéphane, already shown in a three-quarter pose, is turned more emphatically towards Misia, who faces Stéphane. The round table between them, accorded great prominence by virtue of its size, by the large floral bouquet resting upon it, and by the highly skewed overhead perspective, places a further barrier between the figures. When one compares Alma-Tadema's approach to portraiture in his screen (Cat. 2), one realizes how little attention he paid and how much consideration Vuillard gave to the folding nature of a screen image.

As can be seen from the illustration of the screen's original state, Vuillard was also concerned with the decorative aspects of the screen and its frame. In his first screen (fig. 81), Vuillard divided the picture surface into three sections. The primary subjects are located in the two uppermost sections, while floral decorations graced the small horizontal panels at the bottom. A broad, multichannel wood frame surrounded the entire ensemble. In the Natanson screen, however, Vuillard made each picture field uniform in size, crowning the screen with a group of curve-cornered rectangles, one atop the other in the two central panels. Like Whistler, Bonnard, and Redon, Vuillard sought to organize every segment of the screen structure into a coherent whole.

1. Jacques Salomon and Claude Roger-Marx, *Edouard Vuillard. Xavier Roussel* (exh. cat., Munich, Haus der Kunst, 1968), cat. no. 15.

2. André Chastel, *Vuillard* (Paris: Librairie Floury, 1946), 40.

3. *E. Vuillard* (exh. cat., London, Arthur Tooth & Sons Ltd., 1969), cat. no. 4.

4. Salomon and Roger-Marx, *Vuillard. Roussel,* cat. no. 42. Each of the screens shown in this and the above mentioned paintings seem to have been covered with the densely patterned floral wallpapers favored by Vuillard and his friends.

5. A photograph of Bonnard and Thadée Natanson taken in Vuillard's studio shows them seated next to a multi-panel oriental screen. This screen also appears in the background of a later painting by Vuillard, *Femme nue devant un paravent japonais* done around 1912. For reproductions, see Thadée Natanson, *Le Bonnard que je pro-*

pose (Geneva: Pierre Cailler, 1951), Fig. 1; and Claude Roger-Marx, *Vuillard* (Paris: Arts et Métiers Graphiques, 1948) no. 47, respectively. Whether the screen was Japanese or Chinese is difficult to say, as it was almost certainly an object made for export. It is similar in subject and style to the Chinese screen acquired by the South Kensington Museum from the 1867 Paris Exposition Universelle (fig. 35).

6. Stéphane was a cousin of the Natanson brothers Alexandre, Alfred, and Thadée, the founders of the avant-garde journal *La Revue blanche.* Stéphane was an architect and designed a home for the Desmarais, who in 1892 commissioned Vuillard to do his first screen along with a series of decorative panels for their new residence. Misia, the sister of Cipa Godebski and like him a talented musician, was the wife of Thadée Natanson.

7.2 Reconstruction of screen with original frame, shown in two folded configurations.

8

MAURICE DENIS

French, 1870-1943

SCREEN WITH DOVES, *ca. 1902*
Oil on canvas. 162.0 x 204.0 (63¾ x 80⅜)
Private Collection, Paris

Maurice Denis' close artistic and personal ties to the Nabis probably influenced his decision to do his only folding screen. Bonnard, Vuillard, and Seguin in fact had each preceded him in this respect, and he surely knew their works in this genre. It is not surprising that Denis would have taken an interest in screens, as his enthusiasm for all kinds of decorative objects was seemingly unbounded. By the turn of the century, he had done mural and ceiling decorations; costumes, stage decorations, and programs for theater productions; painted papers, stained glass; painted ceramic tiles; and designs for mosaics; as well as paintings, prints, and drawings.[1] And as was so often the case in the last quarter of the nineteenth century, the art of Japan played at least a minor role in the artist's decision to do a screen. Late in 1890 Denis wrote to his friend Lugné-Poë that he had "received from Mme. T[rarieux] . . . a splendid Japanese folding screen."[2] Denis even went on to purchase several more oriental screens in 1908.[3]

The *Screen with Doves* (8.1) consists of four panels supported at each edge by small, blocklike feet. In the first panel there are marks indicating the location of the original frame, now lost. This frame no doubt covered those areas that presently appear as unpainted canvas. At the right a pair of doves feeds on the ground, while another pair drinks from a fountain located at the base of a two-columned portico. In the background, women pick flowers or stroll through the tree-filled garden. The foreground and background spaces are divided by a fence running diagonally from left to right and from back to front.[4] The fence shifts directions several times, first laterally and then forward, and each time except the first, these changes occur precisely at the breaks between the

screen panels. When the screen is folded (8.2), the fence's changing directions are accentuated further. In addition, the foreground emphasis on the potted flowers in the first panel and on the fountain in the third is offset by more distant middle-ground focal points in the second and fourth panels. A compositional balance is thereby struck across all four panels of this masterfully composed folding image.

8.2 *Screen with Doves,* folded position.

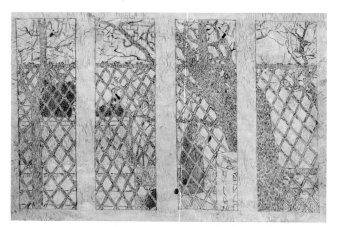

8.3 Ker-Xavier Roussel, French, 1867-1944, *Study for a Screen*, ca. 1895, ink on paper. Paris, Musées Nationaux, Musée d'Orsay.

Both the composition and the subject for Denis' screen derive from several related works. The strongly asymmetric arrangement of the scene certainly indicates an oriental influence, and similar fence motifs can occasionally be found in Japanese prints.[5] Ker-Xavier Roussel, another member of the Nabi group, also did a screen design (8.3)[6] around 1895 which makes use of such a fence, though not nearly in so dynamic a fashion. Denis himself had used the motif in his 1892 painting *April* and in his lithograph frontispiece for Edouard Dujardin's *Réponse de la*

bergère au berger from the same year.[7] Denis' *Garden in the Convent* of 1892 also shows a fenced garden similar to that in the screen; as the title of that painting implies, the locale depicted in the screen is almost certainly a convent in Saint Germain-en-Laye.[8] Even the motif of the young woman leaning against a tree appears in other works by the artist: an 1897 painting, *Figures in a Spring Landscape*;[9] and in reverse, an undated fan design of the mid-to late 1890s.[10]

Shortly after Denis' death, the artist's heirs accorded the screen a date of 1904.[11] A pastel and a crayon sketch for it have recently come to light, however, which suggest that the screen may in fact date from a few years earlier. The undated crayon sketch (8.4) shows the artist's first thoughts for the composition, with the fence consisting of vertical rather than diagonal components. The later pastel (8.5) includes all the essential elements for the final composition. Interestingly, the crayon sketch was done on the back of a letter written to the artist on 5 December 1895 from the Paris gallery L'Art Nouveau S. Bing.[12] Whether Denis was planning his screen at that date is difficult to say, as its composition is also closely related to at least two works dating from 1903. In that year Denis received a commission to do wall, ceiling, and stained glass decorations for the chapel of the Sacred Heart in the parish church of St. Marguerite in Le Vésinet, located some three kilometers east of Saint Germain.[13] A study for one of the windows for the chapel (8.6) shows clearly

8.4 Study for *Screen with Doves*, ca. 1902, crayon on paper. Saint Germain-en-Laye, Private Collection.

8.5 Study for *Screen with Doves*, ca. 1902, pastel on paper. Saint Germain-en-Laye, Private Collection.

8.1

that its fountain of life is nearly identical to the fountain in the screen's third panel. In proceeding from the window design to the screen, Denis compressed the composition slightly in this panel, removing a small section of fence. This change suggests strongly that he was working on both projects at the same time, with the screen probably dating from around 1902.

The only significant difference between the window and the third screen panel is that Denis omitted in the screen the chalice and host that appear in the center of the portico lintel. One should not presume, however, that the screen's subject is purely secular. What set Denis apart from his avant-garde Nabi contemporaries was his lifelong love of and devotion to religious painting. For the most part he considered himself a Christian, that is Catholic, artist. The title of the chapel window, whose design is so closely related to the screen's third panel is *Ego flos campi*, which refers to a passage in the Song of Solomon (2.12-13):

> *The flowers appear on the earth,*
> *the time of singing has come,*
> *and the voice of the turtledove*
> *is heard in our land.*
> *The fig tree puts forth its figs,*
> *and the vines are in blossom;*
> *they give forth fragrance.*
> *Arise, my love, my fair one,*
> *and come away.*

The Song of Solomon, apocryphally attributed to the Hebraic king, is a book whose lyrical, sensuous poetry is thought to have been read or sung at weddings. Although the book has no overt religious content, its mystical language is assumed to be an allegory of the love of Christ for his bride. The second chapter is a dialogue between lovers, and the passages to which Denis' windows refer describe the time in spring when the lover comes to summon his bride.

The presence of the doves, the fountain, and the enclosed garden, then, would seem to have a christological significance: the doves as symbols of Christ; the fountain and the tree from which the water springs as symbols of everlasting life provided by his sacrifice; and the enclosed abundant garden as simultaneous symbols for the purity of Christ's brides who stand in it, and for the fruits offered by his love. It is no accident that Denis also used a

8.6 Study for *Ego flos campi* window, ca. 1903, gouache on paper. Saint Germain-en-Laye, Musée du Prieuré.

variant of the fence and fountain motif in an illustration in the 1903 Vollard edition of *L'Imitation de Jesus-Christ;* there the illustration accompanies the fourth chapter, which is dedicated to the faithful souls who receive communion and therefore God's grace regularly.[14]

Contemporary garb and setting were often used by Denis in his religious pictures, and the Christian content of the screen is entirely consistent with the artist's deeply felt faith. It is no surprise, either, that the mystical and highly figurative nature of the Song of Solomon would have appealed to Denis, who matured as an artist when the literary and pictorial symbolist movements took hold in France at the end of the nineteenth century. The *Screen with Doves* therefore uniquely combines the stylistic conventions of the symbolist movement with more traditional Christian iconography.

1. See *Musée du Prieuré. Symbolistes et Nabis. Maurice Denis et son temps* (Saint Germain-en-Laye: Musée Départmental du Prieuré, n.d.), cat. nos. 1-326, for a listing of these various projects.

2. Lugné-Poë, *La Parade: Le Sot du Tremplin, souvenirs et impressions de théâtre* (Paris: Librairie Gallimard, 1931), 266.

3. Reported to the author in a letter from Dominique Denis, dated 18 March 1983. I am deeply indebted to him for providing continuous assistance in all phases of my research on his father's screen.

4. This type of fence can be seen in the background of Denis' 1897 painting *Dessert in the Garden*, which shows the artist and his first wife Marthe in the garden of their Villa Montrouge in Fourqueux where they lived after their marriage in 1893. For an illustration, see Maurice Denis (exh. cat., Paris, Orangerie des Tuilleries, 1970), cat. no. 103.

5. See Siegfried Wichmann, *Japonismus: Ostasien-Europa, Begegnungen in der Kunst des 19. und 20. Jahrhunderts* (Herrsching: Schuler Verlag, 1980), 237, no. 627.

6. Roussel, who like Denis exhibited frequently with the Nabis, did a number of screen designs, none of which is known to have been executed. My thanks to Antoine Salomon for this information.

7. For illustrations see *Musée du Prieuré,* cat. no. 23; and Pierre Cailler, *Catalogue raisonné de l'oeuvre gravé et lithographié de Maurice Denis* (Geneva: Editions Pierre Cailler, 1968), no. 6.

8. The painting is in the collection of Dominique Denis, who identified the setting as this convent in his letter to the author of 18 March 1983.

9. Now in the Hermitage, Leningrad.

10. *Musée du Prieuré,* cat. no. 66.

11. Reported in M. Denis' March 1983 letter; see also *Maurice Denis* (exh. cat., Tokyo, National Museum of Western Art, 1981), cat. no. 60; and Paris, *Maurice Denis,* where the screen is dated 1904.

12. See "A Perfect Gem of Art," 85.

13. Denis' first commission for this church was in 1901, when he did decorations for the adjoining chapel of the Virgin. See *Musée du Prieuré,* cat. nos. 197-321, for a list of these decorations and related studies.

14. In an adjacent window with the title *Et lilium convallium,* also referring to a nearby passage in the Song of Solomon, Denis reversed the fountain motif. See *Musée du Prieuré,* cat. nos. 279-280.

9.1

154 | *The Folding Image*

9

PAUL KLEE

Swiss, 1879-1940

FIVE-PANEL SCREEN (AARE RIVER LANDSCAPE), *1900*
Oil on canvas with gilded wood frame. 144.0 x 240.0 ($567/16 x 94^{1}/2$)
Collection of Felix Klee, Bern

Only recently has Paul Klee's early work begun to attract serious scholarly attention.[1] A gifted and precocious draftsman who made his first drawings at the age of four, Klee was signing and dating his accomplished landscape drawings and caricatures, compiling them in orderly notebooks, by the age of thirteen. He was also a talented violinist whose profound love for and sensitivity toward music very nearly swayed him from his decision to become an artist. Once having made that decision, Klee traveled to Munich in October 1898 with hopes of entering the academy there. Refused admittance because of his inexperience in figure drawing, he entered Heinrich Knirr's private drawing school to improve his skills. There Klee directed his energies not only to figure drawing, but also to painting and etching. An 1899 entry in his diary noted his progress: "Painting was difficult, but I soon attained a certain manual dexterity and brought off bold studies."[2] In April 1900 his growing abilities warranted his acceptance to Franz Stuck's fall class at the Munich Academy, and Klee was certain of his career decision: "The conviction that painting is the right profession grows stronger and stronger in me."[3]

Sometime after his return to Bern in May 1900, Klee received a commission from Frau Wachter, a friend of his mother, to do a painted folding screen.[4] The screen (9.1) consists of five panels (now unhinged) whose subjects are scenes of the Aare River wending its way through the rising hills near Bern.[5] The choice of subject was surely to Klee's liking; he speaks often in his diary of outings into the hills around Bern, where he sought relaxation and solitude. Broadly painted in horizontal bands of tans, browns, blues, and greens, the screen is stylistically reminiscent of works by Dachau school painters such as

Ludwig Dill and Walter Leistikow.[6] The most obvious characteristic of the screen is that the landscape is not continuous, but shows instead five separate though related views of the Aare River valley. Even more peculiar at first glance is that the second and fourth panels are mirror images of each other. By repeating the composition in these two panels, Klee may have wished to give a limited decorative unity to the overall composition, especially when folded as seen here (9.2). Despite the apparently discordant nature of the screen as a whole, however, it should not be dismissed as the work of a not yet mature artist. Instead, one must seek to understand the reasons for Klee's conscious choice to depict a familiar landscape in this unorthodox fashion.

From his time in Munich, Klee would have had ample opportunities to see various screens by the increasingly popular Jugendstil artists.[7] Yet his own screen clearly denies any links to the linear or sculptural stylizations of this movement. The Munich painter Carl Spitzweg did several vertical format landscape paintings, dating from as early as the mid-1860s, which may have provided a model for the screen panels;[8] by the time Klee arrived in Munich, the late Spitzweg had established a formidable reputation. Klee also probably knew the tall format landscape illustrations which appeared frequently in the pages of *Jugend*, one of the most popular of Munich's turn-of-the-century periodicals. One such illustration by Joseph Damberger (9.3), with its motif of a winding river making its way through a gentle valley complete with high horizon line as in the screen panels, is so close to Klee's conception as to imply a direct influence.[9]

Klee mentioned the screen in a 2 September 1900 letter to his future wife Lily Stumpf: "I am writing letters only

9.2 *Aare River Landscape*, maquette showing screen in folded position.

not to appear unjust, because I have found myself for some time in a fermenting and consuming situation, thus a very pleasurable activity. Notwithstanding, we want to wait and see what kind of vintage 1900 will be, instead of complaining beforehand. Presently I am in a quandary: creative activity in place of indigestible folding screens — five life-sized landscape panels — and postcards with landscape views. And thus I am looking forward excitedly to Munich where the solution of several other problems that do not please me either may very well await me." [10] Klee's language is both highly colloquial and personally expressive here, making translation difficult. It is clear from his choice of words, however, that he saw himself in a situation where his own creative abilities were maturing, like grapes on the vine at harvest time. He emphasizes this idea by comparing his curiosity about the end result of his work with what kind of wine the 1900 vintage will be. His description of the screen as indigestible is also to be understood in this context: it was not yet complete in the sense that a wine is not drinkable until it ferments and matures. It seems, too, that Klee was generally pleased with his progress, though it was by no means without difficulty.

Devoid of figures or any other anecdotal elements, the screen's silent landscapes seem designed to have a disquieting effect. The expressively contoured shapes within them and the separateness of the panel compositions emphasize this sense of loneliness. The viewer is thus forced to reevaluate his relationship with each scene.

9.3 Joseph Damberger, German, 1867-1951, *Landscape*, 1897, illustrated in *Jugend*, 1897, no. 22.

An entry in Klee's diary written in autumn 1900, when the screen was nearly or just finished, may offer a further clue to understanding the composition: "The comparison of my soul with the various moods of the countryside frequently returns as a motif. My poetic-personal idea of landscape lies at the root of this."[11] Thus the juxtaposition of the brighter, warmer colors of the second panel with the darker, more somber hues of the mirror-image fourth panel can be understood. Klee opted for a symbolic presentation of his emotional state as conveyed by depictions of the familiar Aare River valley. By intentionally subverting the potentially unifying role of a continuous composition, he strangely anticipated a similar approach chosen by Jim Dine in his 1968 *Landscape Screen*.[12] Finally, Klee's emphasis on discontinuity where continuity is most expected led to a fractionalization of the image's formal elements, a concept which would later serve the artist in his experiments with Cubism.[13]

1. See *Paul Klee: Das Frühwerk 1883-1922* (exh. cat., Munich, Lenbachhaus, 1980).

2. *The Diaries of Paul Klee* (Berkeley: University of California Press, 1964), no. 20.

3. *Diaries*, no. 93. By the end of 1899 Klee had done at least 268 drawings. In the next year, however, he did hardly any, suggesting further his dedication to painting. See Jurgen Glaesmer, *Paul Klee: Handzeichnung I. Kindheit bis 1920* (Bern: Kunstmuseum Bern, 1973), 1-102, for the early drawings.

4. Ironically, Klee's mother liked the screen so much that she kept it for herself. It has remained in the family's possession. See Marcel Franciscono, "Paul Klee um die Jahrhundertwende," in *Paul Klee: Das Frühwerk 1883-1922*, 41-47 and cat. no. 32. The artist's son Felix Klee confirmed the screen's history during an interview in Bern in June 1981. According to him, there are no photographs which show the screen's intended environment, making it impossible to assess whether there were any factors which could have affected its ultimate appearance. No known studies exist for the screen, which is no longer in its original frames.

5. The locale seems to be somewhere along the Aare north or northwest of Bern. Klee was born in Münchenbuchsee, several kilometers north of the city. By 1886, when Klee started school, the family had moved to the Länggasse in Bern.

6. Franciscono, "Paul Klee," 41.

7. In 1899 Henri Van de Velde's wood and glass screen (fig. 100) was shown at the Munich Secession exhibition at the famous Munich Glaspalast. See *Deutsche Kunst und Dekoration* 5 (October 1899-March 1900): 17. Berhard Pankok, Bruno Paul, Hermann Obrist, Charles Rennie Mackintosh, and Louis Comfort Tiffany, all of whom are known to have done screens, exhibited at this important exhibition of modern decorative arts. See *Münchner Secession und ihre Galerie* (exh. cat., Munich, Stadtmuseum, 1975), 23-24. In 1900 the tenth annual arts and crafts exhibition took place at the Glaspalast; this display was a preview of those objects to be sent to the forthcoming Exposition Universelle in Paris later that year. In the Munich show was Otto and Anna Ubbelohde's fabric and wood screen (fig. 98). Klee very likely could have known these or other Jugendstil screens.

8. See also Jens Christian Jensen, *Carl Spitzweg* (Cologne: Verlag M. Dumont, 1971), plate 15; Erich Höhne, *Carl Spitzweg* (Leipzig: E. A. Seemann Buch- und Kunstverlag, 1972), ills. 84, 85, 93, and 95; and Siegfried Wichmann, *Meister, Schüler, Themen: Münchener Landschaftsmalerei im 19. Jahrhundert* (Herrsching: Schuler Verlags, 1981), "Das steile Hochformat als Einblick in die Weite."

9. Damberger (1867-1951) was also a member of the Munich Secession. See Michael Weisser, *Im Stil der "Jugend"* (Frankfurt: Verlag Dieter Fricke GmbH, 1979), 214, ill. 244. Franciscono's contention that "Klee took over a somewhat more current Jugendstil scheme in which autonomous figures or decorative fields are placed next to each other, as in Asian branch and flower screens," suggested in his comparative illustration "Paul Klee," is not convincing.

10. *Paul Klee, Briefe an die Familie 1893-1940*, ed. Felix Klee (Cologne: Dumont Buchverlag, 1979), 95-96. The text of the letter is as follows: "Ich schreibe Briefe, nur um nicht ungerecht zu scheinen, weil ich mich seit geraumer Zeit in einem gährenden und verarbeitenden Zustande befinde, also eine sehr vergnügte Hauptbeschäftigung habe. Doch wollen wir abwarten, was der 1900-er für eine Sorte wird, anstatt zum Voraus zu jammern. Vorläufig tut mir not: künstlerische Arbeit an Stelle unverdaulicher spanischer Wände – fünf Blatt Landschaften lebensgross – und Ansichtspostkarten. Und so freue ich mich rasend auf München, wo meiner die Erlösung von verschiedenem Anderen, was mich auch nicht freut, harren dürfte." My thanks to Anne-Marie Logan of the Yale Center for British Art for help in translating this letter. It is interesting to note that one of the two German words meaning folding screen, *spanische Wände*, literally means "Spanish walls," perhaps referring to the fact that many earlier western folding screens were made of Spanish leather. The other German term, *Wandschirm*, meaning "screen wall" or "protector wall" is much closer to the Japanese word *byobu*, which means "protection against the wind."

11. *Diaries*, no. 109. See also nos. 56 and 72; both indicate the powerful influence Klee's surroundings had on him, even from an early age.

12. See Cat. 37.

13. Franciscono, "Paul Klee," 44.

10.1

THOMAS WILMER DEWING

American, 1851-1938

MORNING GLORIES, *1900*
Oil on canvas on a multilayered panel with gilded wood and gesso frame
189.2 x 195.6 (74¹/₂ x 77)
Museum of Art, Carnegie Institute, Pittsburgh
Museum Purchase: Gift of the Sarah Mellon Scaife Family, 1973

Along with Albert Pinkham Ryder, Thomas Dewing was one of the few major American artists to have experimented with the screen format in the last half of the nineteenth century. Between 1896 and 1900 Dewing did at least three two-panel and four four-panel screens,[1] making him America's most prolific screenmaker of the period. *Morning Glories* (10.1) and its companion *Cherry Blossoms* were the second of two pairs of screens commissioned by the Detroit businessman Colonel Frank Hecker, a business partner and friend of Charles Freer, who had already commissioned a pair of two-panel screens from the artist in 1896. In 1897/1898 Hecker received the first pair of screens from Dewing, *Classical Figures* and its unnamed, now lost pendant. Two years later Dewing finished *Morning Glories* and its now lost companion *Cherry Blossoms*. Both pairs of screens were intended for the drawing room of Hecker's French Renaissance style mansion, and their nearly identical frames were almost certainly designed by the architect Stanford White.[2] White's frames correspond closely, in fact, to the columns in Hecker's drawing room (10.2).[3]

The two pairs of screens have in common the classically inspired female figures that dominate much of Dewing's art. The figures in the screens were derived from fourth and third-century B.C. Greek terra cotta Tanagra figurines, which Dewing could have known from a number of sources.[4] Their graceful proportions, rhythmic lines, and elegant silhouettes were all esthetic attributes that the late Victorian public believed to be embodiments of the Greek's inner spiritual state and harmony of body and mind. To these attributes Dewing

added those of his ideal of the modern woman: refined and delicate in her idyllic landscape setting, she acts as a spiritual and artistic mediator between nature and human intellect.[5]

10.2 Drawing room, Frank Hecker residence, Detroit, ca. 1891. Photograph, Burton Historical Collection, Detroit Public Library.

Because the pendants to both the *Classical Figures* and *Morning Glories* have disappeared, it is difficult to know the intended compositional relationships between the figures, or if there may have been any optimal folded positions for the screens. A few observations can be made, however. In *Morning Glories* not only did Dewing abandon the darker tonalities of his earlier screens, but he also chose to present a far more defined landscape background. The clarity of the blooming morning glories contrasts sharply with the diaphanously rendered figures and with the hazy, washlike treatment of the grass beneath them. In effect, Dewing emphasized the visual importance of the decorative background in a reversal of the traditional figure-ground relationship.[6] In addition, one senses that the figures' three-dimensionality results primarily from their juxtaposition with this flat background rather than from any attempt to render them in a sculptural manner—despite the figures' evolution from the small-scale Tanagra sculptures.[7]

Dewing's familiarity with Japanese screens in Freer's collections led the artist to this particular treatment. In 1897 Freer purchased this pair of Rimpa school, gold-ground screens (10.3). The emphatic patterning of boldy colored flowers and foliage visible in these screens appealed to most late nineteenth century collectors of oriental art, and apparently to Dewing as well: the slightly diagonal disposition of flowers and foliage in the background and foreground of these Japanese screens is also found in the *Morning Glories* screen. Dewing separated the foreground and background more distinctly, and of course included figures in his composition, but the conceptual similarities between the Japanese screens and Dewing's are undeniable. Even the small, meandering stream in the former has its parallel in Dewing's screen, in

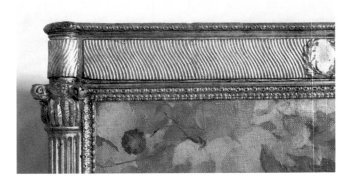

10.4 Detail showing Stanford White frame.

the form of a blossoming morning glory branch which drifts gently across the surface.

The role of Stanford White's frame is crucial in understanding the impact of Dewing's screen. The frame consists of two fluted columns with Corinthian capitals, which support an entablature (10.4) scored with diagonally curved lines emanating in opposite directions from a laurel wreath at the center of each panel. The screen is supported at the bottom by four acanthus-covered ball feet. Within these external framing elements is a simple molding, followed by a more complex foliated molding and beading. The verso has the same framing elements surrounding plain gold leaf, which covers the entire central field of the panels. What is unusual is that the frame is entirely external in its function: there are no framing elements between the panels to disrupt the coherence of the painted images, and all of Dewing's screens are framed in this way. The distinctly architectural quality of the screen virtually encapsulates the paintings within;

10.3 *Pair of Six Panel Screens*, Japanese, 18th-19th century, Rimpa school, watercolor and gold on paper, 124.8 x 579.4 (49⅛ x 228⅛). Washington, Freer Gallery of Art.

even the way in which the ball feet raise the screen from the floor tends to emphasize the precious nature of what is contained within the frame.

White's classically inspired frame accommodates itself perfectly to Dewing's own Tanagra classicisms, and restrained elegance is the dominant result of their collaborative effort. Though Dewing's *Morning Glories* appears esthetically distant from the contemporary curvilinear arabesques of European art nouveau, it nevertheless demonstrates similar concerns for the total integration of the image within its frame, and, more importantly, of the screen within a larger decorative ensemble.

1. Kathleen Pyne's excellent article "*Classical Figures,* A Folding Screen by Thomas Dewing," *Bulletin of the Detroit Institute of Arts* 59, (Spring 1981): 4-15, provided much of the factual information for this entry. Pyne was unaware, however, of the existence of another Dewing screen entitled *Music and Dance.* The two panels of this screen have been removed from their original frames and separated; *Music* is now in the Brooklyn Museum (75.206), and *Dance* is in the Cleveland Museum of Art (40.372). For an illustration of the screen as it originally appeared, see the 8 February 1923 American Art Galleries' *Illustrated Catalogue* from the sale of N. E. Montross' collection, no. 63. Montross was Dewing's dealer.

2. Pyne, "Dewing," 10, 13 and note 41. The frame for the Detroit screen is slightly different from the Carnegie's in the detailing of the pediment, the column bases, the ball feet, and other minor features.

3. The similarity between the screen frames' columns and those in the drawing room can also be explained by the fact that the architect for Hecker's home, Louis Kamper, studied with Stanford White from 1880 to 1888.

4. Hecker himself collected Tanagra figures, one of which is actually visible on the mantelpiece of the drawing room. Whistler, whom Dewing once visited, also owned them. In addition, major museums in London, Paris, Berlin, and Boston all collected Tanagra figures in the late 1880s and early 1890s. See Pyne, "Dewing," 10. They might also have been the sources for the female figures in a four-panel screen painted by the English artist, Amy Sawyer, illustrated in *Studio* 2 (1894): 25.

5. Pyne, "Dewing," 6.

6. The regularized, almost stencil-like leaf patterns are painted in a low impasto, in contrast to the relatively unmodulated surface treatment accorded the figures and foreground. In this respect *Morning Glories* recalls more closely Dewing's first screen, *Four Sylvan Sounds,* done for Charles Freer in 1896 (fig. 115).

7. Pyne's claim that the Tanagra figures were important for their spiritual and psychological implications is consequently strengthened.

There is an additional structural difference between the two screens. *Classical Figures* is painted screens. *Classical Figures* is painted on canvas mounted on panel, as is *Morning Glories,* but the former's panel is a single piece of wood which has warped considerably over the years. Both the *Morning Glories* and *Music and Dance* screens, however, were painted on canvas on a multilayered panel whose construction equalized to a large degree the pushing and pulling forces caused by expanding and contracting wood fibers. I am grateful to William Talbot and the late Del Spurlock at the Cleveland Museum of Art for their assistance in examining their Dewing *Dance* panel.

11.1

II

LOUIS COMFORT TIFFANY

American, 1848-1933

THREE-PANEL SCREEN, *ca. 1900*
Leaded opalescent glass in a bronze frame. 178.7 x 225.6 (703/8 x 88¹³/16)
Lillian Nassau Ltd., New York

Tiffany Studios in New York was responsible for several types of colored glass screens, all of which were made around the turn of the century. They produced small-scale tea or table screens in a number of designs,[1] as well as single-panel firescreens.[2] Among the most famous of Tiffany's works was the stationary glass screen which once adorned the entrance hall of the White House, done in 1881-1882 during the presidency of Chester Arthur.[3] Certainly the most adventurous of Tiffany's screens was this three-panel folding screen (11.1), the only known example of the artist's work in this particular genre.

Tiffany's interest in screens probably derived from both oriental and western sources. Like so many of his screenmaking contemporaries, Tiffany was fascinated with Japanese art, and presumably with Japanese screens: at least two are known to have been in the artist's Oyster Bay mansion, Laurelton Hall.[4] In addition, Tiffany may have known of other oriental screens through his friend and supporter, Samuel Bing, who sold all kinds of Japanese objects through his Paris gallery. Tiffany's involvement in producing stained glass windows for Bing from designs by Bonnard, Vuillard, Roussel, and others may also have provided him with the chance to see folding screens done by these Nabi painters.

Until very recently, this particular three-panel screen was known only from a reproduction thought to have been taken from a Tiffany Studios brochure dating from around 1902.[5] The screen was almost certainly created for the 1900 Exposition Universelle in Paris,[6] and its sudden emergence from a private collection in upstate New York offers the opportunity for a fuller understanding of the artist's screenmaking activities. It consists of three arch-topped stained glass windows mounted in a

bronze frame. Each window is further subdivided by the frame into a triptychlike configuration. Below the windows is a translucent green glass "base" which makes the screen appear as if it were a tripartite window mounted over a marble parapet. This green glass is also broken by the bronze frame into a symmetric grid of squares set at the corners of a central rectangle.

Each of the windows has its own subject. In the first is a *Clematis* vine with purple flowers, most of which are clumped together at the upper left corner. The *Clematis* spreads into the next panel, where five yellow-orange gourds hang down from their vines. Tiffany may have borrowed the gourd subject from a window he executed after a design by the English artist Frank Brangwyn in 1899,[7] though Tiffany's lifelong interest in botany provided a constant source of material for his designs. The third panel shows bunches of ripening grapes that range in color from deep purple to pale green, indicating different stages of maturity. Tiffany's considerable technical skill is also evident in the rendering of these bunches: each cluster of grapes is palpably three-dimensional, extending beyond the window's background plane. The artist also sought to link the three panels compositionally by allowing elements from one window to carry into the next.

Stained glass is indeed an unusual material for a folding screen, one of whose functions was ostensibly to offer privacy in a domestic interior. The translucent colored glass screen could allow daylight to pass through it without necessarily revealing what might be taking place beyond it. Because the screen had to be placed between the viewer and a light source for these color effects to be visible, it is likely that the screen was intended to be used in a large public space in a house, such as a dining room or living room. Though the screen's format and framing elements are somewhat awkward in comparison to most other turn-of-the-century examples, the brilliant handling of materials makes it one of the more spectacular achievements in this period.[8]

1. See "A Perfect Gem of Art," 108.

2. For an illustration see Alastair Duncan, *Tiffany at Auction* (New York: Rizzoli International Publications, Inc., 1981), no. 997.

3. Illustrated in Robert Koch, *Louis C. Tiffany, Rebel in Glass* (New York: Crown Publishers, 1982), 45; see also discussions on pages 21-22. The screen was destroyed at the request of President Theodore Roosevelt when the White House was renovated in 1902 by McKim, Mead & White.

4. One is reproduced in Koch, *Louis C. Tiffany*, 196; and another, in Alastair Duncan, *Tiffany Windows* (New York: Simon and Schuster, 1980), 161.

5. Reported by Robert Koch in a conversation in April 1981. The screen is also reproduced from this brochure illustration in Koch's *Louis C. Tiffany's Glass-Bronzes-Lamps* (New York: Crown Publishers, Inc., 1971), 36, Fig. 27, 36; and in Duncan, *Tiffany Windows*, 81.

6. According to Duncan, the screen was illustrated in an English-language article about the Tiffany exhibits at the 1900 Exposition Universelle in Paris. The article is in a scrapbook kept by Tiffany Studios, and it also shows one window whose present whereabouts is known and a second window whose location has never been traced. The scrapbook is now in private hands. My thanks to Alastair Duncan for providing this information.

7. Entitled *Girl Picking Gourds*, the window was exhibited at the Grafton Galleries in London in 1899. Tiffany later installed it in the living room of Laurelton Hall. It is reproduced in color in Koch, *Rebel in Glass*, iii, and can be seen in a photograph of Laurelton Hall in Duncan, *Tiffany Windows*, 161.

8. At least one American glass screen is known to have survived, although it is very modest by comparison to Tiffany's; see "A Perfect Gem of Art," 100-101 and fig. 113. Stained glass screens seem to have been only slightly more common in Europe, with examples from the circle of Burne-Jones (see fig. 63); by Georg Hagnauer (seen in the Galerie Mostini, Paris, in July 1982); by Huber-Feldkirch (in Munich's Stadtmuseum, accession number 62/121); and by Josef Maria Olbrich (see "A Perfect Gem of Art," note 163. All of these screens date from ca. 1885-1900. Whether there were more screens in this material is difficult to say, but the obvious fragility of glass suggests there were. It is no small miracle that the Tiffany screen itself survived because its considerable weight and size rest precariously on six small casters.

12

ALFONS MUCHA
Czechoslovakian, 1860-1944

and

JOSEF ROUS
Czechoslovakian, 1872-1942

FOUR TIMES OF DAY, *ca. 1900*
Color lithographs with painted and gilded wood frame. 189.0 x 190.0 (74 3/8 x 76 3/4)
Městské Museum, Žamberk, Czechoslovakia

Alfons Mucha, in his avowed agreement with the esthetic and to a lesser degree the social tenets of William Morris, was inclined even more than his French contemporaries to embark upon decorative projects. His early training also prepared him for works of this type. He first did stage sets for a firm in Vienna, and his first commission was to do a number of wall decorations for Count Khuen-Belasi's country estate, Castle Emmahof, near Hrušovany, Moravia. This commission occupied Mucha through 1888, by which time the artist had had several lengthy stays in Paris. He turned his energies next to book and journal illustration, and soon after did his first lithographs with Lemercier et Cie in Paris. He then joined forces with the lithographic printer Champenois, whose business acumen blended well with Mucha's growing artistic skills. It was ultimately through their prints and posters that Mucha established his reputation.

Mucha's experiments with the screen format began sometime between 1885 and 1888, when he made a three-panel painted screen (12.1)[1] as part of the decorations for Count Khuen-Belasi. In its central panel, Pan plays his pipes for a young female companion in a tropical, forestlike setting. In the first panel is a young, laurel-wreathed figure raising a cup. The figure stands well behind and slightly above a large and prominent still life of grapes, melons, and gourds. In the third panel, two winged, Cupid-like creatures are situated in the midst of a large, floral still life. Although the subject matter of the

screen seems rather uninspired compared to Mucha's later works, the interest in flora and fauna and in the idealized female figure within an idyllic outdoor setting are elements that reappear in his works throughout his

12.1 *Three-Panel Screen*, 1888, oil on canvas, 185.0 x 192.0 (72³/4 x 75⁹/16). Brno, Moravska Galerie.

12.2 *Four Seasons*, 1896, lithograph, 43.0 x 61.0 (16¾ x 24). Prague, Collection of Jiří Mucha.

12.3 Photograph of the artist's studio with a screen in the background, ca. 1897. In Mucha et al., *Alphonse Mucha: Posters and Photographs*, 1971.

career. The screen shape itself departs in each panel from the usual rectangular format: the central panel has a broad arched top, and the bottoms of each of the two side panels take on an inverted pointed arch shape. The frame is rather somber and has a base reminiscent of church altarpieces.

All of Mucha's other experiments with the screen format were confined to lithography. In the small *Four Seasons* of 1896, one can trace the artist's continuing interest in the genre (12.2). It was done in the form of a four-panel folding screen, with each season depicted separately in a single "panel," complete with a decorative border that imitates an actual frame.[2] This format was the one he followed in producing a number of folding screens in the next several years. A photograph of Mucha's studio taken in 1897 (12.3) shows a model standing in front of a three-panel screen, which the artist's son remembers as "only a wooden frame covered with greenish satin velvet, and three posters—*Gismonda*, *La Dame aux camélias*, and *La Trappistine* [which] were fixed with golden brades onto it, mounted on canvas."[3] These early efforts culminated in a full-size screen with the *Four Seasons* lithographs, shown at the 1897 Salon des Cents in Paris and the first of Mucha's commercially produced folding screens.[4] Shortly thereafter, Mucha contracted with the furniture firm of F. Topič in Prague to do two different screens: an elaborately framed three-panel version, and a more simply framed four-panel version (12.4).[5] This latter screen is shown in the advertisement with the 1899 lithographic series, the *Four Times of Day*, and has survived in at least four examples.[6]

The success of these commercially produced screens probably led to the unique example now in the Městské Museum (12.5). It was commissioned by Jarka Charfreitag, who owned a beer hall in the small Bohemian town of Žamberk. Charfreitag asked his friend Josef Rous, a wood sculptor, to make the ornate gilded, painted, and carved frame. After taking over his father's woodcarving shop in 1894, Rous gained a substantial local reputation as a carver of altars, frames, chandeliers, and furniture; in 1898 he received a medal from the Prague Museum of Art and Industry for one of his carved frames.[7] Although Mucha and Topič's collaborative efforts certainly inspired Charfreitag's commission, Mucha himself seems not to have been involved in it.

Rous' screen frame, however, relates closely to the decorative border motifs in the *Four Times of Day* litho-

12.5

graphs. The floral patterns at the top of the prints correspond to the friezelike band of lotus blossoms in the frame just above; and the curvilinear swirls in the lithographs' lower borders are echoed both in the spandrels of the ogival arch and in the splayed, tripartite legs which support the screen. Even the regular, symmetrically arranged tendrils in the topmost portion of the frame are at least generically similar to the linear border designs within the lithographs. The frame still bears a closer resemblance to Rous' native Bohemian carving tradition that to the curvilinear stylizations of Parisian art nouveau which one normally associates with Mucha. Their different stylistic approaches are especially evident when one compares Rous' frame with the one envisioned by Mucha in his 1896 *Four Seasons* lithograph.

The separate but related efforts of Mucha and Rous resulted in a screen whose impact derives primarily from the former's bold, colorful lithographic images. In the *Four Times of Day* screen, there is both an implied temporal unity between the panels created by the subject; and a compositional unity from the repetitive decorative patterns in the lithographs. Moreover, Rous' frame design has its own staggered organizational rhythms which lend a certain vitality to the screen's overall appearance. At the top, the floral patterns[8] in the two left panels are matched by those in the two right panels, while at the bottom the pointed arch and splayed legs are repeated in each panel. The band of tulips running across the entire width of the screen near the top seems to be an attempt to link the four panels horizontally. The two-dimensional lithographic images, then, have been extended into the third dimension by Rous' carved frame, wedding frame and image in a vitally new way.

12.4 *The Adornment of the Home*, ca. 1900, F. Topič, publisher.

1. The screen is now in the Moravská Galerie, Brno. Count Khuen-Belasi discovered Mucha's talent, and sent him to study in Munich and Paris. See also Brian Reade, *Art Nouveau and Alphonse Mucha* (London: Her Majesty's Stationery Office, 1967), 6-12, for a discussion of the artist's early career.

2. According to the artist's son Jiří Mucha, this lithograph was "used probably for display in shop-windows." Letter to the author, 20 September 1982. I am deeply indebted to Jiří Mucha for providing so much information essential to this study of the artist's screenmaking activities.

3. Letter to the author, 2 April 1982. The posters have since been removed from the screen because of their deteriorating condition, and they remain in Jiří Mucha's collection.

4. See *La Plume. Littéraire, Artistique et Sociale. Numéro Consacré à Alphonse Mucha*, no. 197 (1 July 1897), no. 92: "Les Saisons, paravent, appartient à Madame Ferniot." On page 436 of the same issue of *La Plume*, Charles Chincholle speaks glowingly of Mucha's *panneaux decoratifs*: "On en fait pour salons, pour salles à manger, pour boudoirs, pour salles de billieards, pour paravents, etc, et on a bien raison. C'est exquis." Chincholle's article, "Les Panneaux de Mucha," appeared originally in the 10 February 1897 issue of *L'Estampe et l'affiche*.

5. The principal distributor of these screens in Prague was the publisher F. Topič, Ferdinandova trida 9, now the location of the Writer's Union publishing house. The title of the undated catalogue is *The Adornment of the Home*. The text reads: "Screens (paravents) composed of Mucha's pictures. Admirable by their subject matter as much as by their color, the charming and sympathetic compositions, mainly *The Four Times of Day, The Flower, The Pen,* and *Reverie* are perfectly suited for use on modern screens (paravents) which are a welcome decoration of every room. These screens are manufactured from stained wood, dark red in color (like mahogany); we can provide these also in other colors or patterns. The price of a threefold screen of stained dark red wood with carvings (the width of the side panels being 33 cm., of the central 53, height 117 cm.) . . . 100K. The price of a fourfold screen of the same color and work, 154 cm. high (center), 143 cm. (sides), 42 cm. width of each panel . . . 125K." My thanks to Hana Demetz of the Slavic Language and Literature Department, Yale University, for providing this translation.

6. Jiří Mucha owns an example of the four-panel screen; one was in the Wuehre 9-Art Deco gallery in Zürich as of July 1982; two other four-panel versions are in private collections in Czechoslovakia, and another is in a private collection in Italy. The three-panel version seems not to have survived. A unusual three-panel screen with Mucha's large-scale *Four Seasons* prints is in a private collection in Kansas City. This last version is unusual because the personifications of Spring, Summer, and Fall are printed on the recto, with that of Winter printed on the central panel of the verso. In addition, the images are printed on fabric. Although Mucha is known to have printed his lithographs on both paper and satin, the material on which these last screen images appear is yet a different, less smooth fabric.

7. See Jaromir Neumann, *Český Sochař. František Rous* (Žamberk: Městské Museum, n.d.), 12 and 28.

8. For the most part the flowers in the lithographs and in the screen frame are identifiable. From left to right, the flowers in the lithographs are: popaver, a field or garden poppy; daisy; daisy or poppy (the flowers in the second and third panels are both of the genus *Chrysanthemum*, but the species is difficult to identify); and popaver. In the upper portion of the screen frame, above the band of lotus blossoms, are daylilies; a daisylike species of chrysanthemum; camellia; and again popaver. My thanks to James E. Rodman, associate professor of Biology and curator of the Herbarium, Peabody Museum, Yale University, for his help in identifying these flowers.

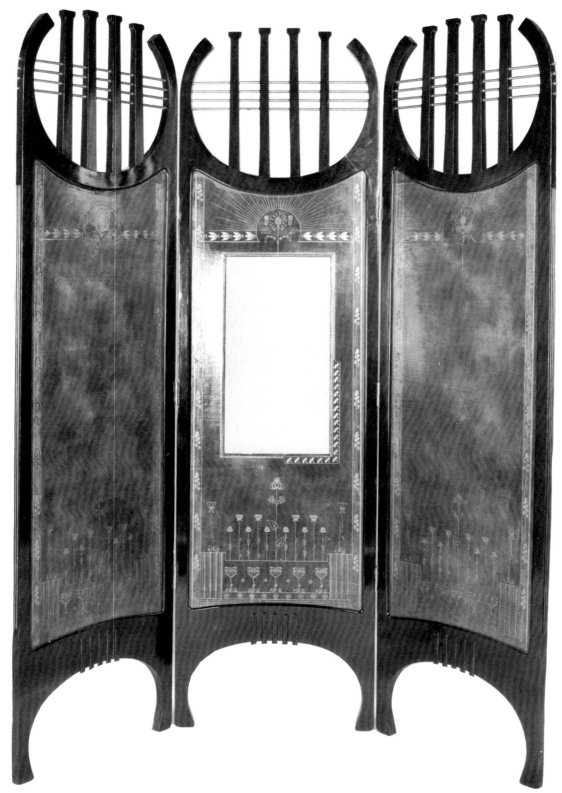

13.1

13
JOSEF HOFFMANN

Austrian, 1870-1956

THREE-PANEL SCREEN, *ca. 1899*
Gilded incised leather panels with ebonized wood frame and brass detailing
156.0 x 123.0 (617/16 x 487/16)
Art Gallery and Museums and the Royal Pavilion, Brighton

This three-panel screen is one of two known to have been designed by the Moravian architect Josef Hoffmann. Trained in the conservative atmosphere of the Academy of Art in Vienna, Hoffmann spent a year traveling and studying classical architecture in Italy before beginning his career in the office of the prominent Viennese architect Otto Wagner. By 1897 Hoffmann and his colleagues Gustav Klimt, Joseph Olbrich, and Kolo Moser broke away from the official art circles of Vienna to form the *Vereinigung bildender Künstler Österreich,* known as the Secession. Their first exhibition took place in 1898, and it was at their third show in 1899 that Hoffmann included his first screen (13.1). He may very well have been influenced in his decision to do a screen by Josef Engelhardt, whose four-panel screen was shown at the first Secession exhibition and which was illustrated in detail in the September 1898 issue of the Secession's publication, *Ver Sacrum.*[1] Olbrich, too, was working on a screen in 1898 for the apartment of a Viennese client.[2]

Hoffmann's screen was illustrated in the 1899 issue of *Studio* magazine, and its similarity in format to the Brighton example (13.2) indicates that both must have been done at very nearly the same time. Unfortunately, this early screen has been lost, and nothing is known about its materials or construction. According to the caption accompanying the *Studio* illustration, it was apparently executed after Hoffmann's design by the Viennese furniture firm of A. Förster, which is still extant today. It is likely that the firm, which retailed high quality furniture and other goods, also sold other screens, as did Liberty's in London. The obvious difference between the two screens is the inclusion of ovals with each of the panels of the lost screen. As far as one can tell, the ovals contained images (painted?) of female figures playing musical instruments. The first plays an ocarina, the second a frame drum, and the third a trumpetlike wind instrument.[3] The Brighton example contains in its central panel a large vertical rectangle, which presumably would have been filled by the purchaser with an image chosen from a selection offered by A. Förster. It is also possible that the purchaser of the screen could have filled this rectangle with a print or photograph from another source, following the earlier tradition of scrap screens.[4]

In addition, the Brighton screen contains in each panel an incised, gilded leather central section decorated with stylized floral and insect motifs. These panels are mounted in an ebonized wood frame detailed with brass rods and inserts, which appears identical to that in *Studio.* The top of each frame section is in the form of a cithara, a lyrelike stringed instrument of Greek origin,[5] a motif obviously in keeping with the musical theme presented in the lost screen.[6] The gently curving oval arch at the top provides a startling and effective variation form the typically rectangular screen panel. This broad arch is repeated at the very bottom, where the screen is supported by slightly inward-splayed legs. Both the arch and leg forms can be seen in pedestals that Hoffmann designed for the third Secession exhibition (13.3).[7] Just as the cithara shape cuts into the leather panels at the top of the screen, the broad arches at the bottom cut into the lower edges of the leather panels. Not only is the rectangle of the leather sections thereby broken, but there is a visual distortion in our perception of the panels as flat, two-dimensional shapes. They almost seem to bend inward, in fact. The dynamics of the screen therefore result from the unusual form of the screen rather than from the relatively insignificant inclusion of an image within it.

Hoffmann's attention to details is evident in other areas of the screen as well. At the top of the screen, for example, square-topped columns form the "strings" of the cithara. They are cut horizontally by four matte-surfaced brass rods whose polished spherical ends protrude slightly beyond the edge of the frame. Three brass inserts run vertically along the left edge of the first panel and along the right edge of the third panel. At the bottom, five pilasterlike relief elements are placed at the center of the broad arches, extending just below the edge of these

arches. They create a subtle but noticeable counterpoint to the top of the screen, where columnar "strings" carefully continue the implied rounded upper edge of the cithara.

The leather panels, however, do not seem to be from Hoffmann's hand. All are virtually identical, save for the central one and which includes a large rectangle bordered all around with an arrow motif and at the lower right corner with an additional double-winged dragonfly design set at an angle. The left and right edges of each of the other panels are bordered with a poppylike motif. Near the top is a stylized chrysanthemum with an incised circle from which concentric rays emanate. To the left and right are more arrowhead shapes, facing toward the chrysanthemum-sunburst pattern. This motif is repeated in miniature as the border for the rectangle in the central panel. At the bottom of each leather section is another stylized floral motif bordered at the right, left, and bottom by abstract geometric designs. Compared to Hoffmann's early border decorations in *Ver Sacrum*, the motifs in these leather panels seem far too flat, even rigid, to have

13.2 *Three-Panel Screen*, 1899 (lost). In *Studio* 16 (1899): 32.

13.3 Detail, pedestal for sculpture in third exhibition of the Vienna Secession, 1899. In *Ver Sacrum*, 1899, no. 8.

been designed by him. They are so distant from the curvilinear intertwined motifs preferred by Hoffmann and his contemporaries Moser and Olbrich, in fact, that it would be difficult to place them within this circle. The deceptively simple, architecturally oriented design solutions for the screen as a whole, however, demonstrate the young Hoffmann's growing ability to manipulate forms in unmistakably innovative ways.

1. *Ver Sacrum*, September 1898, 2-8. For a brief biography on Engelhart, see Christian M. Nebehay, *Ver Sacrum: 1898-1903* (Vienna: Edition Tusch, 1975), 74-76.

2. See Wilhelm Schollermann, "Art in Vienna," *Studio* 16 (1899): 30-38.

3. My thanks to Richard Rephann and Nicholas Renouf from the Collection of Musical Instruments, Yale University, for their help in identifying these instruments.

4. See Cat. 2.

5. See A. J. Neubecker, *Altgriechische Musik* (Darmstadt: Wissenschaftliche Buchgesellschaft, 1977), plate 1.

6. Hoffmann may have seen depictions of such instruments on Greek vases when he traveled through Italy in 1891. Hoffmann was also musically inclined, having studied the violin as a child. See Hoffmann's "Selbstbibliographie" in *Ver Sacrum: Neue Heft für Kunst und Literatur* 72 (1972): 105.

7. For an illustration see *Ver Sacrum*, no. 8 (1898): 25.

14.1

14

GEORGE LOGAN

Scottish, 1866-1939

and

JESSE MARION KING

Scottish, 1875-1949

THREE-PANEL SCREEN, 1902
*Walnut veneer with silver and mother-of-pearl inlay, turquoise, red amethyst
and an unidentified white stone. 172.1 x 137.2 (67¾ x 54)
Collection of Mrs. Patrick Higson, Glasgow*

This elegant, understated, three-panel screen (14.1) designed by George Logan was a highlight of the Scottish section at the 1902 Esposizione Internazionale in Turin.[1] Both the screen and a matching desk[2] were manufactured by the well-known Glasgow furniture firm of Wylie and Lochhead.[3] The screen contains in its central panel a watercolor and ink drawing by Jesse King entitled *Princesses of the Red Rose* (14.2).[4] The inclusion of a relatively small image within the larger screen design is an idea that had its origin in earlier scrap screens, but which was revived at the turn of the century by Josef Hoffmann and others.[5] In this instance, though, the image relates directly to the silver rose appliqués which embellish the screen's surface. In addition, the garments of the figures in the watercolor are clasped together by drooping chains similar to those which hang from the tops of the ovals in the left and right screen panels. The relationship between the image and the screen's decorative details is consequently far more cohesive than that achieved by Hoffmann.

Few details about George Logan's life have emerged, other than his participation in the Turin exhibition. He was one of several talented furniture designers working in Glasgow around 1900, most of whose creations have been unnecessarily overshadowed by the extraordinary accomplishments of the architect-designer Charles Rennie Mackintosh. In addition, many of these artists, including Mackintosh, also produced folding screens.[6]

Logan surpasses all of them, however, in the use and handling of precious materials, and more impor- tantly in the inventive approach to form. The screen's most striking features are the large oval cutouts (14.3), covered partially by three parallel vertical silver bars and which are inserted in the right and left panels. These cutouts mark what is probably the first attempt by an artist to physically deny, however genteelly, one of the traditional functions of a screen – to prevent one from seeing beyond or through it. This concept was to be exploited to far greater lengths by Eileen Gray in the 1920s and again by Lucas Samaras in the 1960s.[7] Practically speaking, one could still dress or undress behind Logan's screen and see or be seen through the ovals, which are conveniently and modestly placed at head level.

Except for these cutouts, the screen's design is quite simple. The basically rectangular panels are broken only by a small V-shaped protrusion at the top center, decorated with an inverted heart-shaped mother-of-pearl inlay; and by the gentle pointed arch at the very bottom. The left and right sides and even the edges of the panels are bordered by linear floral motifs executed in shallow relief. The ovals and the square containing the Jesse King watercolor are also surrounded by these shallow carved relief moldings, and are adorned with stylized silver roses and mother-of-pearl teardrop inlays. These moldings drip down the center of each panel to the bottom of the screen, and the silver bars in each of the ovals echo the verti-

14.2 Jesse Marion King, *Princesses of the Red Rose*, 1902, watercolor and ink on vellum.

14.3 Detail, silver oval.

cality of these moldings. In addition, three shorter drip moldings on either side of the center in the panels, each of different length, are capped by pendantlike silver hearts whose weight "pulls" them downward, a quality further emphasized by the delicate silver and turquoise pendants hanging from the top of each panel. The large silver ovals are also encrusted with mother-of-pearl, red amethyst, turquoise, an unidentified white stone, and silver hearts. The large ovals are surrounded by a slightly broader but more thinly drawn silver oval whose center holds an upside-down heart.

Even the verso of the screen (14.4) is subtly adorned with purposeful decorative details. The walnut ovals are gently rounded and protrude beyond the surface of the panels, as do the silver ovals on the recto. An oval line, in shallow relief in the center and punctuated on each side by three circular depressions, emphasizes the oval shape. Silver roses and mother-of-pearl motifs are placed at the same height across the panels, and even in the central panel where the King watercolor is backed by walnut, there is a single silver rose. Care has also been taken, as on the recto, to match the grain of the walnut veneer that spans the screen surface. The beauty and impact of Logan's screen derive largely from this wealth of gracefully designed and exquisitely crafted surface detail.[8]

14.4 Verso.

1. Vittorio Pica, *L'Arte Decorativa all'Esposizione di Torino del 1902* (Bergamo: Istituto Italiano d'Arti Grafiche, 1903), especially pages 221-222.

2. The screen and desk were purchased by Walter S. Strang, a Scotsman who immigrated to Australia in the 1890s. On one of his trips to Europe between 1902 and 1906 he bought the screen, perhaps even from the Turin exhibition itself. Both the screen and desk were then brought to Australia in 1906 and remained there until 1929. When Strang's daughter married in Scotland that year, she took the screen and desk with her as part of her dowry. In 1937 Mrs. Scott's home burned to the ground, destroying the desk. In the travels between Scotland, Australia, and back, and perhaps as a result of the fire, the screen also suffered some damage. The silver bars in the ovals have been remade for this exhibition, and the silver chains at the top were restored and reinstalled.

3. See Gerald and Celia Larner, *The Glasgow Style* (New York: Taplinger Publishing Company, 1979), 14-19, especially page 15. Wylie and Lochhead are noted as the makers of the screen in Pica, *L'Arte Decorativa*, 236, listed incorrectly as "Wylie and Loethead." The man-

ufacturer also made screens of lesser quality; a ca. 1905 catalogue shows screens done in Louis XV and Louis XVI styles, and at the bottom of the page a note indicates that a "Special catalogue and designs of screens, etc., may be had on application." My thanks to Juliet Kinchin, assistant keeper of Decorative Art, Glasgow Museums and Art Galleries, for this reference.

4. For information on this artist, see Larner, *Glasgow Style*, 12-14 and *Jesse M. King and E. A. Taylor from the Collection of Miss Merle Taylor*, a Sotheby's sale catalogue from 21 June 1977, published by Paul Harris and Sotheby's Belgravia, London.

5. See "A Perfect Gem of Art," 91; and Cat. 13.

6. See "A Perfect Gem of Art," 96-98.

7. Cat. 24 and 36.

8. Like many of the Glasgow School products, these details demonstrate clearly how design elements are ultimately two-dimensional in character. One can literally sense how these elements would have first been laid out in a drawing or sketch and then transferred exactly to the three-dimensional object, while still adhering to their planar source.

15.2

15

CARLO BUGATTI

Italian, 1856-1940

THREE-PANEL SCREEN, *ca. 1900*
Varnished wood with metal and mother-of-pearl inlay. 203.0 x 188.0 (79¹⁵/₁₆ x 74)
Collection of Philippe Morane, Paris

Of all the artists who played a role in the development of art nouveau, Carlo Bugatti was the only Italian artist to gain an international reputation for his work. He begun his career in the late 1870s as a student in architecture, first at the Brera in Milan, then at the Beaux-Arts in Paris. Even at this early date, his penchant for unusual combinations of vaguely Moorish forms was evident.[1] He gradually became interested in cabinetmaking, and in 1880 he designed a suite of bedroom furniture for his sister and her husband, the painter Giovanni Segantini.[2] His earliest screen (fig. 91) dates from 1888 and was shown at the Italian Exhibition at Earl's Court in London, where its eccentric style attracted critical attention.[3] In the next decade Bugatti designed at least five other folding screens while winning medals for his work at the 1900 Exposition Universelle in Paris and at the 1902 Esposizione Internationale in Turin.

Two screens in particular show the extremes of Bugatti's singular style as well as the high level of his technical skills. The first (15.1), dating from around 1900, is a fanciful three-panel screen whose basic rectangular form is broken by the addition of two silk-tasseled, multi-tiered, carved wooden spires. The panels are made of parchment, stretched over a wooden frame. Near the center of each panel and supported by a parchment "pedestal" is an elaborate copper repoussé ebony-inlaid disc, which contains at its center another silk tassel. Such disc forms appear frequently in Bugatti's furniture, sometimes intricately detailed, as in this case, or simply as broad, arched voids. Each panel is also decorated along the edges and at the bottom with a variety of repeating arrow- and star-shaped patterns. The success of Bugatti's screen stems from his decision to delineate

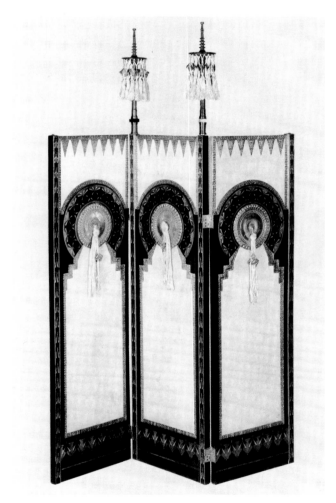

15.1 *Three-Panel Screen*, ca. 1900, ebonized wood, metal inlay, parchment, copper repoussé, with silk tassels, 160.0 x 212.1 (63 x 83½). Private Collection.

the bold geometric features of the design with these minutely detailed borders and from his use of exotic materials in the most unlikely combinations. In contrast to the practices of nearly all his European contemporaries in the field of furniture design, Bugatti himself participated in the completion of the designs.[4]

Another aspect of Bugatti's genius is revealed by this second screen dating from the same period (15.2). Its design is dominated by two enormous inverted black arrows, each spanning two screen panels. It is almost as if Bugatti enlarged one of the decorative details from the border of the silk-tasseled screen discussed above. These arrows, executed in varnished wood contrast sharply with the warm, richly grained unadorned wood below. The V-shape of the black arrows is emphasized by a similarly shaped tip containing a six-petal floral motif. The flowers consist of five- or six-pointed stars constructed in purely symmetrical fashion. The prosaic handling of this motif provides welcome relief from the stark intensity of the overall design. To either side of the flower pattern is a border of diamond-shaped lozenges

laid end to end and set within two pairs of parallel lines. Each of these handsomely conceived details is superbly executed in a mother-of-pearl inlay. Unlike the previous example, the design here is meaningfully altered by folding: the large black V-shapes become narrower and more assertively dynamic as the screen panels are placed closer together.

The contrast between the two screens is indeed striking. An unusual mixture of materials is accompanied by a witty approach to form in the first. Both material and formal components are severely limited in the second, resulting in a design of restrained elegance. Rarely in the history of western screenmaking has an artist so successfully applied such vastly differing esthetic viewpoints.

1. See Philippe Garner, "Carlo Bugatti," in *The Amazing Bugattis* (exh. cat., London, Royal College of Art, 1979), 13, and accompanying illustration.

2. Philippe Dejean, *Carlo-Rembrandt-Ettore-Jean Bugatti* (Paris, Editions du Regard, 1982), 29.

3. *Journal of Decorative Art* 7 (1888): 158-159; see also "A Perfect Gem of Art," 87-88.

4. Garner, "Carlo Bugatti," 8.

16

ANTONIO GAUDÍ Y CORNET

Spanish, 1852-1926

PAIR OF FIVE-PANEL SCREENS, *ca. 1906-1910*
Oak and rose-colored glass
200.0 x 178.5 (78 3/4 x 70 1/4) left half; 196.5 x 200.8 (77 3/8 x 79) right half
Courtesy Allan Stone, New York

In 1906 Pedro Milà i Camps and his wife Doña Rosario Segimón i Artells asked the then-established Catalan architect Antonio Gaudí to build a large apartment house for them at the corner of the Paseo de Gracia and the Calle Provenza, in one of the most fashionable neighborhoods of Barcelona. Gaudí responded with a design of astounding originality, incorporating some elements from the Casa Batlló, located nearby in the Paseo de Gracia and whose construction occupied the architect between 1904 and 1906.[1] The owners' spacious apartment on the second floor of Casa Milà consisted of more than twenty rooms, many of them quite large, including a private chapel and a theater-salon. This pair of five-panel screens (16.1) was intended for the Milà family apartment; they are the only screens done by Gaudí, who only occasionally designed furniture.[2] One of the panels carries a peculiar insignia (16.2) comprised of a capital "R," a heart, and a small cross. Since Gaudí himself did not actually construct the furniture he designed, it is likely that these marks are the maker's signature.[3]

The screen consists of ten irregularly shaped panels of varying heights and widths, each punctured by rose-colored rippled glass windows and elaborated by carved reliefs below. These window openings originally contained etched green glass,[4] probably intended to harmonize with the pale green floor tile used in many of the apartments.[5] The screens' upper edges not only rise and fall in height, but they also undulate in a sinuous play of line in space (16.3). The window heights generally follow those of the oak panels that contain them, emphasizing further the wavelike rhythm of forms across the screens' surfaces. Some of the window shapes approximate

parabolic ovals and some are slightly skewed round-cornered trapezoids, while other defy geometric analogy.[6] The shapes of the oak reliefs below are similarly unpredictable. Gaudí's conception of the screen as an occasion for interplay between asymmetric, biomorphic, and structurally related forms is without parallel even in the fertile and innovative screenmaking environment of European art nouveau.

Though intended for the owner's apartment in the Casa Milà, the screens correspond closely to the interior decorations for the slightly earlier Casa Batlló. The unusual window shapes in the screen almost certainly derived from Gaudí's decidedly sculptural façade for Casa Batlló. Within the nearly pure rectangle of the house's outer walls, the architect broke the interior into irregularly shaped rooms with curved walls, a concept which Gaudí had also planned to use for the Casa Milà.[7] Some of the larger spaces in Casa Batlló, such as the salon (16.4) and the dining room (16.5), were connected to adjacent rooms by multisectioned wood and glass doors whose design and materials are obviously similar to the screens.[8] A slightly less adventurous solution was chosen for the interior in Casa Milà, but a comparison of the shallow relief treatment of the ceiling in some of the apartments there (16.6) still indicates how Gaudí conformed the general stylistic features of his screens to those of the interior.

Unfortunately, nothing is known of the intended location for the screens if indeed there was one. Judging from their considerable dimensions, it seems certain that they would have been best suited for the largest spaces in the apartment. Because of the close formal relationship between the two halves of the screen, it is likely that they

16.1

16.2 Detail, insignia.

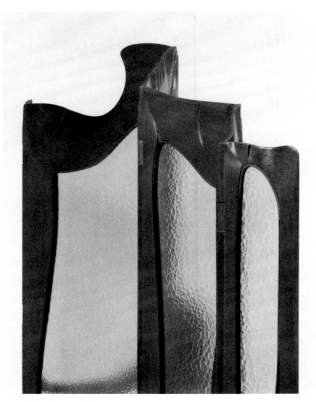

16.3 Detail, top edge.

16.4 Casa Batlló, salon, 1905-1907. Photograph, Barcelona, Archivo Mas.

16.5 Casa Batlló. dining room, 1905-1907. Photograph, Barcelona, Archivo Mas.

functioned together. When the screens were closed they could restrict access between rooms; when opened, they could allow passage between spaces. In either case, light could still pass through the windows in this flexible wall partition. The original green glass was probably sufficiently opaque, however, to offer privacy to people located on either side of the screens.

The beauty of Gaudí's design is that the irregular panel shapes permit a nearly limitless variation of dynamic relationships, changing with the degree to which the screens were opened or closed. Any one of these folded configurations is as effective as another. The screen obviously does not fall into the category of the folding image, but in its masterful balance of layered solids and voids, opaque and semitransparent materials, Gaudí fashioned a unique response to the formal challenges inherent in the folding screen. Moreover, the strongly sculptural character of the screens, certainly in keeping with the nature of Gaudí's architecture, presages an approach to the screen found in works by present-day artists such as Patsy Norvell (Cat. 43).

1. The most thorough description of Gaudí's designs for Casa Milà and Casa Batlló, and for his work in general, is Cesar Martinell's *Gaudí: His Life, His Theories, His Work* (Cambridge: MIT Press, 1967). See especially pages 372-409. A less exhaustive but also useful overview is provided in George Collins' *Antonio Gaudí* (New York: George Braziller, Inc., 1960).

2. For illustrations of Gaudí's furniture, see Collins, *Antonio Gaudí*, Fig. 96-107; and Martinell, *Gaudí*, 216-218.

3. Gaudí's furniture was usually fabricated by Casas y Bardés of Barcelona. In the case of Casa Milà, Gaudí was forced to abandon the project before it was completed, leaving many details to his talented assistants. Juan Bassegoda Nonell, who first published the screens as Gaudí's work in his article "Un Mueble de la Pedrera," *La Prensa* (31 January 1974), apparently did not notice the "R" and cross marks; nor did he mention them in *La Pedrera de Gaudí* (Barcelona: Editores Tecnicos Associados, s.a., 1980), where the screen is discussed briefly on page 75. In a 12 June 1983 letter to the author, Nonell suggested that the marks might refer either to Jose Maria Jujol, or to Juan Rubió Bellver, both of whom worked with Gaudí. Nonell acknowledged, however, that neither suggestion was entirely consistent with the marks on the screen.

4. Nonell, "Un Mueble de la Pedrera."

5. Collins, *Antonio Gaudí*, 127, note 69.

6. See Martinell, *Gaudí*, 374, ill. 434 for an illustration of Gaudí's original plans.

7. See Martinell, *Gaudí*, 372, ill. 433 for a reproduction of the Casa Batlló floor plan as it was executed; and pages 384-386 for the various floor plans for Casa Milà. In the latter, Gaudí was forced to abandon the idea of curved walls, opting finally for asymmetric polygonal rooms.

8. A second door in the Batlló dining room contains some of the biomorphic windows, also done in rippled glass, that appear in the screen. See Martinell, *Gaudí*, 381, ill. 447.

16.6 Casa Milà, ceiling, 1906-1910. Photograph, Barcelona, Archivo Mas.

17.1

17

CHRIS LEBEAU

Dutch, 1878-1944

THREE-PANEL SCREEN, *ca. 1904*
Batik on silk with mahogany frame. 130.0 x 150.0 (50 15/16 x 59 1/4)
Stedelijk Museum, Amsterdam

Chris Lebeau was one of several young Dutch artists who were experimenting with modern concepts of decoration at the turn of the century. Lebeau, whose work is virtually unknown in the United States, was born in Amsterdam. He spent much of his youth in near total poverty, his fervently socialist father working at a variety of odd jobs and his mother cleaning and sewing to earn what they could for the family's basic necessities.[1] His artistic inclinations developed during his teens, and he managed to enter the Kunstnijverheidsschool (Arts and Crafts School) in Amsterdam. By 1899, he was able to secure a teaching position in art at the Burgeravondsschool there. His professional career began shortly thereafter with a commission to do wall decorations for the Netherlands pavilion at the 1900 Exposition Universelle in Paris.[2]

It was also at this time that Lebeau began working in the batik technique in the shop of Agathe Wegerif-Gravenstein in Apeldoorn.[3] The 1883 International Colonial Exhibition in Amsterdam stimulated many Dutch artists to employ this centuries-old stencil printing process in their work.[4] Gerrit Willem Dijsselhof and Thorn Prijker preceded Lebeau in their use of batik; by 1894 Dijsselhof had even done a folding screen with batik-printed designs (fig. 103).[5] Among other things, Lebeau is known to have done nearly a dozen folding screens in batik, some of which were double-sided.[6]

This particular screen (17.1) consists largely of a dense, tightly organized geometric design. What appears to be a combination of abstract motifs, however, is actually a carefully planned decorative and iconographic ensemble. The recto of the screen shows in each panel a pair of storks standing a ground made up of repetitive segmented arches; similar arch motifs, possibly borrowed from

Japanese prototypes, may also be seen in a screen by Bonnard.[7] Directly behind the storks rises the trunk of a highly stylized tree, culminating in resplendent foliage consisting of circular-patterned leaves. A shorter, less leafy tree can be seen to the left and right in each panel; to the left and right of these smaller trees are others, shorter and less densely foliated. A purely decorative border surrounds them all, contributing by the repetition of decorative designs to the rigidly symmetric nature of the screen's image.

The verso (17.2) presents a far more restrained contrast to the recto. The first two panels are unadorned deep blue fabric, whereas the third panel contains a winged, presumably male figure hovering near a glowing yellow sun whose rays emanate to all corners of the surface. When the screen is folded for storage or a less space-consuming placement in a room, only this panel is visible. The figure in this panel is presumed to be Icarus, his youthful pride leading him to ignore his father's admonition not to fly too close to the sun. The conclusion of this Greek tale, of course, was that the heat melted the wax holding Icarus' feathered wings to his body, and he fell into the sea and drowned. The juxtaposition of storks on the recto with the figure of Icarus on the verso has more than one possible interpretation. One may view it as a contrast between life – the stork is a near-universal symbol of birth – and death, caused by Icarus's foolish pride.

There is no parallel in Lebeau's work for this symbolic content, nor is there any event in his personal life which would explain its use.[8] Nevertheless, the choice of subject and its blatant symbolic meaning could not have been the result of chance. There is a possibility that Icarus' presence on the screen has another interpretation. His ability

17.2 Verso.

to fly was made possible by the use of wax, which held his feathered wings together; wax is also the material which makes the batik process possible. It is plausible to consider Icarus' ability to fly as a symbol of human ingenuity, and Lebeau's presentation of this part of the myth as an affirmation of the creativity inherent in the artistic process.

1. His unwanted arrival into the world was announced in the newspaper *De Worksmanbode* (The Workman's Messenger) by his siblings, who stated bluntly they would have far less food and clothing for themselves. What little information is known about Lebeau's life and work can be found in *Chris Lebeau* (exh. cat., The Hague, Gemeentemuseum, 1966), which also lists other bibliographical sources.

2. Lebeau's brother Charles, with whom Chris had worked as a house painter a few years before, helped in the completion of this decoration. Their work was done in a studio which the brothers rented in The Hague. See *Chris Lebeau*, 10-12.

3. See *Studio* 23 (1901): 209-210 for a photograph of the Apeldoorn workshop and some of their products.

4. This process was borrowed from the Dutch colonies in Indonesia. In the batik process, a design is first drawn on the surface to be printed, usually fabric. The areas not to be dyed are covered with wax on both sides of the fabric. The material is then dipped into a vat of dye. After drying, the wax is removed either by boiling the fabric or by scraping it off. The process is repeated for each color in the design; wax is used to stop out areas not to be dyed. By the middle of the nineteenth century, copper blocks known as *tjaps* were used to facilitate the stopping-out process, as they allowed for repetition of regularized designs. *Tjaps* were almost certainly used to print the repeated geometric patterns in Lebeau's screens. For further information on batik, see Susan Macmillan Arensberg, *Javanese Batiks* (exh. cat., Boston, Museum of Fine Arts, 1978); Leo O. Donahue, *Encyclopedia of Batik Design* (Philadelphia: Art Alliance Press, 1981), especially pages 17-41 for a more thorough description and illustration of the process; and *Chris Lebeau*, pages 38-39.

5. See Vittorio Pica, *L'Arte Decorativa all'Esposizione di Torino del 1902* (Bergamo: Istituto Italiano d'Arti Grafiche, 1903), 266-267, and "A Perfect Gem of Art," 94-95. Thorn Prijker is also known to have done a screen, though in wood rather than batik. See *Nieuwe Kunst rond 1900: De Nederlandse toegepaste kunst en architectur van 1885-1910* (exh. cat., The Hague, Gemeentemuseum, 1960), cat. no. 562.

6. Mechteld de Bois at the Provincial Museum Drenthe, Assen, will soon publish the results of her considerable research on Lebeau's screens.

7. See "A Perfect Gem of Art," 72-73 and fig. 73.

8. Lebeau, like his father, held socialist beliefs throughout his life, and did not have any strong religious ties. He was eventually imprisoned by the Nazis as a result of his beliefs, and died in 1944 at Dachau.

18

CHARLES PRENDERGAST

American, 1863-1948

THREE-PANEL SCREEN, *ca. 1916-1921*
Mixed media with gilt over gesso on panel with gilded and painted wood frame
192.0 x 206.5 (75 5/8 x 81 1/4)
Collection of Mrs. Duncan Phillips, Washington

Charles Prendergast's career has been inextricable from that of his more well-known brother Maurice.[1] Beginning his career as a custom woodworker, the younger Charles decided in 1895 to become a framemaker. He was an avid student of art, and traveled to England in 1898. In 1911-1912 he visited the museums and churches of Venice, Florence, Pisa, Siena, and probably Orvieto and Ravenna, making notes on the frames he saw along the way. In 1913 Charles provided frames for objects at the Armory Show in New York.[2] His career as an artist did not begin until 1912, when at the age of fifty he made his first decorative panel.

Sometime between 1916 and 1921, Charles Prendergast made the first of his three folding screens (18.1 and 18.2).[3] It consists of three panels, each with elaborately carved, painted, and gilded frames. The images on both sides of the screen were executed by first drawing the design on the prepared wood panel, and incising the deeper lines with a gouge. Next, coats of gesso were applied, and the more delicate lines traced with a stylus. Colors were applied after the gold leaf, in many areas painted over ungilded gesso. Occasionally the underdrawing is visible, as for example in the halos of the large angel figures on the verso. Prendergast deliberately chose to leave some areas unfinished to add to the mystery of the screen subjects.[4]

On the recto are three separate but related scenes of figures and animals in an idyllic landscape of mountains, trees, ponds, streams, and waterfalls. The subject matter here has a vaguely religious character: at the middle left portion of the third panel, for example, a haloed and winged female figure holding a palm-leafed staff approaches a winged horse. The verso, of course, shows

three nearly life-size winged female angels hovering against uniformly colored or gilded backgrounds. The gentle spirituality of these angels recalls Byzantine-inspired mosaics which Prendergast may have seen on his travels in Italy. The scenes on the recto, however, are not specifically identifiable, and it seems that the depiction of an Eden-like paradise was probably meant to evoke a sense of charm and mystery rather than to suggest any overt Christian, or even mythological, reference.[5]

Interestingly, Prendergast created the scenes on the recto by compiling various smaller, previously completed decorative panels into this larger, denser ensemble. The female figure holding a horned goat in the upper right of the first panel is borrowed from the right-hand portion of the artist's *Fantasy Panel* (18.3). The entire *Figures* decorative panel (18.4) is repeated verbatim in the upper right of the screen's second panel, as is the entire *Riders* group (18.5) in the lower half of the same screen panel. These decorative panels were reused at very nearly the same size in the screen, making the story of its evolution unmistakably clear.

Prendergast's naive and expressive style is generally considered to derive from his interest in Persian miniatures.[6] Indeed, the vertical orientation of the composition, the rounded shorthand description of landscape elements, and the emphasis on strong hues, and the use of gold are all found in fifteenth- and sixteenth-century Persian manuscript illuminations (18.6). Some of the same formal qualities are also found within America's own folk tradition.[7] The fanciful decoration and simplistic renderings of mythological and sometimes biblical themes in eighteenth- and nineteenth-century Pennsylvania German chests are very close in spirit to Prender-

18.1

18.2 Verso.

18.3 *Fantasy*, ca. 1917, oil on panel, 50.8 x 60.9 (20 x 24). Collection of Mr. and Mrs. William Fuller, Fort Worth.

gast's work. Even the pointed arch motif in the central panel of this Pennsylvania German chest (18.7) can be seen in the screen. Prendergast, in fact, made several similarly decorated chests.

The question of sources aside, however, one must consider how Prendergast's screen functions. There was obviously no concern for how folding might affect the image: on the recto its impact derives from a rich combination of pictorial elements woven across all three panels, with no attempt to emphasize one panel over another; while on the verso, each panel is a self-sufficient unit. The activity of small-scale narrative elements on the one side contrasts sharply with the iconic, large-scale figures and boldly colored backgrounds on the other.[8] It is almost as if the two sides of the screen present us with a visual and metaphorical contrast of the active and contemplative, though it is unlikely that Prendergast himself thought of the work in such terms. The predominant use

18.4 *Figures*, ca. 1916-1917, oil on panel, 70.5 x 57.1 (27¾ x 22½). Newark Museum, Felix Fuld Bequest.

18.5 *Riders*, ca. 1916-1917, oil on panel, 76.2 x 58.4 (30 x 23). Collection of Mrs. Charles Prendergast.

18.6 *Shirin Bathing*, attributed to Sultan-Muhammad, from *Khamsa of Nizami*, 1539-1543. London, British Museum.

18.7 Pennsylvania-German *Chest*, 1788, painted and carved tulip wood, 72.1 x 127.0 x 60.9 (28⅜ x 50 x 24). Winterthur, Delaware, Henry Francis du Pont Winterthur Museum.

of primary colors throughout the screen also provides a certain decorative unity. The framing elements in each panel on the recto are painted in red, blue, and gold respectively; on the verso the backgrounds for the figures are in red, gold, and blue, with the framing elements painted to accentuate this mixture of primaries. Prendergast probably wished simply to create a screen whose images and decoration would both charm and intrigue the viewer, and in this goal he was remarkably successful.

1. Richard J. Wattenmaker, *The Art of Charles Prendergast* (exh. cat., Rutgers University Art Gallery and Boston Museum of Fine Arts, 1968), is the most thorough study of the artist's work, and includes the sparse bibliographical references on him. The biographical information in this entry is taken from Wattenmaker's essay.

2. Prendergast might have seen the dozen folding screens exhibited there by Robert Winthrop Chanler, although there are no real correspondences between their works.

3. Few of Prendergast's works are dated, and the consistency of style over long periods makes precise dating even more difficult. Wattenmaker dated the screen to 1916-1917, apparently on stylistic grounds. Mrs. Duncan Phillips reported in an interview of November 1982 that her husband had bought the screen as a gift for her in 1921. The other two three-panel screens by Prendergast are in private collections in Fort Worth and New York, and date from at least a decade later.

4. Reported by Mrs. Phillips in an interview, November 1982.

5. Several other decorative panels have identifiable Christian subjects: *Madonna and Child*, ca. 1912-1914 and *Calling of Sts. Peter and Andrew*, ca. 1914; angels also appear on one of Prendergast's carved chests and on one of his carved mirrors; and two sculptures have biblical subjects, *Eve*, ca. 1912-1914 and *Angel*, ca. 1915. See Wattenmaker, *The Art of Charles Prendergast*, cat. nos. 2, 3, 52, 54, 57, and 58.

6. Wattenmaker, *The Art of Charles Prendergast*, 22.

7. This interest in naively rendered biblical subjects can also be found in the works and writings of Henry Chapman Mercer (1865-1930). The gifted Mercer was an archaeologist, anthropologist, lawyer, collector, architect, and museum founder. Early in his career he produced a study of early American cast-iron stoves, some of which were decorated with subjects stylistically and spiritually close to those in Prendergast's screens, chests, and panels. See Mercer, *The Bible in Iron* (Doylestown: Bucks County Historical Society, 1961), reprint of 1914 ed., particularly ills. 32 and 42. Mercer was also a designer and manufacturer of ceramic tiles, produced in his Moravian Pottery and Tile Works in Doylestown, Pennsylvania. Many of these tiles shared the folk spirit of Prendergast's works. Though no direct link between the works of these two men is suggested here, it is nevertheless interesting to witness another aspect of a continuing American folk tradition in the early part of the twentieth century. For information on Mercer, see *The Mercer Mile: The Story of Dr. Henry Chapman Mercer and His Concrete Buildings* (Doylestown: Bucks County Historical Society, 1972); and the catalogue of reproductions of Mercer's tiles entitled simply *Moravian Pottery and Tile Works* (Doylestown: n.d.).

8. Thomas Dewing also depicted large-scale female figures, and made ample use of gold framing elements in his screens dating from the turn of the century. See Cat. 10.

Virginia F. Butera
THE SCREEN AS METAPHOR

THE FASCINATION felt by western artists over the last century for the folding screen as an esthetic device has developed because of its very special structure and its long history of symbolic associations. A vehicle for extending an artist's range of expression, the screen is aligned with the human condition, existing in a space shared by the viewer rather than separated and isolated on a wall or pedestal. For these artists, the folding screen functions on four levels. The first is purely utilitarian: it is a barrier against drafts, light, and vision, and a flexible wall which creates privacy and separates space within space. On the second level, the folding screen is simultaneously decorative and functional. Within the third and the fourth levels, the metaphorical possibilities inherent in the screen as art form predominate, although the functional aspect still may be present.

On the third level, artists manipulate the structural qualities uniquely present in a screen to correspond with the image created on and by the screen. The shape of the panels, their double-sidedness, the convex and concave angling of the structure, and the notion of movement have been exploited by the artists. Carrying these experiments to an extreme, artists often so fully negate the screen's practical function that geometrically shaped canvases or purely sculptural objects result.

On the fourth level an image is invented which is based on, yet plays with and contradicts, the viewer's understanding of the screen's historical associations. Some of the most poignant metaphors concentrate on the screen as a barrier between people, especially men and women—a boudoir object behind which people dress, a closed door to a private space, or a standing altarpiece.

Altering the conventional shape of a screen's panels is the first way artists may impose new concepts on the format. In her *Block Screen* of 1923 (Cat. 24), Eileen Gray heralded these experiments by eliminating the solid, unbroken panels typical of most screens in favor of a grid of small, regularly spaced rectangles. Unlike Eileen Gray

whose many versions of this screen consist of crisp, sedate lines, Lucas Samaras designed his 1967 *Screen* (Cat. 36) to consist of cutout, biomorphic shapes. The undulating arrangement of the holes in Samaras' work clashes in squeamish tension with the rectangular and acute parallelogram forms of the actual panels. A similar juxtaposition exists in Tom Hill's screen (fig. 124), commissioned by the New York City disco, Danceteria. Hill, whose amorphous, "new wave" shapes perforate the screen's

FIG. 124 Tom Hill, American, born 1954, *Untitled*, 1982, enamel on wood and masonite, 182.9 x 182.9 (72 x 72). Courtesy Danceteria, New York.

surface, devised the piece so that neon lights sitting in the bottom between the front and rear panels illuminate the form. Jack Youngerman's cut metal, two-panel screen, *Tabriz* (fig. 125), one the other hand, avoids the tension inherent in the screens by Samaras and Hill. The frond-like forms in *Tabriz* recall, in fact, the luxurious curvilinearity of art nouveau. A young French artist, Kim Hamisky, carves the wooden panels in his screen (fig. 126), lifting the flaps higher and higher on each successive section. Juxtaposing void and solid, Hamisky uses his screen as a symbol for exposure and enclosure, two of the screen's traditional functions.

Other methods of integrating panel shape and subject enable the screen to transcend its secondary role as neutral surface to gain a symbolic function. Essential to Giacomo Balla's ca. 1918 futurist screen image (Cat. 21) of landscape and velocity lines is the implied passage of the automobile through the landscape, depicted by these lines. In order to enhance this sensation, Balla designed a curve in one of the panels to signify motion and allude to the curving hills in the background of the image. The uneven heights of the panels also add to Balla's dynamic intent and create the impression that the screen is actually moving.

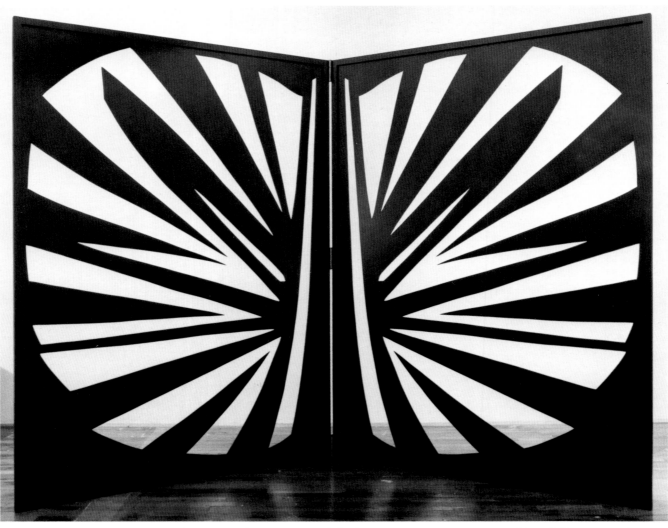

FIG. 125 Jack Youngerman, American, born 1926, *Tabriz,* 1980, painted aluminum, 187.9 x 314.9 (74 x 124). Washburn Gallery, New York.

FIG. 126 Kim Hamisky, French, born 1943, *Untitled*, 1980, carved wood, 280.0 x 320.0 (110½ x 126). Collection of Mr. and Mrs. A. M. Pilaro, Southampton, New York.

FIG. 127 Kenneth Armitage, English, born 1916, *Five-Panel Folding Screen*, 1974, mixed media, 179.2 x 274.3 (84 x 108). Library, Nottingham University.

Throughout his oeuvre, the British sculptor Kenneth Armitage has integrated the human figure within the structure of the screen form. Some of Armitage's screens (Cat. 38 and fig. 127) contain figures whose arms and legs protrude so that the figures seem to be walking out into the viewer's space. In *Screen (Folded Arms)* (Cat. 38), Armitage also integrates screen shape and subject by suggesting that the screen itself has consumed a human

FIG. 128 Patsy Norvell, American, born 1942, *Traveller* (in foreground, with *Jungle Wall* in background), 1982, etched glass, 238.8 x 482.6 (94 x 190). Courtesy of the Artist.

figure, with only its folded arms remaining as a mute reminder of life. The portrayal of man as an inanimate, impenetrable wall is the ominous intent.

Two contemporary American artists, Patsy Norvell and Louise Crandell, have shaped their screen panels to fuse with the images of nature depicted on them. The undulating cut glass panels in Norvell's *Jungle Wall* (Cat. 43) and *Traveller* (fig. 128) echo the actual shapes of the leaves etched into the screens' surfaces. The screen and nature, their subject, are completely intermeshed so that the screen, signifying growth, seems to be alive. By enlarging the tiny shell to human size, Louise Crandell imbues her *Scallop Screen* (fig. 129) with a rocklike solidity mitigated only by the fluted shell form. The shell which once protected a sea creature now assumes a similar function in a domestic human environment.

Screens may be decorated on two sides and many artists have been successful in using this feature to indicate opposition, change, or the passage of time. Eileen Gray, Ansel Adams, and Ed Moses are three artists, all working in different media, who use the screen as a signifier of contrast. In her vermilion lacquer screen of 1914, *Le Destin* (fig. 130), Gray maps out her artistic lineage. Idealized classical figures from Greco-Roman art on the verso give way to an image of geometric abstraction on

FIG. 129 Louise Crandell, American, born 1948, *Scallop Screen*, 1981, acrylic with lacquer on wood, 121.9 x 152.4 (48 x 60). Courtesy of the Artist.

the other, indicating the direction Gray followed as an early twentieth-century modernist.

Ansel Adams also exhibits on his double-sided screen, *Clearing Storm, Sonoma County/Oak Tree, Rain* (Cat. 31), the duality of his photographic vision. Adams' photographs of nature capture either immense landscape vistas or more intimate scenes. The expanse of the untamable mountain and sky in *Clearing Storm* is the antithesis of the more human-scale image of young oaks behind a fence in *Oak Tree, Rain* symbolizing the civilizing influence of man. Ed Moses too designed his *Rose Screen* (Cat. 32) as a double-sided piece. The densely-packed rose bush on the recto is an emblem of fullness and activity. On the verso the screen is blank except for one tiny rose in the lower right corner. Moses uses this emptiness as a symbol of calm and reprieve, offering a stark contrast to the energy-filled image of the rose bush on the recto.

By working on both sides of the screen, changing imagery, coloration, and style, artists have succinctly symbolized the passage of time and have implied notions of continuity and circularity. In proceeding from the recto to the verso of his two-panel screen, Giacomo Balla (Cat. 21) shifted the colors of his force lines from red, pink, and blue to orange, white, and blue in order to emphasize a

different moment in time and place. On the recto of his *Marble Canyon* screen (Cat. 42), Jim Jacobs depicted morning, with its greens and golds sparkling on the arching river. On the verso these colors are transformed into the violets, pinks, and silvers of late afternoon. Similarly, to signify day passing into night, Joanna Pousette Dart painted both sides of *Untitled (Free Standing Wall)* (fig. 131) with increasingly dark colors and an abstract style whose gestures build momentum and power.

Susan Crile and Malcolm Morley each have a different way of manipulating their images on both sides of a screen.[1] Crile's double-sided topographical landscape in *Lake Dancers* (fig. 132) is an aerial perspective. One follows the scene not by traveling horizontally around the screen, but by following the forms over the top of the screen and down the other side. As in the air, there is no right side up. The ground, normally perpendicular to the viewer, is now tipped parallel as in Duncan Grant's abstraction of a lilypond in his *Lilypond Screen* (fig. 133).[2]

Malcolm Morley's motivation is altogether different: half of his screen is clearly upside down. As in the folding postcards which were the model for his enormous screen, half of the views of the monuments in *N.Y.C. Foldout* are standing on end. Clearly, as the viewer encircles any of these double-sided screens, he or she is presented with vastly different compositional, spatial, and temporal experiences. Such multilevel encounters are unique to the folding screen format — one of the primary reasons for its immense popularity among contemporary artists.

For a screenmaker, the separate yet hinged sections and their capacity to be positioned at varied angles elicit the metaphoric power of a folding image when combined with the appropriate subject matter. Even Whistler's two-panel *Blue and Silver: Screen with Old Battersea Bridge* (fig. 54) is a paradigm of this interplay. The painted image of the bridge crossing two banks signifies separation and juncture as well as passage between the two sides of the Thames. This metaphor, moreover, is physically embodied by the two panels as they come together or move apart, visually and symbolically sustained by the image of the Battersea span. Considered from this conceptual vantage point, the centrally hinged frame may be read as a support pylon for the bridge/ screen.

Ellsworth Kelly manipulated the folded sections of his 1950-1951 *La Combe II* (Cat. 30) to achieve a very differ-

FIG. 130 Eileen Gray, Irish, 1879-1976, *Le Destin*, 1914 (recto), lacquered wood, 199.0 x 216.0 (78¼ x 84). Private Collection, London.

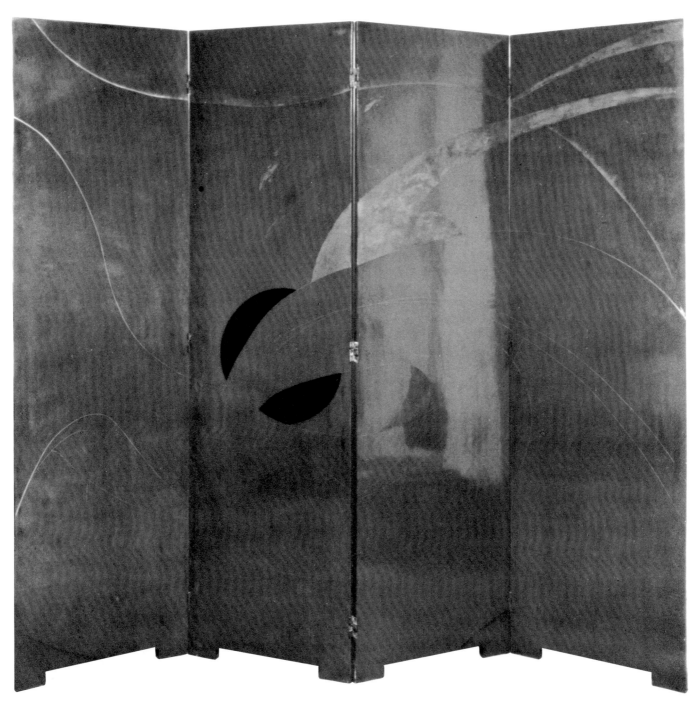

FIG. 130 verso.

FIG. 131 Joanna Pousette Dart, American, born 1947, *Untitled (Free Standing Wall) Dayside/Nightside,* 1981-1983 (recto and verso), oil and metallic pigment on canvas, 243.8 x 396.2 (96 x 156). Courtesy Susan Caldwell, Inc., New York.

FIG. 132 Susan Crile, American, born 1942, *Lake Dancers*, 1975, oil on canvas, 182.9 x 548.6 (72 x 216). Courtesy of the Artist.

ent intent in an image which he also had painted on a flat canvas. In his screen the crisp angling of panels physically and symbolically represents the rise of the steps upon which the shadows of a railing fall. Kelly captured this visual sensation by creating a screen to simulate the zig-zag configuration of a flight of stairs and to demonstrate better the interplay of the shadows in a three-dimensional field.

Francesco Clemente, too, fuses image and structure through the screen's angles. Depicting female and male genitalia along the folds of *Screen #1* (fig. 134), he implies, as does Armitage, that a screen may be considered a metaphor for the human body.

The panels in George Woodman's *Five-Fold Screen* (fig. 135) coalesce like contiguous frames on a film strip. Although the bell-shaped flower images remain the same throughout, a subtle shift in hue or pattern evolves across the sections, creating a rhythmic motion.[3] Woodman's images are metaphors for changing light, time of day, and the vacillation of optical perception.

In a further twist, David Hockney reversed most precedents for the way a screen is to be folded. He has indicated that his three-panel *Midnight Pool (Paper Pool 10)* (Cat. 40) should be arranged so that the central panel projects forward and the two sides angle back. The

viewer then has the true perspective of one standing on the diving board looking out over the pool. In any other configuration, this sensation does not occur.

The folding screen is also an emblem for movement. Every structural element of the Giacomo Balla screen, for example, seems to enhance the dynamic nature of his imagery. As the screen panels are folded to approach a ninety-degree angle, a deeper perspective is given to the landscape image as it takes on a more believable and logical perspective. This perpendicular formation also accelerates the swoop of the force lines through the landscape, signifying the car which we sense but do not see. Paul Klee and Jim Jacobs use the format in vastly different ways. Each of the five panels of Klee's screen (Cat. 9) represents an isolated vista, not one continuous view, along the course of the Aare River. In Jacobs' piece (Cat. 42) the undulation of the screen is synonymous with the unbroken twisting and turning of the Colorado River.

Panels and image fluctuate in Frank Faulkner's 1982 patterned *Snake Carpet* (fig. 136) or in Ellen Lanyon's 1982-1983 *Transformations II (Endangered)* (fig. 137).[4] Designed initially as a folding book, Lanyon's monumental screen displays a complex narrative of fantasy, magic, and nature, and of life's continuing metamorphosis.

FIG. 133 Duncan Grant, English, 1885-1978, *Lilypond Screen*, 1913, oil on panel, 217.0 x 244.0 (85 7/16 x 96). Courtauld Institute Galleries, London.

FIG. 134 Francesco Clemente, Italian, born 1952, *Screen #1*, 1982, watercolor on paper, 182.0 x 234.9 (72 x 92½). Courtesy Daniel Templon, Paris.

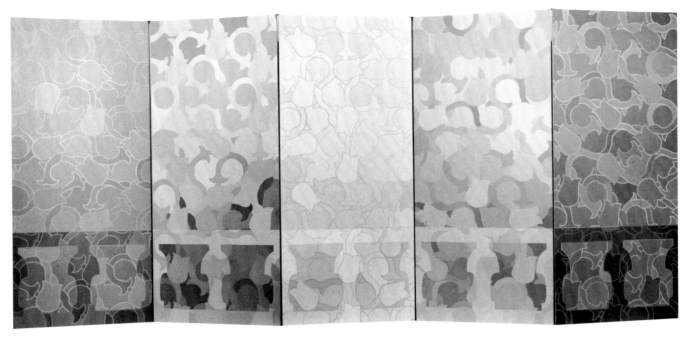

FIG. 135 George Woodman, American, born 1932, *Five-Fold Screen*, 1979, acrylic on canvas, 213.4 x 457.2 (84 x 180). Collection of the Artist.

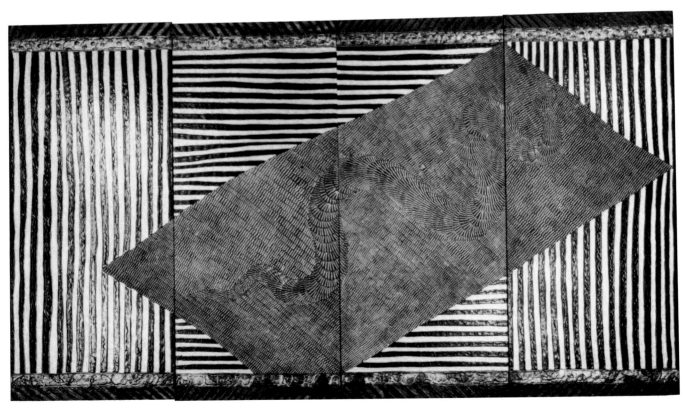

FIG. 136 Frank Faulkner, American, born 1946, *Snake Carpet*, 1982, acrylic on canvas, 213.4 x 365.8 (84 x 144). Collection of the Equitable Life Assurance Society of the United States, New York.

204 / *The Folding Image*

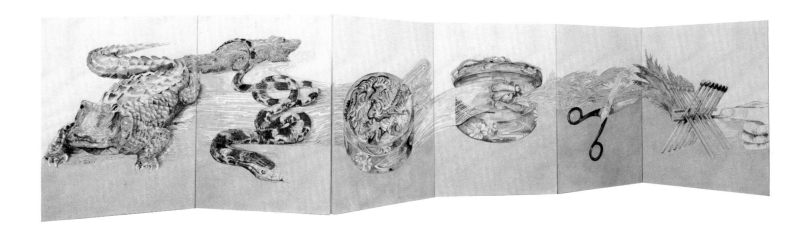

FIG. 137 Ellen Lanyon, American, born 1928, *Transformations II (Endangered)*, 1982-1983, acrylic on canvas, 182.9 x 2,032.0 (72 x 800). Courtesy Susan Caldwell, Inc., New York.

Both the bridge in Whistler's *Blue and Silver: Screen with Old Battersea Bridge* (fig. 54) and the arcing rainbow of Marc's three-panel piece signify structural mobility as well as compositional and symbolic unity. For Marc the rainbow and the overall harmony of the screen's composition are metaphors for the spiritual unity he was seeking in nature itself.[5] Marc surmounted the tip of the mountain with the apex of the rainbow, directing the viewer's eye, and soul, toward heaven.

The dynamic format of the screen is frequently enhanced by diagonal compositional elements such as the giant red parallelogram that takes off across the expanse of white in Leon Polk Smith's *Seven Involvements in One: Correspondence: Red/White* (Cat. 35). Smith's flying carpet form is equivalent to the angled boat waiting for a rower and action in Jack Beal's *Rowboat* (Cat. 39). To create a similar tension and vitality, Jack Youngerman captures waves just as they are about to crash in *High Tide* (Cat. 41).

Irving Kriesberg has been the most elaborate with the metaphor of movement. Although he has made conventional folding screens, Kriesberg, a filmmaker, wanted a structure which would convey more clearly a revolving sequence of images.[6] In *Chrysalis* (fig. 138), he suspended four panels on central bars top and bottom. Painting each section on both sides, Kriesberg fabricated a screen which has twenty-four possible image configurations, seen in an infinite number of angles and from countless points of view.

FIG. 139 Jennifer Bartlett, American, born 1941, *Up the Creek*, 1981-1982, testors enamel on cherry, maple, oak, pine, poplar, walnut, 182.9 x 278.1 (72 x 109½). Courtesy Paula Cooper Gallery, New York.

FIG. 140 Kim MacConnel, American, born 1946, *Pagode*, 1974, painted refrigerator cartons with painted cloth inserts. 525.8 x 251.5 (207 x 99). Collection Ludwig, Aachen.

FIG. 138 Irving Kriesberg, American, born 1919, *Chrysalis*, 1960, assembled and mounted in metal frame, oil on canvas. 132.1 x 213.4 (52 x 84). Collection of the Graham Gallery, New York.

The old notion of art as an isolated object for intellectual contemplation was suppressed in the 1960s in the wake of multimedia environmental "happenings." Within this period's philosophical and esthetic turmoil, the folding screen offered artists another way to take painting down from the wall, and to manipulate three-dimensional space. Leon Polk Smith's 1966 screen, *Seven Involvements in One* (Cat. 35), epitomizes the possibilities of a "folding painting."[7] Retaining the two-dimensional surface, Smith enhanced the optical and spatial investigations of his abstract chromatic harmonies through the folding and thereby the three-dimensional formation of his screen.

Jennifer Bartlett employs screens as sculptural painting extensions of her mixed media wall works as in *Up the Creek* (fig. 139),[8] whereas Kim MacConnel folds his painted screens in *Pagode* (fig. 140) to form an hexagonal sculptural and architectural performance set.[9] MacConnel designed his structure with cut-out refrigerator cartons and translucent cloth to symbolize a music box. *Pagode* isolated the four musicians who played music inside from the audience who gradually gathered outside, peering overtop the screens and looking through the cloth panels.

Further developments led to the complete transformation of the screen into sculpture. Piercing the panel surfaces in *Screen* (Cat. 36) Samaras compelled the actual depth of his screen to be integral to the viewing experience. Forcing the screen further into the realm of sculpture, Jim Jacobs purposefully undermines accepted notions of both flexibility and stability. He interlocks the double-sided sections of his *Marble Canyon* screen (Cat. 42) so they barely touch the floor and are even cantilevered above it. Only Richard Serra has eliminated the folds entirely, amplifying the perimeter to make his outdoor sculpture, *St. Johns Rotary Arc*, 1980, function as both wall and screen (fig. 141).

Historically, one of the connotations of a screen is as barrier: shielding woman from man, hiding an undressing man or woman, or separating people from one another. Since Marcel Duchamp's *The Bride Stripped Bare by Her Bachelors, Even* (fig. 142), several artists have exploited this rich pool of metaphors when making their screens. Duchamp's *Large Glass*, as it is commonly called, is obviously not a folding screen. It does possess, however, some of the characteristics of the screen as a physical barrier, although it consists of two horizontally separated panels. In Katherine S. Dreier's home, in fact, the *Large Glass* served as a partition in her library (fig. 143). As has been well documented, the image on the glass is the undressing and deflowering of the bride in the top panel by the nine bachelors in the bottom panel. Instead of protecting the bride from the bachelors and from the viewers as a traditional screen might, Duchamp's screen, made of transparent glass, becomes the locus of the sexual event for all to see. Duchamp even included in the piece three peeping toms *(témoins oculistes)*.[10] Given Duchamp's ironic sense of humor, the *Large Glass* should be analyzed in the light of the screen metaphor, in addition to its customary interpretations.

Duchamp exemplifies the ambivalent attitude toward women that permeates dada and surrealist art.[11] Man Ray, Duchamp's close friend, also dealt with sexual innuendo in his art. His 1935 screen (Cat. 29) is a continuation of the metaphor Duchamp had begun. Tradition dictates that the action of disrobing should take place

FIG. 141 Richard Serra, American, born 1939, *St. Johns Rotary Arc*, 1980, corten steel, 365.8 x 6,096.0 (144 x 2400). Courtesy Leo Castelli Gallery, New York.

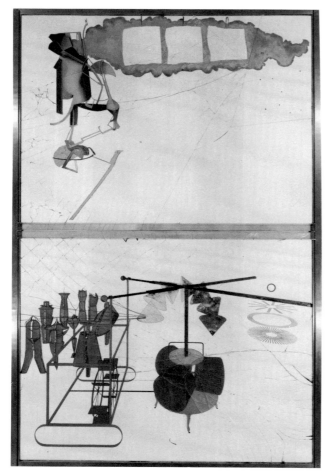

behind the screen, but now the act occupies center stage. Man Ray assumes our knowledge of the screen as a cover and dressing partition, and shocks us with his reversal of its functional role.

Elaborately patterned folding Moorish screens are so ubiquitous in the easel paintings of Henri Matisse that it seems impossible he did not create a real screen.[12] Yet, not a single example by Matisse has been discovered. What is important here, however, is not whether Matisse made standing floor screens, but how he used them in his painting. In his works from the 1920s, Matisse changes the patterns in his screens to fit the mood of the paintings, the women, and their harem clothing. As a signifier for woman, for undressing, and for the sexual act, the screens in Matisse's paintings simultaneously form a

FIG. 142 (top) Marcel Duchamp, French, 1887-1968, *The Large Glass,* 1915-1923, mixed media, 227.5 x 175.8 (109¼ x 69¼). Philadelphia Museum of Art, Bequest of Katherine S. Dreier, 1953.

FIG. 143 (bottom) As seen in the library of The Haven, Dreier's Milford, Connecticut home, 1936.

FIG. 144 Marc Chaimowicz, English, born 1945, *Screen,* 1979, oil on black and white photographs over acrylic on plywood, 182.9 x 182.9 (72 x 72). Courtesy Nigel Greenwood Gallery, London.

barrier between a male viewer (or the male artist) and the seductive yet painted and therefore untouchable woman.

Although lacking an image, the perforated screens by Gray (Cat. 24), Samaras (Cat. 36), and Youngerman (Cat. 41) reveal an ever-changing vista when placed other than against the wall. Samaras' screen in particular is like a many-lensed camera, fundamentally voyeuristic and erotic in the artist's hands.[13] This work is not a screen

but a see-through web made for the titillation of those on the other side.

The delicacy and intimacy of Marc Chaimowicz's photograph screen (fig. 144) is in sharp contrast to Francesco Clemente's *Screen #1*, in part because Chaimowicz uses the screen not just as a sexual metaphor, but as a signifier for intimacy with another person.[14] The series of photographs pasted on the screen reveals the story of a relationship, its sharing, its secrets,

FIG. 145 Pablo Ruiz Picasso, Spanish, 1881-1973, *Two Musicians*, 1921, mixed media on cheesecloth, 177.8 x 187.9 (70 x 74). Photograph shows the work in its original state before the panels were mounted flat. Private Collection, Maryland.

its misunderstandings, and the ultimate separateness of people for whom the screen is the emblem.

Picasso also fruitfully manipulated the concept of separation in his four-panel *Two Musicians* screen of 1921 (fig. 145).[15] In the two center panels, with the end two left effectively blank, Pulcinella and Harlequin confront each other, one facing front, the other with his back toward us. The opposition of the two *Commedia dell'Arte* characters, their costumes, instruments, and stances, is underscored by the screen as divider. Here, as well, Picasso has separated our real world from the imaginary, theatrical one. Jeff Way's screen (fig. 146) in his performance, *Transformations*, acts both as a shield between actor and audience and as a dressing partition.[16] Dancing around and hiding behind the screen, Way changes masks and peels off layers of his costume which echoes the screen's collaged xerox images of skeletons, faces, and undersea creatures.

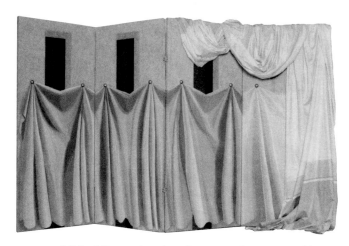

FIG. 147 Michael Graves, American, born 1934, *Decorative Folding Screen*, 1982, acrylic on canvas with fabric, 203.2 x 304.8 (80 x 120). Courtesy Michael Graves and Rizzoli Gallery, New York.

FIG. 146 Jeff Way, American, born 1942, *Transformations*, 1979, color xerox and acrylic on frame and core, 106.7 x 243.8 (42 x 96). Way is shown in his solo performance. Collection of the Artist.

FIG. 148 Seton Smith, American, born 1955, *Mayan Temple*, 1981, oil on canvas with metallic leaf, 182.9 x 228.6 (72 x 90). Collection of the Artist.

The physical and metaphorical implementation of the screen as a barrier is further extended by a group of images of open or closed doors. Hanging on the wall, an easel painting has traditionally been treated by artists as a metaphor for a window. Because the screen stands on the floor and is frequently life-size – five to six feet high or taller – it is more like a wall or a doorway through which the viewer may step to participate in the scene. David Hockney, Daniel Goldstein, Seton Smith, and architects Robert Stern and Michael Graves for example, are all concerned with specific references to the screen as door.[17]

The diving board in Hockney's *Midnight Pool (Paper Pool 10)* (Cat. 40) which doubles as a black door, is conceptually similar to the impenetrable black openings in Graves' screen (fig. 147). Seton Smith, has provided us with stairs to the temple entrance in *Mayan Temple* (fig.

148) while in *The Red Room Screen* (fig. 149), Goldstein offers a play of the screen as a doorway leading to doorways, more doorways, and then to windows. Fittingly, in *Window of the Mind* (fig. 150) Robert Stern blends architectural elements of a broken golden architrave, lime green wainscoting, *faux-marbre* baseboards, and mirrors to simulate French floor-to-ceiling doors which in real houses also function as windows. With mirrors rather than glass, Stern's "doors" are an entrance to, and a reflection of, the viewer's world and his mind, as his title explains.

The folding screen also bears a structural relationship to a folding altarpiece. An altarpiece, however, does not stand on the floor but rather on or above an altar. Closed at certain times during the Christian year, the side panels are often half the size of the central one so as to meet and

FIG. 149 Daniel Goldstein, American, born 1950, *The Red Room Screen,* 1983, paper cutout, 177.8 x 325.1 (70 x 128). Collection of the Artist.

not overlap. The analogy in the mind of the artist when considering the screen as altarpiece nevertheless results in a religious/secular confrontation.

For his carved and painted wooden screen, *Three Women* (fig. 151) Adrian Kellard has adopted the Biblical figures of the three Marys from El Greco's painting, *The Disrobing of Christ.* In the painting, the women turn their heads in sorrow away from Christ as he is being stripped of his garments prior to his trip to Calvary and ultimate death. On the screen, however, we do not see the Christ figure and thus the reason for the look of horror in the women's eyes. Instead, the screen metaphorically blocks our view of the disrobing, so that whoever undresses behind the screen finds himself symbolically in the place of Christ.

Bruce Conner began *Partition* (Cat. 33) in 1961 as an altarpiece, with pictures of Christ collaged on the central panel of one side. As he continued to work, he attached to the surface of the screen bits of the clothing one would expect to remove when undressing behind it. Layering on nylon stockings, lace, broken beads, rhinestones, and bracelets, Conner gave *Partition* the appearance of a prostitute's dressing room. The juxtaposition of these two metaphors, one for religion and the other for sexual gratification, implies yet a third one: man, in a state of original sin, is surrounded by the seducer, woman. The screen therefore signifies the state of the world—an uneasy balance between salvation and temptation.

FIG. 150 Robert A. M. Stern, American, born 1939, and assistant Alan J. Gerber, American, born 1956, *Window of the Mind*, 1982, wood, mirrored glass, taffeta, faux-marbre, and gold leaf, 213.4 x 274.3 (84 x 108). Courtesy Rizzoli Gallery, New York.

FIG. 151 Adrian Kellard, American, born 1959, *Three Women*, 1981, wood, latex paint, ink, 213.4 x 131.4 (84 x 51¾). Courtesy of the Artist.

Western artists in the twentieth century have altered significantly the purpose, image, and structure of the folding screen, challenging the traditional notions about this ancient form. Beyond usefulness and form is the idea, which always separates art from craft. The folding image of the twentieth century screen, however, reveals the power of fusing concept with structure. Embracing function and decoration, the screen is now free to become sculpture and metaphor.

NOTES

1. Susan Crile has made two double-sided folding screens. See Kenneth Baker, "Susan Crile: Abstracting the Image," *Arts Magazine* 50 (December 1975): 54-55. For information on Morley see Michael Compton, *Malcolm Morley, Paintings 1965-1982* (exh. cat., London, Whitechapel Art Gallery, 1983). The pop artists Allen Jones (Cat. 34), Jim Dine (Cat. 37), Andy Warhol, and Billy Al Bengston have made folding screens.

2. The painted pattern of brilliantly colored, amorphous shapes was one Grant had used previously on the tops of rectangular dining room tables designed by the founder of the Omega Workshop, Roger Fry. The lilypond, which one would normally stand above and look down into, has been tilted ninety degrees so that the viewer has the sensation of floating over the pond. If one were to have sat at the "lilypond" table, next to the lilypond screen, the effect must have been overpowering – a successful fusion of art and life, Omega-style.

3. Many artists working within the 1970s style of pattern and decoration have used the format of the screen for their chromatic and imagistic experiments. They include Frank Faulkner, Jane Kaufman, Kim Mac-Connel, Arlene Slavin, George Sugarman, and Robert Zakanitch. See Janet Kardon, *The Decorative Impulse* (exh. cat., Philadelphia, Institute of Contemporary Art, University of Pennsylvania, 1979); and Robert Jensen and Patricia Conway, *Ornamentalism* (New York, 1982).

4. Ellen Lanyon has created three large folding screens and has executed panels for several others. See Lucy Lippard, "Under the Wing of Survival: Ellen Lanyon," in *Ellen Lanyon* (exh. cat., Chicago, N.A.M.E. Gallery, 1983), 4-5.

5. Frederick S. Levine, *The Apocalyptic Vision: The Art of Franz Marc as German Expressionist* (New York: Harper & Row, 1979), 47.

6. Allan Kaprow, "Nature in the Art of Irving Kriesberg," *Art International* 7 (January 1964): 29-31.

7. Leon Polk Smith characterizes his standing floor pieces as "folding paintings" since he does not intend them to serve any function other than as art.

8. John Russell, "Jennifer Bartlett Creates an Archetypal New Found Land," *New York Times* (23 May 1982), 35.

9. Carrie Rickey, "Decor," *Dekor* (exh. cat., Mannheim, Kunstverein, 1979), 10.

10. Richard Hamilton, "The Large Glass," in *Marcel Duchamp*, ed. Anne d'Harnoncourt and Kynaston McShine (exh. cat., New York, Museum of Modern Art, 1973), 66.

11. See Whitney Chadwick, "Eros or Thanatos – the Surrealist Cult of Love Reexamined," *Artforum* 14 (November 1975): 46-56.

12. In 1945 Matisse finished painting a set of doors for Señor and Señora Enchorrena in Paris. The doors have recently been mounted onto a screen structure; see Alfred J. Barr, Jr., *Matisse: His Art and His Public* (New York: Museum of Modern Art, 1951), 493.

13. Samaras is also a photographer and has worked extensively with the polaroid camera. See Arnold Glimscher, *Photo-Transformations*, ed. Constance Glenn (exh. cat., Long Beach, California State University, 1975) and Carter Ratcliff, *Sittings 8x10* (exh. cat., New York, Pace Gallery, 1980).

14. Tate Gallery, *Artists and Performance* (exh. cat., London, Tate Gallery, 1981), 4.

15. This Picasso screen, not recorded in Zervos, was authenticated by the artist himself at the time of a 1961 exhibition, *Bonne Fête Monsieur Picasso* (exh. cat., Frederick S. Wight Art Gallery, University of California, Los Angeles, 1961), ill. 89. The screen designed for Madame Eugenia Errazuriz, derives from the sets of motifs of the third ballet, *Pulcinella*, Picasso designed for Diaghilev and his Ballet Russe: Douglas Cooper, *Picasso Theatre* (New York, 1968), 47-49. Many other artists who designed sets for Diaghilev including Jean Cocteau, Giacomo Balla, Natalia Gontcharova, Robert Delaunay, and Jose-Maria Sert also made folding screens.

16. Kay Larson, "Through the Maskes, Darkly," *Village Voice* (2 June 1980), 85.

17. Rizzoli Gallery recently commissioned the painter Richard Haas and four other architects, Thomas Beeby, Michael Graves, Robert Stern, and Stanley Tigerman to make folding screens for an exhibition at Rizzoli Gallery in New York, December 1982-January 1983.

Catalogue II : 1913 - 1982

19.1

19

VANESSA BELL

English, 1879-1961

BATHERS IN A LANDSCAPE, *1913*
Gouache on paper mounted on canvas. 178.8 x 201.9 (70³/8 x 79¹/2)
Victoria and Albert Museum, London

Vanessa Bell's folding screen, *Bathers in a Landscape* (19.1), was painted a few months after the July 1913 opening of the Omega Workshop in London.[1] The Workshop, where Bell was a co-director, sold textiles, rugs, chairs, tables, and pottery designed and/or painted by some of England's young avant-garde artists. Screens, however, were a specialty and offered Omega artists the basic compositional opportunities of easel painting, though considerably complicated by the folding, multipartite screen structure.[2]

Bathers in a Landscape is based on a sketch (19.2) Bell made in August 1913 while on holiday in Norfolk.[3] The study shows five male and female figures seated on the ground or on chairs in front of the opening of a pitched tent. The apex of the entrance is somewhat right of center. When Bell translated this composition into a screen, she eliminated one of the figures, and transformed the rest into females. In addition, many details were simplified, and the landscape and tent structure were tightly compressed. Although the women in the composition are described as bathers, the lack of water and their languid poses would suggest otherwise.

19.2 *Summer Camp*, 1913, oil on canvas. Painted at Brandon Camp near Thetford, Norfolk. Private Collection.

19.3 Paul Cézanne, French, 1839-1906, *Large Bathers*, oil on canvas. Philadelphia Museum of Art, W. P. Wilstach Collection.

Trained at the Royal Academy School under John Singer Sargent from 1901 to 1904, Bell progressed rapidly in her painting style. Her relatively traditional approach was replaced by one that embraced the newest means of expression. During her excursions to Paris and to the 1910 and 1912 London exhibitions of post-impressionist art organized by her fellow Omega artist Roger Fry, she had the opportunity to study works by Cézanne, Matisse, and Gauguin.[4] The triangular arrangement of figures in Bell's screen, in fact, recalls Cézanne's *Large Bathers* (19.3). Bell, who in 1912 wrote her husband Clive that she wanted to buy a picture by Cézanne, was obviously familiar with this type of Cézanne composition.[5] Fry's 1912 post-impressionist exhibition was even enlarged in January 1913 by the addition of numerous Cézanne watercolors sent from Paris by Galerie Bernheim-Jeune, strengthening the probability that Bell was influenced by the French master.[6] Furthermore, the areas of bright color in the screen, outlined in black, recall the style of Japanese woodcuts and of paintings by the Fauves and Nabis with which Bell was familiar.

The success of *Bathers in a Landscape* is dependent on its folding format. With the central fold coming forward, the tent acquires a pyramidal definition, and space and volume are enlarged as the terrain is broken and angled by the folding structure. Although the folds impede the purity of the diagonal lines, they create the cohesive tension in this painting of reverie.

19.5 *Music Room Screen*, 1932, 132.1 x 182.9 (52 x 72). Portsmouth Museum of Art.

19.4 Vanessa Bell and Duncan Grant, *The Music Room*, 1932. Installation view, Lefevre Gallery, London.

Although Bell had not intended this screen to harmonize with specific Omega products, several projects on which she worked during her career demanded an integration of objects through a planned decorative environment. In 1932 Bell and her companion, former Omega painter Duncan Grant, were asked to collaborate on the design of a music room as a showpiece installation in the Lefevre Gallery in London (19.4).[7] As part of the furnishings, Bell designed a three-panel screen with curving tops and circle motifs that repeated decorative patterns used in the furniture, carpets, curtains, and wall paintings. On the screen (19.5) she painted a trio of graceful nudes who pluck stringed instruments and sing. Through its subject the screen offered visual accompaniment for anyone playing the piano in the music room. Interestingly, this *Music Room Screen* was purchased by Bell's sister, Virginia Woolf.

1. It seems likely that this screen was the one shown in the January 1914 exhibition of the Grafton Group, which consisted primarily of works by Omega artists. Bell exhibited six paintings and one screen in that exhibition. See Richard Shone, *Bloomsbury Portraits* (Oxford: Phaidon, 1976), 260.

2. Vanessa Bell worked in the Omega Workshop with its founder Roger Fry, and with Duncan Grant and Wyndham Lewis, all of whom painted folding screens; see Shone, *Bloomsbury Portraits*, 99, 102-104, 109, 125, 180.

3. Shone, *Bloomsbury Portraits*, 88.

4. Grafton Galleries, *Manet and the Post-Impressionists* (London, 1910); and *The Second Post-Impressionist Exhibition* (London, 1912).

5. Frances Spalding, *Vanessa Bell* (New Haven: Ticknor and Fields, 1983), 109.

6. Spalding, *Bell*, 116.

7. Richard Shone and Judith Collins, *Duncan Grant Designer* (exh. cat., Liverpool, Bluecoat Gallery, 1980), 20; and Shone, *Bloomsbury Portraits*, 239-242.

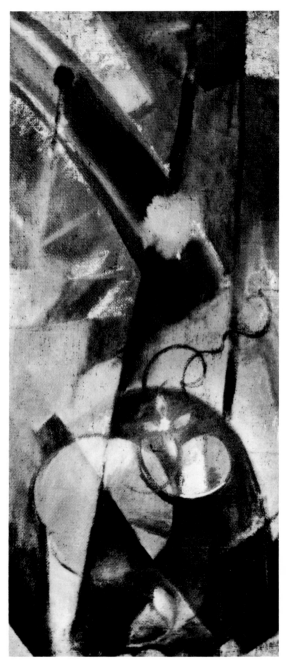

20.1

20

FRANZ MARC
German, 1880-1916

THREE-PANEL SCREEN, *1913*
Oil on canvas. 116.0 x 165.5 (45 5/8 x 65 13/16)
Private Collection
Städtisches Museum, Mülheim an der Ruhr, West Germany
Städtisches Museum Abteiberg, Mönchen-Gladbach, West Germany

Perhaps indicative of the relative disuse into which such objects had fallen by the late fifties, Franz Marc's three-panel screen (20.1) was broken up and each of its panels sold in separate sales in 1958 and 1959.[1] The panels have been reunited for the first time since these sales, for purposes of this exhibition. The "firescreen with landscape and animal-like representations"[2] was painted in 1913 while Marc and his wife Maria were living in Sindelsdorf, a small village in upper Bavaria not far from Murnau, the home of Marc's friend and fellow Blaue Reiter artist Wassily Kandinsky. The screen's provenance suggests it was painted by Marc for his own home,[3] just as its diminutive size suggests it might have been used, albeit carefully, as a firescreen.[4] Other small-scale examples from the turn of the century, however, such as those by Arthur Mackmurdo (fig. 66) and Chris Lebeau (Cat. 17) were intended both to carve out intimate spaces within larger ones, and to block drafts along the floor. One can easily imagine, in fact, that Marc used the screen for this latter purpose, perhaps in the dining room at his Sindelsdorf home.[5]

The screen is one of the few utilitarian objects designed by Marc during his short but brilliant career as a painter, printmaker, and writer. Between 1905 and 1911 he occasionally made sculpture, bronze clasps, and even cups; in 1912 he painted decorations on the four sides of an iron chest.[6] The exact reasons for the artist's interest in the screen format are unknown, yet there are ample grounds for speculation. Marc, like his friends Kandinsky and Klee, studied at the Munich Academy in 1900, the height

of the Jugendstil movement in Germany. Several artists from this movement made folding screens, some of which were produced commercially (fig. 98 and 99). Marc might even have known Klee's own 1900 screen (Cat. 9). In addition, Kandinsky and August Macke, another member of the Blaue Reiter group and Marc's friend as well, designed various types of decorative objects such as vases, embroidery, and clothing in the early 1900s.[7] More importantly, from 1911 to 1913 Kandinsky made several pieces of painted furniture;[8] the primitive decorations on these pieces recall the Bavarian folk tradition, but they also signal an application of modern forms of expression used in painting to common household objects.

In his major foray into the realm of decoration, Marc also chose the medium and materials of easel painting. His three-panel screen, now lacking its original frame, is thinly painted on a rough, burlaplike canvas. Marc's use of the *Sackleinwand* support may very well have been a conscious effort to deny the facility and elegance associated with most Jugendstil products, infusing the object with a certain material primitivism that he and Kandinsky strove for stylistically and symbolically in their works.

The screen shows an abstract landscape with a brilliant rainbow arcing across the upper portions of the scene. In the left hand panel, just below the rainbow at the right, a multifaceted and multicolored star glows near a mountain peak. At the very bottom of the panel, barely discernible because of Marc's typical fractionalization of form into color fragments, is an oval-shaped creature. Upon closer inspection, this creature is seen to be a deer whose head and single visible pointed ear is tucked close to its body, as if asleep. The deer's bent leg and hoof are visible at the bottom edge of the panel. In the center panel, a bright yellow sun shines just below the rainbow. A large horse's head, seen frontally, emerges from the complex colored background at the very center of this panel, just above a tree-covered mountain. Finally, in the right hand panel, the rainbow plummets earthward, ending in a large yellow rectangle which has been tipped on one of its edges. At the left, the blackened top of what seems to be a yellow evergreen tree angles upward into the rainbow, while a small red and white flower blooms near the bottom center. Just below this flower is another oval-shaped deer; its single-eared head bends down so that the top of its head nearly touches the ground.

The many-layered symbolism of Marc's imagery here, and its purposeful accommodation to the folding format require careful consideration. The most obvious feature of the composition is the rainbow. A common element in Marc's work, rainbows carry several possible symbolic meanings. In the now lost and slightly earlier *Tower of the Blue Horses* of 1913,[9] the rainbow can be understood

as a sacred altar symbol and as an apocalyptic motif in this picture where heroic horses yearn for spiritual union with the heavens above.[10] As Mark Rosenthal has convincingly shown, the rainbows in Marc's paintings often encircle and protect what is below them, and, like the appearance of a rainbow to Noah after the flood, symbolize pardon or reconciliation given by God to humanity.[11] In the peaceful, paradisiacal setting of the screen, the rainbow's significance as protector and provider seems especially likely.

Animals, and horses in particular, figure prominently in the content-filled, spiritual works of Franz Marc. He was a great lover of animals and made sketches of them on visits to the Munich zoo. Marc's primary interest in them was not anatomical, however. He wrote that "people with their lack of piety, especially men, never touched my true feelings. But animals with their virginal sense of life awakened all that is good in me."[12] From 1907 on, Marc increasingly depicted animals in his works to convey his contradicting views of the world as a place where either union with nature or apocalyptic doom was possible. In the screen, the peacefully sleeping deer at the left and right suggest Marc chose the former view; deer

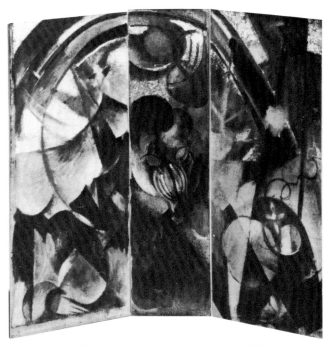 

20.2 and 20.3 Maquette of screen showing alternate folded positions.

were often used by the artist to symbolize an ideal, harmonious relationship with nature. Indeed, the joyous comforting presence of the rainbow reinforces this interpretation.

Yet there is something unsettling about the horse's head in the central panel. Although it seems to assume a cosmic benevolence in the way it peers down over the landscape below, the horse's head is grotesquely out of scale with its surroundings. Moreover, this disembodied head emerges like an apparition from a color-swirled sky. Marc's uncharacteristically frontal view of the horse's head also intensifies its magical appearance. In addition, the head is placed directly below the rainbow and above a triangular mountain. From 1911 onward, the triangle shape was used by both Marc and Kandinsky to symbolize the aspiring soul of the individual and humanity in general.[13] The vertical and frontal arrangement of mountain, horse, and rainbow may be interpreted as a sort of summary statement of Marc's pantheistic creed: our striving for harmony can best be achieved by confronting and understanding the spirituality that is so evident in nature and, by implication, so rarely found in man.

But what of the screen format itself—how does it affect the formal aspects of the composition or our interpretation of the imagery? The most common configurations for a three-panel screen would be with the central panel parallel to the viewer, with the side panels angled toward or away from the viewer. In either case, the changes are dramatic (20.2 and 20.3). The curving lines of the rainbow bend, and we sense that it surrounds us even more or that it reaches farther back. Our reading of the space is thereby significantly altered in the same way as in Balla's slightly later screen (Cat. 21). Marc had seen an exhibition of futurist works in 1912 at the Sturm gallery in Berlin,[14] and it is conceivable this disruption of the curving rainbow may be a personal variation of the Italian artist's use of velocity lines. As we know from Balla's screen, these lines also suggest passage of time, and Marc's placement of a star in the first panel, and a bright sun in the second, clearly presents a meteorological if not a temporal contradiction. In addition, the visual and symbolic impact of the horse's head is also affected. The head either looms out at us with even greater intensity, or it becomes consumed within its surroundings while still maintaining its focal position in the image. For Marc the folding format therefore becomes an instrument by which he makes his message more forceful and direct, just as the rainbow is a metaphor for the spiritual unity he was seeking within nature.

1. The left-hand panel was listed as no. 688 in the 20-21 May 1958 sale of the *Stuttgarter Kunstkabinett. 31. Auktion. Moderne Kunst;* the central panel was listed als no. 524 in the 20-21 November 1959 sale of the same Stuttgart auction house in *34. Auktion. Moderne Kunst;* and the right-hand panel was listed as no. 636 in the 21-22 November 1958 sale in *32. Auktion. Moderne Kunst.* The arduous, year-long search for the present owners and locations of the screen panels was successful only through the assistance and generosity of Roman Norbert Ketterer. I am also grateful to Dr. Karin Frank von Maur of the Staatsgalerie, Stuttgart, and to Friedl Wimmer of Galerie Würthle in Vienna for their help in locating the panels.

2. Klaus Lankheit, *Franz Marc. Katalog der Werke* (Cologne: Verlag M. DuMont Schauberg, 1970), no. 883.

3. According to Alois Schardt, *Franz Marc* (Berlin: Rembrandt Verlag G.m.b.H., 1936), 174, in section IX "Kunstgewerbliche Arbeiten. Malereien," no. 3, the screen was owned by Frau Maria Marc Reid, the artist's widow. The various Stuttgarter Kunstkabinett sale catalogues mentioned above indicate that the screen was later in Schardt's collection in Berlin.

4. A painted fabric screen must obviously be used with some caution when placed near an open fireplace. There is a long tradition of fabric, usually embroidered, single-panel screens being used for this purpose. See for example fig. 25.

5. See the ca. 1913 photograph of Marc at his coffee table, reproduced in Rosel Goliek et al., *Franz Marc. 1880-1916* (exh. cat., Munich, Städtische Galerie im Lenbachhaus, 1980), 42.

6. See Lankheit, *Franz Marc*, nos. 896-917.

7. See Peg Weiss et al., *Kandinsky in Munich. 1896-1914* (exh. cat., New York, Solomon R. Guggenheim Museum, 1982), particularly nos. 149-164.

8. Weiss, *Kandinsky in Munich*, nos. 30-32. These pieces of furniture were presumably made by Kandinsky for the home he and Gabriele Münter shared in Murnau, and surely would have been seen by Marc.

9. See Klaus Lankheit, *Der Turm der Blauen Pferde* (Stuttgart: Phillip Reclam jun., 1961). It is known that Marc encountered considerable intellectual and artistic difficulty in the first half of 1913. By the summer, however, these difficulties seem to have been resolved, and Marc went on to produce some of the most important works of his career by the end of the year. It seems likely that it was in this satisfying period of renewed activity at Sindelsdorf that Marc did the screen.

10. Klaus Lankheit, *Franz Marc. Sein Leben und Seine Kunst* (Cologne: Verlag M. DuMont Schauberg, 1976), 120; and Marion Wolf, "Biblia Omnii: Timeliness and Timelessness in the Work of Franz Marc," *Art Journal* 33 (Spring 1974): 230.

11. Mark Rosenthal, "Franz Marc: Pioneer of Visual Abstraction," in *Franz Marc: 1880-1916* (exh. cat., Berkeley, University Art Museum, 1979), 25.

12. Quoted from Rosenthal, "Franz Marc," 8.

13. Kandinsky first formulated the symbolism of the triangle in his 1911 publication, *Concerning the Spiritual in Art* (New York; Wittenborn, 1947), 27-30. See also Rosenthal, "Franz Marc," 15-16.

14. For an analysis of the futurists' influence on Marc's work, see Frederick S. Levine, *The Apocalyptic Vison: The Art of Franz Marc as German Expressionism* (New York: Harper & Row, 1979), 69-75.

21.5 Verso.

21.4

GIACOMO BALLA

Italian, 1871-1958

SCREEN (VELOCITY LINES AND LANDSCAPE), *ca. 1918*
Oil on canvas. 151.0 x 126.5 (59⁷/16 x 49³/16)
Galerie Rudolf Zwirner, Cologne

On 1 March 1915, the Italian futurist painter Giacomo Balla published a manifesto describing the *Futurist Reconstruction of the Universe*. One section, entitled "Artificial Landscape," summarized Balla's revolutionary concept of landscape:

Developing the first synthesis of the speeding automobile, Balla arrived at the first plastic construction (No. 1). This revealed to us an abstract landscape consisting of cones, pyramids, polyhedrons, spirals of mountains, rivers, lights, shadows. There exists a profound analogy between the essential linear forces of speed and the essential linear forces of a landscape.[1]

The manifesto describes images Balla had been creating since 1913, as in *Triptych: Abstract Speed; Abstract Speed + Noise; Abstract Speed – Wake of Speeding Automobile* (21.1).[2] Until the end of the decade he continued to experiment, depicting speed and landscapes in a series of paintings, drawings, and collages such as *Velocity Lines + Landscape*, 1918 (21.2).[3] These experiments led him to his unique 1916-1917 set design for the

21.1 and 21.2 Left: *Triptych: Wake of Speeding Automobile* (third panel of triptych), 1913, oil on canvas, 50.2 x 63.1 (19¹³/16 x 24¹³/16). Courtesy Marlborough Gallery, New York.   Right: *Velocity Lines* + Landscape, 1918, collage, 35.0 x 28.5 (13¹³/16 x 11¼). Courtesy Carus Gallery, New York.

21.3 Set design for Stravinsky-Diaghelev ballet, *Fireworks*, 1916-1917.

21.6 Study for screen, ca. 1916, watercolor on paper, 36.5 x 24.5 (14⅜ x 9⁹/₁₆). Collection of Milena, Ugolini and Silvana Stipa, Rome.

Stravinsky-Diaghilev ballet, *Fireworks*, for which he constructed a rounded and conical terrain (21.3) resembling those in his paintings and in his manifesto.[4] There were no dancers in this ballet, however; instead, more than seventy light changes, directed by Balla, produced flashing light effects, undulating shapes, modulations of color, and an intense sense of motion.

Shortly thereafter Balla painted a double-sided, irregularly-shaped folding screen (21.4 and 21.5) where he utilized those same dramatic qualities seen in the *Fireworks* ballet.[5] The two-panel screen was created in 1918 for the Princess Bassiano, an American living in Rome who collected a large number of Balla's works.[6] The screen, recently restored, has been dated to 1918-1919 on stylistic grounds.[7] The collage, *Velocity Lines + Landscape* (21.2) from 1918 suggests the earlier date for the screen, although the Balla chronology is difficult to pinpoint.

On the recto of the screen (21.4) Balla painted a scene of a wide white road curving from the foreground into the background toward rounded light and dark green hills. The deep blue of the sky is pierced with two bands of light blue which streak from the top of the screen into tiny points at the bottom. These velocity lines in Balla's vocabulary indicate the passing of an automobile and whip through the composition in arcing red and pink lightning

21.7 *Worker's Day*, 1904, oil on paper. Collection Balla, Rome.

shapes.[8] The image as a whole echoes the stepped structure of the screen and its movable panels. A study for the screen (21.6) shows that Balla began with a shape not made to stand by itself. As the screen panels approach a ninety degree angle, the rush of perspective and vitality increase in the scene, thus underlining the three-dimensional illusion of the landscape. The verso of the screen (21.5) reveals a road through the same landscape, but painted from the opposing perspective. The orange, white, and light blue velocity lines are more agitated, as though the invisible car had passed more recently along this part of the road. Through the screen's double-sided image, Balla also signified simultaneous movement in time and space. He had experimented with the effect as early as 1904 in his painting, *Workers' Day* (21.7);[9] later paintings such as *Dynamism of a Dog on a Leash*, 1912, document the importance for Balla of depicting this kind of simultaneity.

During his career Balla painted and made designs for several other screens. With each one, Balla altered the subject matter and its relationship to the folding format. In another two-panel screen commissioned by Princess Bassiano he employed diagonal and spiral shapes to depict an abstract human form fusing with the structure. (21.8).[10] Stretching its fingertips and toes to the edges of the screen, the figure alludes to Leonardo's perfectly proportioned man. In contrast, the verso of the screen (21.9), and the preliminary study for it, show two distinct panels: in the left panel are undulating abstract shapes, while in the right panel, there are pointed geometric forms.

The implied physical intimacy of Balla's two-panel screens is not present in his designs for three- and four-panel pieces (21.10). Balla portrayed his images laterally across the screen though the shaped panels help to convey a sense of vitality. In his ca. 1925-1930 screen (21.11),

21.8 *Two-Panel Screen* (recto), 1918, oil on wood, height 124.0 (48 13/16). Collection Balla, Rome.

21.9 *Two-Panel Screen* (verso).

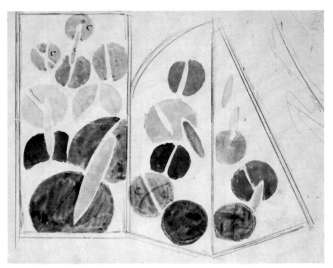

21.10 Study for a three-panel screen, ca. 1916-1918, pencil and watercolor on paper. Collection Balla, Rome.

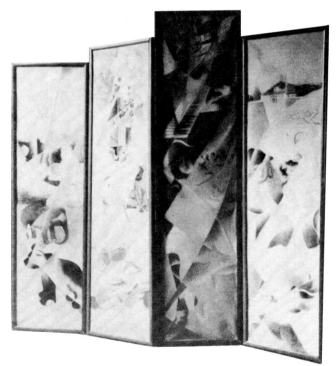

21.11 *Four-Panel Screen*, ca. 1925-1930. Painted for Princess Caetani. Present whereabouts unknown.

painted in a more figurative style, the force lines and simultaneous action still create a dynamism which is accentuated by the folding structure.

Although known primarily as a painter, Balla also applied his talents to the decoration of clothing, fans, chairs, rugs, tapestries, and to the fabrication of his painted wood "futurist flowers." The opportunity to decorate whole interiors, such as a nursery, his own dining room, or the Bal-Tik-Tak cabaret, allowed him to transmit his dynamic visual themes to a variety of surfaces, spaces, and structures.[11] The inherent mobility of the folding screen's hinged panels, combined with Balla's activated forms, however, transformed the folding screen into an appropriate futurist object.

1. Translated from Virginia Dortch Dorazio, *Giacomo Balla: An Album of His Life and Work* (New York, 1969), unpaginated. For the original text see: Maria Drudi Gambillo and Teresa Fiori, *Archivi del Futurismo*, 2 vols. (Rome, 1962), 1:51.

2. "Giacomo Balla intended that these three paintings should be hung together to form a triptych. He wished to portray three different moments of a speeding car penetrating the atmosphere. On the right is his visual perception of a car speeding on a highway within a green landscape; in the center, the same "abstract speed lines" of the car are seen with the addition of zig-zag lines indicating the noise produced by the roaring car; and on the left, the speeding car and noise have passed and the highway remains in a empty landscape. The frames were painted by the artist." Dorazio, *Balla*.

3. For other works in this series see Giovanni Lista, *Balla* (Modena, 1982), Fig. 311-314, 331-334, 362-370, 373, 379, 501, 505, 524.

4. For a detailed description of the performance and of the construction of the stage, see Michael Kirby, *Futurist Performance* (New York, 1971), 83-86. For drawings and photographs of a reconstruction of the set, see Lista, *Balla*, Fig. 466-470.

5. *Giacomo Balla* (exh. cat., Rome, Galleria Nazionale d'Arte Moderna, 1972); Enrico Crispolti, *Ricostruzione futurista dell'universo* (exh. cat., Torino, Musei Civici, 1980); and Lista, *Balla*, Fig. 522a, 522b.

6. Letter from Luce Balla to the author, 27 August 1982.

7. *Balla*, Galleria Nazionale.

8. Balla took the lead from Futurism's leader, Tomaso Filippo Marinetti, who wrote in his founding manifesto of 20 February 1909: "We declare that the world's splendor has been enriched by a new beauty: the beauty of speed. A racing car . . . is more beautiful than the *Winged Victory of Samothrace*" Raffaele Carrieri, *Futurism* [Milan, 1963], 12.

9. "The composition recreates and unites three different moments in a simultaneous experience (space-time) in anticipation of the Futurist concept of sumultaneity." Dorazio, *Balla*, plate 30; and for further discussion see Gerald Silk, "Fu Balla e Balla Futurista," *Art Journal* 41 (Winter 1981): 328-336.

10. Human forms are also evident in the furniture Balla designed for a children's nursery; see Lista, *Balla*, Fig. 759-763.

11. Lista, *Balla*, Fig. 706-721.

22

THOMAS HART BENTON

American, 1889-1975

SCREEN WITH ABSTRACT SEA MOTIF, *ca. 1925-1926*
Oil on canvas with aluminum and painted wood frame. 171.1 x 201.3 (67³/8 x 79¹/4)
Lent Anonymously

Bold, brilliantly colored forms dance across the painted surface of Thomas Hart Benton's four-panel *Screen with Abstract Sea Motif* (22.1 and cover). At the top, undulating, red-edged brownish clouds roll across a deep navy blue sky, contrasting with the calm, waveless light blue sea below. In the foreground, dominating the composition, a massive wave structure grows. These sculpted shapes are an abstraction of the crashing sea which Benton studied and painted firsthand repeatedly during summers on Cape Cod.[1] By depicting the sea subject in a folding screen format, the artist was able to create layered planes and a sense of three-dimensional volume in his composition. Moreover, the screen's folds accentuate the

breaks in the horizon line, carrying the eye farther back into space (22.2).

The image, proceeding from right to left in the oriental manner, and the flattened design underscore Benton's debt to Japanese prints, specifically to Katsushika Hokusai's well-known color woodblock print, *The Great Wave off Kanagawa* (22.3). During his early training at the Art Institute of Chicago, Benton saw an exhibition of Japanese color prints held there in 1908.[2] In a memoir, he described their importance: "I obtained also in Chicago my first insights into the art of designing – of consciously planning, or composing, pictures before attempting to execute them. Japanese prints were, very

22.2 Folded.

22.3 Katsushika Hokusai, Japanese, 1760-1849, *The Great Wave off Kanagawa*, color woodblock print. Yale University Art Gallery.

largely because of James McNeill Whistler's influence, much in favor at this time. Frederick Oswald, my favorite teacher at the Institute, was enthusiastic about these [prints] and encouraged continuous study of the way they were put together. Through continued observation of the prints I learned to arrange my pictures in definite patterns and acquired a taste, from such artists as Hokusai, for flowing lines which lasted all my life."[3] While living in Paris from 1908 to 1911, Benton collected Japanese prints for his studio walls and noted that he "never painted a still life without including one in the background."[4]

Benton's techniques also reflect his study of modern French artists, especially Gauguin and Matisse: "The influence of Gauguin was almost as strong as that of Cézanne and almost directly opposite in its effects. Its orientalist patterns, now being reintroduced by Matisse, were at this time coming into much prominence. Both Gauguin's and Matisse's methods were more closely allied to my own ways of composing than were those of Cézanne, dealing as they did with silhouettes rather than volumes."[5] On the surface of his screen, Benton combined vibrating, sensual tones derived from Gauguin with the colorful abstract forms borrowed from Japanese prints. The screen is also a result of Benton's association with Synchromism, an early twentieth-century chromatic painting style developed by the Americans, Stanton

22.6 Sports Den, Albert M. Briggs home, Garden City, Long Island, with decorations by Thomas Hart Benton, 1925.

MacDonald Wright and Morgan Russell.[6] The Synchromists' emphasis on brightly colored compositions, often consisting of abstract forms, had a wide impact on American art from 1915 to 1930 and influenced the style of Jay Van Everen's screen (Cat. 23) as well.

Benton's screen was probably commissioned in 1925 by Mr. and Mrs. Albert M. Briggs of Garden City, Long Island. Mr. Briggs, whose hobby was fishing, wanted to have his sports den decorated, and chose Benton to do the project. The artist responded by designing four individual decorative wall panels (22.4, 22.5), a rug, and the screen for the room (22.6).[7] The panels, located on the walls between mounted fish, depict four separate oceanic and animal still lifes. An abstract wave formation, similar to that in the screen, serves as the backdrop for the panels' compositions. A three-part rug depicting horses and sailfish in curling bands of red, yellow, and white completed Benton's scheme.

Screen with Abstract Sea Motif is a functional and stylistic complement to the other two elements of the decorative program. The screen, however, contains an unusual feature: each panel is surrounded by aluminum strips and then by a painted wood frame. The painted panels are actually hinged to the intrados of the frame and can be pulled open to reveal a shallow niche (22.7).

22.4 Left: *Sea Fantasy,* 1925, oil on tin mounted on board, 162.6 x 121.9 (64 x 48). Courtesy Salander O'Reilly Gallery, New York.

22.5 Right: *Animalistic Fantasy,* 1925, oil on tin, 157.5 x 120.6 (62 x 47½). Marjorie and Charles Benton Collection.

22.1

22.7 *Screen with Abstract Sea Motif,* shown with outer painted panels open.

According to the screen's current owner, these niches were created by Benton for Mr. Briggs to mount photographs of his fishing expeditions. The screen thereby became another type of trophy display, and the fish in the photographs would have been symbolically placed "in" the waters shown in the screen.

Benton designed a second screen around 1930 (22.8), now lost, which may have been commercially produced.

The architect Frederick Kiesler described the screen: "Abstract design executed in different materials: paper, wood, colored sandpapers, emery board, and grass texture. It is typical of modern screens, that the outlines of their parts are irregular. A great variation may be obtained through the different heights and widths of each part."[8] Indeed, the form of the screen recalls Donald Deskey's *Three-Panel Screen,* ca. 1929 (Cat. 26), while some of its stylized, curved motifs are similar to those in Benton's earlier screen. *Screen with Abstract Sea Motif,* however, reveals more clearly how Benton reconciled his painterly aims within a decorative format.

1. Thomas Hart Benton, "An American in Art: A Professional and Technical Autobiography," *Kansas Quarterly* (Spring 1969). A contemporary painting, *Moonlight, Martha's Vineyard,* shows a relatively more naturalistic treatment of the wave motif; see no. 121 in the Sotheby Parke-Bernet New York sale catalogue (4 December 1980).

2. Philip Dennis Cate, *Thomas Hart Benton: A Retrospective of His Early Years, 1907-1929* (exh. cat., New Brunswick, New Jersey, Rutgers University Art Gallery, 1972).

3. Benton, "An American in Art," 12.

4. Benton, "An American in Art," 21.

5. Benton, "An American in Art," 23.

6. See William C. Agee, *Synchromism and Color Principles in American Painting, 1910-1930* (exh. cat., New York, M. Knoedler & Co., Inc., 1965); and Gail M. Levin, *Synchromism and American Color Abstraction, 1910-1925* (exh. cat., New York, Whitney Museum of American Art, 1978).

7. The present owner of the screen reported in an interview in 1982 that when her parents bought the Briggs' house, the third-floor sports den was still intact, complete with the screen, three panels, and the rug. The panels were sold at auction at Parke-Bernet Galleries, New York, 23 May 1951. Benton indicated he had made four panels in 1925 – one remains unaccounted for; see Benton, "An American in Art," 58. The rug has also been described as "made especially for the residence of Mrs. A. M. Briggs [which] makes the floor of great decorative importance with its themes of horses and sailfish." See Walter Randell Storey, "American Rugs of the Modern Age," *Creative Art* 9 (July 1931), 50.

8. See Frederick Kiesler, *Contemporary Art Applied to the Store and Its Display* (New York: Brentano's Publishers, 1930), unpaginated. My thanks to Scott Braznell for pointing out this reference.

22.8 *Five-Panel Screen,* ca. 1930. Present whereabouts unknown.

23

JAY VAN EVEREN
American, 1875-1947

ABSTRACT SCREEN, *ca. 1920-1927*
Oil on wood panels with carved wood (probably Chinese) frame
100.3 x 101.6 (39¹/₂ x 40)
National Museum of American Art, Smithsonian Institution, Washington, Gift of Henry M. Reed

One Christmas between 1924 and 1927, Jay Van Everen presented a small, two-panel screen (23.1) to Marjorie Mansfield, whom he later married in 1930.[1] The screen, with its brightly colored image, was painted in the earlier part of the 1920s when Van Everen was most involved with modern notions of abstraction. Blues, greens, yellows, reds, and oranges, arranged in geometrically patterned forms, swirl around white centers, like the glass in a kaleidoscope. The white centers extend the depth of the composition, forming the vortex of this color whirlpool, and create a pulsating tension with their surrounding areas. At the top, in a format unusual for a screen, are two horizontal strips with vertical prismatic bands of color. Slightly less brilliant in hue than those in the body of the screen, these bands are mirror images and visually draw the screen together, while the color forms below in the center of the screen optically expand the screen's dimensions.

Throughout his career, Van Everen frequently created art for functional situations: murals, tile designs for New York City subway stations, and book illustrations.[2] *Abstract Screen* provided another challenging format, and reveals several facets of Van Everen's artistic training. Although he graduated from Cornell University's School of Architecture, he decided to become a painter and studied at several art schools in New York including the Art Students League.[3] Working first in an academic style, he then turned to abstraction in 1918 because of his exposure to painters James Daugherty, Arthur B. Frost, Jr., and to their interest in the color theories of Synchromism.[4]

From 1918 through 1930, Van Everen formulated his own idiosyncratic yet sophisticated style, exhibiting his

work with Katherine S. Dreier and Marcel Duchamp's Société Anonyme.[5] He experimented by manipulating hand-cut stencils and small blocks in geometric shapes to create his early nonfigurative pieces which resemble some of Kandinsky's abstractions.[6] The delicate stacking of forms in the painted *Abstract Arrangement* (23.2) was fashioned through this process; consequently, the formal and chromatic intentions in this oil closely parallel those

23.2 *Abstract Arrangement*, ca. 1925-1926, oil on canvas. Collection of the Whitney Museum of American Art, New York, Gift of Mr. and Mrs. Henry M. Reed.

23.3 *Abstraction*, ca. 1926, oil on canvas. Collection of the Whitney Museum of American Art, New York, Gift of Mr. and Mrs. Henry M. Reed.

in the screen. In other works, such as *Abstraction* (23.3), Van Everen's efforts to formulate further illusions of vacillating depth and space are accentuated by an area at the bottom of the canvas. Painted in colors less vibrant than the main part of the image, the designs are employed as a framing device and as a formal counterpoint. They serve a visual function similar to that served by the strips at the top of *Abstract Screen*.

Van Everen was also interested in Aztec and Mayan art, and collected oriental rugs and semiprecious stones.[7] The flat abstract patterns, the borders around his paintings, and the jewel-like quality of his color shapes are the obvious reflections of these interests. His widow also recalls that Van Everen frequented antique shops, and was fascinated with Chinese and Japanese art.[8] Since Van Everen did not make the frame for *Abstract Screen*, she believes it was another of his oriental purchases. The frame's small size and deep carvings support this assumption.[9]

Two of Van Everen's contemporaries, Thomas Hart Benton (Cat. 22) and Carl Newman (23.4), also incorporated synchromist experiments in their screens. Van Everen, however, was the only one to insist on a totally abstract image, therefore closely related to certain rhythmic and geometric preoccupations found in contemporary art déco works. Although Benton's and Newman's larger and semifigural screens are more

readily understood as functional objects, to see Van Everen's smaller work as purely decorative would be to miss the artist's pointed intention to experiment artistically even within a functional idiom.

1. Marjorie Mansfield Jaynes, Jay Van Everen's widow, explained in a 12 October 1982 telephone interview her recollections of the origins of *Abstract Screen*.

2. My thanks to Ruth Bohan, whose research on Van Everen was the basis for parts of this entry. More detailed information will appear in the forthcoming publication, a catalogue raisonné of the Société Anonyme Collection at Yale.

3. Marcia Tucker, *Jay Van Everen* (exh. cat., New York, Whitney Museum of American Art, 1972), 2.

4. William Innes Homer et al., *Avant-Garde Painting and Sculpture in America 1910-1925* (exh. cat., Wilmington, Delaware Art Museum, 1975), 140; and Gail M. Levin, *Synchromism and American Color Abstraction, 1910-1925* (exh. cat., New York, Whitney Museum of American Art, 1978), 144.

5. Katherine S. Dreier, *The Société Anonyme at the Brooklyn Museum* (exh. cat., Brooklyn Museum, 1926), 107.

6. Ruth Bohan suggested in a 20 May 1983 letter to the author that "the use of floating geometric shapes may demonstrate Van Everen's response to the work of Kandinsky and the Constructivists, whose paintings were exhibited throughout the 1920s by the Société Anonyme which also showed Van Everen's work." For example, see the discussion of Kandinsky in Katherine S. Dreier, *Western Art and the New Era: An Introduction to Modern Art* (New York: Brentano's, 1923), 102-105, which Van Everen must have seen.

7. My thanks to Ruth Bohan for this information; see also Tucker, *Jay Van Everen*, 3.

8. Reported by Mrs. Jaynes in the 1982 interview with the author.

9. See "A Perfect Gem of Art," 57 and 67 for other examples of these dwarf screens.

23.4 Carl Newman, American, 1858-1932, *Spirit of Christmas*, ca. 1915-1920, oil and tempera on fiberboard, 170.2 x 233.6 (67 x 92). National Museum of American Art, Smithsonian Institution, Gift of Anna McCleery Newton.

23.1

24.1

24

EILEEN GRAY

Irish, 1879-1976

BLOCK SCREEN, *1923*
Lacquered wood with aluminum rods. 181.6 x 178.4 (71 1/2 x 70 1/4)
Collection of Sydney and Frances Lewis, Richmond

While a drawing student at London's Slade School in 1898, Eileen Gray happened on D. Charles' shop at 92 Dean Street, where a sign outside the entrance announced the repair of old lacquer screens. Curious, the young lady went upstairs and was introduced by the shop's craftsmen to the complex and time-consuming process of making lacquer.[1] Eileen Gray later explained, "I was very interested, because I'd always wanted to learn lacquer; and so I said, 'I suppose I could never come here and work,' and they said, 'But you can — of course you can. Start Monday if you like.'"[2] With this fortuitous discovery of D. Charles' shop, Eileen Gray began her career as a designer and maker of lacquer furniture.[3] Her attempts to master the technique continued after her move to Paris in 1902. In 1907 she met there the Japanese lacquer master Sugawara, who aided her in learning more about the demanding process.[4] In 1914 Jacques Doucet, famed collector and bibliophile for whom Eileen Gray had already made two lacquer tables, acquired from the artist her four-panel, double-sided *Le Destin* screen, the only known, signed and dated example of her work.[5]

Over the next two decades Eileen Gray produced some twenty screens, nearly all of them imaginatively designed and brilliantly executed, not only in lacquer, but also metal, celluloid, and cork.[6] The astonishing variety and quality of her screens make it difficult to choose any one over another for purposes of this exhibition. The so-called *Block Screen* (24.1), however, seems to stand out from the rest in its originality and as a portent of the screen form. It derived from a decorative scheme by Gray done for Madame Mathieu Levy (Suzanne Talbot) to use in her rue de Lota, Paris apartment between 1919 and 1922. For the walls of a gallery leading from Mme. Levy's salon to her bedroom, the artist designed a *paravent*

consisting of 450 wood blocks, each lacquered and textured with powdered stone (24.2). Small spaces were allowed between the blocks, resulting in a bricklike wall surface that mitigated the long, narrow feeling of the gallery itself. At the end of the gallery, much for the same purpose, Gray turned the "walls" toward the doorway to permit glimpses into the private spaces of Mme. Levy's bedroom. By turning the lacquer blocks in this fashion, Gray also made the gallery seem shorter, and at the same time gave added visual importance to the double door centered on the far wall.[7]

This brilliant spatial solution led almost naturally to the block screen, which Gray began producing around 1923 from her newly-opened (1922) gallery called "Jean Desert." The block screen exists in both black and white versions, some of whose lacquer blocks are articulated

24.2 *Apartment for Mme. Mathieu Levy, Rue de Lota*, Paris, 1919-1920. Courtesy Museum of Modern Art, New York.

with slightly raised, centralized rectangles.[8] All these screens consist of horizontal rows of lacquered blocks joined together vertically by rods.[9] The rods protrude slightly at the top and bottom, where they function as feet for the screens. This particular example contains seven horizontal rows of five or six blocks each,[10] connected by five pairs of aluminum rods. The apparent simplicity of the screen and its components belies the sophisticated design and functional concepts which underlie it. Its blocks are staggered in position so that the edge of one block comes to rest at the middle of the block below it. As a result, the screen has vertical "panels" of sorts, overlapping each other and whose vertical continuity is interrupted by every other row. Because of the vertical rods, the arrangement of the panels is enormously flexible: the screen can be compressed or stretched, relatively closed or relatively open. Consequently, some of the traditional functions of the screen are very nearly eliminated. The playful oval cutouts in George Logan's 1902 screen (Cat. 14) are timid by comparison. It is clear, however, that this and other block screens by Eileen Gray still perform an architectural function, dividing space within a larger room. They also anticipate by several decades the contemporary inclination to approach the screen as a type of floor sculpture.

There is obviously no image in this screen, thus, its inclusion in an exhibition predicated upon the notion of folding images may seem at first somewhat out of place. The orientation of the lacquer blocks, though, in their very openness and flexibility, allows one to see through the screen into the surrounding environment. In the interiors created by Eileen Gray (24.3), there are glimpses of walls and her own decorative panels through the screen openings. Depending on where the screen was placed, and from what point one entered the room, there undoubtedly would have been similar views of doors, windows, and furniture familiar in a domestic interior. For Eileen Gray, the image was not to be applied to the block screen, but instead resulted from the interaction between the screen and its setting. The clarity of the image was consequently fragmented by the staggered arrangement of blocks and spaces within the screen. In this context, the block screens are among the most innovative of the twentieth century, foreshadowing, too, the aggressive cutout screens of Lucas Samaras (Cat. 36).

1. "Oriental lacquer is made by building up numerous thin layers of a resin (obtained from the Rhus Vernicifera, a tree in the acacia family), which when hardened forms a lustrous surface that is impenetrable to water. The process by which lacquer is made is extraordinarily demanding, requiring both patience and diligence – patience because each layer must be allowed three days in a humid room to harden before the next can be applied; diligence not the least because the resin is noxious and lacquer workers are subject to painful rashes. At least twenty-two steps are required in making lacquer. First a thin coat of natural lacquer is applied to a smooth surface of wood. When this has dried, a second coat mixed with a fine earth imported from Japan is added in order to fill in any cracks in the wood; and onto this is laid a piece of stretched cloth, the purpose of which is to form a uniform base for subsequent coats of lacquer and to cushion any shocks or breaks that might damage the finished surface and permit the infiltration of water. From this point onward, as far as the artist is concerned, the object becomes lacquer, the wooden core having disappeared. Upon this base eight coats of lacquer and Japanese earth are added, each of which, when hardened, is carefully pumiced to make it absolutely smooth and unblemished. An eleventh coat of pure natural lacquer is applied to stabilize the layers beneath it. Then six more coats of lacquer mixed with extremely fine Japanese earth are added. The eighteenth coat is the first into which pigment is introduced, and it is followed by two more coats, each of which is meticulously pumiced. Finally, several coats may be added introducing applied decoration (including such foreign materials as gold or silver leaf, bits of eggshell, or mother-of-pearl)." From J. Stewart Johnson, *Eileen Gray: Designer 1879-1976* (exh. cat., New York, Museum of Modern Art, 1979), 14.

2. Johnson, *Eileen Gray*, 11. This exhibition catalogue is the most thorough and best-documented treatment of the artist's life and career. It does not contain a bibliography, however, and one must resort to either Lamia Doumato, *Eileen Gray, 1879-1976*, No. A-412 in the Vance Architectural Bibliography Series (Monticello, Illinois, 1981) or Annette Rinn's *Eileen Gray*, a seminar project published by the author in 1978 for the Technical University, Munich.

24.3 *"Bedroom-boudoir for Monte Carlo," 14th Salon des Artistes Décorateurs*, Paris, 1923. Courtesy Museum of Modern Art, New York.

3. By 1930 Eileen Gray began a second career as an architect, although she continued to design furniture for these domestic buildings.

4. Sugawara also worked with Jean Dunand in 1912. See Philippe Garner, "The Lacquer Work of Eileen Gray and Jean Dunand," *Connoisseur* 183, no. 735 (1973): 9.

5. See fig. 130.

6. For other examples of her screens, see the sale catalogue from Sotheby Parke Bernet Monaco S.A., *Collection Eileen Gray: Mobilier, objets et projets de sa création* (25 May 1980), nos. 250, 251, 265, and 269. The City of Bristol Museum owns an example of Gray's wood and cork screen (Na. 222), as does the Leicestershire Museums and Art Galleries.

7. Johnson, *Eileen Gray,* 19-20.

8. Six black lacquer versions are known: the example in this exhibition; one at the Museum of Modern Art, New York (Johnson, *Eileen Gray,* 30); one in the Walker Collection, see Marina Vaizey, "The Collection of Mr. and Mrs. Robert Walker, Part 2," *Connoisseur* 183, no. 734 (1973): 233, ill. 3; one in the Victoria and Albert Museum, London, illustrated in *Victorian and Edwardian Decorative Art. The Handley-Read Collection* (exh. cat., London, Royal Academy of Arts, 1972), no. H.2; one in a London private collection (Garner, "Lacquer Work" 7, ill. 7); and one in the Sotheby Monaco sale catalogue (25 May 1980), no. 247. This last version is identical to the London private collection version, and may in fact be the same one. Three examples of the white version are known: one in the Sotheby Monaco catalogue (25 May 1980), no. 259; and two identical ones exhibited in the 14th Salon des Artistes Décorateurs by the artist in 1923 (illustrated in Johnson, *Eileen Gray,* 32-33).

9. The Handley-Read Collection version at the Victoria and Albert has brass rods.

10. Some variants have as many as eleven rows but no fewer than seven, with as few as three and as many as six blocks per row.

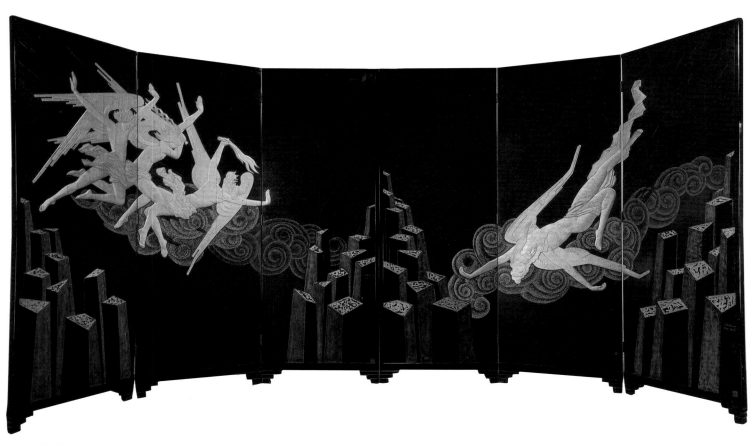

25.1

25

SERAPHIN SOUDBININE
Russian, 1870-1944

and

JEAN DUNAND
Swiss, 1877-1942

BATTLE OF THE ANGELS: CRESCENDO AND PIANISSIMO, 1925-1926
Lacquered wood with eggshell and gold dust. 248.9 x 266.7 (98 x 105), each three-panel pair
Metropolitan Museum of Art, New York. Gift of Mrs. Solomon R. Guggenheim

Jean Dunand, along with Eileen Gray and Leon Jallot, was one of the foremost lacquer artists working in France in the 1920s and 1930s. He began his career as a metal-worker, and by 1910 was decorating some of his copper vases with lacquer. In 1912 Dunand studied lacquer techniques with the Japanese master Sugawara, who also trained Eileen Gray. Gradually Dunand focused his efforts almost entirely on the medium, producing dozens of folding screens and numerous panels, tables, and cabinets in his crowded Paris workshop.[1] On this pair of three-panel screens (25.1), Dunand collaborated with the relatively unknown Russian sculptor Seraphin Soudbinine. Because Dunand's screens almost always consist of geometric patterns or landscape subjects, one would have to conclude that Soudbinine was responsible here for the overall design and for making the low-relief angel figures, while Dunand was probably called upon to do the lacquer work.

In 1924 Mr. and Mrs. Solomon R. Guggenheim purchased the Port Washington, New York, home that had been left vacant by the death of one of Mr. Guggenheim's brothers. Mrs. Guggenheim apparently took over responsibility for remodeling the mansion, and she prevailed upon a friend's son, Rowland Burdon-Muller, to help her. As he later recalled, "They did not want a decorator and she did not know what to do and liked our house in England. I was busy and had never done such work but she begged and begged me so that eventually I

did it, and it was most exhausting as it was a huge house but everything went in place."[2] Burdon-Muller recognized his task from the beginning: "[the house] was well built, but abominably decorated in modern machine-made furniture with every room a different period. I cleaned it up and eliminated much excess decoration.... I also eliminated glass doors in the music room."[3] He replaced these doors in the music room with a pair of lacquer doors at one end and the pair of three-panel lacquer screens at the other (25.2 and 25.3), all done jointly by Soudbinine and Dunand. Burdon-Muller's modest alterations to the room resulted in a conservative if not peculiar mixture of art déco accoutrements in what was otherwise a late beaux-arts interior.

Burdon-Muller approached the Russian-born sculptor Soudbinine early in 1924 to make the doors and screens. In a letter dated 15 December of that year, Soudbinine wrote him that "it is very difficult to calculate in advance how much gold will be needed for this work, because at least ⅓ of the gold will be lost, that is to say embedded in the lacquer, it is inevitable.... The work on the screens and doors is progressing normally and the incrustation of the egg shells is arleady done. Now I am overseeing the incrustation of the gold. The sculpture and the bas-reliefs are also done. You can tell Mrs. Guggenheim that everything will be finished by the anticipated date, in March.... I have already been working for eight months without rest."[4] Soudbinine's confidence was apparently not justified, for in a letter from Dunand to Soudbinine nearly a year later (10 December 1925), Dunand reported that at the latter's request he had begun to lay down layers of gold dust in the doors and screens. The amount of gold needed, in fact, cost more than anticipated, and Dunand wrote to ask for a reimbursement of $500 that he had been forced to pay himself.[5]

The heroic subjects for the screens and doors in the music room were chosen by Soudbinine, probably in collaboration with Burdon-Muller and Mrs. Guggenheim. In the left-hand screen, entitled *Crescendo,* three winged angels tumble downward in front of a cloudy sky in a mountainous landscape of squarish, columnar rock formations. In the right-hand pendant, entitled *Pianissimo,* a lone angel floats upward on his back in a similar rock- and cloud-filled landscape. The musical overtones in the contrast of tumultuous action in the first screen with restrained action in the second were particularly appropriate for the screens' music room location. They were placed at one end of the room with the organ console between them. At the opposite end was the pair of two-section doors whose exotically attired, bronze-skinned angel figures blow shofarlike horns. These figures mutely signal one's entrance into the room, while at the same time symbolically announce the room's purpose.

The screens were used to block two doorways at the organ end of the music room. Judging from the placement of the screens indicated in the period photograph of the room, and from their considerable size and weight, it is likely that they were intended to serve as more or less permanent, albeit flexible, partitions. In comparison to the doors, which of course opened and closed, the screens appear to have been conceived more as folded than folding images. The contrast of the static, ceremonial character of the door compositions with the dynamic downward and upward compositional rhythms in the screens offers an unexpected decorative counterbalance to these functional conceptions.

Both these screens and doors contain skillfully executed passages in which sumptuous materials were used. Against a deep greenish-turquoise sky bordered in black, majestic gilded angels fall and rise in a bank of clouds. These clouds consist of swirls of crushed eggshell embedded in the lacquer, highlighted as well by clouds of gold dust. The figures were carved and then applied to the wooden core with round-headed nails. The rest of the screen was then lacquered before the angels were gilded. With the exception of these figures, which contain several vertical cracks, the screens are in superb condition and convey thoroughly the reasons for Dunand's reputation as a lacquer artist par excellence.

1. The most useful reference source on Dunand's work is *Jean Dunand. Jean Goulden* (exh. cat., Paris, Galerie du Luxembourg, 1973), which contains a thorough bibliography and many illustrations.

2. Letter from Rowland Burdon-Muller to the Metropolitan Museum of Art, dated 19 February 1973.

3. Letter from Burdon-Muller to the Metropolitan Museum, dated 4 December 1971.

4. Letter from Soudbinine to Burdon-Muller, dated 15 December 1924, in the files of the Metropolitan Museum.

5. Letter from Soudbinine to Dunand, dated 10 December 1925, in the files of the Metropolitan Museum.

25.2 and 25.3 Music Room of Solomon R. Guggenheim home, Port Washington, New York, with doors and screens by Soudbinine and Dunand.

26

DONALD DESKEY

American, born 1894

THREE-PANEL SCREEN, *ca. 1929*
Oil paint and metal leaf on canvas. 197.5 x 152.4 (77³/4 x 60)
Collection of the Sydney and Francis Lewis Foundation, Richmond

As a visitor to the famous 1925 exhibition of contemporary decorative arts in Paris, Donald Deskey was among the first American artists to become familiar with the achievements of French avant-garde designers of the 1920s. Deskey previously studied painting and architecture at the University of California, and later went to Paris to study painting at the Ecole de la Grande Chaumière. By 1922 Deskey was in New York, where he began his own architectural and interior design firm. He is perhaps best known for his 1932 interior decorations at Radio City Music Hall. From 1937 on, as head of Donald Deskey Associates, he established his reputation as one of America's foremost industrial designers. His clients included Procter and Gamble, Coca-Cola, General Electric, Sears Roebuck and Company, Johnson and Johnson, and many other major corporations.[1]

Around 1927 Deskey met Phillip Vollmer, probably at the home of fellow designer Paul Frankl. Shortly thereafter the two joined forces, Deskey as designer and Vollmer as business manager of Deskey Vollmer in New York. Until they disbanded in the early 1930s, they successfully produced small editions of custom-made lamps, tables, screens, and other pieces of household furniture. These objects were made from Deskey's designs under his supervision at small local workshops. The few painted screens[2] known to have been done at this time, however, were almost certainly made by Deskey himself; each was a unique example, and Deskey's love for painting prevented him from allowing anyone else to carry out his designs.[3]

The screen in this exhibition (26.1) was purchased probably in 1929 by Mr. and Mrs. Glendon Allvine for their newly built Long Beach, Long Island, home. Mr.

Allvine, an advertising executive with the Fox Film Corporation, had hired architect Warren Shephard Matthews to build a house in the modern style. The house was finished in 1929, and the Allvines soon began to decorate it with furniture by Deskey and others.[4] An early reviewer of the Allvine-Matthews beach house described the interior: "A number of the chairs are framed in tubular metal lacquered in silver and upholstered in red fabrikoid. A screen in black and white in the zig zag motive, designed by Deskey Vollmer is included in the essential furnishings. In some of the rooms the walls are painted, as in the dining room adjoining, done in bright – almost an independence – blue in striking contrast to the black linoleum floor, the tubular metal chairs in red and silver, and a screen, decorated in flat planes of red, black and silver."[5] The screen was surely part of a consistent decorative scheme in the dining room, even though it was probably not designed specifically for the Allvine home.

This dining room screen, like the example in the Philadelphia Museum of Art (26.2), consists of three panels staggered in height with the tallest at the left. This "step down" configuration recalls features in skyscrapers of the 1920s, but it also relates to both exterior and interior architectural elements in the Allvine home.[6] The irregular form of the screen and the discontinuity of the design caused by the breaks between the panels create an active geometric rhythm across the surface. The energy of this image is further enhanced when the screen is folded. The screen's bright red parallel bands shoot off in all directions over the black solids and silvery voids, intensifying the dynamic character of the design. The way in which these lines and shapes purport to extend beyond the object's physical borders also may be seen as a decora-

26.2 *Three-Panel Screen*, ca 1925, silver and bronze leaf, leather and oil on canvas with wood frame. 196.8 x 149.9 (77½ x 59). Philadelphia Museum of Art, Thomas S. Harrison Fund

tive simplification of paintings by Piet Mondrian and other De Stijl artists in which the canvas edges seem to cut off geometric fragments from an invisible yet palpable cosmic whole.[7]

Deskey's awareness of modern painting styles can be seen as well in his so-called *Lysistrata* screen from about 1930. The screen was a gift for Gilbert Seldes, a noted drama critic and a friend of Deskey who was then writing an adaptation of Aristophanes' play.[8] In this gouache design for the screen (26.3), one sees Deskey's highly stylized portrait of the heroine Lysistrata, facing to our left, her wavy hair cascading downward. In the first and second panels her shoulder and dress are also discernible. The witty combination of geometric forms in the portrait recalls contemporaneous works by Archipenko,[9] Picabia,

and other Dada artists, which Deskey surely could have seen in New York. Deskey's vocabulary, however, was less complex, with greater emphasis on the clarity of relationships between recognizable figural elements; he had no intentions of altering spatial or surface perceptions as in cubist or cubist-inspired works. Characteristically, Deskey refused to apply ornament to the surface of his screens, allowing the flatness and purity of his designs to dominate instead.[10] Insofar as his screens are concerned, Deskey's contribution lay in his ability to fuse these formal elements of modern painting into an idiom more appropriate for these large-scale decorative yet functional objects.

1. This biographical outline is condensed from several autobiographical statements in the Deskey archives at the Cooper-Hewitt Museum.
2. Other screens done by Deskey include an example at the Philadelphia Museum of Art and the *Lysistrata* screen, illustrated in Christie's New York sale catalogue, *Art Nouveau, Art Deco, and Moderne* (9 October 1982), no. 226, both of which are discussed later in this

26.3 Study for *Lysistrata* screen, ca. 1930, gouache on paper. Cooper-Hewitt Museum, Smithsonian Institution's National Museum of Design, New York, Gift of Donald Deskey.

26.1

entry. In addition, photographs in the Deskey archives at the Cooper-Hewitt confirm that he did at least four other painted screens in this period (before 1935), one of which was used in a window display at the Franklin Simon store in New York. Gouache on paper designs for four other screens are also in the Cooper-Hewitt Museum (1975.11.13, 1975.11.14, 1975.11.16, and 1975.11.17), though none of these seem to have been carried out as actual screens.

3. From an interview with Derek Ostergard of David Hanks Associates. Mr. Ostergard is currently preparing a book on Deskey's work from 1926-1946. My thanks also to Karen Davies, a graduate student in the history of art at Yale University, for sharing with me the results of her research on Deskey for the 1983 Yale University Art Gallery exhibition, *At Home in Manhattan: Modern Decorative Arts, 1925 to the Depression*.

4. See Christie's sale catalogue, *Furniture from America's First Modernistic Home: The De Lorenzo Collection*, cat. no. 5005A (New York, 4 October 1980).

5. See Harriet Sisson Gillespie, "A Modernistic House on the Atlantic Beach," *Arts and Decoration* (January 1930): 96-98. From this description it seems there were in fact two screens by Deskey in the house: "A screen in black and white in zig zag ootive, [and] a screen, decorated in flat planes of red, black and silver." The former screen has not been located.

6. See Gillespie, "A Modernistic House," 53, for illustrations.

7. Deskey may have seen works from this group in Paris, but he more likely could have seen paintings by Mondrian and Caesar Domela in the 1926-1927 exhibition of the Collection Société Anonyme. See *Brooklyn Museum Catalogue of an International Exhibition of Modern Art*, 19 November 1926–1 January 1927, nos. 117 and 118 (Mondrian), and nos. 115 and 116 (Domela).

8. According to the Christie's catalogue (see note 2), Deskey designed several rooms for Seldes; the furniture was produced by the firm of Schmieg, Hungate, and Kotzian. The screen, done in lacquered plywood with chrome detailing (213 x 135), has since been sold to a private collector in Australia.

9. See for example, Archipenko's *Woman* (known as *Metal Lady*), illustrated in Robert L. Herbert et al., *The Société Anonyme and the Dreier Bequest at Yale University: A Catalogue Raisonné* (New Haven: Yale University Press, 1984), cat. no. 12.

10. For Deskey's comments on the evolution of modern design, see Giulio Veronesi, *Style and Design, 1909-1929* (New York: George Braziller, 1968), 215.

27

ALBERT ARMAND RATEAU

French, 1882-1938

THREE-PANEL SCREEN, *ca. 1930*
*Oil gilding in silver leaf on burnished water-gilding in silver leaf on
white gesso ground, with forged iron frame*
300.0 x 240.0 (118¹/8 x 94¹/2)
Art Gallery and Museums and the Royal Pavilion, Brighton

Albert Armand Rateau first studied drawing and wood sculpture at the Ecole Boule in Paris, and at the age of sixteen was already carrying out designs by decorators such as Georges Hoentschell. From 1905 to 1914 Rateau was the director of the Ateliers de Décoration de la Maison Alavoine, and in 1918 he set out on his own. In the 1920s Rateau completed a number of decorative interiors for both private and commercial clients, among them Jeanne Lanvin, the Duchess of Albi, and the Baron Eugène de Rothschild. Rateau was also one of the main exhibitors at the French section of the 1925 Exposition des Arts Décoratifs.[1]

The Brighton screen (27.1) is one of several pieces of furniture Rateau designed for his Quai de Conti apartment in Paris in 1930. His earliest attempt at screenmaking was in 1921-1922, when he designed a huge pair of screens for the dining room in Jeanne Lavin's spacious Paris apartment (27.2). The lively, richly foliated scenes on these lacquered wood screens are also present on the second lacquer screen that Rateau did for his own apartment (27.3). It was intended for his living room, where its six panels concealed a window and a stairway landing, masking as well two doorways into the bedroom of Rateau's son.[2] The three-panel Brighton screen parallels

27.2 Pair of screens by Rateau for Mme. Jeanne Lanvin's Paris apartment, 1921-1922. Courtesy Musée des Arts Décoratifs, Paris.

27.3 *Six-Panel Screen*, 1930, yellow, brown and clear lacquer on wood with forged iron frame, 310.0 x 420.0 (120⁷/8 x 163⁷/8). Musée des Arts Décoratifs, Paris.

closely the style and subject matter of these earlier works. The artist also decorated a small bed (27.4) that surely is a pendant to the Brighton screen.

In his choice of materials for both the bed and screen, however, Rateau departed considerably from his earlier work. The scenes on both pieces were executed with consummate technical skill in two distinct silver leaf finishes, matte and polished. The subtle tonal differences between them allowed Rateau to delineate the various details of the subject, with the matte areas appearing to stand out in shallow relief from the brighter, polished areas. In the screen a low railing establishes the foreground plane and partially obscures a group of cacti below. Beyond is a grove of olive trees before a loosely rendered landscape background. The screen image is surrounded by a forged iron frame embellished with rosettes, and is raised slightly off the floor by small feet consisting of a stylized acanthus leaf and rosette motif.

How, or even if, the screen's image was affected by folding seems not to have concerned Rateau. The homogeneous decorative treatment of the subject across the Brighton panels virtually assured an identical result no matter how the screen may have been arranged. Rateau was far more interested in transforming the appearance of his apartment by filling its interior with these vast, shimmering exotic scenes. The Mediterranean subjects were no doubt in striking contrast to the busy metropolitan setting in which the apartment was located.

Rateau also concentrated his efforts on lending the apartment a sense of luxury and elegance through the brilliant handling of the silver surface. The two finishes reflect and refract light to differing degrees, so that as one moves in front of the screen (or as the light source moves), the appearance of the glistening surface changes as well. Only in this private and essentially physical context can one appreciate the high level of Rateau's achievement.

1. Rateau's screens have been exhibited several times, with the same bibliographical and factual material cited in each of the catalogues: *Les Années "25"* (exh. cat., Paris, Musée des Arts Décoratifs, 1966), 59-69 and cat. no. 627; *Art Déco 1925* (exh. cat., Brussels, Société Générale de Banque, 1975), 22-23 and cat. no. 59; and *Cinquantenaire de l'Exposition de 1925* (exh. cat., Paris, Musée des Arts Décoratifs, 1976), 101-103, 143, and cat. no. 753. See also Paul Maenz, *Art Deco. Forme Zwischen Zwei Kriegen* (Schauberg: Verlag M. Dumont, 1974), nos. 124 and 132 for examples of Rateau's furniture.

2. *Cinquantenaire*, cat. no. 753.

27.4 Bed, ca. 1930. Art Gallery and Museums and the Royal Pavilion, Brighton.

27.1

28.1

28

YVES TANGUY

French, 1900-1955

FOUR-PANEL SCREEN, *1928*
Oil on wood. 200.0 x 240.0 (78³/4 x 94¹/2)
Private Collection, Paris

The young surrealist artist, Yves Tanguy, had only been painting for five years when in 1928 he executed an eight-panel folding screen in two parts (28.1 and 28.2).[1] It seems probable that Tanguy was commissioned by a patron to paint the screens, the largest works of his career, but there is no firm documentation. Lacking money and a large living or studio space, Tanguy most likely would not have initiated such a large and expensive project on his own.[2]

Biomorphic shapes, typical of this period in Tanguy's work, inhabit the black ground. The artist mottled the inky color and heavily scratched its surface to give texture to the essentially flat area. Although seemingly straight,

the horizon line is actually uneven, implying the presence of hills in the distant background. The upper third of the composition is gray, flecked with tiny white clouds, and the unfamiliar world depicted in the screen has been labeled "prehistoric" and "alien."[3]

Viewed flat, the screen's composition is calm, distended, and lacks the tension and internal cohesion of Tanguy's other contemporaneous paintings such as *L'Humeur des temps*, 1928 (28.3) or *Vieil Horizon*, 1928 (28.4). When the screen is folded, the landscape acquires animation and depth, as if seen from a floor-length window. Analyzed together, the two four-section screens form an eerie panorama: a theatrical backdrop and

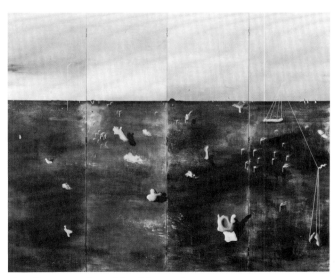

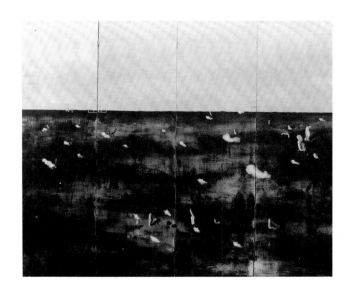

28.2 Reconstruction of the eight-panel screen.

dream landscape of human scale. Tanguy's angled paintings display an oriental-like perspective as seen in Chinese and Japanese landscape screens.[4]

In 1932, Tanguy created another four-panel screen, seventy centimeters shorter than its predecessors.[5] He carefully compensated for the smaller scale. The elongated sky forms the necessary balance for a terrain dense with more elaborate and specific shapes than those found in Tanguy's earlier screens.

The screen as a functional and decorative object was extremely popular at the end of the twenties and the beginning of the thirties in France. At the 1925 Paris *Exposition Internationale des Arts Décoratifs*, which Tanguy may have visited, many designers and artists exhibited their modern furniture, including screens.

The predominant use of black in Tanguy's screens is not unusual in the subdued palette he was using at this time. The color, however, may allude to the shiny black lacquer screens by Jean Dunand (Cat. 25) and Eileen Gray (Cat. 24) both of whom had exhibited in the Exposition. They also dealt with the surface of the screen as a strictly two-dimensional plane, allowing the folds to create volume.

Tanguy was the first of many Surrealists, including Man Ray (Cat. 29) and Salvador Dali, and their followers, to devise a folding screen.[6] He anticipated this group's interest in constructing art using formats other than the traditional easel painting. The signed and dated screen in the exhibition demonstrates the allowances Tanguy made for a new type of structure.

28.3 *L'Humeur des temps*, 1928, oil on canvas. Collection of the Museum of Modern Art, New York, James Thrall Soby Bequest.

28.4 *Vieil Horizon*, 1928, oil on canvas. Pierre Matisse Gallery, New York.

1. James Thrall Soby, *Yves Tanguy* (exh. cat., New York, Museum of Modern Art, 1955), 11.

2. Pierre Matisse, a lifelong friend of Tanguy, confirmed this deduction.

3. J. H. Matthews, *Eight Painters: The Surrealist Context* (Syracuse, 1982), 68; and John Ashberry, "Yves Tanguy, Geometer of Dreams," *Art in America* 62 (November-December 1974), 71.

4. José Pierre, "Le Peintre surréaliste par excellence," *Yves Tanguy* (exh. cat., Paris, Centre Georges Pompidou, Musée National d'Art Moderne, 1982), 51.

5. Kay Sage, *Yves Tanguy, A Summary of His Works* (New York: Pierre Matisse Gallery, 1963), 82.

6. See entry on Man Ray (Cat. 29). For screens by Dali see Leopold Diego Sanchez, *Jean-Michel Frank* (Paris, 1981). Both Max Ernst and Marcel Jean made folding screens in 1973.

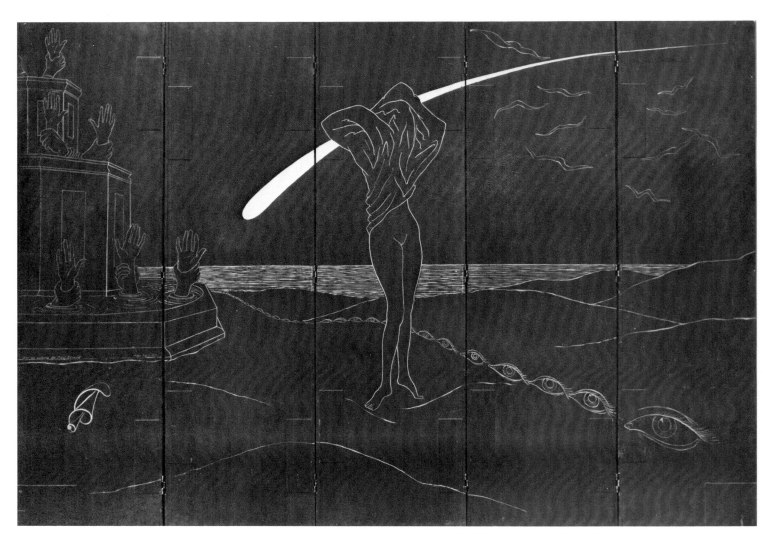

29.1

29
MAN RAY
American, 1890-1976

SCREEN, *1935*
Oil on wood. 179.0 x 250.0 (70^{1}/$_{2}$ x 98 7/16)
Collection of Giorgio Marconi, Milan

In 1934, the French surrealist writer Paul Eluard dedicated a poem to his friend, Philadelphia-born artist and photographer, Man Ray.[1] One of the stanzas in the poem so inspired Man Ray that in the following year, he painted a five-panel folding screen whose imagery was based on the poem (29.1).[2] Figured in the central panel is a lithe young woman pulling her dress over her head so that neither her face nor her hands are visible. She stands between a row of red staring eyes and a three-tiered fountain filled with hands, rising from pools of water.

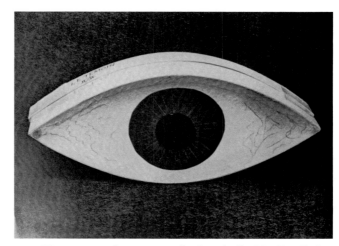

29.4 *Witness*, 1941, oil on paper. Collection of Juliet Man Ray, Paris.

29.2 Left: *Lampshade*, 1919-1959, painted metal. Collection of Juliet Man Ray, Paris.

29.3 Right: *Indestructible Object*, 1923-1958, metronome with photograph. Collection of Juliet Man Ray, Paris.

Behind her, a comet—described by Eluard as a rocketlike tear—plunges toward the blue sea below.

Incorporating emblems important in both his own work and in surrealist iconography in general, Man Ray endowed the screen with a sense of drama that is intensified by the angled position of the panels. The scene may be considered a twentieth-century interpretation of the birth of Venus. In contrast to Sandro Botticelli's famed 1482 version, however, Man Ray's goddess of love is half-clothed, portrayed as a sexual object performing a striptease. Tangled in the membranelike web of her clothing, she embodies the surrealist duality: desire coupled with fear of castration.[3] In the lower left panel Man Ray painted an image of his spiraling lampshade (29.2), like the woman, partially concealing and partially revealing.

29.5 *Beautiful Hand*, from Paul Eluard, *Les Mains libres* (Paris: Jeanne Bucher, 1937).

The disembodied hands constitute another surrealist image. Although they symbolize the sense of touch, the hands are restraining each other from reaching out. The spermlike meteor falling into the life-giving ocean further emphasizes the bristling sexuality of the scene painted by Man Ray onto an object traditionally intended to hide woman from man.

Man Ray reworked the themes from the screen on other occasions. His illustrations for Eluard's book of poems, *Les Mains libres*, published in 1937, include a similar female figure and emblems of hands and eyes in fantasy settings, drawn in the same crisp linear style

The procession of eyes into the sea forms one of the perspectival orthogonals which link the four sections of the screen. These eyes are as hypnotic as the collaged eye in *Indestructible Object*, 1923-1958 (29.3), and as watchful as the bloodshot eye in *Witness*, 1941 (29.4). At ground level the ocular sockets serve simultaneously as footlights and as an allusion to viewers contemplating the screen. From this low vantage point, the unblinking eyes are as vulnerable as the eye about to be slashed in the opening scene of Luis Buñuel and Salvador Dali's 1929 film, *The Andalusian Dog*.

29.6 *Paravent*, 1944, tempera on paper on board, 30.6 x 43.5 (12 x 17⅛). Courtesy Studio Marconi, Milan.

29.7 *La Forêt dorée*, 1950, oil on wood, 152.4 x 182.9 (60 x 72). Collection of Juliet Man Ray, Paris.

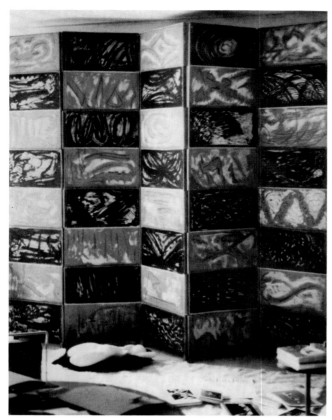

29.8 *Twenty Days and Nights of Juliet*, 1952, oil on canvas, 243.8 x 304.8 (96 x 120). Collection of Juliet Man Ray, Paris.

Man Ray's screens of the 1950s represent a change in his style and iconography. Whereas the 1935 *Screen* had been a figurative visualization of a literary subject, the screens from 1950 and 1952 reflect increasingly abstract and more personal imagery. Living in California in 1950, Man Ray painted a three-panel screen entitled *La Forêt dorée* (29.7). The brownish surface infused with vertical streaks of gold was Man Ray's vision of sunlight streaming through a redwood forest.[4] The 1952 screen (29.8), the *Twenty Days and Nights of Juliet*, was also made for his own home (29.9). In his autobiography, *Self-Portrait*, Man Ray describes its creation:

Among the objects and paintings that accumulated, there stood always in the studio the large screen, no longer serving any purpose since there were more permanent partitions for kitchen, bath and bedroom. It seemed to challenge me to attack it, but I bided my time. . . . I began by dividing it up into forty rectangles, like a chessboard.

(29.5). The artist also re-created the image from Eluard's poem and the 1935 screen in a 1973 color lithograph, *My First Love*.

Man Ray was characterized by André Breton, the leader of the surrealist movement, as "the great scrutinizer of decoration for everyday life." A 1944 drawing and three other screens demonstrate that Man Ray was indeed intensely interested in the esthetic potential of this functional object. The drawing (29.6), which foreshadows some of Kenneth Armitage's screen concepts (Cat. 38), shows a massive truncated human figure trying to extricate himself from an eight-panel screen, recalling Laocoon's struggles in the serpent's coils. The domestic object has taken on menacing qualities: man is being merged into screen.

29.9 Man Ray's studio in the rue Ferou. Courtesy Galeria Il Fauno.

One of the first assignments I'd give a pupil in painting was to lay out a chessboard. I explained that this was the basis of all art: a picture could be modified as dictated by the subject, maintaining the contrasts of light and dark patterns, or blending them as required. On the screen I followed my theory, but conserved the chessboard effect, filling in each panel with an improvised motif that was neither abstract nor figurative. One could see anything one wished in these panels. I alternated their values, light and dark, as in a chessboard. The screen now became a part of the studio.[5]

The weave of dark and light squares parallels the angling of the panels and emphasizes the pulsating quality of a piece which is a clock, a calendar, and a visual domestic diary. Man Ray had conceived this screen as an embodiment of his feeling and thoughts of his wife Juliet while she was away at the beach. Its image as a chessboard also alludes to Man Ray himself, and to the chess games with his fellow artist, Marcel Duchamp.

Another screen served a more dramatic function. When commissioned to design a backdrop for a solo dance performance, Man Ray found a six-panel screen made entirely of mirrors. Installing it as the only object on the set, he turned the single dancer into an illusionary *corps de ballet*, whose image was almost infinitely multiplied by the screen's reflective, angled surfaces.[6] In each of his screens, done over a period of three decades, Man Ray developed new ways to incorporate his imagery within a folding structure, thereby extending his esthetic vision through this multipurpose functional object.

1. The inscription at the base of the fountain in the screen reads "par un poème de Paul Eluard" (from a poem by Paul Eluard). During the author's conversation with Juliet Man Ray on 4 July 1983, she confirmed that Man Ray painted the screen because of the poem. The poem itself was part of a longer work, *La Rose publique*; see Paul Eluard, *Oeuvres complètes* (Paris, 1968), 1: 450-451. The translated verse pertaining to the screen is as follows:

> In the ebb and flow of a body which undresses
> Resembling the breast of twilight,
> The eye forms a chain on the neglected dunes
> Where fountains hold in their clutches
> naked hands
> Vestiges of a bare forehead pale cheeks
> beneath the eyelashes of the horizon
> a rocket-like tear betrothed to the past
> To know that the light was fertile
> Childish swallows mistake the earth for
> the sky.

2. Bussmann, "Überlegungen zur Malerei und zur den Objekten von Man Ray," *Man Ray: Inventionen und Interpretationen* (exh. cat., Frankfurt, Kunstverein, 1979), 80; and William Copley, *Man Ray: Inventor/Painter/Poet* (exh. cat., New York Cultural Center, 1974); and Maurizio Fagiolo, *Man Ray: Opere 1914-1973* (exh. cat., Rome, Il Collezionista d'Arte Contemporanea, 1973); Arturo Schwarz, *Man Ray, the Rigour of Imagination* (New York: Rizzoli, 1977), 72.
3. Whitney Chadwick, "Eros or Thanatos – the Surrealist Cult of Love Reexamined," *Artforum* 14 (November 1975): 46-56.
4. Reported by Juliet Man Ray in the 1983 interview with the author.
5. Man Ray, *Self-Portrait* (Boston: Little, Brown and Co., 1963), 385-386.
6. Pierre Bourgeade, *Bonsoir, Man Ray* (Paris: Pierre Belford, 1972), 50-51.

30

ELLSWORTH KELLY

American, born 1923

LA COMBE II, *1950-1951*
Oil on wood. 99.4 x 117.2 (39 1/8 x 46 1/8)
Private Collection, New York

While living in Paris in 1951, Ellsworth Kelly created a nine-panel folding screen, *La Combe II* (30.1).[1] The screen is one in a series of three paintings whose images record the shadow of a crisscrossed railing as it falls across a set of nine sunwashed outdoor metal steps. Kelly developed the idea for the image in August 1950 while visiting a villa called "La Combe" outside Paris.[2] He

photographed the steps (30.2) and then made sketches (30.3) to show the shadows' changing patterns at different intervals during the day.[3] He eliminated, however, any visible reference to the railing or the steps' embossed designs, and to hide the painting's source, he turned the image ninety degrees. A related collage (30.4) also preceded the screen.

Kelly was motivated by several factors in deciding to make a screen.[4] At that time, he wanted to create a piece using wood panels. In addition, the folding structures of Japanese screens and Grünewald's *Isenheim Altarpiece*, which Kelly had studied, influenced him. Equally important was his pursuit of a means of freeing form from

30.2 Shadows on a staircase at La Combe, 1950. Photograph, Ellsworth Kelly.

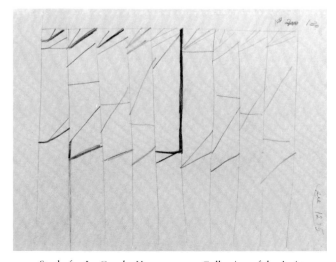

30.3 Study for *La Combe II*, 1950-1951. Collection of the Artist.

30.4 Study for *La Combe II*, 1950-1951, collage, 65.1 x 80.6 (25⅝ x 31¾). Collection of the Artist.

30.5 *La Combe I*, 1950, oil on canvas. Collection of the Artist.

son, the respective red and blue patterns on the flat canvases of *La Combe I*, 1950 (30.5) and *La Combe III*, 1951 (30.6) convey vastly different abstract sensations. In these works the steps are delineated only by the unconnected shadow lines which break visually, not physically, in nine measured intervals across the surface.

La Combe II is one of Kelly's many paintings, collages, and relief constructions of the late forties and early fifties in which he concentrated primarily on depicting accidental light and shadow falling on water, walls, and windows.[5] These preoccupations figured in the 1951 *Cité*, a twenty-panel oil (30.7), and in the 1956 sculptures for Philadelphia's Transportation Building, where influence of *La Combe II* is evident.[6]

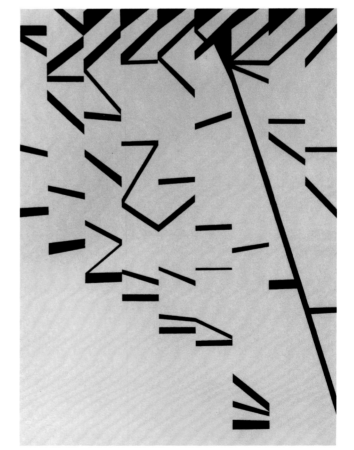

ground: by painting shapes on the free-standing, three-dimensional form of a screen, Kelly hoped to establish space as the ground of the painting, thus completely liberating the image depicted on the surface of the screen.

In *La Combe II* the black shadow bands are released from the white background by the folding structure, while at the same time Kelly still simulates the stairway form and records his chromatic experience. By compari-

30.6 *La Combe III*, 1951, oil on canvas. Collection of the Artist.

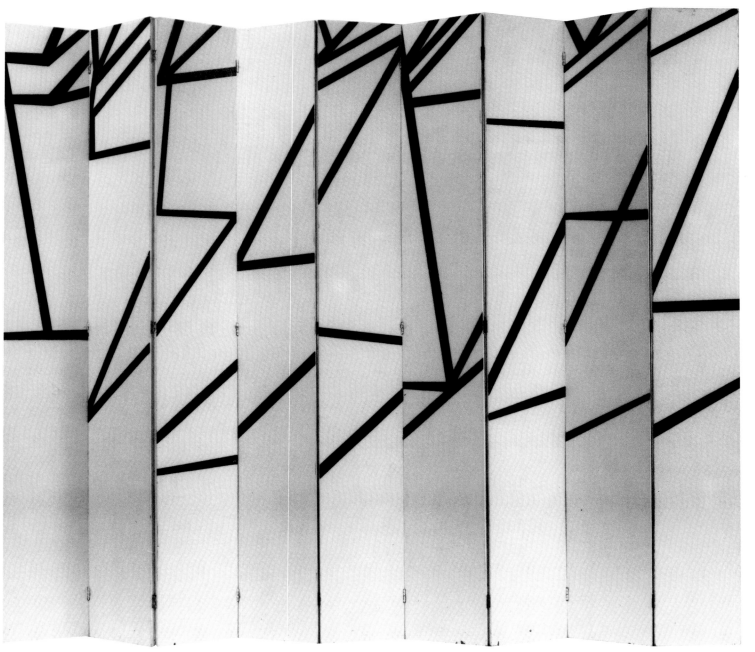

30.1

30.7 *Cité*, 1951, oil on wood. Collection of the Artist.

30.9 *Sculpture Model (Monsanto)*, 1957, cardboard, wood, and wire, 41.9 x 36.8 x 19.1 (16½ x 14½ x 7½). Collection Henry Persche, Ghent, New York.

30.8 *Seven Sculptural Screens in Brass*, 1957, brass, 137.2 x 152.4 x 30.5 (54 x 60 x 12), each screen. Originally installed at the Post House Restaurant, Transportation Building, Penn Center, Philadelphia. Present whereabouts unknown. Courtesy Ellsworth Kelly.

30.10 *Gate*, 1959.

Kelly further developed the format in the *Seven Sculptural Screens in Brass* (30.8) and in a series of proposals for various corporate commissions. The all-white *Sculpture Model (Monsanto)*, 1957 (30.9) and the multicolor *Sculpture Model*, 1958 emphasize the interrelationship between line, plane, and three-dimensional structure.[7] The suspended, geometrically segmented forms of these maquettes recall not only *La Combe II*, but also the visual effects and format of Eileen Gray's 1923 *Block Screen* (Cat. 24). In addition, *La Combe II* may be considered the ancestor of Kelly's 1959 metal sculptures such as *Pony* and *Gate* (30.10), where light falling on these bent forms modulates their flat colors, creating shadow and thus another kind of folding image.

Kelly's abstraction of reality into edge and shape, light and shadow, is the central issue at work in his art; but it is the act of seeing which is always the subject,[8] nowhere more evident than in *La Combe II*.

1. *La Combe II* has been discussed in detail in John Coplans, *Ellsworth Kelly* (New York, 1972), 36; Eugene Goossen, *Ellsworth Kelly* (exh. cat., New York, Museum of Modern Art, 1973), 35; and Patterson Sims and Emily Rauh Pulitzer, *Ellsworth Kelly: Sculpture* (exh. cat., New York, Whitney Museum of American Art, 1982), 54-55. Kelly exhibited *La Combe II* only once before in a 1951 exhibition of his relief constructions at Galerie Arnaud, Paris. Although a visitor to the exhibition wanted to purchase the screen, Kelly did not wish to sell it.

2. The villa La Combe belonged to the Seyrigs, Jack Youngerman's in-laws.

3. Goossen has argued convincingly that Kelly's World War II military training in camouflage inspired his early works. See Goossen, *Kelly*, 12 and 14.

4. During an April 1983 interview, Kelly explained his reasons for making a folding screen.

5. Goossen, *Kelly*, 24 and 30.

6. Sims and Pulitzer, *Kelly*, 60.

7. Sims and Pulitzer, *Kelly*, 62.

8. Sims and Pulitzer, *Kelly*, 11.

31.7

31
ANSEL ADAMS
American, born 1902

CLEARING STORM, SONOMA COUNTY *(recto)*, OAK TREE, RAIN *(verso)*, 1951-1970
Silver print. 193.0 x 299.7 (76 x 118)
Collection of Dr. Seeley W. Mudd, II, Carmel

Quite early in his career, the photographer Ansel Adams became absorbed with the esthetic and technical problems inherent in large scale photomurals. His interest in screens developed from these experiments, and he made the first of thirteen folding screens in 1936 for a one-man exhibition at the Katherine Kuh Gallery in Chicago.[1] The subject was *Leaves, Mills College* (31.1). Adams wrote that a screen image should comprise "patterns of leaves, natural or mechanical forms... patterns not dissimilar to tapestry effects, or to semi-abstract compositions."[2] Each of his subsequent screens, *Pine Needles and Pool*,

ca. 1938 (31.2);[3] *Wooden Wheels*, from the late 1930s (31.3);[4] and *Fresh Snow, Yosemite*, 1963 (31.4)[5] utilizes this close-up view, where middleground and background are eliminated and the viewer approaches the screen as though peering through a giant microscope.[6] The effect is necessarily decorative, an aspect of art and photography which Adams encourages in his essays on photoscreens and photomurals.

31.1 *Leaves, Mills College*, ca. 1931, 185.4 x 232.5 (73 x 77½).
Courtesy Ansel Adams.

31.2 *Pine Needles and Pool*, ca. 1938, 167.6 x 154.3 (66 x 60¾).
Collection of David Hunter McAlpin.

31.3 *Wooden Wheels*, ca. 1935-1940. Courtesy Ansel Adams.

31.4 *Fresh Snow, Yosemite*, 1963. Installation photograph from *The Eloquent Light* exhibition, M. H. De Young Memorial Museum, San Francisco, 1963.

According to Adams, *Clearing Storm, Sonoma County/Oak Tree, Rain* is his most successful and ambitious folding screen.[7] He first enlarged the negatives of the two photographs in 1951 to create a five-panel, double-sided screen, commissioned as a room divider by an architect who was redesigning the California home of Mr. and Mrs. Jack Skirball.[8] This first version of the screen stood on legs and could be easily opened and closed. In its original setting, the screen's storm clouds,

31.5 *Clearing Storm, Sonoma County*, Skirball Ranch. Courtesy Ansel Adams.

31.6 *Oak Tree, Rain, Sonoma County*, Skirball Ranch. Courtesy Ansel Adams.

31.8 Verso.

rolling off the hills in *Clearing Storm, Sonoma County*, created an expansive picture window view for the occupants of the living room (31.5). *Oak Tree, Rain* (31.6) offered a calm pastoral backdrop for those eating in the dining room.

Partially limited by the forty-inch width of his photographic paper,[9] and partially to accommodate the screen to the dimensions of the room for which it was intended, Adams made this first version in five panels. When he assembled two subsequent versions, such as the one exhibited here (31.7 and 31.8), however, he eliminated a panel and cropped the images at different points to achieve a slightly altered effect. On the *Clearing Storm* side, the image has been cropped on the right and expanded on the left. *Oak Tree, Rain*, however, has been completely reversed. Because the newer versions rest flush with the floor rather than stand on legs, Adams made further adjustments at the upper and lower edges of the landscape views. The landscapes in the screen shown here have been expanded at the top, but have been diminished at the bottom foreground.

In *Clearing Storm, Sonoma County* Adams captured a monumental vista of nature. It is a vision reminiscent of those he proposed in his well-known photographs of Yosemite, the Sierra Nevadas, and the southwest desert. The folding format of a screen enhances the impact of the image and provides a further allusion of the three-dimensional space depicted in the photographs. This six and one-half foot high screen envelops and awes the viewer, a simulation of the actual landscape experience rather than a mere record of the moment. In *Oak Tree, Rain*, a fence zigzags across the image in the middle-ground, its diagonal path accentuated by the screen's angled position; a similar use of a fence motif can also be seen in Maurice Denis' ca. 1902 screen (Cat. 8). The small size of the young oak trees seems to scale the scene to human proportion – a striking contrast to the expansive, almost overpowering view on the recto.

In his continuing dialogue with nature and his insistence on flattening his images to produce partially abstract patterns and shapes, Adams approaches Japanese sensibility. *Clearing Storm, Sonoma County*, especially, alludes to the entire genre of Chinese and Japanese landscape paintings.[10] The success of Adams' screens derives from his ability to choose arresting and appropriate subject matter, and from his ability to crop his images to produce a coherent, continuous composition. In creating three-dimensional folding screens, Adams subordinates the role of his photographs and allows the viewer to experience both the full power of his line and texture, as well as his love of the American wilderness.

1. Adams wrote to his wife about that exhibition: "It seems that Katherine Kuh has really done a very great amount of work in my behalf. The show looks very fine and the screen is a knockout." See Nancy Newhall, *Ansel Adams* (San Francisco: Sierra Club, 1963), 1: 129.

2. Ansel Adams, *The Print: Contact Printing and Enlarging* (Hastings-on-Hudson: Morgan and Morgan, Inc., 1967), 105 and 111.

3. David McAlpin describes how Adams made the 1938 folding screen *Pine Needles and Pool*: "Our principal camp was in the valley of Lyell Fork of the Merced River, looking across a quiet pool to the summits of Rodgers and Electra Peaks. Adams made a fine 'decorative' picture looking straight down into the pool with pine needles floating on its surface. My wife and I were greatly pleased with a photographic screen, composed of three sections, five feet high, made from this 4 x 5 inch negative. This was one of his [Adams'] first experiments in large fine-print making." See "Photographic Experience with Ansel Adams," an unpaginated essay by McAlpin in *Ansel Adams: Singular Images* (Dobbs Ferry, New York: Morgan and Morgan, Inc., 1974), with texts by Edwin Land, David H. McAlpin, Jon Holmes, and Ansel Adams.

4. Adams made *Wooden Wheels* in the late 1930s. He remembers leaving the screen behind during his move from San Francisco to Carmel in 1962, and its present whereabouts is unknown. The author is grateful to Andrea Gray whose 20 November 1978 letter contained this information. See also Ansel Adams, "Photo-Murals," *U.S. Camera* 12 (Autumn 1940): 53.

5. *Fresh Snow, Yosemite* was made for the 1963 exhibition of Adams' work at the De Young Museum in San Francisco; the exhibition was entitled *The Eloquent Light*.

6. Adams' thirteen screens were made from ten different photographs. All of them are three-panel and single-sided with the exception of the three versions of *Clearing Storm, Sonoma County/Oak Tree, Rain*, which is double-sided and exists in four- and five-panel examples.

7. Recorded in an interview with the artist by the author, 31 August 1982. The author is also grateful to Andrea Gray, former assistant to Ansel Adams; to Mary Alinder, Adams' current assistant; and to John Pultz and the Museum of Modern Art, New York, for providing information on Adams' screens and photomurals.

8. When the Skirballs moved from that home in the 1970s, the screen was disassembled due to lack of space, and it now hangs as ten individually framed panels in their new home.

9. Letter from Andrea Gray to the author, 20 November 1978: "I think the screens are all more or less the same size for each panel since this was governed by the width of photographic paper that Ansel could buy – and that is 40 inches wide."

10. Adams reported in the August 1982 interview with the author that he did not specifically attempt to emulate Japanese folding screens; rather he wanted to enlarge his own vision of the American landscape.

32

ED MOSES

American, born 1926

ROSE SCREEN, *1963*
Graphite on paper with painted wood frame. 152.1 x 218.4 (597/8 x 86)
Hereditary Disease Foundation, Beverly Hills

The Japanese, Mexican, and American Indian cultures have each had a pervasive influence on the work of the California artist, Ed Moses. In the *Rose Screen* (32.1 and 32.2) Moses combines philosophical and esthetic allusions to these cultures with the formal characteristics of Los Angeles abstract and pop art of the early 1960s.[1] From a distance, the four-panel screen seems to show a dark, amorphous mass spreading over the surface. On closer inspection, it is clear that the screen is comprised of

small, shaded blocks placed next to each other – a thick and variegated shape randomly punctured with white forms intended to be roses.

The artist derived the rose motif from a piece of Mexican oilcloth purchased on one of his trips south.[2] As did many artists of the early sixties, for example Warhol, Johns, and Rauschenberg, Moses incorporated motifs and designs from banal sources into his artistic vocabulary.[3] Moses was interested in how the artist, like the

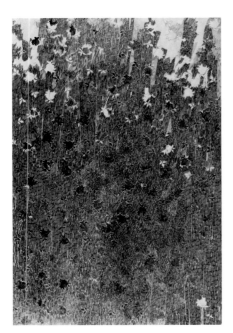

32.3 Left: *Rose #1*, 1961, graphite on paper, 152.4 x 101.6 (60 x 40). Courtesy Ed Moses.   32.4 Center: *Rose #4*, 1963, silver paint and graphite on paper, 152.4 x 101.6 (60 x 40). Courtesy Ed Moses.   32.5 Right: *Rose #5*, 1963, graphite on paper, 152.4 x 101.6 (60 x 40). Courtesy Ed Moses.

American Indian medicine man, could extract the psychic from the prosaic.[4] Beginning in 1961 and working principally in 1963, Moses traced the Mexican fabric to derive the outline of the roses and the leaves, developing a common formal structure for a group of seven drawings (32.3, 32.4, and 32.5).[5] Employing various techniques of shading, Moses manipulated the free-form pattern in the drawings to formulate different levels of surface and depth. *Rose Screen* was the culmination of this series.

Moses designed the screen, itself an allusion to Japanese landscape screens, as an integral element of a room's environment and yet as a visual, psychological escape from that environment.[6] Forms move forward and then sink back into the composition, offering a pulsating focus for meditation. At the edge of the sand-colored Strathmore board surface, the roses range in tone from white to almost black, similar to bees buzzing in and out of a hive. Slowly, an alarming image emerges: these roses resemble crabs with pinching claws, an image more fully realized in the artist's 1964 assemblage, *The Crab* (32.6).

The *Rose Screen* embodies contrasting themes of solidity and vacuity in both its imagery and structure. The almost claustrophobic feeling in individual panels and across the surface of the screen is dramatically relieved on the verso (32.2), where a single dark rose appears on a nearly blank ground, an emblematic reference to the screen's primary image. The rectilinear gray frame, a grid

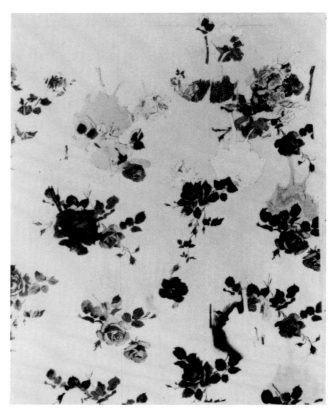

32.6 *The Crab*, 1964, graphite, paint, and collage over printed image of roses, 152.4 x 171.8 (60 x 44). From Henry Hopkins, "West Coast Style," *Art Voices* (Fall 1966). Present whereabouts unknown.

32.2 Verso.

devised and fabricated by the artist, confines the expressive free-form image but also allows it to float, suspended above the ground.[7] According to the artist, he wanted "to paint a plane with no support being visible,"[8] as an emanation of power. The energy inherent in Moses' folding screen derives also from the tension between the small passages of delicately rendered shading and the throbbing, sprawling mass of the overall image.

1. Moses exhibited regularly at the avant-garde Ferus Gallery in Los Angeles during the 1950s and 1960s; see Betty Turnbull, *The Last Time I Saw Ferus* (exh. cat., Newport Beach, Newport Harbor Art Museum, 1976).

2. Reported by the artist in an interview with the author, 12 September 1982. See also Joseph Masheck, *Ed Moses: Drawings, 1958-1976* (exh. cat., Los Angeles, Frederick S. Wight Art Gallery, University of California, 1976); and Susan C. Larson "Los Angeles Painting in the Sixties: A Tradition in Transition," in *Art in Los Angeles*, Maurice Tuchman, ed. (exh. cat., Los Angeles County Museum of Art, 1981), 19.

32.1

3. Masheck, *Ed Moses: Drawings.*

4. Reported by the artist in the September 1982 interview.

5. Tuchman, *Art in Los Angeles,* 48, 86-88.

6. Moses also reported to the author that his desire to make a screen came from his exposure to Japanese screens and art during summers spent in Hawaii, from exhibitions of Japanese art in the Los Angeles museums, and especially from a 1950 trip to Japan when he first became interested in Zen Buddhism.

7. Masheck, *Ed Moses: Drawings,* discusses Moses' tendencies toward expressive organic motifs and constructive geometric emphases. Some of Moses' graphite grid drawings from 1965-1966 are also reproduced in this exhibition catalogue.

8. Ed Moses and Stephanie Barron, *Ed Moses: New Paintings,* (exh. cat., Los Angeles County Museum of Art, 1976), 4. The grid structure in the frame reappears in drawings from 1966-1967; see Masheck, *Ed Moses: Drawings.*

33

BRUCE CONNER

American, born 1933

PARTITION, *1961-1964*
Mixed media. 182.0 x 222.0 (71 5/8 x 87 3/8)
Musée National d'Art Moderne, Paris

Bruce Conner's double-sided *Partition* (33.1 and 33.2) is a complicated assemblage of photographs, newspaper, candle wax and string, nylon stockings, feathers, ribbons, lace, sequins, jewelry, and paint adhered to a wood core. Conner initially conceived the screen as a divider to separate his dining room from his kitchen. During the three years he spent fashioning the piece, he gradually evolved *Partition's* structure and consequently its imagery on an increasingly symbolic level.

Conner began the screen while living in Mexico City in 1961.[1] He designed the pointed-top cedar structure and had it built to his specifications by a local carpenter. Shaped like a tripartite altarpiece, the screen and the objects attached to its surface — Mexican popular prints with Christ images and candles placed on top of the structure — were meant to correspond to the Last Supper composition painted by Conner on the surface of his dining room table.[2] Although he conceived of the screen as a room divider, he also meant it to function in an additional manner, as a backdrop for the Catholic mass ritual in which he participated symbolically with his dinner guests (33.3). By extended allusion, Conner, seated at the table in front of the screen, then became a priest in his own home. Compared to the Christological symbolism in Denis' *Screen with Doves* (Cat. 8), the multileveled symbolism of Conner's partition seems far more aggressive if not blasphemous.

Other works by Conner in the early sixties also focus on an almost "surrealist reassembling of Catholic catechism."[3] The 1963 *Suitcase* (33.4), for example, a representation of the Trinity collaged on its side with candles flanking the handle, attests to Conner's interpretation of the destitute state of religion, its rites, and its iconography.

When Conner moved to Wichita, Kansas, and later Brookline, Massachusetts (1962-1964), he continued to alter *Partition*. He intermingled Mexican religious metaphors with the theme of the seductive female. The many robings and disrobings which normally take place behind a screen are recorded on *Partition's* surface, particularly on the verso (33.2). Vast accumulations of nylon stockings sheath the panels like a caterpillar's cocoon. Lace, ribbons, bits of mirror, hairs, and a lingerie bag litter the screen. The attached costume jewelry, broken and dusty, is depicted as if to symbolize favors won and lost. Other works contemporary with *Partition*, such as *Señorita* and *La Novia* from 1962 convey the tawdry horror of the prostitute. These images are an allusion to the baudy Victorian past of San Francisco where Conner now lives.[4]

33.3 *Partition*, as seen in artist's home.

33.1

33.2 Verso.

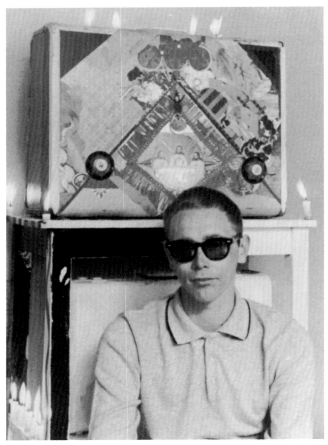

33.4 *Suitcase*, 1963, as seen in artist's home.

1. During a 29 April 1983 interview with the author, Bruce Conner described the philosophy and construction of *Partition*.

2. "Late in 1961 Conner traveled to Mexico and remained there during the following year. Many works assembled during this stay and after his return reflect his appreciation of that country's crude but dramatic popular art." Joan Siegfried, *Bruce Conner: Sculpture/Assemblages/Collages/Drawings/Films* (exh. cat., Philadelphia, Institute of Contemporary Art, University of Pennsylvania, 1967), unpaginated.

3. Reported in an interview with the artist, 29 April 1983.

4. See Joan Siegfried's discussion of this erotic imagery in *Bruce Conner;* and in Thomas H. Garver, *Bruce Conner, Sculpture/Assemblages/Drawings/Films* (exh. cat., Waltham, Massachusetts, Rose Art Museum, Brandeis University, 1965), unpaginated.

5. See especially Anne Bartless Ayres, "Berman and Kienholz: Progenitors of Los Angeles Assemblage," in *Art in Los Angeles: Seventeen Artists in the Sixites* (exh. cat., Los Angeles County Museum of Art, 1981), 11.

Conner's style, techniques, and symbolism can be seen as a direct outgrowth of dadaist and surrealist practices. They relate even more closely, however, to principles of representation advocated by Edward Kienholz and Wallace Berman, both of whom were actively pursuing a new esthetic vision while working in California in the late 1950s and early 1960s.[5] By using trash and discarded items in *Partition*, Conner contrasts religious purity and devotion with sexual amorality. Moreover, by daring to interweave themes of religion and sex on the screen, he separates and equates the seductive qualities of each, a powerful social commentary of a type often found in the works of Kienholz and Berman as well.

34

ALLEN JONES

English, born 1937

SCREEN, *1965 (recto), 1973 (verso)*
Oil on pine panels. 182.9 x 215.9 (72 x 85)
Private Collection, London

While living in New York City in 1965, Allen Jones was commissioned by the fashion photographer Bert Stern to make a folding screen (34.1) for his home.[1] According to Jones, Stern was interested in the pop art movement with which Jones was identified.[2] The folding screen appealed to Stern as an object close to both functional and fine art. For Jones, who was not limited by his patron in the choice of subject matter, the structure offered an opportunity to extend his images into the viewer's space, rather than isolating them on a wall.

Jones remembers that he had first been intrigued by the format of the folding screen in 1959 while a student at the Royal College of Art, London, where David Hockney (Cat. 40) was a classmate. Jones often passed a screen in the corridor of the nearby Victoria and Albert Museum, and each time he observed the unusual way its narrative was developed across the panels; like a story in the frames of a comic strip, a simultaneous passage of time and space

was implied. Jones emulated this quality as he evolved his own idea for a screen.

The subject for the screen came to Jones partially by accident. His newly painted *Female and Male Diptych*, 1965 (34.2), was in two pieces in his studio. Both canvases were lying on their sides, so that the feet of the figures were resting on the floor of the studio. With the screen in mind, Jones responded immediately. Like other pop artists, Jones rarely establishes a middleground or background in his paintings, and seeks other methods to express reality. By painting the feet at the bottom edge of the screen, and by depicting the image on grainy wooden door panels rather than on stretched and primed canvas, Jones hoped to enhance the illusion of three-dimensional space already implied by the screen's bent surface.

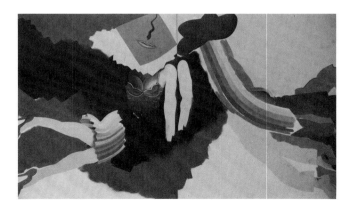

34.2 *Female and Male Diptych*, 1965, oil and pencil on canvas, 183.3 x 305.5 (71⅛ x 120⅜). Hirshhorn Museum and Sculpture Garden, Smithsonian Institution.

34.3 *2nd Bus*, 1962, oil on canvas. Collection Granada Television, Manchester, England.

Since the early sixties, Jones has used shaped canvases, as in *2nd Bus*, 1962, (34.3), to amplify the meaning of his subject. In *Screen,* the women's striding legs and the billowing smoke embody the kineticism implicit in the folding format. Sexual energy is symbolized as well by the women's painfully high-heeled shoes, one of Jones' favorite motifs. The diamond shapes at the top of the composition are formal devices, Jungian mandalas signifying the women's heads and also the unconscious self.[3] Representing the contemplative aspect of life, the diamond shapes function as a symbolic antithesis to the lower part of the screen, whose imagery is an emblem for activity.

In 1973 Jones agreed to paint an image on the verso (34.4) for the screen's new owner. Continuing the yellow, red, and black shapes from the front, he combined the snaking, phallic form with a mandala to create a "male" side for the screen. A trip to Japan in 1974 inspired the artist to draw sketches for additional screens (34.5), abstracting trees into floating, gestural areas of color. The five-panel screen of 1965-1973, however, remains his only realized work in this format.

1. During a 20 July 1983 interview, the artist explained the circumstances under which he made his screen. See also Marco Livingstone, *Allen Jones: Retrospective of Paintings 1957-1978* (exh. cat., Liverpool, Walker Art Gallery, 1979).

2. Bert Stern, known for his photographs of Marilyn Monroe taken shortly before her death, has influenced British pop art through his work. See Lawrence Alloway, "The Development of British Pop," *Pop Art,* ed. Lucy R. Lippard (New York: F. A. Praeger, 1966), 47.

3. Christopher Finch, "Allen Jones," *Art International* 11 (Summer 1967): 48; and Marco Livingstone, *Sheer Magic* (London, 1979), 44.

34.4   Verso of 34.1

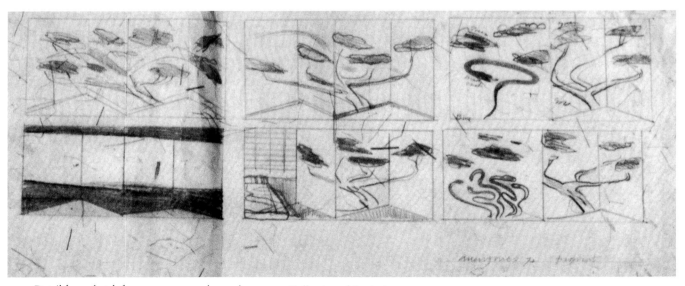

34.5   Detail from sketch for screens, 1974, charcoal on paper. Collection of the Artist.

34.1

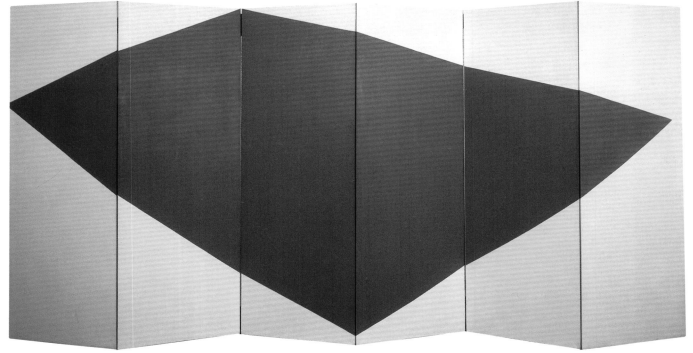

35.5

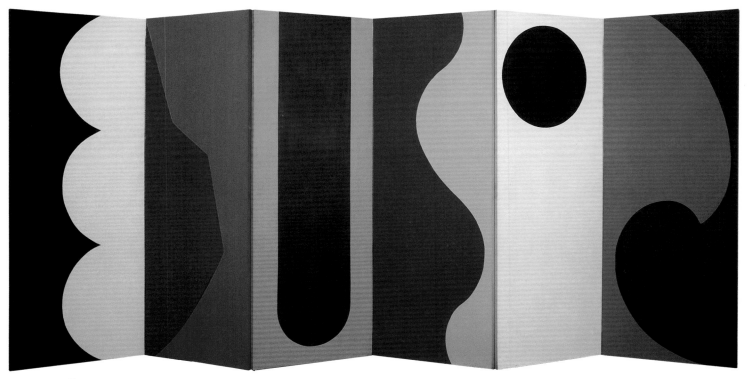

35.6 Verso.

35

LEON POLK SMITH

American, born 1906

SEVEN INVOLVEMENTS IN ONE
CORRESPONDENCE: RED/WHITE *(recto)* SIX INVOLVEMENTS *(verso)*, 1966
Oil on canvas. 218.4 x 487.7 (86 x 192)
Washburn Gallery, New York

For more than four decades, Leon Polk Smith has been continually and specifically concerned with the formal interactions between space and color. While adhering to Mondrian's principle of the interchangeability of form and space, Smith was eager to move beyond the lessons of his Dutch mentor. He wanted to accomplish in other formats what Mondrian had evolved on rectangular and diamond shaped canvases.[1]

Throughout the 1940s and 1950s Smith produced paintings of unhinged panels hung side by side. In other experiments, he focused on creating space and balance in a circular canvas (tondo) by juxtaposing curving configurations of unmodulated color. A 1951 commission to make a wooden lattice and translucent *shoji* screen for a client's Connecticut home (35.1) led Smith to confront a

functional situation while still working with his concepts of light and shape.

In his first screen, *Two Involvements in One*, 1961 (35.2 and 35.3), Smith explored the visual intersection of a curved shape painted on a flat surface, while the hinging

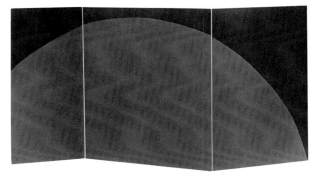

35.2 *Two Involvements in One* (recto), 1961, oil on canvas, 208.3 x 396.2 (82 x 156). Courtesy Leon Polk Smith.

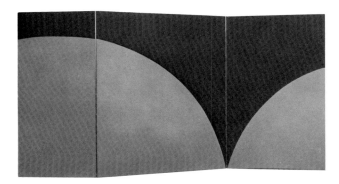

35.3 Verso.

35.1 *Shoji* screen, 1951, as seen in Connecticut client's home. Courtesy Leon Polk Smith.

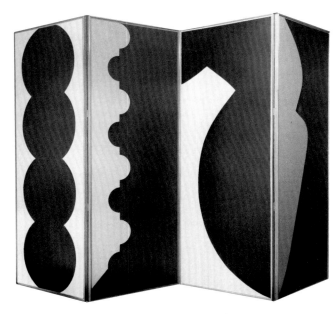

35.4 *Four Involvements in One,* 1964-1965, oil on canvas, 107.0 x 158.4 (42⅛ x 62⅜). Courtesy Galerie Chalette, New York.

of the panels bent this image into three dimensions. Using sections of different widths, Smith carefully controlled the cadence of the image. Diversity of form and rhythm was also the goal in Smith's second screen,[2] *Four Involvements in One,* 1964-1965 (35.4). Here the artist explored the juxtapositions of shape and color correspondences on an even larger scale.

The huge six-panel, double-sided *Seven Involvements in One* (35.5 and 35.6) derives directly from these experiments. On the recto a red parallelogram soars like a flying carpet across the surface, while on the verso is an unsuspected staccato of colored shapes.[3] Stretched diagonally over the crisp white ground, the red form on *Correspondence: Red/White* (35.5) creates a tension with the horizontal axis of the screen.[4] Because of the folded format, the light hitting each section of the screen makes the red hue vary in tone from panel to panel, causing six different correspondences of red to white. Perceived in its totality, the red parallelogram pulsates forward and backward to give the sensation both of unviolated flat surface and of infinite depth. When the panels are squeezed together, however, each section is seen as isolated from the whole, so that the resulting red shape acquires a new character.

35.7 Four tabletop folding paintings, 1961-1962. Courtesy Leon Polk Smith.

The reverse of the screen, *Six Involvements* (35.6), also exemplifies Smith's concept of correspondences. According to the artist, any two colors can correspond or be juxtaposed, provided that the correct proportion of each is found.[5] By changing tones and forms in each panel, Smith forces the viewer to examine the relationships carefully: a black negative space contrasts with a swelling white one; a blue angled shape is balanced against a red; a navy curve thrusts into its orange complement; blue and yellow forms undulate symbiotically; a black sun floats in a white sky; and an orange wave engulfs a blue. The unity found on the recto dissolves into a series of contrapuntal relationships on the verso.

Smith insists that his small, tabletop folding paintings (35.7) reflect his interest in the format as much as his larger ones.[6] The painted shapes and the more irregular, nonrectangular forms of the panels in these small versions, in fact, suggest that Smith's innovations often occurred here. While the function of his screens is a moot issue to Smith (hence his description of them as folding paintings rather than as screens), their sculptural bases are not. He has achieved in his folding paintings a sense of multidirectional movement in space, an entirely three-dimensional notion. Moreover, Smith acknowledges that his screens influenced the direction of his work when the series of Correspondences ended in 1967. The subsequent group of shaped wall reliefs called *Constellations* indicates the artist's continuing fascination with altering exterior form and interior imagery, concepts derived from his folded paintings and their quasi-sculptural properties.

1. Lawrence Alloway, "Leon Polk Smith: Dealings in Equivalence," in *Art in America* 62 (July-August 1974): 59.
2. As Alloway has noted, Smith in his folding screens has made it "impossible for the spectator in motion to avoid combinations of head-on and foreshortened views of the panels. . . . The jump from one canvas to the next . . . is abrupt but works brilliantly to transfer to the group of panels as a whole the diversity of incident that cannot be contained within one of them. The diversification which he properly excludes from his paintings, given the color usage and the space concept on which they are based, appears in another way on some screens." See Lawrence Alloway, *Leon Polk Smith* (exh. cat., San Francisco Museum of Modern Art, 1968), 8.
3. *Seven Involvements in One* is made of two separate six-panel structures which abut back to back and are fastened to stabilize the object as a whole. This construction differs from that used in almost all other double-sided screens whose two sides share the same stretcher or support.
4. Ted Castle, "Leon Polk Smith: The Completely Self-Referential Object," in *Artforum* 18 (September 1979): 36.
5. Reported by the artist in an interview with the author on 3 February 1983.
6. Reported by the artist in the February 1983 interview.

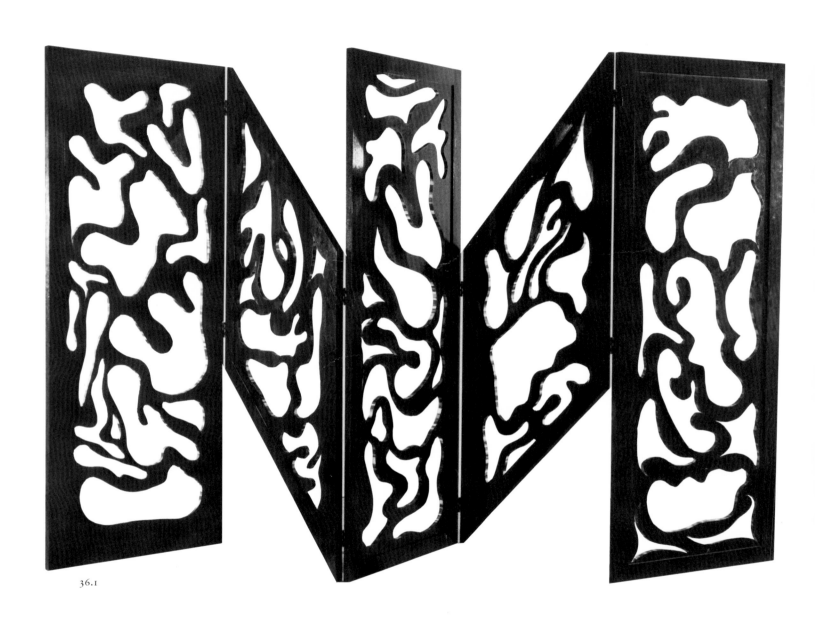

36.1

36
LUCAS SAMARAS
American, born Greece 1936

SCREEN, *1967*
Painted wood. 150.5 x 354.3 (59 1/4 x 139 1/2)
Pace Gallery, New York

When he moved into a new apartment in 1967, Lucas Samaras designed for himself a set of furniture, including a table, six chairs, and this folding screen (36.1).[1] The screen was carved out of plywood from the artist's design by a carpenter, and then decorated by Samaras himself. The panels' surfaces are painted a flat black; the half-inch deep edges of the jigsaw cutouts, however, are striped with thin sets of rainbow colors. Despite the transparency caused by these cutouts, the screen is often used to surround or partially conceal photographic equipment in the artist's living room.

In planning the work, Samaras made a series of ten pencil drawings (36.2) to experiment with different concepts of the screen format. The drawings establish that it was never Samaras' intention to use a traditional arrangement of uniformly-sized and shaped panels. These designs symbolize motion and permutation, and his desire to transform the screen from a functional object into a humorous fantasy as he has done with chairs, boxes, and eyeglasses. *Screen* consists of five sections organized in an ABACA rhythm of rectangles and acute parallelograms which contrast with the biomorphic cutouts. Panels fold in both directions and shift from a stable vertical to an active diagonal. Violation and perforation

36.2 Series of drawings for screens, 1967, pencil on paper. Collection of the Artist.

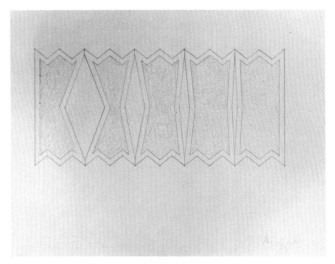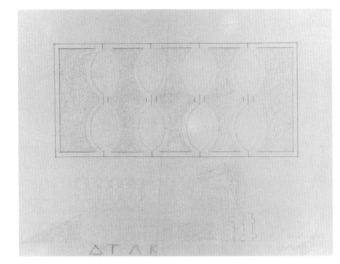

36.2 Series of drawings for screens, 1967, pencil on paper. Collection of the Artist.

of an object's surface were nothing new for Samaras; his paper cutouts and his pierced *Book* demonstrate his fascination with the concept.[2]

By its very structure, *Screen* contradicts the more traditional functions of blocking a view, light, or a draft. Although still furniture, it articulates space in a sculptural manner, as did Eileen Gray's 1923 *Block Screen* (Cat. 24). The "image" of Samaras' screen is more intricate, however; its striations of rainbow hues intimately involve the

viewer with the carved and painted interior of the screen rather than with its surface.

The 1967 *Screen* is not the first of Samaras' career. While studying at Rutgers University from 1955 to 1959, Samaras made a series of at least six tiny tabletop screens.[3] Adopting a scale commensurate with the restricted spaces of his studio-apartment, Samaras taped small glass panels together. He then covered them with tissue paper, and painted and decorated them with silver

36.3 Two tabletop screens, 1958-1959, glass, tissue paper, and gold leaf. Collection of the Artist.

or gold leaf. Illuminated from behind, the images on these screens (usually floral) glow with diffused light (36.3). Samaras considers these diminutive screens as finished works of art, not simply as maquettes for larger versions. In their size they recall so-called tea screens by Tiffany and Gorham which were popular at the turn of the century (fig. 121 and 122).

A blue and silver double-sided painted screen, *Untitled*, was done in 1958-1959 (36.4 and 36.5), and according to Samaras was commissioned by Rutgers.[4] He remembers that a university restorer brought him an old screen, saying that the university would pay him, then a student, if he would paint a new image on the panels. As with Samaras' other easel paintings from that period, this screen's image contains vibrating, concentric vertical rectangles in relatively subdued tones.[5] The infinite perspective of the corridors depicted in each panel prefigure the dizzying sensation of being inside Samaras' 1966 *Mirrored Room #2*.[6] By covering the lower third of the screen's recto with silver-colored liquid aluminum paint, Samaras isolated and suspended the images from the floor as though they were paintings hung on a wall.[7]

Evolving his concept of the screen, Samaras' intent was to manipulate space with the structure of the screen and within its surface design. Depth, defined by the passage of light in the tiny glass screens, and illusionistically depicted in *Untitled*, is a concept more fully explored in the airy panorama of the 1967 *Screen*.

1. Kim Levin, *Lucas Samaras* (New York: Harry N. Abrams, 1975), 77.

2. "The actuality is a flat two-dimensional surface, like the surfaces of his furniture and the pages of *Book*. By the end of 1967 absolute flatness replaced the illusion of space in his work, and the only space was actual space – the environment filtering through the holes." Levin, *Samaras*, 78.

3. Reported to the author in a November 1982 interview with the artist. Samaras owns two of these screens, but fears the others may have been destroyed. They relate to an *Untitled* 1958-1959 work which resembles an altarpiece. See Levin, *Samaras*, ill. 53.

4. The author is grateful to Philip Dennis Cate, director, and Jeffrey Wechsler, curator, at the Rutgers University Art Gallery for information on this screen.

5. Levin, *Samaras*, ill. 52.

6. Levin, *Samaras*, ill. 158.

7. For other liquid aluminum works, see Levin, *Samaras*, ill. 82 and 86.

36.4 *Untitled*, 1958-1959, oil on wood, 174.6 x 117.5 (69¾ x 46¼). Jane Voorhees Zimmerli Art Museum, Rutgers University.

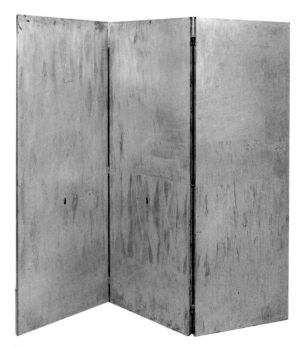

36.5 Verso.

37.1

37

JIM DINE
American, born 1935

LANDSCAPE SCREEN (RAINBOW, SNOW, GRASS, SUN, SKY), *1969*
Acrylic over silkscreen on linen. 187.3 x 228.6 (73 3/4 x 90)
Pace Gallery, New York

"The landscape around you starts closing in," Jim Dine once said, *"and you've got to do something about it."* [1]

Although Jim Dine characterizes *Landscape Screen* (37.1 and 37.2) as a purely decorative piece, its formal and imagistic elements are thoroughly consistent with the artist's concerns of the 1960s.[2] When he lived in London in 1969, Dine had an opportunity to study Bonnard's lithographic screen, *Promenade des nourrices, Frise des fiacres* (Cat. 6), in a friend's home.[3] Immersed almost exclusively in printmaking at that time,[4] Dine followed

Bonnard's example and produced a five-panel color silkscreen on canvas screen (37.3).[5] Mounted on stretchers, the double-sided printed screen is identical on front and back.

The *Landscape Screen* exhibited here, however, is unique. Bonnard had developed his lithograph screen in 1896 as a nearly exact replica of his 1894 painted screen of the same subject (fig. 80). Dine reversed the order; after he completed the silkscreen version, he painted over the entire print in acrylic. Following the original silkscreen images on one side of the screen, Dine intensified each

37.2 Verso.

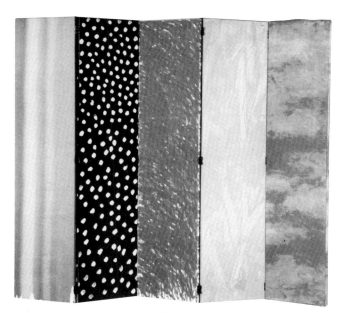

37.3 *Landscape Screen,* 1969, silkscreen on canvas, 183.0 x 227.5 (71⅜ x 88¾). Courtesy Petersburgh Press, New York and London.

37.4 *Studio Landscape,* 1963, oil on canvas. Collection of A. Alfred Taubman, Bloomfield Hills, Michigan.

hue, and with agressive brush strokes, he added surface textures. The *Grass* panel, for instance, has a boldness of gesture which results from the addition of the acrylic paint. Dine also altered the verso of the screen where each panel is now solid black with the exception of a scrawled white title identifying the image on the recto.

The screen presents an abstract landscape consisting of terrestrial and atmospheric elements – a rainbow, a nighttime snowstorm, grass, sunlight, and a sky dotted with white cumulus clouds – which are juxtaposed vertically within the screen panels rather than depicted horizontally across them. Similarly innovative depictions of natural phenomena occur in Dine's *Studio Landscape,* 1963 (37.4), and in *The Creation (Rainbow),* 1965, a seven-part lithograph commissioned by the Jewish Museum in New York. In his folding screen, Dine isolated familiar components of landscape which we all encounter, but turned these components on their side, a decision typical of the pop artist's intent to shock, surprise, and parody. The isolation of these natural elements within the individual screen panels leads the viewer to become totally absorbed with each single image and sensation. When viewed as a dynamic, folding whole, however, the screen becomes a changing seasonal, temporal, and spatial experience.[6] Dine's response to the impact of landscape in his folding screen recalls that of Paul Klee, who sought in his five-panel screen of 1900 (Cat. 9) to force the viewers of his screen to reevaluate their notions of and therefore their relationship to nature.

The *Landscape Screen* has also been described as an arrangement of "varied aspects of nature, like so many

patterns of kitchen wallpaper."[7] In works such as *Landscape Robe,* 1969, in fact, Dine logically alludes to fabric motifs. By reducing nature to strips of pattern in his screen, Dine captures nature, transforming it into a human and artistic creation. The screen is also emphatically about color; Dine consistently uses chromatic variation in his works to express emotion. In *Hearts with Hammer,* 1960 (37.5), for example, the tones describe the range of human feelings. The colors of *Landscape Screen* similarly function as barometers of the artist's state of mind, again recalling the expressive handling of color in Klee's screen. Because Dine has chosen a folding format for his presentation, one has the prerogative of arranging it in a variety of configurations, each to reflect a color, weather, or mood preference. As a result, Dine has allowed the work to retain its function while also permitting it to alter expressively its surrounding environment.

1. John Russell, "Jim Dine," in *Jim Dine: Complete Graphics,* ed. Michael S. Cullen (Stuttgart, 1970), unpaginated.

2. Reported by the artist in a 14 January 1983 interview with the author. Dine's other decorative projects include an interior for the Biltmore Hotel, Los Angeles, containing rugs and plaster reliefs of tools.

3. Reported by the artist in the 1983 interview.

4. Constance Glenn, *Jim Dine: Figure Drawings, 1975-1979* (New York: Harper & Row, 1979), 9.

5. "No prisoner of the traditional rectangle, Dine will make prints in any format that suits him. "They can even come boxed and tied up like ribbons, like candy. He likes to bring the print into life, not to lock it away in a conceptual Solander case." From John Russell, *Jim Dine.*

6. Russell, *Jim Dine.*

7. Riva Castleman, *Jim Dine: Prints 1970-77* (exh. cat., New York, Museum of Modern Art, 1976), 37.

37.5 *Hearts with Hammer,* 1960, mixed media on paper, 103.5 x 88.1 (40¾ x 30¾). Pace Gallery, New York.

38

KENNETH ARMITAGE

English, born 1916

SCREEN (FOLDED ARMS), *1967-1968*
Painted cast and plate aluminum. 175.0 x 195.0 x 65.0 (687/8 x 763/4 x 255/8)
Collection of the Artist, London

The sculptor Kenneth Armitage recalls that the format of the folding screen appeared in his work quite by accident.[1] In the late forties he rented a studio in which he "made two or three folding screen frames and covered them with corrugated paper" to hide some furniture the landlady wanted to keep there. As if by osmosis, the angled, webbed concept of the screen crept into his sculpture. As early as 1952, in a bronze, *Standing Group (2)* (38.1), the artist had already applied the screen as a symbol for the human torso, a theme which has never left Armitage's work.[2]

By the mid-sixties, Armitage's references to the human figure were reduced even more. He was working not in the figural manner of Henry Moore or Barbara Hepworth, two of his early mentors,[3] but in a more violent, angry mode. In *The Forest*, 1965 (38.2), for example, bodies were abstracted into appendages projecting from a bronze monolith.

Armitage's interest in manipulating the human figure is continued in *Screen (Folded Arms)* (38.3). While living and working in Germany, he "had the idea of making some large folded arms projecting from a continuous wall in a building, but the opportunity never came." He eventually decided to incorporate the image of the arms into a screen. Modeled first in plaster, the work was cast in aluminum at the Foundry Noack in Berlin. The artist has eliminated the torso completely, with the screen itself taking on that anatomical function. Symbolically, the folded arms suggest the format of the triparite structure, while their locked position directly refers to the fact that the panels are rigidly attached to one another and cannot

38.1 *Standing Group (2)*, large version, 1952-1954, bronze, height 104.5 (41⅛). Courtesy Kenneth Armitage.

be moved. Psychologically, the heavy gray painted screen has an oppressive effect, and the rigidly folded arms imply the closed attitude of an icy person. A sense of power and brooding remoteness permeates the entire piece. Like *The Bed* and a later series of *Chairs*, the screen has lost all functional qualities.

In 1974-1975, Nottingham University commissioned a piece of sculpture for their new library, and Armitage responded by creating the double-sided *Five-Panel Folding Screen* (fig. 127). The figures and composition were based on two double-sided folding screens Armitage had constructed from foam core and bromide paper. In contrast to his intentions for *Screen (Folded Arms)*, Armitage merged structure and human figure in the Nottingham piece to symbolize activity. His two-color silk-screen image depicts students leaving the library; the building's windows are symbolized by vertical shaded bands. Each of the four abstract figures stretch out over several panels so that hands and feet extend beyond the boundaries of the surface.

The screen for Armitage, then, vacillates between being a benign and a menacing structure. In his 1977 *Fleeing Figure*, for example, one sees the figure struggling to escape from the screen's entangling web. Armitage admits to being drawn to screens because of "the zig-zag simplicity of form and the economic occupation of space by means of a geometric-confined membrane." As a result, the folding format is for him an instrument of uniting man within as well as separating him from his environment.

1. Armitage explained to the author in a 9 October 1982 letter his interest in the folding screen format, and specifically the genesis of *Screen (Folded Arms)*. All quotations were taken from this letter.

2. Armitage has searched "for a formal unity in the resulting sculpture, [finding] it by emphasizing flatness, often using a screen-like structure to bind his figures together." Alan Bowness, *Kenneth Armitage* (exh. cat., London, Arts Council of Great Britain, 1972), unpaginated.

3. Roland Penrose, *Kenneth Armitage*, vol. 7 of *Artists of Our Time* (Amriswil, Switzerland, 1960), 6-7.

38.2 *The Forest*, 1965, bronze, height 170.2 (67). Collection Metro de Caracas.

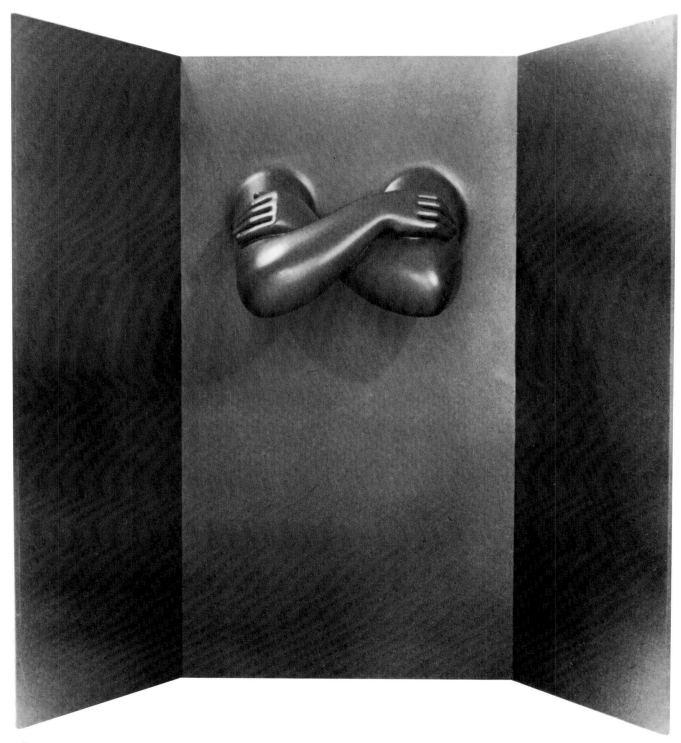

38.3

39.1

39

JACK BEAL

American, born 1931

ROWBOAT, *1977*
Color silkscreen with wood frame. 181.6 x 242.6 (71 1/2 x 95 1/2)
Courtesy Brooke Alexander, Inc., New York

Jack Beal, a realist painter and printmaker, had always wanted to make a folding screen.[1] As a student at the Art Institute of Chicago in 1954, he avidly studied its collection of Japanese screens, especially those by Ogata Korin, one of Japan's greatest screenmakers. Beal also recalls making prints emulating Japanese woodcuts and their method of depicting the natural landscape through flattened planes and outlined shapes. Beal had long been aware that late nineteenth-century French artists, such as Bonnard (Cat. 6) and Vuillard (Cat. 7), had produced folding screens. *Rowboat* (39.1), printed in 1977 in an edition of twenty-four and mounted on a traditional Japanese layered paper screen, offers homage to these Japanese and French predecessors.[2]

The creation of *Rowboat* was preceded by several studies and false starts. During the summer of 1969, Beal was working on a painting entitled *Peace* (39.2). Two-thirds of the image in the painting reveals an abstract view of the countryside through the open slats in Beal's barn-studio in Oneonta, New York. Beal felt that this section of the painting would translate well into a folding screen.

39.3 Study for *Rowboat*, 1977, pastel, 15.2 x 20.3 (6 x 8). Courtesy Brooke Alexander, Inc., New York.

He sketched his idea in charcoal on a canvas on which he had already delineated the screen's four sections. He never continued work on this screen, however, and the charcoal on canvas drawing is now lost.

A new idea for a screen occurred to Beal during the following summer, after he had finished a pastel study (39.3) of waterlilies in a pond owned by his neighbors. Beal realized that the subject, an allusion to Monet's famous series, would provide a calm background which he considered suitable for a screen.[3] The main subject, however would be a folding rowboat; Beal used to go fishing in a fold-up boat called a Kalamazoo Kanoe. The artist then executed a new charcoal sketch on canvas for a

39.2 *Peace,* 1969, oil on canvas. Courtesy Allan Frumkin Gallery, New York.

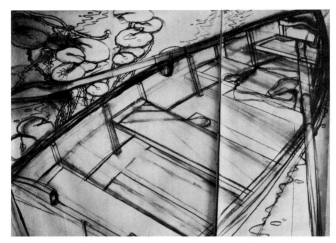

39.4 Study for *Rowboat*, 1971, charcoal on canvas. Present whereabouts unknown.

three-panel screen (39.4), but still did not make the actual object.

In 1977 when Beal finished *The History of American Labor* murals for the Department of Labor in Washington, he was urged by his friend, the printer and artist William Weege, to return to the idea of making a screen. For three months Beal worked intensively on the image he had sketched seven years before. The completed *Rowboat* screen, printed by Weege, shows the gray and blue boat angled up and out of the picture, as if straining to escape the confines of the screen. The green oars, dangling overboard, define the horizontal and vertical axes. As Beal was developing his plan for the screen, he added for visual balance a fourth panel depicting only water and lilypads. Although Beal's subject matter is always figurative, the angled configuration of the screen isolates the images from individual panels as abstract forms. The resulting disjuncture throws into even sharper relief the agitated surfaces of the water and lilypads, surfaces which contrast with the flat, unvaried surface of the wooden boat.

The artist's decision to produce *Rowboat* as a print rather than as a painting was motivated at least partially by his desire to have his screen available in greater numbers, and to see his art become more integrated with everyday life. In this sense, Beal was following the example set by Bonnard and Mucha, both of whom chose to do printed folding screens (Cat. 6 and 12). Surely, the inclusion of Beal's peaceful image in a domestic environment would have a quieting effect on the surroundings. Yet the image is not without a bit of surprise: as one looks down into the boat and at the empty cushion, it seems that Beal's rowboat happily has provided the viewer with an escape from the frenetic world.

1. During a 15 March 1983 interview with the author, Jack Beal explained in detail the evolution of *Rowboat*. Unless otherwise noted, all factual information pertaining to the development of Beal's screen comes from this interview.

2. The paper screen supports were made by Hisad Hana Fusa, owner of Miya-Shoji in New York.

3. Beal was inspired not only by Monet's *Waterlilies* but also by the manner in which Hugo van der Goes painted lilies in the *Portinari Altarpiece*, now in the Uffizi, Florence. Subsequent to the 1970 *Waterlilies* pastel is a gouache of the same subject, followed by a lithograph made by Beal as part of a portfolio for Skowhegan Art School. See *Jack Beal: Prints and Related Drawings* (exh. cat., Madison, Wisconsin, Madison Art Center, 1977), 4-5.

40
DAVID HOCKNEY
English, born 1937

MIDNIGHT POOL (PAPER POOL 10), *1978*
Handmade paper. 182.9 x 217.1 (72 x 85 1/2)
Collection of André Emmerich, New York

One of a series of twenty-nine handmade paper pieces created by Hockney in 1978, *Midnight Pool* (40.1) is a summary statement of the artist's symbolism, his constant technical and stylistic experimentation, and his application of theatrical techniques.[1] The swimming pool became one of Hockney's most important subjects after his first trip to Los Angeles in 1964.[2] Not only was he fascinated with how to depict light reflecting on water, and the objects seen below and on its surface, but he also saw the pool as a metaphorical expression of emptiness, transparency, and solidity. His paintings of that period, such as the 1964 *Picture of a Hollywood Swimming Pool*, similarly emphasize curvilinear surface patterns, delineations of form into flat color planes that are an allusion to both western art nouveau and Japanese woodblock prints. The same treatment is found in Hockney's *Paper Pools*, but the tactile qualities of the handmade paper used in these images provides a far richer, denser, and far more emotionally charged surface.

In the summer of 1978, on his way to California, Hockney stopped at Ken Tyler's graphic workshop in Bedford, New York. Tyler persuaded Hockney to exper-

40.2 *Autumn Pool (Pool #29)*, 1978, colored and pressed paper pulp, 182.9 x 217.2 (72 x 85½). Courtesy Tyler Graphics Ltd., Bedford Village, New York.

40.3 *Pool on sprayed blue paper with purple top (Pool #25)*, 1978, colored and pressed paper pulp, 182.9 x 217.2 (72 x 85½). Courtesy Tyler Graphics Ltd., Bedford Village, New York.

iment for the first time with the technique of painting with liquid colored paper pulp in a mold to form his images. After the water is drained from the mold, the still soggy pulp is removed and dried to form a sheet of color-infused paper. As Hockney became familiar with the process, he evolved the idea of depicting Tyler's swimming pool at varying times of day and night.[3] He studied the subject by taking polaroid snapshots of every part of the pool and water during changing light and weather conditions. The scale of the resulting compositions required Hockney to use six sheets of paper to complete each of the *Paper Pools*.

Seventeen of the twenty-nine *Paper Pools* present the same configuration of diving board and pool as in *Midnight Pool*; only the chromatic variations alter the mood and perception of the scene (40.2 and 40.3).[4] In the daytime versions, the diving board is either sunlit yellow or cloudy grayish-white, while in *Midnight Pool*, the diving board is an ominous black. The blue water in most of the images in the series is dappled with whites, greens, and purples; the water in *Midnight Pool*, illuminated by underwater lights rather than above from the sun, is colored in concentric rings of blues and turquoise. The brilliant light and bright colors of the grass found in the

40.5 *Looking at Pictures on a Screen*, 1977, oil on canvas. Courtesy André Emmerich Gallery, New York.

40.4 Maquette of *Midnight Pool (Paper Pool 10)*, showing optimal folded position.

morning and afternoon *Pools* are replaced with nighttime hues of deep greens in the midnight rendition.

Hockney initially planned to frame all *Paper Pools* as folding screens,[5] and each of the compositions seems to have been devised to benefit from the folding structure. Hockney has indicated, in fact, that the optimal position of *Midnight Pool* is with its central panel thrust forward and the two side panels angled back (40.4). The swimming pool becomes threatening and mysterious as a result, an icon of intangibility and solitude.[6] The diving board is transformed into a gang plank to the rectangular womb of the pool, a gaping door into aqueous uncertainty. The intentionally dramatic, if not theatrical, effects of folding on the composition derive from Hockney's work on stage sets for *The Rake's Progress* and *The Magic Flute*, which he had just completed before arriving at Tyler Graphics.[7] Hockney has even equated the screen with stage flats: both turn corners and create an illusion of space and perspective.

Hockney's interest in the screen format may also have been fueled by his exposure to oriental art during a 1971 trip to Japan. In addition, Hockney's drawings from

40.1

1973 suggest the artist's familiarity with the angled images Picasso created in his cut out and folded metal sculptures dating from 1953.[8] Hockney also included a screen in one of his 1977 paintings, *Looking at Pictures on a Screen* (40.5). He depicted paintings by Vermeer, Piero della Francesca, Van Gogh, and Degas attached to the surface of the screen as a symbol for separation, progression of artistic development, and time. As part of the *Paper Pool* series, *Midnight Pool* also represents a temporal metaphor, but its arresting image, broken by the folds of the screen structure, takes on a far more abstract and timeless quality.

1. Nikos Stangos, ed., *David Hockney: Paper Pools* (London, 1980), 5-7.

2. Marco Livingstone, *David Hockney* (New York, 1981), 68.

3. Jan Butterfield, "David Hockney: Blue Hedonistic Pools," *Print Collector's Newsletter* 10 (July-August 1979): 70-76.

4. The entire series is documented and illustrated in Stangos, *Paper Pools*.

5. According to Tyler Graphics, only two *Paper Pools* were framed as screens; one has already been remounted in a flat frame for storage purposes.

6. In a 9 September 1982 interview with the artist, the author showed Hockney a small photographic reproduction of the screen. Although the actual screen has been exhibited with its central panel receding behind the forward-angled side panels, Hockney in the interview immediately reversed the configuration in the three-dimensional reproduction and indicated his preference for this arrangement.

7. Butterfield, "David Hockney," 74. For descriptions and illustrations of these two productions see Livingstone, *David Hockney*, 173-180, 200-208.

8. Reported by the artist in the 1982 interview. Hockney also thinks of his stage sets as large three-dimensional pictures which are often angled to ensure that each spectator, depending on his or her location in the audience, will get a slightly different view. This is, of course, what happens as one walks around a folded screen. See Livingstone, *David Hockney*, 178.

41

JACK YOUNGERMAN

American, born 1926

HIGH TIDE, *1978*
Oil on luan mahogany panels. 182.9 x 436.9 (72 x 172)
Washburn Gallery, New York

Billowing skyblue forms soar out of a belt of dark blue and maroon in *High Tide* (41.1), the most recent of Jack Youngerman's ten screens. The right to left cadence of the image is rhythmically accentuated by the thrusting and retreating folds of the screen structure. Youngerman purposefully employs the angled surfaces to echo the undulations of the crashing wave and flowing tide shapes that wash off the screen, an allusion to Hokusai's *The Great Wave off Kanagawa* (22.3) and indirectly to Thomas Hart Benton's own *Screen with Abstract Sea Motif* (Cat. 22). The rectangularity of the panels in Youngerman's screen, and its expansive width confine and freeze the wave motion.

Youngerman created at least eleven versions of the momentary, splashing wave image on small, oil-on-cardboard maquettes, in which the forms, the number of panels, and the color combinations are manipulated (41.2). In contrast to most of his other screens, which are painted in acrylic and/or oil on raw linen, *High Tide* has been painted on luan mahogany. The artist chose this particular support to add unexpected surface quality.[1] The vertical texture of the wood grain creates a tension with the horizontal and diagonal painted forms, and symbolizes for Youngerman a mystical infinity, as does the traditional gold ground in Japanese screens.[2]

During his student days in the early 1950s at the Ecole des Beaux-Arts in Paris where Ellsworth Kelly became a good friend (see Cat. 30), Youngerman focused on the formal aspects of images, inventing from memory and sensation shapes based on organic abstractions.[3] His experiments were affected by Mondrian's use of primary colors, Arp's shaped wall reliefs, and Matisse's rich palette and lyrical cutout forms.[4] The structure of the folding screen allowed Youngerman to interweave these concerns for surface, form, color, and motion in an object whose properties lie between painting and sculpture.[5]

Japanese examples also affected Youngerman's screenmaking activities.[6] After studying the progression of a stream or bridge across the composition in a Japanese screen (such as 10.3), Youngerman reinterpreted the spatial experiment in *Mecox Bay* (41.3). He admits that his nature images and use of broad areas of unmodulated color derive from his exposure to both Japanese prints and screens.

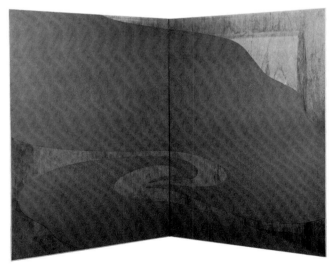

41.3 *Mecox Bay*, 1978, acrylic on wood, 182.9 x 243.8 (72 x 96). Courtesy Washburn Gallery, New York.

41.4 *Pale Gray*, 1972 (recto and verso), acrylic on canvas, 186.7 x 265.4 (73½ x 104½). Courtesy Washburn Gallery, New York.

41.2 Six maquettes for folding screens, oil on cardboard. Collection of the Artist.

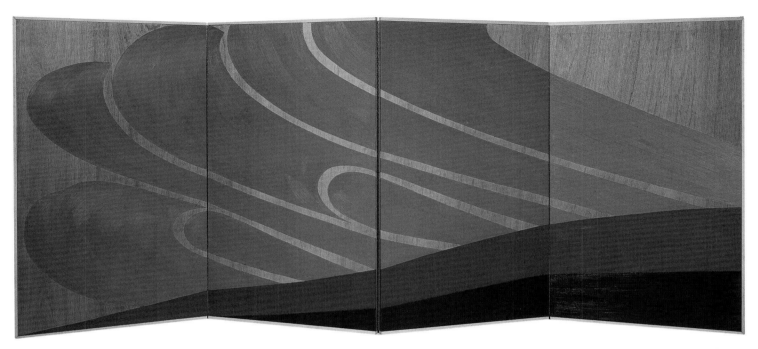

41.1

Youngerman emphasizes his debt to another non-western culture.[7] He was inspired by the Moroccan patterned screens which appear in Matisse's paintings of the 1920s. His screens also relate to the omnipresent wooden window grilles of Damascus, which Youngerman saw on a trip there in the early 1950s. These grilles protect modest Arab women from prying male glances, and Youngerman's metal see-through sculptural screen *Tabriz* (fig. 125), alludes to this middle eastern precedent. Both grille and screen partially block a view, at the same time creating a splintered one in its place. The function of the grille as barrier between men and women, so typical in the Middle East, is also found in the West, where the screen often serves to provide privacy while dressing or undressing. Moreover, the transparency and three-dimensional volume of Youngerman's metal screens recur pictorially in his painted ones. The image in *High Tide* and in the 1972 *Pale Gray* (41.4), Youngerman's earliest screen, like screens themselves, have both two- and three-dimensional existences.

1. Reported by the artist in a 19 January 1983 interview with the author.

2. In 1975 Youngerman remarked, "A painting is an object, and there is always the participation of the canvas to consider. The background must be dealt with in such a way that the surrounding space becomes part of a pictorial interaction. The 'ground' in my paintings completes and forms a shape so that it is impossible to separate figure from ground . . . in sculpture, real space completes the form, but the shape has its own definition. In painting, there are definite boundaries to the canvas but sculptural space is unbounded infinite space." D. Bratton, "An Interview with Jack Youngerman: The New Sculpture," *Arts Magazine* 50 (December 1975): 91.

3. Reported by the artist in the 1983 interview. See also Daniel Catton Rich, *Paintings and Drawings by Jack Youngerman* (exh. cat., Worcester Art Museum, 1965), 5; and April Kingsley, "Exhibition Review: Jack Youngerman," *Artforum* 11 (December 1972): 81.

4. Roger Bordier, "Youngerman, or Dialogue with Forms," *Cimaise* 112 (May-August 1973): 56; and Colette Roberts, "Jack Youngerman," *Archives of American Art Journal* 12 (1972): 6.

5. "The screens blur the lines between painting and sculpture. They are flat, as stretched canvases are, yet they stand free like sculptures. By disregarding the borders between mediums, Youngerman is able to map the edges of his forms with ever-greater accuracy. Their outlines are the only lines which count in his art. The ground may shift, the figure may evolve from an Action Painter's roughness to Matissian elegance and farther, to those reminiscences of Art Nouveau which glide through so much of Youngerman's new work, yet the exclusiveness of his concern persists." From Carter Ratcliff, "Jack Youngerman at Washburn," *Art in America* 69 (November 1981): 174.

6. Youngerman specifically cites the exhibition, *Masterpieces of Japanese Screen Painting*, Pace Gallery, October-November 1977, as inspiration for his concentrated production of screens in 1978.

7. Reported by the artist in the 1983 interview.

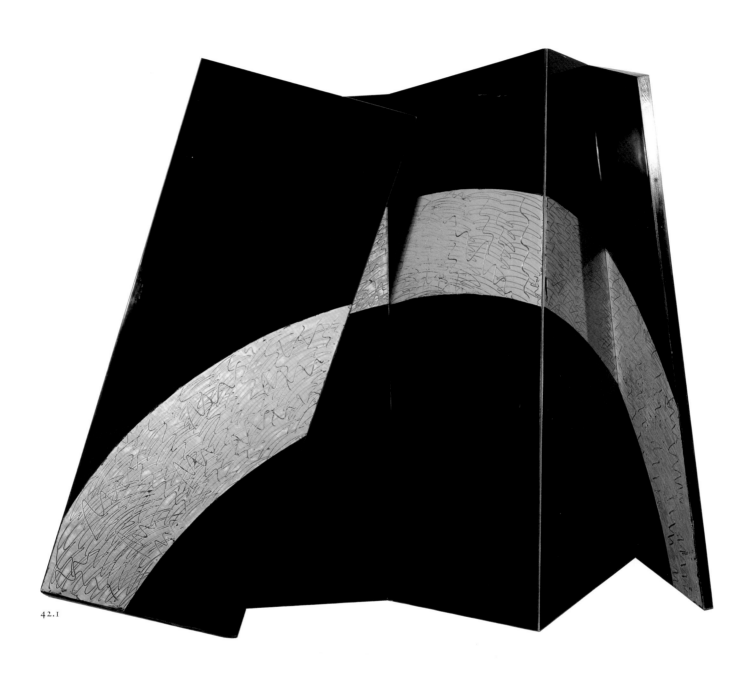

42.1

42
JIM JACOBS

American, born 1945

MARBLE CANYON, *1980-1982*
Lacquered wood. 187.9 x 228.6 (74 x 90)
Collection of the Artist, New York

Cantilevered off the floor by means of its six interlocking, stationary panels, *Marble Canyon* (42.1) is a witty commentary on the folding screen's staid oriental ancestors. By combining the ancient and painstaking lacquer medium with a daring folded structure, Jim Jacobs extends the concept of the screen to a purely sculptural conclusion. The image of the Colorado River which appears on both sides of *Marble Canyon* was derived from a series of drawings the artist made from a small aircraft during a trip across the United States. This abstraction of aerial perspective drawings finds its way onto Jacobs' other screens, such as *Abilene*, 1982 (42.2), where a sunlit expanse, depicted by yellow lacquer, is punctuated only by the floating gray and rust of a harvest-time field. In *Marble Canyon*, the Colorado River snakes and folds across the black panels as it winds in and out of the angled mountain passes. On one side the river sparkles in morning light, highlighted in silver, turquoise and yellow; while on the other side, the water reflects the purples, greens, and golds of a sunset's dying light. For Jacobs the fan-shaped arc of the multicolored river signifies the force of nature charging through the blackness of the universe.

The antecedents for Jacobs' screens are both ancient and contemporary. In response to John Chamberlain's unwritten theory that alteration of form creates energy in an art work, Jacobs sought to embody that energy in his screens.[1] As Chamberlain's studio assistant from 1969 to 1973, Jacobs was influenced by Chamberlain's "scrunching" of automobile parts and metal pieces to create elements for sculpture. Rather than working with junk metal and its inherent symbolism, Jacobs chose to transfer the concept to the screen format. He also experimented with another technique to which Chamberlain

had exposed him—lacquer making.[2] The creation of Jacobs' lacquer screens is a complicated process and requires a lengthy explanation. He begins by folding and crunching small pieces of cardboard until he attains the desired multipanel shape, the more precarious the better.[3] The cardboard models are then given to Billy Russell and Paul Nippes, owners of the New York furniture design firm, Ace Jointers. They fabricate each of the screen panels by laminating Montecure, a medium-density fiber board, to either side of a wooden frame. Bedrail hinges, a Russell invention, are installed so that the panels will lock into a nonfolding position.

42.1 Verso.

42.2 *Abilene*, 1982, lacquered wood, 182.9 x 99.1 (72 x 39). Collection of the Artist.

sculpt on the lacquer surface, Jacobs eventually developed a way to draw in the lacquer. To the surface of the Montecure-coated wood panels, he applies a quick-drying liquid plastic known as Bondo in the areas where he intends to draw his image. When the Bondo has dried, Jacobs carves his image into the surface with sculptor's tools, later sanding flush with the rest of the surface the ridge at the extreme edges of the Bondo-covered area so as to eliminate possible cracking. Only then are the many coats of lacquer applied.[5]

Unlike his oriental predecessors, whose natural lacquers were created from the resin of the *Rhus vernicifera* tree, Jacobs uses both an organic nitrocellulose and a chemical-based acrylic lacquer. He first applies twelve coats of primer, sanding after every three coats. He

Then Jacobs goes to work. At first, he did not know a method which would allow him to draw freely in the lacquer. The imagery on the earliest of Jacobs' twelve screens, such as *Durango* (42.3) and *Warsaw, Virginia* (42.4), both from 1981, consists of hard edge, geometric forms which have been built up simultaneously with planes of deeply hued lacquer. Although the subject matter is still ostensibly about landscape, the designs on these early screens are extensions of Jacobs' earlier lacquer paintings which satirize the abstract vocabulary of artists such as Piet Mondrian, Josef Albers, and Barnet Newman.[4]

Whereas all previous artists were obliged to paint or

42.3 *Durango*, 1981, lacquered wood, 203.2 x 167.6 x 81.3 (80 x 66 x 32). Collection of the Artist.

42.4 *Warsaw, Virginia,* 1981, lacquered wood, 190.5 x 243.8 (75 x 96). Private Collection.

sprays, pours, or squeegees subsequent coats of colored liquid lacquer onto the surface. Several layers of different colors of lacquer are gradually built up with Jacobs sanding the surface smooth after every five coats. As many as forty base-color coats may be applied in all. Once dried, Jacobs sands down the upper layers, revealing portions of the different colored lower layers to create the multihued abstract images which cut across the surfaces of his recent screens such as *Marble Canyon.* Unlike painters who build up layers of color to produce an image, Jacobs takes away layers of color to achieve the effect he wants. Once the primary image has been defined, Jacobs then tapes over it and adds ten to thirty additional coats of lacquer, again sanding after every five, to give the screen its main overall color. Finally, the entire surface is polished with six different gradations of stones.

The use of Bondo allowed Jacobs to alter the intersection of surface and design in his screens. The textured abstractions, as in *Theseus and the Minotaur* (42.5) and *Stone Creek* (42.6), violate the purity of the smooth lacquer with an esthetic entirely divergent from that of both

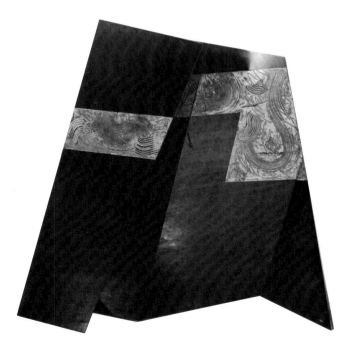

42.5 *Theseus and the Minotaur,* 1982, lacquered wood, 187.9 x 187.9 (74 x 74). Collection of the Artist.

42.6 *Stone Creek,* 1983, lacquered wood, 187.9 x 279.4 (74 x 110). Collection of the Artist.

the oriental tradition and the twentieth-century western adaptations of that tradition (Cat. 24 and 25). Furthermore, due to the methods of interlocking the screen panels, Jacobs' screens are neither portable nor can their shapes be altered to accommodate the demands of a space or the inhabitants of that space. With their unusual cantilevered trajectories, and double-sided imagery, Jacobs' screens are meant to be studied from multiple vantage points. The calligraphic and sculptural qualities of Jacobs' unique lacquer screens posit a thoroughly new alternative for the ancient screenmaking tradition.

1. Reported by the artist in a 16 February 1983 interview with the author.
2. As Tony Towle has noted in *Jim Jacobs* (exh. cat., Miami, South Campus Art Gallery, Miami-Dade Community College, 1983), 1, Jacobs "saw some plain lacquer panels that Chamberlain had done in the early sixties, that nobody had liked or bought – except Donald Judd. . . . These panels stuck in Jacobs' mind. The actual technique of lacquering, though, he first learned later, while working for the French artist Arman in the south of France."
3. Reported by the artist in the 1983 interview.
4. Towle, *Jim Jacobs*, 2.
5. Jacobs described his lacquering process to the author during the 1983 interview.

43

PATSY NORVELL

American, born 1942

JUNGLE WALL, *1981-1982*
Etched glass. 208.3 x 457.2 (82 x 180)
Collection of the Artist, New York

Made of five irregularly shaped etched glass panels, Patsy Norvell's *Jungle Wall* (43.1) interweaves her concerns with transparency, nature and sculpture.[1] Through her translucent screen, Norvell brings the lush *Rhododendron giganteum* leaves into our interior environment. The shimmering of textures on the surface of the one-half inch thick plate glass is reinforced by the undulating top and side edges of the unframed panels, and arranged in a snaking configuration. As light strikes the carved surface and as the viewer moves around the piece, subtle nuances of white, blue, gray, and green tones emerge from the overlapped leaves, etched on both sides of the glass. Forming a transparent impasse, the screen remains both a theoretical and a physical dichotomy.

Norvell learned how to etch glass with a sandblasting gun in 1980 during her appointment as the first artist-in-residence at the New York Experimental Glass Workshop.[2] Although etched glass is not a new medium, Norvell's innovation has been to utilize the technique to carve into rather than merely apply decoration to the glass surface.

As an environmental sculptor from 1977 to 1979, Norvell employed various types of fencing, as in *Garden Variety*, 1979 (43.2), to delineate space and line outdoors, and to create a barrier between the viewer and nature.[3] In her first three screens, *Morning Glory Screen*, 1980, *Grapevine*, 1980-1981 (43.3), and *Rosetrellis*, 1981 (43.4), Norvell combined images of earlier work. She etched fence hatching and plant motifs, recalling her

43.2 *Garden Variety*, 1979, wood, paint, and galvanized poles, 248.9 x 1,219.2 (98 x 480). Courtesy A. I. R. Gallery, New York.

43.3 *Grapevine*, 1980-1981, sandblasted glass with maple frame, 182.9 x 317.5 (72 x 125). Courtesy Patsy Norvell.

43.4 *Rosetrellis*, 1981, sandblasted glass with maple frame, 176.5 x 266.7 (69½ x 105). Collection of the Artist.

43.5 *Glass Garden*, 1979-1980, etched glass, wood, "Wood-Life," paint, plants, and flowers, 238.8 x 228.6 x 259.1 (94 x 90 x 102). Courtesy Patsy Norvell.

43.6 Patsy Norvell and Robert S. Zakanitch, American, born 1935, *Towards the Forest*, 1982, sandblasted glass, acrylic on canvas, 335.3 x 731.5 x 701.0 (132 x 288 x 276). Courtesy Patsy Norvell.

outdoor sculptures and her greenhouse piece, *Glass Garden* 1979-1980 (43.5).[4] Each panel of these early screens is also framed in wood, giving them a more traditional appearance.

Although she had already eliminated the confining fence motif in her fourth screen, *Winter Palm*, 1981, Norvell formulated *Jungle Wall* using other structural and visual innovations. She developed a hinging system with metal clamps which allowed her to abandon the wooden frame altogether, with the result that the glass panels seem to dissolve into the air, without any external edges. While the clamp system does not permit the screen to fold or be moved without being disassembled, the fixed position of *Jungle Wall* establishes its sculptural rather than its functional aspects. Norvell, furthermore, was able to design panels of vastly irregular shapes and sizes. *Jungle Wall*'s leaf forms determine the screen's outer edges, and therefore define the internal spatial boundaries of the space in which it is placed.

Her most recent screens – she has done seven in all – are an extension of the experiments begun in *Jungle Wall*. In *Traveller*, 1982 (fig. 128), the plain unetched panel symbolizes the ultimate transparency/barrier in her work. We expect an image there, but we can only look through it and are forced to impose our own. Collaborating with her husband, painter Robert Zakanitch, Norvell united two screens with a huge acrylic on canvas painting to create *Towards the Forest*, 1982 (43.6).[5] The folding structures function as sculptural wings – physical and metaphorical continuations of the two-dimensional painting. In *Jungle Wall*, images of the plants similarly remind us of where we are not. We want to walk through them, pushing the foliage away to clear our path. As a

43.1

screen, *Jungle Wall* does not obstruct light or vision, posing another dichotomy in our interpretation of it. It is a barrier preventing passage, but not perception. As sculpture, it is ever-changing in its transparency, dependent on the external environment, consequently presenting yet another conceptual definition of the contemporary screen.

1. Grace Glueck, "The Screen Comes into Its Own," *New York Times*, 19 September 1982, 27-28; and Jean E. Feinberg, "Patsy Norvell," *Content in Abstraction: The Uses of Nature* (exh. cat., Atlanta, High Museum of Art, 1983), 21.

2. Reported by the artist in a 25 January 1983 interview with the author.

3. Jean E. Feinberg, "Patsy Norvell: Ten Years 1969-1979," in *Patsy Norvell*, (exh. cat., Poughkeepsie, New York, Vassar College Art Gallery, 1979), 7-8.

4. John Perrault, "The Greenhouse Effect," *Soho News*, 9 April 1980, 23.

5. The Norton Gallery and School of Art in West Palm Beach invited Norvell and Zakanitch to collaborate on pieces for an exhibition. For a discussion of *Towards the Forest* see Bruce Weber and Sally Webster, *A Collaboration: Patsy Norvell & Robert Zakanitch* (exh. cat., West Palm Beach, Florida, Norton Gallery and School of Art, 1982), 15-16.

PHOTOGRAPH CREDITS